Redesigning Rural Development

THE JOHNS HOPKINS STUDIES IN DEVELOPMENT
Vernon W. Ruttan and Anne O. Krueger, Consulting Editors

ASIAN VILLAGE ECONOMY AT THE CROSSROADS
An Economic Approach to Institutional Change
Yujiro Hayami and Masao Kikuchi

THE AGRARIAN QUESTION AND REFORMISM
IN LATIN AMERICA
Alain de Janvry

REDESIGNING RURAL DEVELOPMENT
A Strategic Perspective
Bruce F. Johnston and William C. Clark

REDESIGNING RURAL DEVELOPMENT
A Strategic Perspective

Bruce F. Johnston and William C. Clark

THE JOHNS HOPKINS UNIVERSITY PRESS
Baltimore and London

The Johns Hopkins University Press, Baltimore, Maryland 21218
The Johns Hopkins Press Ltd., London

Library of Congress Cataloging in Publication Data

Johnston, Bruce F., 1919–
  Redesigning rural development.

  Bibliography: p. 273
  Includes index.
  1. Rural development. I. Clark, William C.
II. Title.
HD1415.J63   338.9′00173′4   81-17138
ISBN 0-8018-2731-0   AACR2
ISBN 0-8018-2732-9 (pbk.)

To Harriet and Anni

Contents

Foreword

An agricultural economist and a systems analyst of resource and environment management have collaborated in an essay on rural development in low-income countries. They have written for practitioners and students of development in general, and I believe that their work will indeed be useful for all cross-sectoral system development problems involving the behavior of people.

My own experience enables me to "test" this from one such field: long-term policies and services benefiting children. I have found many of their approaches and conclusions to be congruent with the experience of UNICEF, as well as enlightening and suggestive of new emphases to be tried out.

The improvement of the situation of children in low-income areas requires as a basis an increase in production. Probably this is also true for improving other aspects of living conditions. Yet, extensive experience shows that although increasing production is a necessary condition, it is by no means a sufficient one. Much of the benefit depends on the way the increase in production is obtained. The authors recommend broad-based agricultural development involving small cultivators rather than only large commercial enterprises.

The authors' value premises require improvement of the situation of the rural poor. The process should involve them—the "choice endurers," as they are called—with a natural right to be involved in making the choice. Further, the process should increase the country's capacity to learn and to deal with its own problems, at the local, regional, and national levels. Similar values have been agreed by the international community in the strategy of the Third Development Decade of the United Nations, adopted by the General Assembly in December 1980 (resolution 35/56).

However, there is no general agreement about how to put these values into practice. Much support to development follows fads and fancies, and is closed off prematurely before there has been time to prove out the line being tried. The authors offer approaches to avoid this.

Their use of systems analysis means consideration of production, consumption (particularly of public services), and organization. One of the original features of their synthesis is the very welcome amount of attention they give to organization; this chapter will be of very general interest, and has application to many fields.

It is refreshing that a firm understanding of system leads not to a technocratic approach but to recommending a common-sense balance of intellectual analysis and exploration and interaction in the field, with a constant emphasis on how much is unknown. The book's many indications of practical methods to be explored and built upon are particularly timely when inflation and economic stagnation are strongly reinforcing the natural tendency for inequality to intensify through the accumulation of power and wealth, to the extent that currently there is every prospect that the poor will continue to become poorer over the next few years, unless specific measures are undertaken.

E.J.R. Heyward
Senior Deputy Executive Director, UNICEF
6 July 1981

Preface

This book by Johnston and Clark is a product of work initiated by Johnston at the International Institute for Applied Systems Analysis (IIASA) during the academic year 1978/79. In the course of that period, however, this work on the process of rural development in the low-income countries was linked informally with an ongoing research project whose purpose was to evolve an adaptive approach to environmental and resource management. This latter work, carried out by a group led by C. S. Holling, drew upon an international network of scientists and managers associated with IIASA and the Institute of Resource Ecology at the University of British Columbia. (These efforts are described in *Adaptive Environmental Assessment and Management*, edited by Holling [1978], and in an IIASA Executive Report, *Expect the Unexpected: An Adaptive Approach to Environmental Management* [1979].)

Clark, a member of the core group from the University of British Columbia that worked at IIASA in 1973 and 1974, returned to IIASA in 1978/79 to draft a book summarizing the principal lessons learned from this collaborative effort about the application of systems analysis to the design and redesign of policies for resource and environmental management. During that time, Johnston and Clark became aware of a striking convergence of interest and viewpoint in considering the even more ill-structured problems of rural development. Following their return to their home institutions, Stanford and the University of British Columbia, in the fall of 1979, they reached a decision to continue and intensify their collaboration. This extended essay is a product of their joint effort to apply a systems analytical perspective to the enormously important but intractable problems of rural development in low-income countries. It is my understanding that it represents the first serious effort to apply such a perspective to the complex, interdisciplinary issues that must be confronted in the design and redesign of strategies for rural development.

It is not necessary to be a specialist in the problems of developing countries to recognize that development is a systems problem which cuts across the traditional bureaucratic and disciplinary boundaries. Even a seemingly technical problem such as the design and construction of a dam is bound to have repercussions in such nontechnical fields as public health, rural sociology, and demography, which should be incorporated in the dam's planning. Even more clearly, the technical innovation of introducing high-yield, fertilizer-responsive crop varieties has had generally unanticipated social and economic ramifications that need to be accounted for in future developments.

I have been convinced for some time that properly conceived and executed systems analyses can help decisionmakers in developing countries to deal with such complex, multi-faceted problems. Most immediately, systems analysis can help to clarify the nature of the problem and the character of the system with which the decisionmaker is concerned. Often, just this change in under-standing can lead to improved policies. The process can be carried further through efforts to anticipate the consequences of alternative courses of action before they are taken. This may involve the use of a variety of different models, for example, to trace the behavior of a complex system in choosing among alternative water control investments. Sometimes, however, models will be infeasible or unreliable because understanding of the major variables and their interrelationships is inadequate. This is especially likely to be true of the many aspects of rural development that depend on the behavior and responses of people—men and women at the village level, agricultural field staff, local health workers, middle-level administrators, decisionmakers in the national capital, and many more. In these cases, carefully designed, small-scale experi-ments may be able to provide enough information to improve the choice among alternatives.

I believe that working out the complex steps needed to implement a favored course of action is a systems problem as well, and it requires careful analysis to identify and sequence the steps to be taken. Therefore, it seems to me to be noteworthy that the authors of this book have examined in considerable detail the complex and important issues of organizational design and management. They stress that programs in developing countries are characterized by a great many uncertainties. Consequently, monitoring and evaluating the success of a program in achieving its goals is imperative. The necessity is even greater be-cause the complexity of the problems often defies comprehensive understand-ing, and because the external environment is changeable, often rapidly and unpredictably. These are just the conditions which occur in complex resource development and environmental protection problems and which establish the relevance of a number of the important lessons derived from the IIASA pro-ject on an adaptive approach to environmental management. For example, that approach emphasizes the importance of recognizing that failures are inev-itable; the need, therefore, is not to avoid failures, which is impossible, but to learn from mistakes and improve performance in a continuing, adaptive pro-cess of policy design and redesign.

This book, then, is the result of a unique collaboration between an econo-mist long interested in rural development in low-income countries and an ecologist concerned with the analysis and management of complex systems under uncertainty. The merging of their approaches has led them to helpful insights about the process of development; the results are a clear demonstration of the benefits that systems analysis can offer to those facing development problems. IIASA is pleased to have served as initiator and catalyst of this notable work.

Roger E. Levien
Director, IIASA

Acknowledgments

We begin by acknowledging our gratitude to the Goddess of Serendipity. This collaborative effort between an agricultural economist and a policy analyst would not have happened in the normal course of events.

As Roger Levien has explained in his Preface, it was the International Institute for Applied Systems Analysis (IIASA), in Laxenburg, Austria, which provided the environment in which we discovered the convergence of our interests and became convinced that a joint effort to apply a policy analysis perspective to the problems of rural development would be both desirable and feasible. We are extremely grateful to Roger Levien, the director of IIASA, and Andrei Rogers, chairman of its Human Settlements and Services Area, for the invitations which brought us to the Institute, a unique institution which provided the environment for initiating this unanticipated interdisciplinary collaboration.

We are also indebted to Roger Levien for writing a Preface to this book and to E.J.R. Heyward, deputy director of UNICEF, for writing the Foreword. The differences between IIASA and UNICEF are many and obvious. We believe, however, that they share some important characteristics as relatively small organizations that have been highly effective because of the intelligent, skillful, and flexible way in which they have pursued their mandates.

Our ability to continue and complete the work that we began at IIASA after we returned, respectively, to Stanford University and the University of British Columbia, depended on quick action to obtain the modest financial support that we required. If we had been obliged to follow the normal procedures of preparing an elaborate grant proposal for review, it simply would not have been possible for us to undertake the relatively short but intensive collaboration which resulted in the writing of this extended essay.

Our first debt is to the Stanford Committee on Human Nutrition, which provided a small grant which enabled Clark to make his first visit to Stanford to initiate work on this book. It soon became apparent that we would need a second and more extended period of joint work at Stanford in order to bring the undertaking to a satisfactory conclusion. L. J. Teply, senior nutritionist at

UNICEF, and Mr. Heyward, as deputy director, were extremely cooperative and flexible in speedily evaluating drafts of our early chapters and making a prompt decision to provide the modest additional support that we needed. Finally, we are indebted to the Food Research Institute, and especially to Walter P. Falcon, as director, for support that ranged from providing Clark with office space to providing both of us with encouragement, criticism, and wise counsel.

While we were shaping our ideas at IIASA, we benefited particularly from the comments and criticism that we received from Andrei Rogers, Brian Arthur, Allen Kelley, Hiromitsu Kaneda, and Warren Sanderson. The present manuscript was read in full by Falcon, J. Price Gittinger of the World Bank's Economic Development Institute, and David Leonard of the University of California, Berkeley. We have also received valuable comments and suggestions from H.J.L. Burgess, James G. Clark, John Cleave, Carl Gotsch, Timothy Josling, Dudley Kirk, James Kocher, David and Frances Korten, Uma Lele, Giandomenico Majone, Reynoldo Martorell, Leon Mears, John Mellor, John Page, Carl Taylor, L. J. Teply, Thomas Walker, and Pan Yotopoulos. Ajay Chibber prepared the subject and name indexes. Alan Piazza provided helpful research assistance.

One thesis of this essay concerns the importance of combining "intellectual cogitation" and "social interaction" in reaching improved understanding of the complex issues of rural development. As noted by Roger Levien in the Preface, Clark has benefited from his participation in the joint efforts of IIASA and a team from the University of British Columbia to evolve a policy (systems) analysis approach to problems of resource and environmental management. Johnston acknowledges his debts to interaction with a number of earlier collaborators, in particular John Mellor, Kazushi Ohkawa, and Peter Kilby. He is also indebted to José Bengoa, Doris Howes Calloway, C. Gopalan, Asok Mitra, and other participants in the Ninth Session of the Joint FAO/WHO Expert Committee on Nutrition for advancing his understanding of the nutrition, health, and family planning components of strategies for rural development.

Finally, we would like to express our special appreciation to Minnie Jurow for the many ways in which she has assisted us, including the speed and skill with which she has typed numerous drafts of the manuscript. Mrs. Jurow has saved us from many errors, especially in references to the extensive literature that we have drawn upon.

Introduction

This essay presents a policy analysis of rural development in the late-developing countries. We have written it for practitioners and students of development who seek a strategic perspective from which to reflect on what they and their colleagues are doing.

We focus on specific interventions in three key program areas: production-oriented interventions, dealing with rural employment opportunities and agricultural development; consumption-oriented interventions, dealing with health, nutrition, and family planning; and organization-oriented interventions, dealing with institutional structures and managerial procedures. We analyze the historical performance of policies in these program areas, identify the competitive and complementary relationships among them, and discuss how they can be combined to design feasible and effective strategies for rural development.

Why a strategic perspective? Because we believe there is a need to emphasize the interactions among, and long-term consequences of, the individual program interventions and policy choices of development. Immediate objectives and actions are indubitably important: if they are infeasible or ineffective nothing can be accomplished. But a preoccupation with tactical considerations also has its costs: human suffering is needlessly prolonged when choices prompted by impatience or short-term perspectives foreclose future options or preclude long-term gains.

The people who make things happen in development must spend most of their time at the tactical level: that is where the work gets done. But as Northrop Frye has remarked in another context, there is no reason why the grand edifice to which these workers are contributing must remain forever invisible to them, like the coral atoll to the polyp.

Similar concerns have motivated a number of sectoral or regional studies of development experience over the years. Our debt to one of the best of these studies—Uma Lele's *The Design of Rural Development*—is evident in both the title and the conceptual structure of this essay. We have attempted to bring together the results of these various local studies to see what can be learned from a comparison of their evidence, insights, and conclusions. Our intent is

1

not to supersede but to complement: to provide a more general and synoptic perspective which will help you, our readers, to reflect on your own activities, to see some of your own ideas in different lights, and to play your role in the development process more efficiently. We therefore do not propose authoritative answers or definitive solutions. Rather, we attempt to organize what is known about rural development in order to cope better with what is not. Our ultimate goal is to facilitate progress in understanding the major issues, trade-offs, constraints, and opportunities that confront contemporary development workers.

The dangers of the synoptic approach are clear enough: Proust's warning that "to generalize is to be an ass" has hung over us throughout our investigations. Nonetheless, a preoccupation with the unique also has its shortcomings. Too often we have heard potentially useful evidence and insight dismissed with a cavalier "Oh, but so-and-so did all his work in India [or wherever]; circumstances here are totally different." Different they may be, but in that case the important questions are, Different in what way? Different for what reason? Different to what effect? We suspect that more often than not those inclined to dismiss others' experience out of hand are simply too lazy, too prejudiced, or too insecure to think seriously about what Mr. So-and-so's experience might mean. We prefer the risk of sounding like a generalized ass. We hope that some of our braying will prove useful to some of our readers; what is of no use to anyone may be discarded with our blessing.

The analytical table of contents, following this introduction, outlines the thrust of our argument. More generally, chapter 1 establishes our point of view. It draws on the experience of policy analysts in other fields to illuminate what we will call the "development debate," the continuing interplay of people and ideas, actions and results that together form the history and make the future of development. We show that the development debate has tended to flit from fad to fad rather than build a cumulative body of fact and informed consensus. Furthermore, we argue that the development community has failed to learn from experience, repeating the same mistakes over and over again. We explore why this is so and reflect on what is going on in contemporary efforts to redesign rural development.

Our approach is that of an essay not a treatise. We therefore focus selectively on a few key dimensions of development problems. These are defined in chapter 2. First we analyze the structural and demographic characteristics of the late-developing countries, in order to establish fundamental constraints on the feasibility of alternative development strategies. In this analysis we emphasize the overriding significance of development in the rural sector. A parallel consideration of basic data on health, malnutrition, and fertility recapitulates this emphasis: it focuses our subsequent attention on the particularly acute needs of infants, small children, and their mothers.

Rather than attempt a comprehensive analysis of development options within these structural, demographic, and human welfare constraints, we concentrate on the specific actions—the programs and interventions—out of which any development strategy must be built. Chapter 3 reviews experience with production-oriented programs. We are particularly concerned with efforts to expand rural employment opportunities and with measures affecting the rate and "pattern" of agricultural development. We discuss the accomplishments of alternative programs and describe the trade-offs and complementarities among their components. The evidence is relatively unambiguous. It argues strongly that broadly based efforts to achieve production gains are superior to efforts that concentrate on a few large, highly organized, and relatively capital-intensive ventures.

Consumption-oriented programs are treated in chapter 4. These programs have a shorter history and are more difficult to analyze than programs concerned with production. We focus on interventions designed to improve the health, nutritional status, and family planning capabilities of the poor. Many programs proposed in these areas have ignored the feasibility constraints discussed earlier, and can be dismissed from pragmatic discussions of policy design. The evidence shows that even programs that are feasible individually often can compete for the same limited resource pool. In addition, however, we find substantial potential for strong complementarities among health, nutrition, and family planning programs. This leads us to argue the merits of an explicitly integrated approach to consumption-oriented development activities. We emphasize, however, that integrated approaches place greater demands on institutional infrastructure and managerial competence than do their piecemeal alternatives. The prospects of meeting these organizational demands are discussed in chapter 5.

The third group of programs we consider comprises programs that enhance a society's ability to organize people for policy redesign and implementation. Organization concerns the institutional, managerial, and administrative linkages among the various actors in the policymaking process. It provides the framework for calculation and control through which groups of individuals determine who should do what and assure that all in fact do what has been agreed upon. Without appropriately designed organizations to make things happen, production and consumption programs will remain only empty intention. Specific interventions to provide the organization required for rural development have been relatively unexplored by practitioners or analysts. In chapter 5 we are therefore reduced to setting out a basic framework for analysis of the diverse and controversial evidence that is just now beginning to accumulate. We focus on two particularly important areas: programs to organize the rural poor and programs to organize the "facilitators," the civil servants and field staff who must link national plans to local actions.

Helping to combine production, consumption, and organization programs into strategies for rural development is the ultimate challenge for policymakers and analysts; it is also their most difficult and uncertain task. In our final chapter, we review the often ambiguous evidence regarding trade-offs and complementarities among these component programs. Experience with various "comprehensive" approaches (including an array of "systems models") suggests that even the most sophisticated "thinking-through" analyses are inadequate for the complex and uncertain world in which development policies must be carried out. We therefore stress the importance for policy design incorporating complementary "acting-out" approaches, ranging from market and political arrangements to trial-and-error experimentation. Above all, we argue that development strategy should include an explicit emphasis on learning *how to learn* from the actual experience of development, and thereby how to contribute more effectively to a continuing process of adaptive implementation and policy redesign. We conclude our essay with some speculations on feasible and desirable directions for the continuing redesign of rural development strategy.

Analytical Table of Contents

Policy Analysis and the Development Process

The Development Mess

A short list of objectives presently ranking high in most developing countries would include accelerating growth of output, expanding employment opportunities, reducing malnutrition and disease, and slowing population growth. These goals are being pursued through a vast number of programs and interventions, from tool design to the promotion of family planning, backed by development-oriented institutions and research organizations throughout the world.

Failures in Development

There are indications, however, that the rural poor have often failed to benefit—indeed have sometimes even suffered—from the development effort. Worse, study after study shows that the same kinds of failures recur in country after country, year after year (e.g., Chenery et al. 1974; Adelman 1975; Huntington and Nelson 1976; Eckstein et al. 1978; Heyer 1979).

Examples are familiar to all. In agriculture there has been a tendency for resources to flow to a few favored areas, such as the irrigated regions in northern Mexico, while investments in research, infrastructure, and organization programs required to achieve more widespread increases in productivity and incomes have remained too limited (Redclift 1980). Rice breeders in India persisted for years in an effort to produce rice varieties which would give high yields without the aid of chemical fertilizers even though experience in Japan, Taiwan, and elsewhere had demonstrated the feasibility and effectiveness of a plant breeding strategy directed at the development of fertilizer-responsive varieties.[1]

In nutrition, despite a "dramatic upswing in international attention," typical programs remain "little more than palliatives, in effect if not in intent" (Field 1977, p. 230n). The World Food Conference of 1974 adopted a universal dec-

---

[1] The strategic importance of high-yield, fertilizer-responsive varieties in Japan's agricultural development was stressed three decades ago (Johnston 1951).

laration calling for the eradication of hunger by 1985. Today, unrealistic proposals, band-aid programs, and lack of consensus on feasible and effective programs continue to undermine serious efforts to meet that desirable goal. The number of people subject to malnutrition and related manifestations of poverty continues to increase.[2]

Efforts to organize the rural poor in self-help efforts have fared no better (Korten 1980a). The rural poor are in fact a very diverse group, including landless workers as well as small marginal farmers.[3] Cooperativelike schemes are still touted as a panacea by some. Yet even a decade ago Hunter (1971, p. 2) could write that perhaps two thirds of all cooperatives attempted in East Africa and India "have proved unviable or semi-viable; and a large proportion of those which have succeeded have . . . resulted in rewards for the . . . 'big men' of rural society as distinct from the humble farmers." Programs of community development, adopted with much to-do in their 1950 "decade of prominence," delivered so little that most were terminated or drastically reduced as early as 1965. Nonetheless, under new names to hide the past, many of the same mistakes are being repeated in today's New Directions programming (see chapter 5).

We recite these failures with no intention of apportioning blame or claiming superior abilities. Rather, we find ourselves sharing with many colleagues what Blaug (1979) has described as "a widespread sense . . . that something has gone wrong of late with development policies" (p. 361). We find ourselves wondering, Why do such fundamental mistakes continue to be made? Why do we fail to learn from past experience?

Some development programs, of course, have made progress.[4] Even in the "low-income developing countries" this is true of certain favorably endowed

---

[2] The gap between expectations and outcome appears to be especially large in Africa. A report for a recent summit of the Organization for African Unity prepared by an Inter Agency Working Group states: "Over the last two decades, the food and agricultural situation in Africa has undergone a drastic deterioration. Today, each person in the Region has, on the average, considerably less access to food than was the case ten years ago, and average dietary standards have fallen below nutritional requirements" (FAO/WFC/ECA Inter Agency Working Group 1980, p. 1; see also Lewis/OECD 1980, chap. 2).

[3] We suggest in chapter 5 that insufficient attention to the divergent interests of various rural groups has been an important reason for the failure of many organization programs.

[4] Our focus on the low-income (late-developing) countries doubtless reinforces our emphasis on the shortcomings of past development efforts. It could be argued that it is no mean achievement that "only" thirty-eight developing countries are classified as "low-income developing countries," whereas there are now fifty-two "middle-income developing countries" (World Bank 1980a, pp. 110–11). But the 1.3 billion persons in the low-income category account for some 25 percent of the world's population; and acute poverty is widespread in many of the middle-income countries because of highly unequal income distribution. We also recognize that most of the contemporary developing countries have achieved good to excellent rates of growth in aggregate output in comparison with earlier historical experience. The very limited progress in raising per capita incomes in the low-income countries is influenced considerably by the remarkable acceleration in their rate of population growth during the past four decades. Unfortunately, as we emphasize in chapters 2 and 4, it is in these low-income developing countries that so little progress has been realized in slowing population growth.

areas, such as India's Punjab. It also applies to public health measures amenable to "mass campaign" attacks and to many vertically structured organizations which have been built around high-value export crops. And these successes, by and large, have been due to pragmatic development workers who have refused to become embroiled in unproductive debates over philosophy and ideology and have instead insisted on "getting on with it." Nonetheless, the historical prevalence of failure, the divergence between intention and accomplishment, and the inability to learn from mistakes all suggest that a tactical concern for "getting on with it" is not sufficient. There is also a need to step back and establish a perspective from which we can better understand what is going on in development.

This essay is our attempt to construct one such strategic perspective. We seek to reflect systematically on the key issues, the large constraints, the feasible opportunities, and the main priorities of the contemporary development debate. In other words, we attempt to build a policy-analysis perspective on rural development. We do not pretend that any perspective can "solve" development problems. We do believe that a range of complementary perspectives can help practitioners, policymakers, and advisors in their continuing efforts to understand development problems and to attack them more effectively.

A Perspective from Policy Analysis

To speak of "the development problem" is to imply a well-structured world of unambiguous objectives, mutually exclusive choices, authoritative decision-makers, and willing decision-endurers. In contrast to this idyllic vision, development actually involves a staggering variety of people and organizations, all pulling, pushing, and otherwise interacting with each other in pursuit of their various interests. Since each actor in this process has a more or less unique perspective on "the development problem," the policy process invariably deals with numerous overlapping problems, or in Ackoff's (1974) phrase, a "mess." Turning messes into problems about which something constructive can be done is one way of viewing the central task of policy analysis.[5]

Our view of policy analysis focuses on people, on their interactions with each other and with their environment. These interactions are mediated through various *organizations*: markets and exchange systems, political organizations, family and community groups, cooperatives, bureaucracies, and so on. We see *policies* as social action programs through which groups of people seek to resolve such questions as, How can we better play our interac-

[5] Our use of the term "policy analysis" follows the political economics path of Lindblom, Heclo, Wildavsky, Majone, and others. We have explored elsewhere (e.g., in Holling 1978) the alternative formalist paths of the decision analysts, the systems modelers, and the economic theorists (e.g., Stokey and Zeckhauser 1978). The virtues of using the formalist approaches are many when the problem is to decide between two well-structured alternatives or to build, say, an inventory control system. As most of the formalists would agree, however, their approaches are inappropriate or insufficient for the messy, political, ill-structured issues we deal with here. We discuss the different approaches in more detail later in this chapter and in chapter 6.

tive role to get what we want? How can we better help to achieve some public purpose? How can we better change the basic structure and organization of interactions to better achieve some purpose?[6]

Policies are intimately bound to policymaking *processes* in which people try to invent, control, and implement resolutions to messes. This view of policy-making processes accommodates tactics of planning, of revolution, of intervention-focused efforts to "try it and see," of institutional reform, and of economic incentives. Equally important, however, is its insistence that policy-making is indeed a process, and an iterative one.

Messes are not solved, but resolved sufficiently to be temporarily removed from the agenda, making room for others that are temporarily more pressing. Policymakers seldom start with a "clean slate" on which to draft their desires. Policies are not designed, but *redesigned* as modifications of existing policies which in turn provide foundations for policies that will follow. As Hirschman (1971) has argued, the critical need is to "think in terms of sequences in the course of which a forward step in one direction will induce others . . ." (pp. 19–20). Policy analysis seeks to understand how policy processes operate and how people can more effectively participate in their redesign.

The great variety of people involved in development should not be underes-timated. Crudely speaking, the participants might include a dozen or so inter-national development agencies, ten times that many regional and national authorities, perhaps ten times again that many research organizations and other scholars, and so on to the millions of villages and clans and the billion or so individuals at whom development policies nominally are directed.

It would be surprising indeed if the interests of all these actors in the devel-opment debate coincided. In fact they do not. Instead, what is seen as a suc-cessful policy- or problem-resolving endeavor from one perspective appears as a failure, a source of problems, or perhaps an opportunity from another.[7] The difficulties inherent in a situation of multiple and often conflicting objectives are compounded because "the new nations are constantly prodded and preached at by competing politico-ideological mentors" (Harrari 1978, p. 178). Those seeking to copy the trappings of advanced Western medicine, for exam-ple, have encouraged construction of large hospitals equipped with modern medical facilities. Other health specialists, however, condemn this concentra-tion of scarce health resources in a few urban centers and advocate health systems that permit broader coverage of the population.

---

[6] We use *policy* and *program* interchangeably throughout this essay. This is partly a matter of convenience. It also reflects our conviction that political policies can usefully be treated as the essentially historical and evolving "program" entities developed by philosopher Imre Laka-tos (1970). Majone (1979) has developed this parallelism at some length.

[7] Conflicting interests are a commonplace. Less frequently noted is the possibility for complementary interests. Discovering or building complementary interests—showing how coop-eration can mean more for all those involved—is a central task of policy analysis and a central concern of this essay.

Development strategies determine not only the size and flavor of the communal pie but also the division of the pie among competing claimants. It follows that development is not necessarily in everyone's best interest. The fight for *whose* interests will be served imparts to the development process an inherent political dimension.

The different interests of development attain particular significance because people enter the policy process armed with vastly different quantities of resources. Banks have money, advisors have articulate expertise, governmental authorities have political power, and all of these actors have alternatives when the development debate goes against them. The poor lack these assets, which is one reason why they are poor. Development thereby becomes something "done to the poor" (Heyer 1979).

In this context, one of the truest but least useful observations that can be made about development programs is that their failures to help the poor are "essentially" political failures. Politics, power, and competing interests have been with man since his emergence from the soup. There is no reason to expect their immediate extinction for the convenience of development workers. Furthermore, bewailing the unequal distribution of power is about as conducive to resolving "essentially political" problems as bewailing the unequal distribution of rainfall is to resolving "essentially agricultural" ones. Good policy analysis, as opposed to good intentions, consists in learning to understand the constraints of power—be it man's or nature's—and in learning to shape feasible programs within the limits they impose.

Power and Persuasion

It is reasonable, indeed necessary, to ask what policy analysis, or planning, or advising, or any other approach based on persuasion rather than power can accomplish in the inherently political world of development. Our answer is that quite a lot can be accomplished, though not as much as some claim or as the poor could use. This is true because self-interest is only one source of development activities detrimental to the poor. Another is simple self-delusion. The poor can suffer just as much from an ill-conceived program designed to help them as from a well-conceived program designed to exploit them. Well-intentioned though ill-conceived development programs are not uncommon. But policy analysts in recent years have tended to let their frustration, rage, and relative impotence regarding the self-interest component of development failures obscure the limited but significant contribution they can make in mitigating effects of the self-delusion component. As analysts, we should be able to do something about self-delusion, or we have no business meddling in the already crowded development debate.

It is all too obvious that when power confronts persuasion head on, power wins. Some development situations are so thoroughly dominated by power-holding interests that the analyst's only honest reply to the question, What can be done? is, Nothing—at least until the power structure is fundamentally changed. The only options are to get power or to get out.

Even under more favorable circumstances, however, planners, advisors, and policy analysts "cannot deal with mass politics. If they really tried to organize at the grass roots they would be dismissed. The dilemma . . . is that if they act like politicians they are removed, and if they do not act like politicians they have no power" (Wildavsky 1978, p. 27). The distinctive competence of persuaders does not lie in attaining a position of power from which to speak their own version of the truth. Rather, it lies in what Wildavsky (1979) calls "speaking truth to power"—and speaking it clearly and persuasively enough that the needs of the needy are advanced to the maximum degree feasible.

Doing this job well involves a delicate balance between a realistic recognition of the political realities which constrain decision-makers and a broader view of constraints and opportunities based on detailed and systematic analysis. There is an art and a craft to this form of policy analysis, just as there is a requirement for a certain humility in professed objectives. Wildavsky is right in warning that if the analyst is seen to be maneuvering for a de jure powerful position, he is likely to disappear or arouse far stronger opposition than he can cope with. Successful practice means not flailing about for power one is incompetent to take or hold but instead seeking to understand how the powers in a particular situation work, and how support for desirable and feasible policies can be mobilized.

It should go without saying that the "truth" which good analysis seeks to speak is at best an incomplete and poorly understood truth. It would be naive to believe that *any* sort of truth is sufficient to carry the day in the world of multiple perspectives, competing interests, and dispersed power which we have described. But another kind of naiveté is shown in the presumption that if only the "right" political ideology could be incanted over the development mess, poverty and malnutrition would somehow disappear. This is nonsense. A country with an average per capita income of $150 on the day before the revolution still has an average per capita income of $150 on the day after. It is the inescapable reality of this fact, and of others like it, which is responsible for the somewhat surprising observation that when realistic and perceptive analysts try speaking truth to power, power sometimes listens. Policy analysts and others engaged in the arts of persuasion must make sure that when such opportunities arise, they have something useful to say.

In the last section of this chapter, we describe our approach to "the art and craft of policy redesign." We do not pretend to know how to do this successfully, but we do know a few of the pitfalls that experience has revealed. Thinking seriously about what we are doing in development involves exploring how these general pitfalls of analysis can help explain the specific failures of past and present development policies. In the next three sections, we discuss three especially relevant pitfalls, under the headings "Feasibility and Desirability," "Ineffectiveness and Consensus," and "Cogitation and Interaction."

Feasibility and Desirability

A prime pitfall of development practitioners and analysts is to equate the feasible with the desirable. The equation is applied in both directions. On the one hand, people assume that what they want can be obtained; on the other, they assume that what they can obtain, they should want. Both assumptions are false. In a world of unlimited resources this might be of little consequence. In this world—where time, money, talent, and effort are never enough for the important tasks at hand—the consequences are serious indeed.

The pitfall of equating the feasible and the desirable is primarily a pitfall of self-delusion—of wishing the world were simpler than it really is. And self-delusion is a source of development failures which careful policy analysis can do something about.

"You Can't Always Get What You Want"

Consider first the common habit of setting development goals without regard to resource availability. This leads to Christmas lists of the sort familiar to all. Thus the World Health Organization argues not only that we must have primary health care for the whole population of the earth by the year 2000 but

> that primary health care should include at least: education concerning prevailing health problems and the methods of identifying, preventing, and controlling them; promotion of food supply and proper nutrition, an adequate supply of safe water, and basic sanitation; maternal and child health care, including family planning; immunization against the major infectious diseases; appropriate treatment of common diseases and injuries; promotion of mental health; and provision of essential drugs (WHO 1978, pp. 24–25).

Nor are such wishful indulgences confined to international organizations with political clienteles. T. P. Schultz (1976, p. 111) opines that before choices among alternative programs for fertility reduction can be made, there is a need for "two advances in the social sciences. . . . First, agreement must be reached on how to characterize a society's interpersonal and intergenerational goals and their trade-offs. Second, a much improved understanding will be required of how economic and demographic variables influence and are influenced by reproductive behavior." Other workers in the development field will have their own examples of similar fancies.

Hyperbole does serve legitimate rhetorical functions, ranging from the building of political consensus to the display of good intentions. But when statements such as those quoted above are taken seriously as guides to action, the people they are helping are not the poor. Scarce resources are directed at glorious but unattainable goals, while less ambitious but more realistic programs wither from lack of support. Expectations are raised to impossible levels only to be dashed amid angry recriminations as the inevitable shortfalls and failures of policy occur. Because we cannot accomplish everything, we begin to believe that nothing can be done.

The dangers of lopsided attention to the desirable are particularly acute for development policies directed at the needs of the very poor. Here the desirable is *so* desirable, the alternatives *so* appalling, that often there seems to be no humane alternative to stressing what is needed in the hope that something will be done. Precisely because the costs—to the poor—of such wishful, try-to-do-everything "policies" are so acute, feasibility questions must be seriously addressed. Development workers do not know how to get—and probably cannot get—everything they want for the poor, or even everything they judge to be absolutely necessary. The goals of the analyst, as we have said before, are to help dispel the self-delusion that these limitations do not exist and to "assist the policymaker in the difficult task of deciding which social objectives are in fact attainable at a given time, and with given resources and organizational skills" (Majone 1975, p. 69).

"You Shouldn't Always Want What You Can Get"

The other side of the feasibility/desirability equation is more subtle. It is at least as likely to hinder emergence of effective development policy. Since accomplishing anything with development-related activities is so difficult, pragmatic politicians, managers, and advisors have an understandable tendency to stick with the few things that have worked in the past, that is, with demonstrably feasible activities. This, of course, is preferable to sticking with things that do not work. It is important to remember, however, that under the constrained circumstances of the development mess doing one thing almost always means not doing something else. Too often, deciding what should be done in terms of feasibility per se precludes the search for actions that might have a much greater impact on improving the conditions of the poor.

This is almost certainly true, for instance, in the case of school lunch programs, which have been a popular element in aid programs throughout the developing world. The health gains secured by such programs have been positive but marginal, and often they have been offset by changed consumption patterns in the home. Moreover, when measured in terms of the forgone opportunities for improving the nutritional status of the most needy mothers and preschool children not reached by the lunch programs, the cost has been enormous. In an important sense the school lunch programs have been too feasible: they have provided a convenient outlet for the urge to "get on with it" and thus have reduced the pressure to search for more efficient and more effective alternatives.

Another popular class of actions comprises those that are eminently doable but actually harm the poorest segments of society. One of the worst examples is the widespread promotion of capital-intensive farm equipment throughout the developing world. Particular harm has been done by policies which have fostered the rapid spread of tractors among large-scale farm units in countries where the opportunity cost of farm labor is still extremely low. In countries as diverse as Tanzania and India the promotion of tractor cultivation has been at the expense of alternative investments which would have benefited the rural poor rather than restricted the growth of opportunities for productive employment (see below, chapter 3). It would be naive to ignore the power politics and conflicting interests inherent in this policy failure. It is clear, nonetheless, that much of the continuing advocacy of tractors is due simply to the relative ease with which the tractor programs can be implemented. Whereas tractor technologies can be transferred with ease, implementation of broad-based, employment-oriented technologies depends on location-specific research, for example, in developing high-yield, fertilizer-responsive varieties.

Our general argument is that just as development workers cannot always get what they most ardently want, so they should not always want what they can most readily get. The commonsense seductiveness of "getting on with it," of doing what works, is all the more reason for making this issue an explicit focus of efforts to think more seriously about what we are doing in development.[8] And perhaps the greatest contribution that policy analysis can make to that thinking is through its radical revision of the received view of means-ends relationships and their bearing on processes of social problem resolution.

The Mutual Adjustment of Ends and Means

The development debate involves a continuing interplay between ends and means. Resolution of the debate, if it occurs at all, is both tenuous and tendentious. Judgments concerning the feasibility of alternative development strategies will always differ. The following observation by Michael Polyani remains as valid today as it was more than a quarter of a century ago:

> The existence of social tasks which appear both desirable and feasible and yet are in fact impracticable has set the stage throughout history for a wide range of human conflicts. All the battles of social reform were fought on these grounds, with conservatives often harshly overstating, the progressives recklessly underestimating the limits of manageability (Polyani 1951, p. 169).

Policy analysis cannot resolve such battles any more than it can assume the roles of power discussed previously. Nonetheless, the need remains to combine questions of feasibility and desirability in policy analyses, simultaneously asking "what changes—social and political, as well as economic—are within the politicians' 'means', and what are not; and what patterns or sequences of change, among those that are practicable, will carry the process of economic development farthest and fastest at the least cost in the politicians' resources?" (Leys 1971, p. 133).

How is this question to be answered? First of all, by rejecting the conventional view of rational problem solving which sees its job as establishing where

---

[8] We realize that this borders on the longstanding debate over "muddling through" or "incremental" approaches to problem-solving versus their "synoptic planning" or "systems analytic" alternatives. Have patience: we will expound our position shortly, under the heading "Cogitation and Interaction."

it wants to go and then determining how to get there. One of the central lessons of applied policy analysis (or, again, applied common sense) is that destinations and routes, ends and means, are not distinct entities. Instead, they are interrelated, determining and determined by each other. Effective problem solving consists not in preoccupation with one or the other but in facilitating mutual adjustment between the two.

The conventional view has so permeated contemporary thought on this matter that it may be worthwhile to illustrate the mutual-adjustment notion. Our favorite is an old tale of an Eskimo carving a piece of bone. He carves a little, not quite knowing what he is making, exploring the bone for its texture, faults, and potential. He pauses, examines, carves a bit more. And again. Finally, a smile of recognition: "Hello seal, I wondered if it might be you." Problem posed and resolved all in the same process. Means and ends, thinking and doing, are one.

Problem solving via mutual adjustment of ends and means is not confined to Eskimos. It is a behavior well adapted to real-world problem solving in areas as diverse as behavioral psychology (Weick 1969) and economics (Alchian 1950). A key concept here is what March and Olsen (1976) have called "the ambiguity of self-interest." People decide what they want only in light of what they think they can get; and they imagine what they can get only in light of what they think they might want. Policy analysis, in the form we use here, seeks to recognize this tangled relationship between means and ends, desirability and feasibility, preferences and resources: "Policy analyses are . . . changers, not maintainers of preferences. How are preferences changed? When they are hammered on the anvil of incompatibility between objectives and resources. Changing our conception of what we ought to prefer under the discipline of our limitations as well as the spur of our aspirations is the highest form of learning" (Wildavsky 1979, p. 39). The means by which that learning can be promoted is one of our major concerns.

Ineffectiveness and Consensus

Development advisors have been generally ineffective in bringing their perspectives, expertise, and knowledge to bear on the design of development strategies. This ineffectiveness surfaces as a lack of consensus among advisors regarding the basic issues, constraints, and possibilities associated with development problems. In the absence of such a consensus, the political impotence of development advice is virtually assured.

One of our goals in this essay is to work towards a more effective consensus on development strategies. We do this by focusing on the sources of present ineffectiveness; by identifying explicitly those established "facts" that should "go without saying" in any policymaking effort; and by suggesting procedures for dealing with areas of continuing controversy and uncertainty.

The Ineffectiveness of Development Studies

One of the most discouraging features of the contemporary development debate is its failure to make cumulative progress in the content of its arguments. The same phenomenon has been observed in a number of would-be scientific fields, where historian Jerome Ravetz calls it a symptom of immaturity: "Watching the activity of a[n immature] field over a period of years, one does not witness the steady cumulation of new facts, perhaps superseding but never completely destroying the old. Instead, there is a succession of leading schools, each with a manifesto which is more impressive than its accomplishments, and each fading into obscurity as its turn on the stage is over" (Ravetz 1971, p. 368). The tendency of the development debate to proceed as a series of fads fits well with this general picture of the ineffective discipline. One year the "in" issue is protein, the next it's calories, one year local government, the next cooperatives, and the pendulum continues to swing. Successive fads (or schools) give little impression of building on the foundations left by their predecessors. Their attitude is more one of dancing on an enemy's grave.

A further indication of the development field's immaturity is its insistence on fighting the same battles over and over again, changing only (and not always) the place and the time of the fight. We noted several examples at the beginning of this chapter, and we will discuss others in more detail later on. The general point is that too many development workers continue to function blissfully unaware of their history, neighbors, or the larger edifice which their efforts are creating.

The difficulties of working in an immature field are particularly acute when, as in the case of development, the field is called upon to address pressing social problems. In such an uncontrolled and perhaps uncontrollable context, where facts are few and political passions many, the relevant immature field functions to a great extent as a "folk science," a body of accepted knowledge whose function is not to provide the basis for further advance but to offer comfort and reassurance to some body of believers (Ravetz 1971, p. 366).

Each of Ravetz's general themes finds a specific incarnation in the development field. The political and practical implications of development ensure that its advisors will always serve to some extent in a folk-science role. This means that they will be asked or encouraged to undertake many *pro forma* studies ("Yes, we have somebody looking at that problem"). This is not necessarily bad, for folk science has played some very useful roles. It does mean, however, that much of the work done by development advisors is never intended for actual implementation.

Another of Ravetz's themes, the hollow pretense of maturity, enters the development debate in numerous guises. The most blatant are the complex formal models we will discuss in chapter 6. Less obvious but more insidious is the emphasis on "uniquely best solutions" taken from the simpler and tamer worlds of physics, optimization, and economic theory. Even the notion of pilot projects as "tests" of development policy "hypotheses" retains a flavor of inappropriate "physics envy" when applied in the development context.[9] Hirschman (1971) has rightly condemned these apings of scientific maturity as counterproductive to development, an argument we will return to throughout this essay.

Finally comes the problematic question of quality control. Ravetz notes that a breakdown of normal procedures for peer review and evaluation is inevitable when an immature field is applied to pressing social problems. He comments that such fields tend to acquire "an accumulation of congenital rebels whose reforming zeal exceeds their scholarly talents." Even worse are the outright charlatans out to make a quick name and money from the urgency of the problems (Ravetz 1971, chap. 14). To suggest that such problems are present in one's own field is not considered good form, but there is no reason to suspect that the development community should be any more virtuous than those studied by Ravetz. A more reasonable presumption is that the incompetence and opportunism are there, cluttering the literature, mucking up even the most straightforward of programs, and contributing to the general ineffectiveness of the field.

Accepting this immaturity and lack of cumulative progress in the contemporary development debate, the question remains, Does it really matter? Sadly, we believe it does—for reasons discussed in the next section.

Controversy and Consensus

We argued earlier that the strength of any persuasive endeavor lies in its ability to speak truth to power in such a manner that power will listen and modify its actions. In a field as complex as development, it is hardly surprising to find that several voices, with several versions of the "truth," invariably speak at once. Some controversy is doubtless for the good. It is a source of the new ideas so desperately needed in development, and it supports a degree of skepticism necessary to combat tendencies towards dogma. While academic pursuits may thrive on conflict and controversy, however, effective implementation of a social action program requires substantial consensus. And consensus is just what the immature and ineffective development debate does not offer.

Political action is much easier to stop than to start. The power of policy analysts (and advisors in general) lies in their ability to devise policies that serve the needs of the poor and, at the same time, appear appropriate to other interests. In this context, the open skepticism and criticism so appropriate in an academic context easily can become counterproductive to the larger goals of development. The inconclusiveness and noncumulative character of the development debate becomes a positive hindrance.

One familiar example of these difficulties is the proliferation of "options" facing those responsible for shaping development strategies. Each "option" is a potential starting point for the process of policy design. In a mature field the

---

[9] The term is from Cohen (1971), who called "physics envy . . . the curse of modern biology."

parallel activities of analysis, consolidation, testing, and synthesis would keep the menu of seriously considered alternatives down to a manageable level of complexity. This is not true, by and large, in the development debate. Instead, those responsible for policy formulation are pulled first one way, then another. A narrow preoccupation with physical capital formation had scarcely given way to an emphasis on employment when the "basic needs approach" was moved to center stage at the 1976 World Conference on Employment (ILO 1976). Claims and counterclaims make it supremely difficult to assemble the high-quality information necessary for rational choice. Their time and attention limited, the policymakers' frequent failures to make the "right purchases" is hardly surprising.

A further consequence of the inconclusive skirmishings among development advisors is that any one opinion—any one effort to "speak the truth to power"—is unlikely to carry much weight with those who think differently. In particular, those bent on self-interested efforts to exploit or to ignore the poor can invariably find some advisory recommendation to interpret as support for their favored programs. Any dissenting view can be countered by some other view of arguably equal weight. "Truth," spoken in a thousand different dialects, is little more than a justification for everyone's doing what he chooses.

More generally, the scattered, vague, and contradictory components of the development debate make it virtually impossible to mobilize the will required for sustained attacks on complex social problems. In the absence of a consensus on what needs doing and how it is to be done, the nay-sayers carry the day. Perhaps even more significant, a narrow concern for the best can easily stand in the way of the good. Advisors and experts often seem more concerned with proving that someone else's proposal is not "optimal" than with building the support necessary to carry any of several good proposals through to effective implementation.[10] Thus development exhibits a history of partially funded programs, prematurely terminated policies, and numerous other symptoms of a field that cannot decide where it's going and therefore wanders in pursuit of the fancies of the moment.

But if consensus matters, is a lack of consensus inevitable? Does the complexity and uncertainty of the development mess condemn the advisory community to ineffective and inconclusive debate? Is the best that can be hoped for a role of bestowing expert sanction on predetermined policies? Experience in other fields suggests that these are all real possibilities but that serious commitment to thinking about what we are doing may be able to improve the situation.

Policy Analysis As Bootstrap

There is no reason that development workers, like Frye's polyp, must remain forever oblivious to the broader implications of their endeavor. The

---

[10] This is Hirschman's (1971) warning about the pursuit of "uniquely correct policies" in another garb.

predicament posed by the immaturity of the development debate, and the political ineffectiveness which its lack of consensus engenders, is a predicament of the field as a whole. We believe that it should be possible for the development community to undertake self-conscious, politically sophisticated efforts to articulate consensus positions on what is known, on what is not known, and on how best to proceed in the face of remaining uncertainty and controversy.

An important part of this enforced self-consciousness involves no more than speaking over and over again about those things which should "go without saying." Development specialists are so busy debating their disagreements that they sometimes forget that certain facts of development experience are now taken for granted by a great majority of informed workers. This essay is in large part devoted to nothing more than spelling out such common knowledge. We argue that precisely because certain things can now be taken for granted, they must not be. They represent the few tentative approximations to "facts" or "truths" which development experience and research have yielded. The cost of their trial-and-error discovery has been extraordinary. To waste or ignore the result of the investment because it is (to some) old hat would be unconscionable. That the same well-known mistakes are repeated in contemporary development programs is clear evidence that these truths are not yet being spoken loudly, clearly, or unanimously enough. There have been too few instances of the development community's rising in unison to declare that "this sort of thing has been tried over and over again and left the poor worse off than they were before. Why is the development agency sponsoring this project intent on hurting the poor?" Before development workers spend too much time bemoaning their lack of political power, they might at least see how far such a consensus on "truth" would take them.

It remains true, however, that whatever consensus can be formed on the basic facts of development, fundamental uncertainties will remain. Most "facts" are only dimly perceived, most "truths" only partial. This, however, is precisely where policy analysis has helped in other fields, and where we believe it can help in development. Particularly important in this context is recognition that a consensus on procedures for debate and problem-solving can be a valuable alternative to consensus on solutions themselves. An accomplished practitioner writes:

> Good policy analysis recognizes that physical truth may be poorly or incompletely known. Its objective is to evaluate, order, and structure incomplete knowledge so as to allow decisions to be made with as complete an understanding as possible of the current state of knowledge, its limitations, and its implications. Like good science, good policy analysis does not draw hard conclusions unless they are warranted by unambiguous data or well-founded theoretical insight. Unlike good science, good policy analysis must deal with opinions, preferences, and values, but it does so in ways that are open and explicit and that allow different people, with different opin-

ions and values, to use the same analysis as an aid in making their own decisions (Morgan 1978, p. 971).

Let us next consider how this sort of procedure can be carried out.

Cogitation and Interaction

There are a great many contemporary approaches to social problem-solving. We find it useful to focus on the two extreme forms which Wildavsky (1979) has called "intellectual cogitation" and "social interaction." These may be distinguished in terms of their views on the relationship between the cognitive competence of human problem-solvers and the interactive complexity of social problems (Lindblom 1977).[11] In brief, the approach of intellectual cogitation presumes that man is up to the task of "thinking through" solutions to his problems. The approach of social interaction presumes that he is not: it seeks instead to "act out" solutions through social processes of voting, markets, bargaining, and the like. Policy analysis emphasizes the complementary potential of the two approaches and seeks a strategy for their integration.

Thinking Through

An optimistic faith in man's ability to think through solutions to social problems engenders hopes for policymaking by intellectual cogitation. This view is latent in centuries-old ideologies stressing the perfectibility of man. It surfaced as political philosophy in Marx, and entered what might be called its technological phase through the successes of operations research in World War II. Nurtured through a subsequent generation of military think tanks, cogitation has since blossomed forth in a bumptious array of applications ranging from systems modeling to cost-benefit analysis and comprehensive economic planning.

In the extreme form which we caricature here, the cogitation approach is synoptic in ambition, emphasizing "the breadth and competence of analysis" (Lindblom 1977, p. 314). Confident of its abilities, cogitation seeks to anticipate all possible policy outcomes by thinking through all possible contingencies. On the basis of its comprehensive analyses, it proceeds to identify optimal or at least efficient solutions and to recommend them for implementation.

Among the foremost selling points of cogitation approaches are their rigor, rationality, and relative freedom from the distortions of special-interest plead-

---

[11] This section draws heavily on the work of Lindblom (1977, chaps. 19, 23); see also Lindblom and Cohen (1979, chap. 2) and Wildavsky (1979). The terms "intellectual cogitation" and "social interaction" are Wildavsky's. He notes their origin in, and their relation to, Lindblom's "Models 1 and 2 of views on the efficacy of intelligence, thought, or analysis when applied to tasks of social organization" (Lindblom 1977, p. 249). We differ from these two authors, however. While they sometimes allow the "interaction" (Model 2) approach to include a large amount of sophisticated cogitation, we prefer to view cogitation and interaction as two extreme archetypes, and to treat their integration as the central task and product of policy analysis.

ing and power politics. These characteristics have made cogitation attractive for many policymakers confronted with the complexity and conflict of real-world development messes. The common interest of practitioners and cogitators—the community of academic advisors—in promoting synoptic cogitation has led to ambitious, not to say absurd, aspirations.[12] The following statement by India's Prime Minister Nehru is typical:

> [Planning] and development have become a sort of mathematical problem which may be worked out scientifically. . . . [Planning] for industrial development is generally accepted as a matter of mathematical formula. . . . [Men] of science, planners, experts, who approach our problems from purely a scientific point of view (rather than an ideological one) . . . agree, broadly, that given certain preconditions of development, industrialization and all that, certain exact conclusions follow almost as a matter of course (quoted in Karanjia 1960, pp. 49 ff.).

The naiveté of such hopes, as well as the counterproductiveness of their pursuit, will seem obvious to some. This, however, has lessened neither the enthusiasm of contemporary cogitators nor the growing demand for their products. We discuss the problem in chapter 6, devoting particular attention to some of the grander "systems models" of rural development which are now receiving attention.

For the moment, it is sufficient to note that however estimable the ends of intellectual cogitation may be, the available means are insufficient for the task of shaping effective development policy. Comprehensive planning is in fact a classic example of those arguably desirable but wholly infeasible goals so common in the development debate. Lindblom (1977, p. 322) notes that synoptic approaches to thinking through development policies can work only to the extent that three conditions are met: (1) the problem being analyzed does not exceed man's cognitive capacities; (2) there exist agreed-upon criteria of goodness or value on which alternative solutions can be judged; and (3) policymakers have sufficient incentive to stay with the formal analysis until it is completed. Unfortunately for cogitation, not one of these conditions is encountered in real-world development messes.[13] Fortunately for development, there exists an alternative approach to problem-solving.

---

[12] Harvey Brooks (1975, p. 259) has commented on this common interest in a different but related context. Brooks notes that cogitators see programs, clients, and eventual publications in a world where bigger and more ambitious is generally better. Politicians seek to do something new, ambitious, and sophisticated. Significantly, consummation of the obvious alliance between the two—an alliance that may be formed with the best of intentions on both sides—removes both from their usual channels of accountability and control. The cogitator no longer operates within anything approaching the peer-review system of normal academia because no academic could possibly have his intimate acquaintance with the particular development problem (model, or whatever). The politician, on the other hand, has obtained a unique piece of expert advice which no other politician has or is competent to criticize. In slightly less altruistic situations, questions of prestige also enter (in the form of tractors, steel plants, weapon systems for the "modern" look), making the situation even more problematical.

[13] We note at the end of this section that comprehensive economic planning is, within limits, feasible and useful in the context of a developed country such as the Netherlands; but in

Acting Out

The acting-out approach to social problem-solving is less ambitious than its thinking-through alternative. It also demands less of analytic talent, political harmony, and leaders' attention. As its method of calculation and control, the acting-out approach employs not intellectual cogitation but social interaction. Rather than trying to think through all possible decisions and ramifications ahead of time, it gets on with the business of acting on one of the possible choices. It then reacts to the situation that develops, thereby promoting incremental improvements in the mess. Acting-out approaches therefore seek to adjust present difficulties rather than to anticipate future ones. Much is obviously lost by such an approach. But practicality and adaptability are gained.

The acting-out approach to social problem-solving takes a relatively skeptical view of man's competence for calculation and analysis, but it is no less rational for its skepticism. On the contrary, as Nobel laureate Herbert Simon argued over a decade ago,

> The dream of thinking everything out before we act, of making certain we have all the facts and know all the consequences, is a sick Hamlet's dream. It is the dream of someone with no appreciation of the seamless web of causation, the limits of human thinking, or the scarcity of human attention. . . . The world outside is itself the greatest storehouse of knowledge. Human reason, drawing upon the pattern and redundancy of nature, can predict some of the consequences of human action. But the world will always remain the largest laboratory, the largest information store, from which we will learn the outcomes, good and bad, of what we have done. Of course it is costly to learn from experience; but it is also costly, and frequently much less reliable, to try through research and analysis to anticipate experience (Simon 1971, p. 47).

A strategy of incremental improvement has always been the pragmatic administrator's alternative to synoptic analysis. It is carried out in most societies through a rich array of social interactions ranging from market systems and exchange traditions to voting and bargaining arrangements. We discuss these interactive mechanisms at length in chapter 5.

Some of the most forceful contemporary advocates for acting-out solutions to development problems are people reacting against excesses of the synoptic cogitators. There has in fact emerged something of a fetish in contemporary development circles for adopting a stance of the no-nonsense pragmatist, defending "what works" and disdainful of "theory," that is, intellectual cogitation, in almost any form. In many ways, this reaction has been for the good, stopping some of the more pretentious nonsense of vacuous thinkers from further confusing the already difficult messes of development. The pendulum can swing too far, however. Pure interaction is as unlikely as is pure cogitation to advance development policies which are truly beneficial to the poor.

---

low-income developing countries such as Niger, Bangladesh, or Indonesia the limitations of a thinking-through approach are severe.

Even the strongest advocates of acting-out approaches to social problem-solving have argued only that interactions works *better* than cogitation (Hirschman and Lindblom 1962). Better is good, but at least in the development field, still not very good. We have already noted that a predilection for "getting on with it" invariably leaves development prey to undesirable long-term consequences of apparently desirable present actions—the feasible is not always desirable. Related difficulties include the unconscious foreclosure of options and the blind pursuit of policies with high opportunity costs. In addition, interaction learns only randomly from its own experience and is wholly incapable of learning from the experience of others. Finally, many people affected by acted-out solutions lack the will or opportunity to participate in the social interactions which determine those solutions. The very poor in the developing countries are more likely than most to face such de facto exclusion. There is little provision in the society's acting-out mechanisms for others to stand in as their surrogates. To serve a surrogate role is one of the goals of policy analysis.

A Guide for the Unknown

Intellectual cogitation and social interaction are incomplete guides to effective action. The design of development strategies cannot come from thinking alone or acting alone or even from thinking and then acting. Just as in our earlier example of the Eskimo carving his bone, effective design emerges from a process in which thinking and doing become one, constantly iterated as alternate phases of the design-and-execution process. Policy analysis seeks to facilitate such a process by explicitly recognizing the strengths and limitations of cogitation and interaction. Adopting neither the role of omniscient seer nor that of the blind stumbler, policy analysis seeks to become, in Feyerabend's words, "a guide who is part of the activity guided and is changed by it" (1978, p. 33). This guiding effort seeks to combine knowledge inherent in the doing of development with systematic but explicitly limited reflection on that doing.

A critical step in beginning this effort is to understand what kind of a problem the "guide" of policy analysis faces. We suggest that the problems are of the sort that Simon (1977) has called "ill-structured," very different from the "well-structured" problems around which most thinking about problem-solving has been carried out.

A well-structured problem, such as designing inventory control or solving a transportation problem, has a well-defined objective, such as arriving at an answer or procedure for managing an inventory. In contrast, in the case of an ill-structured problem, there is no well-defined "problem" but rather a "mess": a general concern to change the functioning of a complex, dynamic system in order to make progress in attaining multiple objectives. Obviously, in rural development messes a great many interacting variables are involved. Many of the behavioral relationships, the organizational capacities, and even some of the technical input-output coefficients are poorly understood.

Policy analysis of ill-structured development problems may seek to provide decision recommendations to policymakers. More frequently it will seek to reflect systematically on the key issues, the large constraints, the feasible opportunities, and the main priorities of the development debate. This reflection becomes a basis and a guide for articulate intervention in the development mess.[14] To paraphrase Lindblom (1977, p. 314), our expectations of that intervention remain modest, seeking primarily to encourage the close interplay between ends and means to which we referred earlier. The supporting policy analysis is less concerned with "correctly" solving a problem than with making an advance from which others will follow, less concerned with a predetermined set of goals than with remedying dissatisfaction over past policy while goals and programs are both reconsidered. Formal analysis is not excluded from this activity; however, it is explicitly limited in its aspirations. It seeks to play a role strategically adapted to these limitations and to existing interactive processes. In brief, policy analysis endeavors to play its role in a way which makes it relevant and useful in the situation in which policymakers and administrators must in fact operate.

What is the relationship between this modest view of the role of intellectual cogitation and the tradition of comprehensive economic planning pioneered by Nobel laureate Jan Tinbergen? The question is important because of the extent to which enthusiasm for planning has influenced research and analysis focused on the problems of developing countries during the quarter-century since Tinbergen published his classic treatise, *Economic Policy: Principles and Design* (1956). In later books, Tinbergen (1958, 1967) applied some of those principles of economic planning and programming to "the design of development." Many economists and development planners have followed in that tradition.[15]

Tinbergen notes that his 1956 treatise derived from his experience in the Netherlands Central Planning Bureau and from discussions in the Dutch political arena. There is much wisdom in this treatise and in his later books that is relevant to developing countries as well as to the relatively well-structured problems of economic policy which he had addressed in the Netherlands. He recognizes, for example, that development policy is so complex that it embraces not only the whole of economic life but important extra-economic phenomena as well. He therefore stresses that analysis must go beyond "quantitative policy" to embrace qualitative analysis as well (Tinbergen 1956, p. 86 and chap. 5). Thus, after noting the relationship between a country's rate of population growth and the "required" rate of investment to achieve a given rate of increase in per capita income, he states that the problem of reducing poverty in less developed countries "is insoluble unless a check on the growth

---

[14] The phrase "articulate intervention" is drawn from a book of that title by Boothroyd (1978), a book which in our opinion provides one of the best and most succinct available introductions to the philosophy and practice of policy analysis.

[15] See, for example, Chenery (1971), Ojala (1967), and Pyatt and Thorbecke (1976).

of population is one of the means used" (Tinbergen 1956, p. 91). He also includes among "the qualitative means" the "institutions chosen by a country as the organisational framework within which its economic and social life take place" (Tinbergen 1967, p. 41).

Among the significant principles emphasized by Tinbergen is the proposition that there must be consistency between the "means of economic policy that are used" and the aims to be achieved. And in language that anticipates our emphasis on the need for mutual adjustment of ends and means, he notes: "Inconsistency of a set of means and aims need not be ascribed to insufficiency of the means considered" because "it may also be attributed to overambitiousness in the aims set" (Tinbergen 1956, p. 26). Some of Tinbergen's prescriptions for developing countries raise questions of feasibility. But shortcomings are much more evident in the work of some of those who have followed in the Tinbergen tradition.[16]

The Art and Craft of Policy Guidance

How does policy analysis play its strategic role as a guide to the unknown? In this essay we emphasize three simultaneous activities of the guide: looking backward, to create a retrospective view of past experience; looking forward, to create a prospective view of future expectations; and looking inward, to create an interactive view of adaptive learning.

Looking Backward: A Retrospective View of Experience

It is one thing to accept the need for utilizing the experience of past development interactions; it is something else to do so, as suggested by the tendency of development workers to repeat past mistakes. One reason is the predilection of analysts to concentrate on prospective studies of what is to be, virtually

[16] Tinbergen suggests that in both developed and developing countries a "general task of government is to provide a minimum of social security . . ." (1956, p. 5). That point of view is echoed in a recent monograph by Pyatt and Thorbecke in which they assert that "the alleviation of poverty in its extreme forms requires subsidies from rich to poor and a reallocation of scarce resources in a way which is unlikely to have any immediate justification in terms of economic efficiency" (Pyatt and Thorbecke 1976, p. 8). The desirability of immediate action to eliminate poverty is not in question. As we will argue in chapter 6, however, an emphasis on short-term, relief-and-welfare measures is bound to have a high opportunity cost in low-income developing countries, where average per capita incomes are exceedingly low and poverty is a huge and pervasive problem. The neglect of the future implications of present actions by Pyatt and Thorbecke is also inconsistent with the emphasis that Tinbergen places on "looking ahead" as a chief element of economic planning (1967, p. 44). In line with the Tinbergen tradition, Pyatt and Thorbecke emphasize that "the feasible policy space" can be expanded by considering "a more ambitious package of policy instruments and structural reforms . . ." (1976, p. 12). Nonetheless, they essentially ignore policies affecting the rate and bias of technical change, the rate of population growth, and administrative capabilities. On the other hand, they give undue emphasis to a thinking-through approach which assumes that measurement is invariably a prerequisite to action. This is evident in the priority that they assign to the organization of national data systems so that the effects of alternative policies can be traced through a "social accounting matrix." We will have more to say on the role of national planning in chapter 6.

excluding retrospective attempts to understand what has been. Majone (1977) calls this predilection the Received View of analysis. He characterizes it in the words of one of its most successful practitioners:

> There is need, first of all, for a systematic investigation of the decision maker's objectives and of the relevant criteria for deciding among the alternatives that promise to achieve these objectives. Next, the alternatives need to be identified, examined for feasibility, and then compared in terms of their effectiveness and cost, taking time and risk into account. Finally, an attempt must be made to design better alternatives and select other goals if those previously examined are found wanting (Quade 1968, p. 11).

There is a place for this prospective approach, and we will describe it shortly. But to view prospective studies as the only legitimate use of analysis and to brand as unprofessional or even unethical efforts to explain policies already undertaken is both naive and destructive.

It is impossible to learn from experience until experience is diagnosed and understood. The diagnosis is rarely self-evident. Policies and programs are undertaken for a variety of reasons, some explicit, some hidden even from the individuals making the choices. What is actually done and actually accomplished through a given policy effort may be radically different from what is generally perceived or advertised. Extraneous factors not obvious to participants and not envisioned ahead of time often play a critical role in determining success or failure of a policy. Until such factors are sorted out—what was done? What occurred? What was the connection between the two?—only self-delusion and propaganda can emerge from the experience of development.

We believe that one of the most challenging and potentially rewarding tasks facing development analysts lies in what Lakatos (1971) has called the "rational reconstruction" of past experience. Such reconstruction consists primarily of efforts to develop a rigorous, defensible conceptual framework within which retrospective studies of development efforts can be conceived, executed, analyzed, and compared. In its least ambitious form the retrospective framework would consist of a simple catalog of historical successes and failures experienced in common development situations. Policymakers and analysts in a variety of countries and settings could then use this catalog to help identify appropriate comparisons between their own development problems and problems addressed in other times and places.[17]

At a minimum, such a retrospective approach should be able to decrease the frequency with which past mistakes are unconsciously repeated. This alone should substantially improve policy formulation and performance in the de-

[17] This recommendation is not made lightly. One of us (Clark) has been involved in an exhaustive review and evaluation of alternative approaches to environmental impact analysis (see Holling 1978). At the completion of this study the best systems analyst in the group, the late Dixon Jones, concluded that a cataloging "system" of the sort described here would benefit most practitioners more than any computer models we were ever likely to see.

velopment field. Conversely, a good catalog of retrospective analyses would identify what sorts of development circumstances are *not* similar and what sorts of comparisons are bound to be superficial and misleading.[18] Finally, to the extent that a retrospective inventory of development experience became widely accepted and used, it would go a long way towards building the consensus of informed opinion which is so important for giving political power to persuasive argument.

Many retrospective frameworks, many systems for cataloging information are possible. The important task of development analysts is to begin identifying key criteria for valid "this-is-like-that" comparisons. Such criteria cannot be asserted a priori, and a single set of criteria will never emerge as "best." There will always be dissent among development workers over what criteria merit priority consideration. Nonetheless, if such dissent develops with some appreciation of its own political significance, the task of building a generally agreed-upon framework will be well underway.

Several beginnings are already being made. The distinction that the World Bank has been making in recent years between low-income and middle-income developing countries is a useful if primitive step towards defining the catalog headings. So, for all its problems, is the quality-of-life index proposed by the Overseas Development Council (See below chapter 2). Another example is the African Rural Development Study, a retrospective analysis which grew out of the World Bank's interest "in finding ways of designing relevant projects that could be accomplished despite limited resources, particularly of money and trained manpower, and that would reach a large proportion of the low-income rural population" (Lele 1975, p.3). The Second Asian Agricultural Survey, sponsored by the Asian Development Bank, also included a serious attempt to examine past experience and to derive policy lessons from it (Asian Development Bank 1978, 1979). The volume on Kenya's agricultural development edited by Heyer, Maitha, and Senga (1976) is a noteworthy example of a national study. The classic treatise by Hayami and Ruttan (1971) and the recent work by Berry and Cline (1979) on agrarian structure and productivity illustrate what systematic examination of evidence and technical analysis can offer in this general area.

We draw on such retrospective studies, in addition to shaping our own, throughout this essay. Our goal is to extract from past experience some enlightening perspectives from which to view problems of redesigning rural development. By better understanding past experience, we hope better to profit from its successes and better to avoid its mistakes.

---

[18] Thus far, we have said little about the problem of unjustified parallels drawn in development debates. Nonetheless, we believe that fallacious comparisons have been almost as damaging to development policy as the more obvious failure to make justifiable comparisons. The tendency of many analysts to apply uncritically lessons learned in middle-income developing countries to the formulation of policies for low-income developing countries is one of the most serious examples of this problem. We consider it and others at length in chapter 2.

Looking Forward: A Prospective View of Futurities

Retrospection alone, however, leads only to results like those obtained through guiding an automobile by means of its rear-view mirror.[19] The approach works only so long as there are no bends in the road, and it is virtually useless for finding the road again after the inevitable plunge into a ditch. We have already noted that social-interaction approaches to problem-solving are particularly prone to such backward-looking accidents. To improve the performance of development policies the backward look must be complemented by an ability to look forward at the long-term consequences of present actions.

The looking forward we have in mind is not synonymous with predicting the future. Rather, it is what business managers call "assessing the futurity" of present decisions. Drucker (1974) illustrates the difference with a logging company's decision to replant an area after harvest. This decision, argues Drucker, is not based on predictions of timber supply, pulp demand, and labor costs half a century hence, when the planted trees will be ready for harvest. Rather, it recognizes that planting now creates a present option of being in the logging business fifty years hence. Not planting now forecloses that option.

We show in subsequent chapters that similar futurity issues arise in development activities ranging from fertility control to agricultural production to institution building. The assessment of futurities is an exercise in identifying option-generating and option-foreclosing actions, in articulating major trade-offs and complementarities, and, generally, in appreciating some of the long-term implications inherent in policy choice.

How are long-term consequences to be assessed in the face of partial, incomplete, and inconclusive information? With partial, incomplete, and inconclusive analysis—analysis that is explicitly aware of and strategically adapted to its own limitations; analysis that aims to support, not replace, ongoing interactive approaches to social problem-solving; analysis, in short, that is the direct antithesis of the synoptic Received View on which Mr. Nehru based the peculiar statement quoted earlier, a Received View which in its essentials is repeated by many contemporary texts on policy analysis.[20]

In our experience, the key to effective strategic analysis is a commitment to simplicity. In a field as complex and immature as development, attempts to analyze everything are futile. At best they produce analyses as intricate and unfathomable as the real world. They are more likely to founder in a limbo of unending data requirements, opaque argument, and general ineffectiveness. In place of a spurious pretense of comprehensive authority, we have found that analysis benefits from being "as ruthlessly parsimonious and economical as possible while still retaining responsiveness to the management objectives and

[19] The analogy comes from Dr. Gordon Baskerville, who points out that this is precisely how many resource management agencies in North America "design" their policies.

[20] For example, the well-known text by Stokey and Zeckhauser (1978) is, we believe, of very limited relevance to ill-structured problems; and it virtually ignores problems of organization and implementation.

actions appropriate for the problem" (Clark, Jones, and Holling 1979, p. 7).[21] Only through such parsimony can the analysis achieve the transparency necessary for political credibility, and the accessibility necessary to become part of the social interactions of real-world problem-solving.

Some guidance is necessary for deciding what few things to include in an analysis and what many things to leave out. Experts often are of little help in providing such guidance. A characteristic of experts is the conviction that their particular specialty is the one thing which absolutely must be considered if an analysis is to have any validity. When the number of participating experts is very large, the chances of conducting a useful analysis becomes correspondingly small.[22]

Our approach to this dilemma puts the experts in service of the analysis instead of vice versa. Instead of asking the experts what they believe to be important, we begin from the perspectives of those who will have to endure the chosen policy and those who will have to implement that policy. We focus first on the most intensely felt needs of the policy endurers. What is wrong with the present situation? What specific evils are most in need of mitigation? What aspects of past policies require correction? We next turn to the specific actions or interventions which policymakers and implementors believe to be potentially feasible and desirable. What might actually be done? What resources are available? What political coalitions are needed and possible? Finally, we proceed to mobilize the small subset of expert knowledge and experience which is necessary to establish relationships between the implementors' actions and the endurers' needs.[23] To be sure, things are left out of such an analysis. Optimal prescriptions are not even aspired to; the modest hope is to find something merely better. With luck and cunning, the exercise has been known to produce insights and progress.

Looking Inward: An Interactive View of Adaptive Learning

The analytic processes of looking backward and looking forward aim to invent perspectives from which to guide and interpret the ongoing experience of development. It remains to look inward with a view towards reorganizing the processes by which policy redesign and implementation actually occur. Our goal is to use what we do know so that we can better contend with what we

---

[21] On the mistaken pursuit of authoritativeness in policy analysis see Lindblom and Cohen (1979).

[22] This phenomenon is well documented in the literature on social "modeling," e.g., Brewer (1973), March and Olsen (1976), Ackerman et al. (1974), Holcomb Research Institute (1976).

[23] The approach outlined here was developed by Carl Walters and his colleagues at the Institute of Resource Ecology, University of British Columbia. It is described in more detail, and illustrated with examples, in Holling (1978, esp. chaps. 4 and 11). In part, it reflects what March and Olsen (1976) have described as the "garbage can model of social choice." Problems and solutions pile up independently, as results of quite different sociopolitical processes. The goal of the problem-resolver is to bring about effective matches between them.

do not—to design the experience of development so that we can better learn from it.

Debate on this learning problem often has polarized around the extremes of "external intervention" and "planning from below." External intervention, in its most pronounced forms, is a relatively pure example of the thinking-through, or intellectual-cogitation, approach to social problem-solving. Its presumption is that professional development experts are the best equipped to solve development problems. The job of local authorities and policy endurers is to implement the experts' calculated solutions. In reality, however, significant improvements in the condition of the rural poor (or of anyone else) require that the individual people with the problem become willing and able to change their way of doing things. To be adopted, the change must be perceived as effective by the people adopting it. It must also be sufficiently in tune with local realities that it does not bring down retribution from either environment or society on the head of the changer. Sensitive adaptation of broad strategy to the aspirations, resources, and constraints existing at the community level is not an activity at which national or international agencies are particularly adept. We argue in chapter 5 that one of the worst consequences of the paternalistic arrogance involved in "doing development to the poor" has been the failure to make use of local knowledge, skills, competence, and perceptions of what "the problems" actually are. This disregard of local circumstances is responsible for many failures of external intervention to produce successful development policies.

The alternative extreme of planning from below has gained popularity in recent years. In part, this reflects the basic sensibility of an implementation-oriented approach; in part it embodies a reaction to the failures of external intervention. The planning-from-below approach reflects the old consultant's adage that "only the man with the problem can solve the problem." It therefore emphasizes local perceptions, capabilities, and constraints; it stresses feasibility; it relies heavily on acting-out methods of policy calculation and control. There seems little question that the procedure often works, after a fashion, where external intervention has failed. A heavy price is paid for this success, however, a price often forgotten or ignored by the advocates of planning from below. Most obviously, approaches viewing the world entirely from below miss the perspective gained from an awareness of other experiences in other locations. In addition, they forgo or downgrade the highly sophisticated development options (genetically improved crop strains, for example) that no amount of local effort can invent. Perhaps most significantly, the planning-from-below approach assumes that the time and energy of the people from below is a free and unlimited resource. This is readily apparent in the current enthusiasms for "maximizing local participation." How extraordinary! Whether it is a housewife trying to fit a health class into her crowded daily schedule or an administrator trying to promote another town meeting, the resource of "planning effort" is exceedingly scarce and in high demand. Listening to some of the more euphoric tales of the planning-from-below advocates, it is easy to conjure a vision of the rural poor doing nothing but sitting in endless meetings and lectures, imitating their advisors to the last full measure of coronary thrombosis.

As guides to learning, the extremes of external intervention and planning from below both have shortcomings. Effective policy redesign requires an integration that recognizes the strengths and limitations of each. Our goal is to promote that integration.

Our first concern is to avoid doing in the name of analysis stupid things which make positions more rigid and learning and adaptation more difficult than they already are. We therefore begin by rejecting analysis of objectives, preferences, or conflicts as a point of departure. If people learn what they want by understanding what they can get, then it makes little sense to ask them what they want and then treat their answers as the last word on the subject, only to discover how many other people want incompatible things. Social-problem resolution is hard enough without this sort of analytic assistance. Once again, our goal is to help preferences change and adapt to reality, not to cast them in cement. The ambiguity of self-interest to which we referred earlier is an asset, not an obstacle to policy redesign. Preferences and conflicts do and should change in the course of successful problem resolutions. Any analysis focused on what those preferences or conflicts were is therefore likely to become rapidly obsolete (Clark, Jones, and Holling 1979, pp. 6–7; Holling 1978, chap. 8). Conflict resolution is indeed one end of analysis, but that end is approached through means of facilitating adjustment, not by accentuating differences.

For the same reasons that we reject conflict analysis and similar approaches as counterproductive, we reemphasize Hirschman's view that an emphasis on "uniquely correct policies" and "absolute priorities" can do little but hurt the development process (1971, pp. 19–20). The Eskimo who insisted that he must carve a falcon from some particular bone would likely be both a bad and a frustrated artist. Absolute priorities too often include some of those many things that the policy process shows to be infeasible or undesirable or both. In addition, the absolute priority, if it has any specificity at all, is a prejudice formed prior to a consideration of what can be obtained at what cost. This is just what our analysis is trying to avoid. As for uniquely correct policies, once it is accepted that we do not yet know where we are going—because of the need for mutual adjustment of ends and means—then there clearly is little to be gained from plotting a road map of how best to get there. Analysis in its uniquely-optimal, absolutely-best mode is as destructive of learning as can possibly be imagined. We believe that there are better ways to play the game.

One of the great challenges for policy analysis is the design of organizational structures which can mobilize local experience and integrate it with improved expertise. In seeking to promote this design function, we therefore emphasize the importance of local organizations for articulating needs and delivering services. We recognize, however, that organizational resources are at least as scarce and valuable as capital, land, and technical knowledge.

Above all, we insist that the design of development must be seen as a trial-and-error learning process. Contrary to the ambitions of the cerebral planners, there can be no trial without error. Contrary to the practice of the let's-get-on-with-it activists, the poor should not be made to endure repeated trials from which nothing is learned.

Whatever approach to policy design and implementation is pursued, many choices will turn out wrong, and many programs will fail. Ultimately, these failures are guaranteed by pervasive ignorance and uncertainty regarding the development mess. All the research and analysis ever done will not eliminate this uncertainty, or even make a large dent in it.

Our goal as advocates of policy redesign is not to eliminate uncertainty but to accommodate it more effectively. In practical terms this means using the best analysis and knowledge that we can muster to help policymakers to see a little further ahead, to comprehend a few more interactions, and to avoid some of the truly disastrous and irreversible mistakes to which development is prone. It means recognizing that mistakes—big, costly ones—will be made anyway. It means viewing failures as a form of unavoidable, dearly paid-for, but potentially invaluable experience which can be the single greatest asset in a continuing adaptive effort to redesign development strategies. And it is important, of course, for the learning to lead as promptly as possible to policy redesign so as to reduce the cost of errors.

The results of our own efforts to better accommodate the uncertainties of development are reported in the next five chapters. As we've said, we are less concerned with convincing you, our readers, of our conclusions than with helping you to reflect on your own actions and experience. For that reason, we concentrate throughout on articulating the major issues, constraints, trade-offs, complementarities, and uncertainties which arise in designing and redesigning policies for rural development. We seek to build a framework that will help you better utilize what is known about development policy in order that you may cope more effectively with what is not. We therefore present our evidence and analysis in a sequence that starts with knowledge that is relatively specific and certain. We build from this foundation of fact up towards the necessarily broader and more speculative issues involved in the redesign of development strategies. Chapter 2 begins the sequence with a review of the fairly solid but conventional evidence which defines the conditions of rural poverty in the late-developing countries, and establishes the constraints within which policies to alleviate that poverty must operate.

CHAPTER TWO

Rural People:
Conditions and Constraints

To attempt to deal with all the dimensions of a problem as vast and complex as rural development would be futile. It is necessary, as we argued in chapter 1, to simplify and bound the problem without losing sight of the elements that are of fundamental importance. It is also useful to begin with an examination of what is known with reasonable confidence about the nature of the rural development problem before going on to discuss intervention programs, where our judgments inevitably are tentative and can rarely yield "hard conclusions."

Introduction

We bound the problem in part by emphasizing things that really matter prior to considering what can be done to change the most unsatisfactory features of the present situation. Our objectives in this chapter are twofold: to identify what really matters as a basis for determining what changes are most *desirable*; and to identify the major constraints, which largely determine what is *feasible*.

The general rubric "developing nations" comprises a large and highly diverse group of countries. Our first step in bounding the problem addressed in this book is to define the subset of developing countries on which our analysis is focused. The economic growth experience of the middle-income developing countries has differed sharply from that of the low-income countries. They not only had substantially higher levels of per capita GNP in 1960 but have subsequently experienced much more rapid rates of growth than the low-income countries. Table 2.1 contrasts average figures for thirty-eight low-income and fifty-two middle-income countries. In addition, the table presents data for ten low-income countries which account for approximately one fourth of the world's population. The selected countries are representative of the variation in income and in other basic indicators that characterize the full set of countries with per capita income of $360 or less in 1978. The eight middle-income countries included in the table represent a more arbitrary selection, but they give a fair indication of the wide variation in income and other characteristics of the fifty-two countries in that category.

Table 2.1. Basic Indicators for Low- and Middle-Income Developing Countries

Country	Population (millions) mid-1978	GNP per capita		Percentage of labor force in agriculture	
		(U.S. dollars) 1978	Average annual growth rate (%) 1960–78	1960	1978
A. Low-Income Countries[a]					
Ethiopia	31.0	120	1.5	88	81
Bangladesh	84.7	90	–0.4	87	74
Zaire	26.8	210	1.1	83	76
India	643.9	180	1.4	74	74
Pakistan	77.3	230	2.8	61	58
Tanzania	16.9	230	2.7	89	83
Madagascar	8.3	250	–0.3	93	86
Sri Lanka	14.3	190	2.0	56	54
Indonesia	136.0	360	4.1	75	60
Kenya	14.7	330	2.2	86	79
Average for 38 countries (total population: 1.3 billion)		200[b]	1.6	77	72
B. Middle-Income Countries[a]					
Nigeria	80.6	560	3.6	71	56
Philippines	45.6	510	2.6	61	48
Colombia	25.6	850	3.0	52	30
Korea, Republic of	36.6	1,160	6.9	66	41
Costa Rica	2.1	1,540	3.3	51	29
Taiwan	17.1	1,400	6.6	56	37
Mexico	65.4	1,290	2.7	55	39
Brazil	119.5	1,570	4.9	52	41
Average for 52 countries (total population: 873 million)		1,250[c]	3.7	58	45
Average for 18 industrialized countries (total population: 668 million)		8,070	3.7	17	6

Source: World Bank (1980*a*), pp. 110–11, 146–47.
[a] Listed according to their estimated per capita GNP in 1976 (World Bank 1978, pp. 76–77).
[b] The range is from $90 to $360.
[c] The range is from $390 to $3,500.

In the sections that follow we highlight some of the most significant characteristics of low- and middle-income countries through comparison of their (1) structural and demographic relationships, (2) changes in mortality rates, life expectancy, and morbidity, and (3) changes in fertility and rates of natural increase. We then summarize some of the evidence concerning food production and the adequacy of food supplies. Our focus on the distinction between low- and middle-income countries is dictated by data limitations and by the lack of agreement on a more meaningful typology.[1] One especially significant

[1] Dissatisfaction with GNP estimates as indicators of "development" has led to a renewal of interest in alternative indicators of "the quality of life." A "Physical Quality of Life Index" (PQLI) has been presented by the Overseas Development Council "as a measure of how effectively various development strategies distribute the most basic benefits of development progress to all parts of society" (ODC 1977, p. 148). It is a composite index (on a scale of one hundred) of three indicators—life expectancy, infant mortality, and literacy. As would be expected, there is consid-

parameter that would be included in a more meaningful typology is the extent to which an overwhelmingly agrarian economy has been transformed by structural change.[2]

Structural and Demographic Features

Of great relevance to the design of strategies for rural development is the contrast between countries where substantial industrial growth has already led to considerable economic diversification and a good deal of structural transformation and countries still predominantly agricultural in terms of the occupational composition of their labor force and the source of GNP. Our focus is on the "late-developing countries," where some 60–80 percent of the labor force is still dependent on agriculture for a livelihood. This contrast based on the degree of structural change has important implications with respect to both the persistence and the current extent of rural poverty. Virtually all countries in the low-income category of developing countries are "late-developing" in this sense; only in Sri Lanka and Burma was appreciably less than 60 percent of the labor force in agriculture in 1978.[3] Most of the middle-income countries had already experienced considerably more structural change by 1960, and the contrast between the two groups of countries had become a good deal more pronounced by 1978 (table 2.1). However, the labor force structure in a number of the "lower-middle-income" countries meets our crude definition of late-developing. Thus in 1978 ten out of twenty middle-income countries with per capita GNP in the range of $390 to $840 still had 60 percent or more of their labor force in agriculture. Among the thirty-two middle-income countries with per capita GNP above $840, only Turkey had 60 percent of its labor force in agriculture in 1978; in Nigeria and Ghana, however, about 55 percent of the labor force was in agriculture. For eighteen industrialized countries, the average share of the labor force dependent on agriculture in 1978 was only 6 percent, as compared with 17 percent in 1960. It

erable correlation between the PQLI estimate and per capita GNP: an average PQLI of 39 for low-income countries; 59 and 67, respectively, for low- and upper-middle-income countries; and 95 for high-income countries. But some of the variations in the PQLI within a particular income category are striking. For example, Sri Lanka is a low-income country with a PQLI of 83; conversely, the middle-income countries Nigeria and Gabon, with PQLIs of only 25 and 21, respectively, rank well below the average for low-income countries. There are marked regional variations in the relationship between a country's income and its PQLI which appear to be related to historical and cultural factors and the availability of natural resources (Brown 1978, p. 84). A recent World Bank publication analyzes those regional patterns in considerable detail (1980a, chap. 7). GNP estimates for less developed countries are subject to statistical problems related to the availability of data, as well as the conceptual problems noted above. The changes between 1976 and 1978 in the rank ordering of a number of the countries in table 2.1 were probably influenced as much by changes in judgment as by actual changes in their "true" GNP over a two-year period.

[2] Some key members of the World Bank's Urban Poverty Task Force have utilized an interesting four-way classification of development situations which is helpful for analyzing problems of managing rapid growth of cities and urban poverty (Beier et al. 1976).

[3] An even lower figure for Benin seems highly questionable (World Bank 1980a, p. 146).

is noteworthy that even in agriculturally oriented high-income countries such as Denmark and New Zealand only 8 percent and 10 percent, respectively, of the labor force was employed in agriculture.

The sources of variation in the composition of the labor force among developing countries were many and complex. Given that agriculture continues to employ a large percentage of the labor force in late-developing countries, in combination with rapid rates of growth in total population and in the labor force, the decrease in the share of the labor force dependent on agriculture will inevitably be slow.

Because of the high correlation between the characteristics "late-developing" and "low-income," we will sometimes use the terms interchangeably to describe the subset of developing countries on which we focus in this essay. Moreover, the generalizations that we advance in later chapters are likely to be most applicable to the intersecting set which has both characteristics. The severity of resource constraints in poor countries, whether "low-" or "lower-middle-" income, necessarily limits the options that are feasible. Limited organizational capacities and lack of trained and experienced manpower are also extremely important constraints and raise issues which we examine at length in chapter 5. Knowledge and understanding of organizational and managerial capabilities, and means of enhancing those capabilities, are woefully inadequate. But it seems obvious that variations in the availability of trained manpower and organizational capacities are only loosely correlated with levels of per capita GNP. India, for example, is much better endowed in those respects, even adjusting for large differences in population, than are countries in Sub-Saharan Africa with considerably higher levels of income (Acharya 1978, pp. 10–15; World Bank 1980a, pp. 87–90).

It is the combination of structural and demographic features in late-developing countries that ensures that for many years the problems of persistent poverty will be concentrated to a large extent among their rural populations. And the predominance of agriculture in a country's total population and labor force also has important implications for the design of agricultural strategies, to which we turn in chapter 3.

Late-developing Countries and the Growth of the
Agricultural Population

By definition, the rate of growth of a country's total labor force equals the rate of growth of the labor force in each sector multiplied by sectoral weights. For countries that are still predominantly agricultural, however, it is illuminating to write that identity in such a way that the rate of change in the agricultural labor force (L'_a) is a "residual" determined "exogenously" by agriculture's initial share in the labor force (L_a/L_t) and the rates of change in the total labor force (L'_t) and in the nonagricultural labor force (L'_n):

$$L'_a \equiv (L'_t - L'_n) \frac{1}{L_a/L_t} + L'_n. \tag{1}$$

The rationale for writing the identity with the rate of change in the agricultural work force (L'_a) as the "dependent variable" has been set forth elsewhere (Johnston 1969, pp. 67–71). The principal qualification to viewing the agricultural labor force as a "dependent variable," especially if income-earning opportunities in agriculture are severely restricted, is that a sizable fraction of the "residual" work force will migrate to urban slums and eke out an existence in petty trade, as casual laborers, or in various illicit activities.

The significance of this "arithmetic of population growth and structural transformation" can be illustrated by hypothetical calculations of the time required to reach the turning point when the agricultural labor force begins to decline in absolute size. The Western European countries and Japan reached their "structural-transformation turning point" without any significant increase in the size of the agricultural labor force. The rates of growth of total population and labor force during their demographic transition were only about 1–1.5 percent, so that a moderate rate of growth of nonfarm employment was sufficient to absorb the annual additions to the labor force. In Japan, agriculture's share in the total labor force was still large in the 1880s. But because the total labor force was growing at a little less than 1 percent while nonfarm employment was increasing at about 3.5 percent, the additions to the labor force were absorbed by the nonfarm sectors, and the percentage of the labor force dependent on agriculture declined rapidly from about 75 percent in the mid-1880s to less than 70 percent in the mid-1890s. During the first three decades of the twentieth century the rate of increase in nonfarm employment declined considerably; but even so, agriculture's share in the labor force was less than 50 percent in 1930, and the absolute size of the farm work force declined from 15.5 million in the mid-1880s to 14.1 million.[4]

Today's developing countries, however, are experiencing substantial growth in the size of their farm labor force because of rapid growth of total population and labor force combined with a high initial share of agriculture in the total labor force. Because it experienced a rapid decline in mortality as early as the 1920s, Taiwan's total labor force was already increasing at a fairly rapid rate of 2.3 percent during the 1930s; and the farm work force increased from 1.2 million in 1930 to 2.0 million in the mid-1960s in spite of a very rapid growth of nonfarm employment.[5]

The hypothetical calculations summarized in figure 2.1 illustrate the sensitivity to the values of the three parameters in equation (1)—the rates of growth of the total labor force and of the nonfarm labor force, and the initial share of agriculture in the total—of the time required to reach the turning point when the agricultural labor force begins to decline. Panel A shows the number of years required to reach the structural-transformation turning point for various combinations of constant growth rates of total and nonagricultural employment when agriculture accounts for 70 percent of the labor force. For exam-

[4] See Johnston and Kilby (1975, appendix tables 2 and 3).
[5] Ibid.

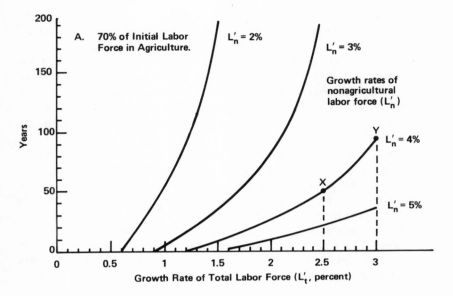

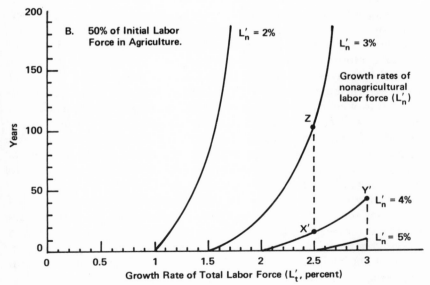

Figure 2.1. Time until the Turning Point When the Agricultural Labor Force Begins to Decline.

Note: The figure shows the number of years until the turning point is reached as a function of the growth rate of the total labor force (L'_t) and of the growth rate of the nonagricultural labor force (L'_n).

ple, if the total labor force increased at 2.5 percent annually, and nonfarm employment at the rapid rate of 4 percent annually, just over fifty years would be required to reach the turning point (at X). But if the total labor force increased at 3 percent instead of 2.5 percent, the time required to reach the turning point (at Y) would nearly double, to ninety-five years. (Obviously, if the rate of growth of nonfarm employment were the same as the growth rate of the total labor force, there would be no change in the relative shares of agriculture and nonagriculture, and the time required to reach a turning point would be infinite.)

Panel B illustrates how a seemingly modest change in agriculture's share in the total labor force, from 70 percent to 50 percent, would drastically reduce the time required to reach a structural-transformation turning point. For example, with a 2.5-percent rate of growth for the total labor force and a 4-percent growth rate in nonfarm employment, the turning point (at X') would be reached in only about fifteen years. With a 2-percent rate of growth for the total labor force, a country would already be at the turning point. However, with 70 percent of the labor force still in agriculture, as in panel A, a 4-percent rate of growth of nonfarm employment would fully absorb the annual increment in the work force only if the growth rate of the total labor force had declined to 1.2 percent. Even with a 3-percent rate of growth for the total labor force, the time required would be only forty-two years (Y' in panel B), as compared with the ninety-five years shown for the same combination of growth rates in panel A. But with a somewhat slower rate of growth of nonfarm employment, 3 percent, and a 2.5-percent rate of growth for the total labor force, 105 years would be required even though agriculture's initial share in the labor force was down to 50 percent (point Z). The corresponding point in panel A is not shown, but assuming that constant growth rates of 2.5 percent and 3 percent were maintained, the turning point would be reached in 210 years. It is of course absurd to suppose that the growth rates of a country's labor force will remain constant for even twenty or thirty years. In fact, awareness of the impact of a rapid rate of growth of a country's total labor force on the process of transforming the structure of a predominantly agricultural economy may reinforce other considerations which motivate governments to adopt programs to slow the rate of population growth.

The conclusion is inescapable that under even the most optimistic of assumptions, the late-developing countries will remain predominantly rural societies into the twenty-first century. Their rural populations may well increase threefold or more before they begin to decline, posing truly staggering problems for the maintenance, much less improvement, of present levels of well-being.

Introducing into the analysis explicit consideration of rural-urban migration and of changing fertility rates leaves the qualitative character of this conclusion unchanged. Andrei Rogers (1978) has explored the future consequences of various assumptions about changes in mortality, fertility, and migration that yield numerical estimates of the future size, age composition, and spatial (urban-rural) distribution of population. The projections in table 2.2 depict the increase in total population and "labor force" (actually the population of "working age," defined as fifteen through sixty-four) over a fifty-year period related to his two alternative assumptions with respect to fertility—fertility unchanged and fertility reduced—and his two assumptions about internal migration—migration unchanged and migration increased (the specific assumptions are summarized in part B of the table).

Inasmuch as the two scenarios with "fertility unchanged" imply an initial rate of natural increase of 3 percent, which increases appreciably over the first thirty years as mortality continues to decline and fertility remains at its initial high levels, the projected growth of population by year fifty is very great in-

Table 2.2. Alternative Projections of Urban and Rural Population and "Labor Force" over a Fifty-Year Period

		Initial Year			Year Fifty	
A. The Four Scenarios		Total Population	Labor force[a]		Total Population	Labor force[a]
1. Fertility and migration unchanged	Urban	0.2	0.1	Urban	2.0	1.0
	Rural	0.8	0.4	Rural	4.7	2.3
	Total	1.0	0.5	Total	6.7	3.3
2. Fertility reduced, migration unchanged		Same		Urban	1.0	.6
				Rural	2.3	1.4
				Total	3.3	2.0
3. Fertility unchanged, migration increased		Same		Urban	4.2	2.1
				Rural	2.2	1.0
				Total	6.4	3.1
4. Fertility reduced, migration increased		Same		Urban	2.0	1.3
				Rural	1.1	.7
				Total	3.1	2.0

B. Rogers's Assumptions Underlying the Four Scenarios
Initial Values (per thousand)   Future Paths

	Urban	Rural		
Death rate	11	15	*Mortality*:	Decline over 25 years (urban) and 35 years (rural) to a level with an expectation of life at birth of 70 years; unchanged thereafter
Birth rate	40	45		
Out-migration rate	10	7	*Fertility*:	In (2) and (4) a reduction of 50 percent over 20 years (urban) and 30 years (rural); unchanged thereafter
			Migration:	In (3) and (4) an increase of 500 percent over 50 years

Source: Rogers (1978), pp. 176–77.
Note: The initial population is normalized to 1.0.
[a] The population of working age, 15 through 64.

deed. The increase from 1.0 million to 6.4 million in scenario 3, which assumes that unchanged fertility is associated with increased migration, is a little less than the increase to 6.7 million in scenario 1, where fertility and migration both are unchanged.[6] This is a consequence of Rogers's assumption that the constant rate of natural increase is slightly lower in urban areas than in rural areas.

Scenarios 3 and 4, in which increased migration is combined, respectively, with unchanged and with reduced fertility, result in a very large increase in the degree of urbanization by year fifty because of the assumption that rural outmigration would increase by 500 percent over the fifty-year period. In terms of "labor force" composition, at the end of fifty years the rural labor force would account for only about a third of the total labor force, as compared with its initial share of 80 percent. In scenarios 1 and 2, in which the rate of migration is unchanged, there is only a small decline, to 70 percent, in spite of the fact that the urban labor force increases much more rapidly than the rural labor force. Even in scenario 2, in which fertility is reduced, there is a 500-percent increase in the urban labor force and a 250-percent increase in the rural labor force. It is also worth noting that the 300-percent increase in the total labor force is considerably larger than the 230-percent increase in total population, reflecting a substantial lag before a reduced rate of natural increase is reflected fully in a slower rate of growth in the working-age population.

Actual rates of structural change and trajectories of growth of population and labor force for late-developing countries that still have high rates of natural increase are likely to fall somewhere between Rogers's alternative assumptions. But under any realistic set of assumptions, it is apparent that the growth of demand for enlarged food supplies merely to keep pace with population growth will be substantial. And the challenge of expanding opportunities for productive employment in pace with the growth of the working-age population is perhaps even more formidable. Even with the combination of reduced fertility and greatly increased migration assumed in scenario 4 there would be a 75-percent increase in the rural work force. Thus, while the problem of declining size of farm units and increased landlessness would remain substantial, it would not be intensified nearly as much as under the less optimistic assumptions of scenarios 1 and 2.

It seems very unlikely that the growth of the rural sector can be substantially mitigated by urban growth rates above those used in Rogers's analyses. The investment and other requirements that would be required to permit the thirteenfold increase of urban employment in his scenario 4 are staggering.

"Urbanization" and "Urban Growth"

Past experience shows a high correlation between a country's level of economic development and its degree of urbanization, that is the percentage of the

---

[6] Since the initial population in table 2.2 is normalized to 1.0, assignment of magnitudes to the proportional changes is arbitrary. The increase from 1.0 million to 6.4 million could just as well be an increase from 10 million to 64 million.

population located in urban areas. In contrast, there is little or no correlation between economic development and the *rate* of urban population growth (Rogers 1978, pp. 192–93). It is not surprising that urbanization is highly correlated with per capita GNP. It reflects the degree of structural change that has taken place in an economy and the growth of specialization and of functional differentiation among educational and research institutions as well as production units. And this spread of specialization and increasing interdependence between sectors such as agriculture and industry as well as among individual firms is both cause and effect of rising levels of productivity and output (Johnston and Kilby 1975, chap. 2). But for today's developing countries, the rapid rate of urban growth is to a large extent merely a reflection of rapid growth of the total population (United Nations Population Division 1980).[7] Hence it is not surprising that there is essentially no correlation between rates of urban growth and rates of growth in per capita GNP.

The rapid urban growth in developing countries during the past twenty-five years has been associated in most instances with a considerable increase in unemployment and underemployment and "pathological" growth of urban slums. The U.N. projections shown in table 2.3 suggest that even by the year 2000, major cities in a number of countries may reach a size that implies staggering problems of urban management: meeting requirements for water, sanitation, and other services and coping with problems of poverty in urban slums. Indeed, such problems seem so enormous that it is hard to believe that the population of Mexico City, for example, will actually approach 32 million by

[7] Keyfitz (1980) has published an elegant analysis of the factors that determine the relative importance of natural increase among the urban population and of net migration in the growth of a country's urban population. In a country characterized by high rates of natural increase among both the rural and the urban population, urban growth comes to depend mainly on natural increase well before the population becomes predominantly urban. For example, in Mexico, in-migration accounted for nearly 60 percent of the 2.8-million increase in the country's urban population between 1940 and 1950. But between 1960 and 1970, natural increase accounted for just over two thirds of the 8.4-million increase in urban population (Keyfitz 1980, p. 146).

Table 2.3. Population Estimates and Projections for Selected Cities in Africa, Asia, and Latin America

City	Population (millions)			Multiple Increase over Base Year	
	1950	1975	2000	1950–75	1975–2000
Nairobi	0.1	0.7	3.4	5.5	4.5
Lagos	0.29	2.1	9.4	7.2	4.6
Jakarta	1.6	5.6	16.9	3.6	3.0
Karachi	1.0	4.5	15.9	4.3	3.6
Mexico City	2.9	10.9	31.6	3.8	2.9
São Paulo	2.4	10.0	26.0	4.1	2.6

Source: United Nations (1976), pp. 77–83.

the year 2000. But given the momentum that characterizes population growth, the main consequence of slower urban growth during the next two decades would be more rapid growth of the rural population. Accelerated growth of towns and smaller cities could, however, reduce the concentration of population in a single metropolitan area such as Mexico City. With a decentralized pattern of growth of manufacturing and service industries, the distinction between a country's "agricultural" and "rural" population and labor force becomes very significant.

Rural-to-Rural Migration

Because of the difficulty of finding even precarious sources of income in urban areas, intensified pressure of population on the land in the better endowed and more populous rural areas can be expected to lead to considerable rural-to-rural as well as rural-to-urban migration wherever arable land is available. This applies especially to the countries of tropical Africa, although even there the potential for expanding the area under cultivation has already been reduced considerably (Johnson 1978, pp. 78–81).

This phenomenon of rural-to-rural migration is strikingly apparent in Machakos District, Kenya, an area just to the east of Nairobi. At the time of the first population census, in 1932, almost 90 percent of the district's population was concentrated on 25 percent of the land area, where it was about equally divided between "high-potential" hill areas with ample and reliable rainfall and the relatively favorable "medium-potential" areas which surround the high-potential areas. The districtwide growth rate of population increased from about 2.5 percent in the 1932–48 period to 2.8 percent between 1948 and 1963 and to 3.5 percent in the 1963–69 period. Until recently, 3.5 percent was the official estimate of the population growth rate of Kenya as a whole; it is now estimated at about 4 percent, the highest in the world (Mott and Mott 1980; World Fertility Survey, [1979?]). The rate of population growth has been declining, however, in the high-potential areas because of out-migration caused by the increasing pressure of population on the land. But in the less favorable, medium-potential areas, characterized by low and erratic rainfall, the growth of population has greatly exceeded the rate of natural increase. Between 1963 and 1969, migration into this marginal zone was so large that population grew by nearly 14 percent per year, whereas in the high-potential zone the rate of growth declined from 2.8 percent in the 1932–48 period to 1.6 percent in the 1963–69 period because the increase in the rate of natural increase was more than offset by out-migration (Lynam 1978, chap. 2).

Although rural-to-rural migration affords some relief from population pressure in the more productive but densely populated farming areas, the influx of population into marginal areas is magnifying the demands for famine relief on the frequent occasions when the level or distribution of rainfall is more unsatisfactory than usual. The increasing hardship experienced by the households affected is accompanied by degradation of the land because of soil erosion, which is aggravated by the cutting of trees and shrubs for firewood and for making charcoal, an especially significant source of income in seasons when crops fail.

This Kenya example is paralleled by similar problems in many developing countries. Although an influx of population into semiarid areas poses especially serious problems, rural-to-rural migration resulting from rapid population growth is a much more widespread phenomenon. Kikuchi and Hayami (1980, p. 24) have presented a particularly interesting analysis of a village in a rice-producing area 90 kilometers southeast of Manila, where the farm population increased at an annual rate of 5.3 percent between 1966 and 1976 because of a high rate of natural increase and substantial net migration into the village. The effects of the resulting increase in the labor force in holding down the increase in returns to labor are examined in chapter 3.

A general conclusion derived from this analysis of demographic-structural relationships needs to be underscored: even when there is a tremendous acceleration in rural-urban migration, rural development strategies in low-income developing countries must take into account that their agricultural population and work force will increase substantially over the next fifty to one hundred years. More generally, the momentum of population growth in these countries means that the rate of rural-urban migration will affect mainly the relative importance of problems of "hyperurbanization" and of "rural overpopulation" (Rogers 1978, p. 190). Opting for, or accepting, hyperurbanization cannot be expected to avoid the problems of development associated with an expanding agricultural population.

Mortality, Life Expectancy, and Morbidity

Mortality, life expectancy, and morbidity constitute a second dimension along which low- and middle-income developing countries are strongly differentiated. These health-related issues also define the special nature, constraints, and extent of development problems in the low-income countries.

Several health-related indicators are summarized in table 2.4 for the same developing countries that were included in table 2.1. Crude death rates in the middle-income countries were less than 60 percent of those in the low-income countries in 1960. The differential narrowed by 1978, possibly because of a larger increase in the relative size of the young age groups in the low-income countries. Virtually all of the developing countries achieved a substantial increase in life expectancy between 1960 and 1975—from an average of forty-two to fifty years in the low-income countries and from fifty-four to sixty-one years in the middle-income countries.[8] For the thirty-eight low-income countries, the decline in the crude death rate (CDR) was from 24 per thousand to 15 per thousand. Of the ten low-income countries listed in table 2.4, the decline of

[8] All of the figures are of course only approximations.

Table 2.4. Mortality and Health-related Indicators

Country[a]	Crude Death Rate (per thousand)		Life Expectancy at Birth		Child Death Rate (per thousand, ages 1–4)[b]	
	1960	1978	1960	1978	1960	1978
A. Low-Income Countries						
Ethiopia	28	25	36	39	43	37
Bangladesh	25	18	40	47	29	23
Zaire	24	19	40	46	37	27
India	21	14	43	51	28	18
Pakistan	23	15	44	52	27	17
Tanzania	22	16	42	51	32	20
Madagascar	27	19	37	46	41	27
Sri Lanka	9	6	62	69	7	2
Indonesia	23	17	41	47	31	20
Kenya	19	14	47	53	25	14
Average for 38 countries	24	15	42	50	30	20
B. Middle-Income Countries						
Nigeria	25	18	39	48	38	24
Philippines	15	9	51	60	16	7
Colombia	14	8	53	62	17	9
Korea, Republic of	13	8	54	63	13	5
Costa Rica	10	5	62	70	10	3
Taiwan	7	5	64	72	8	1
Mexico	12	8	58	65	14	6
Brazil	11	9	57	62	13	9
Average for 52 countries	14	11	54	61	18	10
Average for 18 industrialized countries	10	9	69	74	1	1

Source: World Bank (1980a), pp. 144–45, 150–51.
[a] The countries are listed in order according to their 1976 per capita income (World Bank 1978, pp. 76–77).
[b] Many of these estimates are rough approximations; see text.

about 10 percent in Ethiopia's CDR (from 28 per thousand to 25 per thousand) was the smallest reduction. The reduction of CDRs in the middle-income countries was from an average level of 14 per thousand in 1960 to 11 per thousand in 1978.

The broad improvements in mortality rates and life expectancy have been influenced to a large extent by reduced mortality among infants and small children. There is, however, great variation in the degree to which infant and child mortality rates have been reduced. Estimates of infant mortality in 1975 in the ten low-income countries ranged from 140 per thousand in Bangladesh to 45 per thousand in Sri Lanka (World Bank 1978, p. 108).[9] Among the

[9] The statistics available concerning infant mortality often represent serious underestimations, and figures for individual countries show a great deal of variation. For example, one 1966 estimate for Madagascar is 102 per thousand, compared with the 69 and 53 per thousand, for

middle-income countries the range of variation was truly enormous—from 163 per thousand in Nigeria to only 14 per thousand in Taiwan.[10]

The estimates of child mortality (deaths per thousand children between the ages of one and four) in table 2.4 for the developing countries are only rough approximations, many of them based on the Coale-Demeny Model life tables (World Bank 1980*a*, p. 164). Nevertheless, the indicated decline between 1960 and 1978 from 30 per thousand to 20 per thousand in the low-income countries is no doubt valid in indicating that a substantial decline occurred. Still, the approximation for 1978 is twice as high as the estimated child mortality in the middle-income countries, and twenty times as high as in the industrialized countries.

According to World Health Organization statistics, despite the reduction of mortality among infants and small children, in 1972 mortality among children under five years still accounted for about half of all deaths in Egypt and Ecuador, and close to 40 percent of all deaths in the Philippines (WHO 1976, p. 83). Estimates for five Central American countries and Panama indicate that deaths in the population under age five accounted for approximately half of all deaths in 1960. By 1975, however, the percentage had declined to about 28 percent in Costa Rica and Panama, but 45 percent of all deaths in Guatemala and close to 40 percent in Honduras and El Salvador (Teller et al. 1979, p. 100).[11] These examples all pertain to middle-income countries. The concentration of deaths in the under-five population might be even greater in some of the low-income developing countries. High fertility, which continues to be characteristic of low-income countries, is itself a significant factor contributing to high infant and child mortality: it increases the percentage of the population in the vulnerable category of children under five; moreover, the mortality risk among infants and small children and their mothers increases significantly after the third birth (World Bank 1980*b*, pp. 20–21).

Changes in negative health indices such as the mortality rate do not provide a very satisfactory measure of the health status of a population. Health is

---

1960 and 1975, respectively, reported by the World Bank (1978, p. 108). Moreover, the 1966 figure was based on a "retrospective survey," an estimation procedure which generally leads to substantial underestimation. In Algeria, for example, infant mortality in 1969 was estimated at 112 per thousand on the basis of retrospective observation, whereas an estimate for 1970 based on repeated-visit surveys is 145 per thousand. A comparison of the two types of estimates in a number of localities in tropical Africa indicates even larger differences (see Vallin 1976, pp. 661–62).

[10] The high figure for Nigeria is not surprising: Nigeria's increase in income is recent and has resulted almost entirely from rapid expansion of petroleum exports, a development which still has had only limited impact on the great mass of the population.

[11] A sharp decline in Costa Rica's crude birth rate (CBR) from 47 per thousand in 1960 to 29 per thousand in 1975, which reduced the proportion of the population under age five, undoubtedly made a significant contribution to the decline in the percentage of total deaths represented by infants and small children from 53.4 percent to 27.6 percent; but a considerable strengthening of rural health services is also a noteworthy factor. In Hong Kong, an even sharper reduction in fertility (from 35 per thousand to 18 per thousand between 1960 and 1975) was associated with a dramatic decline in the proportion of all deaths accounted for by children under age five from more than 30 percent in 1960 to less than 10 percent in 1972 (WHO 1976, p. 83).

difficult to define, and in developing countries, "morbidity data are scarce, poorly standardized, and cannot be quantified" (WHO 1976, p. 10). It is tempting to make inferences about improvements in health and in the "quality of life" on the basis of the available evidence concerning reduced mortality. Thus T. W. Schultz has argued: "The increase in the survival rate of children is the most telling indirect evidence . . . that supports the hypothesis that child quality has been increasing in low-income countries" (1979, p. 16). And lower death rates among infants and children mean that parents do not experience the tragic loss of children as frequently as in the past. However, the medical and nutritional scientists who participated in the ninth session of the Joint FAO/WHO Expert Committee on Nutrition asserted that in many situations "there is no corresponding improvement in health of the children who survive"; the gains represented by reduced mortality "are illusory" because "the health and well-being of many of the survivors is at an appallingly low level" (FAO/WHO 1976, p. 8).

The high level of morbidity is illustrated by a recent study in a Guatemalan village: just over half of the one- to three-year-old children were sick on an average day (Martorell 1979a). On the basis of anthropometric measurements carried out in conjunction with a series of nutrition surveys in Central America, it has been estimated that 71 percent of children under five were malnourished; 3.4 percent were subject to severe Protein-Energy Malnutrition (PEM); 21 percent to moderate PEM; and 47 percent to mild PEM (Martorell 1979b, p. 6). An analysis of changes in three Central American countries between 1965 and 1975 in mortality and in the prevalence of second- and third-degree malnutrition is especially pertinent to the view that reductions in mortality frequently have not been associated with improved health of the surviving children. In Costa Rica, a decline in mortality among the under-five population was associated with a reduction of second- and third-degree malnutrition in that age group from 13 percent to 11.7 percent. But Costa Rica is unusual among Latin American countries in implementing effective rural health programs and in realizing broad participation of its population in socioeconomic advance. In contrast, reduced child mortality in Guatemala and Panama between 1965 and 1975 appears to have been associated with an increase in second- and third-degree malnutrition among the under-five population: from 26.7 percent to 32.5 percent in Guatemala and from 11.1 percent to 20.4 percent in Panama (Teller et al. 1979, p. 102; Valverde et al. 1980). High rates of malnutrition and morbidity among infants and small children seem to persist in other developing regions as well. For example, nutrition survey data reported in Kenya's development plan for 1979–83 indicate that 5 percent of all preschool children are subject to severe PEM, and 30 percent to moderate or mild PEM (Kenya 1979a, p. 151). Similar estimates exist for many other developing countries.

Evidence from a number of surveys in Asia, Africa, and Latin America shows that the frequency, duration, and severity of infectious diseases and many other health problems are much greater in developing nations than in high-income countries.[12] Moreover, the main health problems concentrated among infants and small children and their mothers are related to multiple causal factors. Thus the summary view expressed in the Sixth Report of the WHO Expert Committee on Maternal and Child Health is that "the priority health problems of mothers and children are related to the synergistic effects of malnutrition, infection, and unregulated fertility together with poor socio-economic conditions, including scarcity of health and other social services" (WHO 1976, p. 10).

A large-scale Inter-American Investigation of Mortality in Children, carried out under the auspices of the Pan American Health Organization, appears to be the best source of information concerning the causes of infant and child mortality in developing countries. A major finding of that study is that in the thirteen Latin American projects analyzed, nutritional deficiency was the underlying or an associated cause of death in 52 percent of 33,826 deaths among children under five years (Puffer and Serano 1973, p. 167).

The interactions between malnutrition and infection appear to be a particularly significant source of persistent high mortality and morbidity among children in low-income countries.[13] On the one hand, there is a good deal of evidence that demonstrates that the body's defense mechanisms against infectious disease are impaired by malnutrition. Of equal importance, however, are the ways in which frequent bouts of diarrhea and other health problems contribute to malnutrition. In part this is a direct result of decreased food intake because of loss of appetite or because of the cultural practice of withholding food when a child is sick. In addition, infection causes defective absorption of nutrients because of vomiting or malabsorption per se. Finally, infection often reduces the availability of protein and other nutrients to a child because of altered metabolism, and in many cases there is loss of iron and other nutrients because of parasitic infestation.

It is important to emphasize that both nutritional and health problems are subject to considerable seasonal variation. In many developing countries the wet season is particularly hazardous for rural households. This is the preharvest period when food stocks are most likely to be depleted, and frequently the incidence of malaria and other diseases is at its highest. It is also a period of peak demand for farm labor, which further increases the risk that food intake will fall below requirements (Chambers et al. 1979).

Studies carried out in Guatemala by the Institute for Nutrition for Central America and Panama (INCAP) provide particularly valuable information

---

[12] David Morley estimates that morbidity rates among infants and small children in less developed countries are typically five to ten times as high as in developed countries (Presentation at a meeting on health delivery systems in developing countries, Laxenburg, Austria: IIASA, 1979).

[13] For a good summary statement see Latham (1975); see also Chandra (1979) and Reddy and Srikantia (1978).

concerning the relations between diet, infectious disease, and the development and health of children. The problems start with the health and size of mothers. The prevalence of intrauterine infection, which is very much higher in developing countries than in the developed countries, is "among the most important causes of fetal growth retardation in Guatemala and, most likely, in similar areas as well" (Martorell 1979a, p. 1).

The relationships between a mother's size and food intake during pregnancy and her infant's size and survival prospects are also highly significant. Nutrition scientists estimate that the total energy cost of a normal pregnancy is approximately 80,000 calories. Some 36,000 calories represent the fat that should be gained during pregnancy for use during lactation. In a study of rural Guatemalan women, it was found that nearly 20 percent of those with an energy supplementation during pregnancy of less than 10,000 calories give birth to low-birth-weight babies, that is, weighing less than 2.5 kg, but less than 10 percent among those with an energy supplementation of 20,000 calories or more. The correlation between mothers' height and the percentage of low-birth-weight babies is also striking: close to a fourth of mothers that measured 141 cm or less had low-birth-weight babies, as compared with a little over 10 percent of mothers whose height was 151 cm or more. Furthermore, for the group of mothers measuring 148 cm or less, mortality among their newborns averaged 96 per thousand, as compared with 24 per thousand for newborns of mothers taller than 151 cm. Those are striking differences "given that these are all women from poor isolated communities with only subtle variations in socio-economic status" (Martorell 1979b, p. 5). The strongest correlation is between maternal head circumference and infant birth weight. Nearly 30 percent of babies born to women with a head circumference of less than 50 cm weighed less than 2.5 kg, whereas only about 3 percent of the mothers with a head circumference of 53 cm or more had low-birth-weight babies.

Although the linkage between birth weight and infant mortality and morbidity is indirect, the prevalence of low birth weights in developing countries and the significance of that linkage are well documented. According to a well-known study of the village of Santa Maria Cauqué in Guatemala, 42 percent of the newborns weighed less than 2.5 kg, as compared with about 10 percent in the United States (Mata 1978; Martorell 1979b). The truly dramatic effects of low birth weight apply to the relatively small percentage of newborns weighing less than 2.0 kg. Over half of the babies with a birth weight between 1.5 and 2.0 kg died, as compared with only 2.3 percent of those weighing more than 3.0 kg. The excess risk was much less among the larger fraction of newborns (34 percent of the total) weighing between 2.0 and 2.5 kg, but even so, infant mortality in that group was three times as high as among newborns weighing more than 3.0 kg. Only 10 percent of the Guatemalan babies had a birth weight over 3.0 kg, as compared with 69 percent of babies in the United States (Martorell 1979b, p. 3).

The high correlation between mothers' head circumference and the frequency of low birth weights among babies directs attention to some of the long-term consequences of malnutrition and ill health in the first years of life. The effects of malnutrition on growth in stature are most pronounced during the first two to three years of life. "In the case of head circumference, any retardation would most likely have to occur in the first two years of life" (Martorell 1979*b*, p. 4). Thus malnutrition and retarded growth in early childhood not only increase the risk of mortality and the prevalence of morbidity for all children but also impair girls' ability to deliver a healthy child.

Malnutrition during the first three years of life often impairs the mental as well as the physical development of children. In the case of severe malnutrition at an early age, this may well be due to physiological factors. The more persuasive evidence, however, is related to the behavioral consequences of the syndrome of malnutrition, frequent illness, and apathy (Ricciuti 1979, p. 302). A village study carried out in Mexico by Alfonso Chávez and coworkers at the National Institute of Nutrition matched two groups of children according to the physical and socioeconomic characteristics of their parents. In one group the mothers received a small food supplement during pregnancy, and their children were given a small supplement from five or six months until age three. The mothers and infants in the control group received no supplement to the normal diet. Carefully trained observers well acquainted with the villagers studied the children and their families for several days at a time throughout the study period. It was found that the children that received no supplemental food spent more time in the crib and less time exploring their environment. But the children that received supplementary food had a higher level of "cognitive stimulation" both because they were more active and because they demanded and received more interaction from their parents and siblings (Levitsky 1976; Chávez and Martínez 1979).

An encouraging implication of the view that impaired mental development is mainly a consequence of the behavioral effects of malnutrition is that the impairment need not be permanent. A study of seventy-five hundred families in Colombia from February 1971 to August 1974 examined the effects of integrated health, nutritional, and educational interventions on the cognitive and motor development of experimental and control groups of children. In order to have reference standards for "normal" physical and psychological development that did not depend on foreign standards, a group of children from families of high socioeconomic status was also included. A variety of cognitive measurements were made at intervals to obtain estimates of "general cognitive ability" of experimental groups that were included in the intervention program for either one, two, three, or four nine-month periods. The most important conclusion of the study was "that combined nutritional, health, and educational treatments between 3½ and 7 years of age can prevent large losses of potential cognitive ability, with significantly greater effect the earlier the treatments begin" (McKay et al. 1978, p. 277). A large deficit in cognitive ability was apparent at age three and a half between the "normal" children from families of high socioeconomic status and children subject to nutritional and other poverty-related deprivations. It seems probable that this cognitive deficit among children from poor families could have been reduced significantly by action to improve their nutritional status and health during the critical period from birth to age three or three and a half. That conclusion is suggested by the Mexican study mentioned earlier (Chávez and Martínez 1979) and more directly by a study of children in Bogotá, Colombia, studied longitudinally until age three. Nutritional supplementation and psychological stimulation each had significant effects on factors influencing cognitive development; and when the two interventions were combined there was also a significant interaction effect (Mora et al. 1979). Nutritional supplementation had an especially marked effect on locomotor development, and psychological stimulation had its greatest effect on speech and language development.

There has been great variation among developing countries in the degree of success achieved in reducing infant and child mortality and the extent and severity of health problems such as protein-energy malnutrition and vitamin A deficiency. The evidence for Central America is especially interesting because of the INCAP studies carried out in that region and the strong presumption that the differences in large measure result from program interventions rather than simply from environmental or cultural differences.

The contrasts between Costa Rica and Guatemala are especially striking. As of 1965, the infant mortality rate in Costa Rica was still 65 per thousand, nearly 75 percent as high as that in Guatemala. But in 1977 the rate in Guatemala was still 70 per thousand, while in Costa Rica the rate was down to 27 per thousand, less than 40 percent of that in Guatemala. The contrast in the reduction in mortality in the group aged one to four was even greater. In Guatemala there was a decline from about 34 per thousand in 1965 to 21 per thousand in 1976; but in Costa Rica there was a drastic reduction from an already low 7 per thousand to less than 2 per thousand over the same period. Survey data for the two countries on changes in the prevalence of growth retardation between the mid-1960s and the late 1970s indicate clearly that Costa Rica's much more impressive gains in health were associated with much greater success than in Guatemala in reducing the prevalence of protein-energy malnutrition (Valverde et al. 1980); the progress in Costa Rica was also related to an unusually vigorous and effective rural health program.

Two highly important conclusions are suggested by this brief review of health conditions in developing countries. First, high levels of mortality and a high incidence of morbidity among infants and small children are especially serious manifestations of poverty in many developing countries. This seems particularly true of the low-income, late-developing countries, but it also applies to many middle-income developing countries. Second, there are strong indications that these are problems which can be affected strongly and fairly quickly by government interventions, a proposition that receives major attention in chapter 4.

Fertility and Rates of Natural Increase

The rapid decline in mortality rates in developing countries began well before the 1960–75 period examined in the preceding section. Of course, the persistence of high fertility rates associated with falling mortality accounts for the 75-percent increase in the world's population from 2.5 billion in 1950 to 4.4 billion in 1980. During that thirty years the population in developing countries nearly doubled; by 1980 they accounted for three quarters of the world's population, as compared with just over two thirds in 1950 (Mauldin 1980, p. 148). The population growth rate in the developing countries had already reached an estimated annual rate of 2.1 percent during the period 1950–55, a rate which rose only moderately to 2.4 percent during 1965–70 and 1970–75 (table 2.5).

During the two decades between 1950–55 and 1970–75, the decline in the crude birth rate in developing countries was slight: from an estimated 42.1 per thousand to 39.5 per thousand (table 2.6). Estimates of fertility in developing countries are of course subject to a substantial margin of uncertainty. "Most developing countries lack adequate vital statistics, so it is necessary to derive estimates of fertility from censuses, which are often sporadic and of questionable accuracy; in some cases even censuses are nonexistent" (Kirk 1979, p. 389).[14] It is apparent from table 2.6 that there are considerable and increasing differences in fertility levels in the major developing regions.

The range of variation among individual countries is now very large; even "by 1970 the signs were clear that major declines were occurring in a widening circle of developing countries" (Kirk 1979, p. 387). Estimates reported by Mauldin and Berelson (1978a, p. 97) indicate that in seventeen out of ninety-three countries the decline in the CBR between 1965 and 1975 exceeded 20 percent. Among fifteen developing countries with a population of 35 million

[14] This recent paper by Kirk (1979) provides a concise and extremely valuable review and analysis of the estimates of crude birth rates and rates of natural increase made by eight organizations, including the U.N. Population Division, the World Bank, and the Population Council.

Table 2.5. Average Annual Rate of Population Growth for the World and the Major Developing Regions (in percent)

Region	1950–55	1955–60	1960–65	1965–70	1970–75	1975–77
World total	1.8	2.0	2.0	2.0	1.9	1.9
Excluding China	1.7	1.9	1.9	1.9	1.9	1.8
Developed	1.3	1.3	1.2	1.0	0.9	0.7
Developing	2.1	2.3	2.3	2.4	2.4	2.3
Excluding China	2.1	2.3	2.4	2.5	2.4	2.4
Africa	2.1	2.3	2.5	2.6	2.7	2.8
Asia	2.0	2.2	2.1	2.3	2.2	2.1
Latin America	2.6	2.8	2.8	2.7	2.6	2.6

Source: U.S. Bureau of the Census; estimates presented in Kirk (1979), p. 398.

Table 2.6. Estimated Crude Birth Rates for the Major Developing Regions

Region	1950–55	1955–60	1960–65	1965–70	1970–75	Percent Decline 1950–75
World total	35.6	34.6	33.7	32.1	31.5	−11.5
Developing	42.1	40.9	39.9	38.4	39.5	−10.9
Developed	22.9	21.9	20.5	18.1	17.2	−24.9
Africa	48.1	48.0	47.7	47.2	46.3	− 3.7
Latin America	41.0	40.5	39.5	38.1	36.9	−10.0
East Asia	35.6	30.9	28.5	27.0	26.2	−26.4
South Asia	44.0	45.1	44.8	42.9	41.9	− 7.1
Southeast Asia	44.7	45.6	44.9	43.4	42.4	− 7.0
Middle South Asia	43.9	45.1	44.9	42.7	41.7	− 7.5
Southwest Asia	46.2	45.9	44.1	43.5	42.8	− 7.4

Source: United Nations (1977); estimates presented in Kirk (1979), p. 396.

or more, eight have had declines in the CBR of 20 percent or more; but in five of the fifteen countries, there was no significant change (see table 2.7). There is, however, considerable variation in the estimates of CBRs in developing countries. Even as a global average for 1975, the estimates range from a low of 26.6 births per thousand (espoused by AID, the Agency for International Development) to 33.7 per thousand (the estimate of the Environmental Fund). "Estimates of the birth rate in China are extremely tenuous," Kirk notes. The two global estimates are influenced strongly by the fact that AID uses a remarkably low figure for China, 14 per thousand, whereas the Environmental Fund uses an extremely high figure, 36 per thousand (Kirk 1979, pp. 391, 394). The World Bank now uses an estimate of 18 per thousand for 1978, as compared with their estimate of 26 per thousand for 1975, published two years earlier (World Bank 1978, p. 105; 1980a, p. 145). Needless to say, that change is more a reflection of a change in experts' perception of fertility levels than a measure of the actual change in fertility during a three-year period.

Fertility levels are influenced by numerous biological factors, such as the extent to which conception is reduced by post-partum amenorrhea, and the attitudinal and societal factors which determine both the motivation to practice family planning and the knowledge of and access to effective contraceptive methods.[15] Indeed the determinants of changes in fertility and in the rate of population growth are so complex that there is still only very limited agreement concerning them. We defer our review of attempts to explain changes in fertility and in population growth until our discussion of population programs in chapter 4.

[15] Changes in a country's crude birth rate are, of course, also influenced by changes in the age composition of the population. The total fertility rate (TFR) is free of that distortion because it is defined as the number of children a woman would have had throughout her childbearing years if she experienced the age-specific fertility rates of all women in that population during the year to which the TFR estimate pertains. There are, however, serious data problems in estimating TFRs for developing countries.

Table 2.7. Crude Birth Rates and Crude Birth Rate Declines for Fifteen Less Developed Countries

Country	1980 Population (millions)	Crude Birth Rate		Percentage Change in Crude Birth Rate, 1965–1975 (or later)
		1965	1975 (or later)	
China	975	34	22[a]	−35
India	694	43	36	−16
Indonesia	152	46	36	−22
Brazil	122	42	33[b]	−21
Bangladesh	89	48	48	[c]
Pakistan	82	47	47	[c]
Nigeria	77	49	49	[c]
Mexico	70	44	37[a]	−16
Philippines	51	44	34[b]	−23
Thailand	48	44	33	−26
Turkey	45	40	34	−16
Egypt	42	41	37	−10
Iran	38	45	45	[c]
South Korea	38	32	22	−29
Burma	35	40	40	[c]
Total	2,523	40	33	−20

Source: Mauldin (1980), p. 153.
Note: The countries each had a population of 35 million or more. Vietnam, with an estimated population of 52 million, is not included, since information on its vital rates over time is not thought to be reliable.
[a] 1978.
[b] 1977.
[c] No significant change.

A significant contrast between the low-income and middle-income developing countries concerns the prospects for slowing population growth during the next two or three decades. Even among the low-income countries, however, there was substantial variation in the change in fertility between 1960 and 1978. In several African countries there were small increases, whereas in Sri Lanka there was a 28-percent decrease (from 36 per thousand to 26 per thousand). In fact, Sri Lanka is the only low-income country that has already achieved a significant reduction in the rate of population growth. According to recent estimates, however, China had a 1978 per capita income comparable to Sri Lanka's, and experienced an even larger decline in fertility and in its rate of natural increase (see table 4.1).

In the low-income countries the crude birth rate (CBR) declined from 48 per thousand in 1960 to 39 per thousand in 1978. This weighted average figure is influenced strongly, however, by the substantial declines in fertility believed to have taken place in India and Indonesia in recent years; these two countries account for 60 percent of the population in the thirty-eight low-income countries. We have followed the approach of the *World Development Report 1980* in reporting group averages weighted by population. In this instance, however, it is important to note that the decline in the unweighted average fertility for the thirty-eight low-income countries between 1960 and 1978 was only from 47 per thousand to 45 per thousand, reflecting the fact that in the great majority of these countries no significant reduction had taken place by 1978.

In terms of the weighted averages, the decline in the CBR from 48 per thousand in 1960 to 39 per thousand in 1978 was just offset by a decline in the CDR from 24 per thousand to 15 per thousand. Hence, the average rate of natural increase remained unchanged at 2.4 percent. In many of the low-income countries, however, the rate of natural increase was higher in 1978 than in 1960, as illustrated by seven of the ten low-income countries included in table 2.8. The 1960 CDR of 24 per thousand was considerably below the "traditional" levels of mortality of some 40–45 per thousand that had prevailed in some countries until the late 1940s. The 2.4-percent rate of growth of population in 1960 was therefore already exceptionally high. In Western Europe, Japan, and most other areas that have passed through the "demographic transition" the rate of

Table 2.8. Fertility, Mortality, and Rates of Natural Increase

Country	Crude Birth Rate (per thousand)		Crude Death Rate (per thousand)		Rate of Natural Increase (percent)	
	1960	1978	1960	1978	1960	1978
A. Low-income countries[a]						
Ethiopia	51	49	28	25	2.3	2.4
Bangladesh	51	46	25	18	2.6	2.8
Zaire	48	46	24	19	2.4	2.7
India	43	35	21	14	2.2	2.1
Pakistan	48	45	23	15	2.5	3.0
Tanzania	48	48	22	16	2.6	3.2
Madagascar	47	45	27	19	2.0	2.6
Sri Lanka	36	26	9	6	2.7	2.0
Indonesia	47	37	23	17	2.4	2.0
Kenya	51	51	19	14	3.2	3.7
Average for 38 countries; weighted	48	39	24	15	2.4	2.4
Unweighted average	47	45				
B. Middle-income countries[a]						
Nigeria	52	50	25	18	2.7	3.2
Philippines	45	35	15	9	3.0	2.6
Colombia	46	31	14	8	3.2	2.3
Korea, Republic of	41	21	13	8	2.8	1.3
Costa Rica	47	28	10	5	3.7	2.3
Taiwan	39	21	7	5	3.2	1.6
Mexico	45	38	12	8	3.3	3.0
Brazil	40	36	11	9	2.9	2.7
Average for 52 countries	40	35	14	11	2.6	2.4
Average for industrialized countries	20	14	10	9	1.0	0.5

Source: World Bank (1980a), pp. 144–45.
[a] Listed in order of 1976 per capita income.

natural increase during periods of rapid population growth was only about 1.0–1.5 percent because of their much more gradual decline in mortality.

Among the middle-income countries, there was even greater variation in the extent to which fertility declined between 1960 and 1978. For the entire group of fifty-two middle-income countries (table 2.8), a decline in the CBR, from 40 per thousand to 35 per thousand, was a little larger than the decline in the CDR, from 14 per thousand to 11 per thousand. Hence the rate of natural increase in that group of countries apparently declined from 2.6 percent to 2.4 percent. The figures for the eight middle-income countries included in table 2.8 indicate the enormous range of variation among individual countries in the middle-income category. Thus in Nigeria it is estimated that the rate of natural increase rose from 2.7 percent to 3.2 percent, whereas in Taiwan there was a sharp decline from 3.2 percent to 1.6 percent because of a dramatic drop in the CBR from 39 per thousand in 1960 to 21 per thousand in 1978.

In the past few years much attention has been given to the fact that a landmark has been reached: the rate of growth of population in the developing countries has begun to decline. According to the estimates in table 2.5, the average population growth rate for the developing world during 1975–77 was 2.3 percent, as compared with the peak levels of 2.4 percent in 1965–70 and 1970–75. The estimated growth rate for the developing countries excluding China is unchanged, however, at 2.4 percent. It is also noteworthy that the population growth rate in Africa has continued to increase, reaching an estimated 2.8 percent in 1975–77 (table 2.5).

Three general conclusions appear to be of great importance. First, there is clear evidence that a growing number of developing countries have entered the phase of the demographic transition in which fertility is declining significantly. Indeed, just as the earlier reduction in mortality levels took place with unprecedented speed, in a number of countries the decline in fertility also has been exceptionally rapid.

Second, in many developing countries, especially among the low-income and late-developing countries, there is still little evidence of a decline in fertility. This is especially true of the countries in tropical Africa, but it also applies to Bangladesh, Pakistan, Nepal, Bolivia, Guatemala, Haiti, Peru, and a number of other Asian and Latin American countries. Moreover, the continuing dominance of the rural population in most of those countries and the persistence of traditional pronatalist attitudes suggest that achieving reductions in fertility will be difficult and slow unless means are found to accelerate the spread of family planning in rural areas.

Finally, it should be emphasized that the population growth in absolute numbers will be an important feature of the developing countries for a long time. This is partly a consequence of the momentum of population growth resulting from the fact that high birth rates during the past two decades already ensure substantial increases in the number of women who will be reaching childbearing age during the next two decades. It is also simply a consequence of the arithmetic of population size. Even the remarkable achievement of a relatively modest rate of natural increase of 1 percent in the year 2000 would imply an addition of some 60 million to the world's population; a growth rate of 2 percent in 1950 represented an addition of "only" 50 million. In general, it is probably the *rate* of growth of population that is most significant in compounding the difficulty of achieving development objectives; but the absolute size of a country's population obviously has a significant impact on the pressure of population on land and other natural resources.

Trends in Food Production and the Adequacy of Food Supplies

Our review of evidence pertaining to changes in mortality and morbidity in developing countries emphasized the critical importance of nutritional status as a determinant of health and well-being. It is generally recognized that widespread malnutrition is one of the most serious manifestations of poverty in less developed countries, and discussions of a "basic needs approach" to development invariably include food as one of the most basic of basic needs.

There is now a fairly general consensus that Protein-Energy Malnutrition is the major nutritional problem in developing countries and that it is most widespread and serious among small children. Other nutritional problems of global significance are vitamin-A deficiency, nutrition anemias (predominantly iron deficiency), and endemic goiter. Rickets and pellagra continue to be serious nutritional problems in more limited areas (FAO/WHO 1976, pp. 9–10).

We will note in chapter 4 that the present emphasis on PEM as the most important nutritional problem represents a shift since the 1960s, when there was a tendency to emphasize a so-called protein gap as the critical problem. Although there is not unanimity, the prevailing view among nutritionists is that nutritional deficiencies, including protein malnutrition, generally "are the result of inadequate intake of *food*, being thus unavoidably associated with inadequate intakes of energy" (FAO/WHO 1976, p. 31).[16] This emphasis on the problem of inadequate food intake directs attention to questions related to the *availability* of food, as determined by the level of production, and *access* to food, as determined by income or by a farm family's capacity to meet its own food requirements.

Recent estimates of the prevalence of malnutrition in developing countries have attempted to take into account the relationship between income level and the level of food consumption. According to recent FAO estimates, the number of persons in developing countries consuming less than a "critical minimum energy intake" increased from 400 million in 1969–71 to over 450 million in 1972–74 (FAO 1977, p. 53). In a World Bank monograph, Reut-

[16] The view that a "protein gap" was the major nutritional problem in less developed countries was the result of an overestimate of protein requirements and an underestimate of the extent to which protein malnutrition is caused by insufficient calorie intake, which reduces the utilization of protein for its distinctive functions (FAO/WHO 1973).

linger and Selowsky estimate that 840 million persons had "calorie deficient" diets in the mid-1960s (Reutlinger and Selowsky 1976, p. 2). And a later publication using the Reutlinger-Selowsky methodology estimates that 1.3 billion persons were "underfed" in 1975 (IFPRI 1977a, p. 16). The large differences between those alternative estimates give an indication of the severe difficulties of quantification which stem from conceptual problems, as well as serious data deficiencies.[17]

There is no need to elaborate on the difficulties that arise in estimating the consumption of foods in a developing country and in converting those figures into estimated intake of energy and other nutrients. It should be emphasized, however, that equal if not greater difficulties arise in estimating nutritional requirements. There is a rather broad range of food intakes that can maintain a satisfactory state of health, and the first effect of deficient nutrient intake is simply to deplete tissue reserves. Moreover, human beings have considerable capacity to "adapt" to substandard levels of nutrient intake. For example, adults have considerable capacity to adjust to low energy intakes, particularly by restricting their level of activity. For children, there are also possibilities for adjustment through a slower rate of growth and a reduction in the body size attained. Needless to say, prolonged restriction of energy intake below energy expenditure will lead to weight loss and eventually death by starvation. But the great majority of those who are "underfed" or have "calorie-deficient" diets are subject to mild or moderate rather than severe malnutrition.

There is in particular a lack of knowledge about the functional significance of different types and degrees of moderate and mild nutrition, which are much more widespread than severe malnutrition.[18] Adjusting even to mild or moderate malnutrition entails a cost to the individual and to society (Gopalan 1978). But relatively little is known about the seriousness of those adjustment costs except in cases involving certain vulnerable groups and semistarvation diets.[19] For infants and small children, it is well established that periods of arrested growth are usually good indicators of serious nutritional and health problems. Thus, surveillance of the nutritional status of infants and small chil-

[17] It has been argued that the Reutlinger-Selowsky methodology leads to a sizable overestimate of the number of persons with inadequate energy intake because it fails to make allowance for individual variations in calorie requirements (Sukhatme 1977).

[18] The nutrition study team that participated in the World Food and Nutrition Study organized by the U.S. National Academy of Sciences gave a high priority to the need for research on the functional consequences of malnutrition (NAS 1977). There seems little doubt about the importance of such research even though it is a difficult and fairly long-range undertaking (Calloway 1977).

[19] A study carried out during World War II by Ancel Keys, Josef Brožek, and their associates at the University of Minnesota remains one of the most valuable sources of information about the effects of semistarvation diets (Franklin et al. 1948; Keys et al. 1950). Following a drastic but controlled reduction of energy intake from over 3,000 calories to a level of roughly 1,550 calories, the young men in the experiment lost on the average about 24 percent of their body weight. In addition to experiencing physiological symptoms such as anemia, edema, and a slowed heartbeat, the subjects substantially reduced their level of activity (except for certain prescribed tasks), tired easily, and showed apathy, a marked lack of endurance, and increased irritability.

dren is not only particularly desirable; it is also more feasible than assessing the effects of malnutrition on the performance of school children and the productivity of adult workers. We have also seen that apathy and seriously restricted activity among small children is likely to result in impaired cognitive development.

The difficulties that arise in attempting to quantify the number of persons subject to malnutrition should not be allowed to obscure the fact that nutritional problems resulting from inadequate levels of food intake are widespread and serious in most developing countries. Even the *average* per capita availability of food energy is marginal in most of the developing countries. In the developed countries the per capita availability of food calories is typically some 20–35 percent above estimated requirements. But according to FAO estimates for 1972–74, the average availability of calories per capita was rarely more than 15 percent above estimated requirements; and for roughly half of the less developed countries, the estimated energy supply was below the estimated requirements (FAO 1977, pp. 77–80).

It is apparent from figure 2.2 that in the period since 1961–65 total food production in the developing countries increased more rapidly than in the developed countries; but the increase in per capita food supplies was limited. During the 1960s, the 3.3-percent rate of increase in food production in the developing market economies was appreciably higher than the 2.6-percent rate of population growth. During the years 1970–76, however, the average rate of

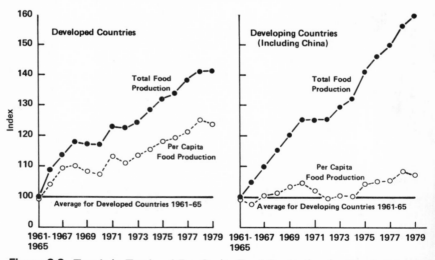

Figure 2.2. Trends in Total and Per Capita Food Production for Developed and Developing Countries.

Note: Production is shown on a relative scale, with 100 defined as the average production within the relevant country group for the period 1961–65.

Source: *FAO Production Yearbook*, vols. 30, pp. 74, 78; and 33, pp. 76, 80.

increase in food production was only marginally higher than the 2.6-percent rate of population growth, so that per capita output increased by only 0.2 percent. Furthermore, in the most seriously affected countries, that is, those identified by the U.N. system as having been affected most adversely by the food shortages and sharp increases in agricultural, petroleum, and fertilizer prices during the 1972–74 period, there was an annual decrease in per capita food production of some 0.4 percent (FAO 1977, p. 4). The indices of per capita food production presented in table 2.9 indicate that in most regions there has been improvement since the 1972–74 period; but in Africa the per capita level of food production has declined in recent years. In fact, per capita food production in 1979 was down about 10 percent in comparison with the 1961–65 average as well as the 1969–71 base used in table 2.9.

Projections of output and of consumption of major staple foods by the International Food Policy Research Institute (IFPRI 1977b) suggest that the shortfall in production in the Developing Market Economies will increase from 37 million metric tons in 1975 to 120–45 million metric tons in 1990 in terms of cereal equivalent.[20] Population growth alone will account for some 70 million tons of the projected deficit in 1990. An additional 50 million tons would be required to satisfy effective demand with slow growth in incomes, whereas the additional quantity required to meet market demand would approximate 75 million tons with higher rates of growth of per capita income.[21] For the low-income developing countries, which have the most serious food deficits and nutritional problems, food production would have to grow at 4.5–4.6 percent per year to overcome existing energy deficits and to meet the growth in demand associated with population growth and modest increases in per capita income. These required growth rates are a third higher than the growth rates obtained over the last two decades. The low-income developing

[20] FAO (1979c p. 39) reports that the cereal deficits for eighty-three developing countries increased from an annual average of 22 million tons in 1961–65 to 47 million tons annually during 1974–76.

[21] According to projections by FAO (1979c, pp. 39, 231), the net cereal-import needs of eighty-three developing countries would increase to 77 million tons in 1990, and 125 million tons by the year 2000, if agricultural growth is accelerated to the "maximum *feasible* extent"—to 115 million and 180 million tons, respectively, according to their "trend scenario."

Table 2.9. Indices of Food Production per Capita

Region	1972	1973	1974	1975	1976	1977	1978	1979
World	99	102	102	103	103	104	107	106
Africa	99	93	98	95	95	91	92	90
North and Central America	100	101	101	105	107	110	111	112
South America	97	99	103	105	109	108	109	110
Asia	98	101	101	105	104	105	107	106

Source: FAO (1979a), p. 16.

Note: 1969–71 = 100. The indices are price-weighted and thus reflect changes in the "quality" (as reflected in market value) as well as the quantity of food produced.

countries thus face the formidable task of achieving a substantial increase in the rate of growth of agricultural output in order to prevent a worsening of the food supply/demand situation, which inevitably would have especially serious consequences for low-income households. Moreover, reduction of the nutritional problems which are concentrated among the low-income rural households will require a pattern of agricultural development that enables disadvantaged groups such as very small farmers and landless laborers to participate in gains in productivity and income so as to raise their food intake levels by increased production and enlarged purchases of food. Our analysis of production programs in chapter 3 therefore gives major attention to factors influencing both the *rate* and the *pattern* of agricultural development.

What We Have Left Out

In seeking to make tractable our analysis of rural development strategies in the chapters that follow, we have restricted and simplified the scope of this essay. Focusing on a few strategic issues, we have explicitly omitted many others.

The international economic order. At one extreme we have left out the issues raised by the ongoing debate concerning a new international economic order (NIEO). Mahbub ul Haq devotes the two concluding chapters of his challenging book on development strategy (1976) to a discussion of the NIEO and a new framework for international resource transfers. Nevertheless, he recognizes that in "thinking about the new international economic order . . . we still seem to be standing on the threshold of new perceptions" (Haq 1976, p. 11). A lucid review of these issues and proposals for a NIEO by Griffin (1978, chap. 5) also emphasizes the tentative nature of the current debate.

The Independent Commission on International Development Issues, under the chairmanship of Willy Brandt, gave particular attention to "the need for a new international order" (Independent Commission 1980, p. 268). Members of the commission came from five continents and included political leaders from very different political systems. Both the "emergency program" outlined by the commission and its longer-term recommendations emphasize "that profound changes are required in international relations, particularly international economic relations" (Independent Commission 1980, p. 297). The commission's report recognizes that a new international economic order will take considerable time to achieve, and it stresses the need for an intensive process of education to prepare public opinion for bold and imaginative initiatives. Major attention is directed to "the burden and waste of the arms race," with total military expenditures approaching $450 billion a year, compared with only $20 billion for official development assistance (Independent Commission 1980, p. 117). So far, the international climate of opinion for the report, released early in 1980, has not been auspicious. It is, however, an eloquent and provocative report which may well have considerable influence over a period of years.

Our reasons for leaving aside these issues of international economic policy are similar to those cited by the task force which carried out the Asian Development Bank's Second Asian Agricultural Survey. The authors of that excellent report recognize the importance of trade patterns and of destabilizing influences from abroad on the development efforts of individual countries. Hence, the achievement of certain development objectives is "beyond the control of the DMCs [developing member countries of the ADB] as individual countries, and largely so even as a group. Yet there are certain crucial areas of policy and action within the competence of the countries concerned which can accelerate the pace and change the pattern of their development" (Asian Development Bank 1978, p. 209).

The effects of the international economic order on trade are particularly important of course. It is significant, however, that W. A. Lewis argues that in the future the "engine of growth should be technological change" rather than international trade; trade's proper role in development is "as lubricating oil not as fuel." He further notes that "the gateway to technological change is through agricultural and industrial revolutions, which are mutually dependent" (Lewis 1978, p. 74). In concluding his essay, he places particular emphasis on the key role of food production: "The most important item on the agenda of development is to transform the food sector, create agricultural surpluses to feed the urban population, and thereby create the domestic basis for industry and modern services. If we can make this domestic change, we shall automatically have a new international economic order" (p. 75). Such efforts "to transform the food sector" should promote not only widespread increases of productivity and of income among the farm population but also the strengthening of social services such as education and health. Our premise in this essay is that action within individual late-developing countries can achieve substantial improvement in the well-being of both the rural and the urban populations, independent of the changes in the international framework envisaged by the advocates of an NIEO. We will, however, have something to say about the influence of foreign-aid policies on the production, consumption, and organization programs undertaken within individual developing countries.

Country-specific factors. At the opposite extreme, we have ignored the specific circumstances of individual countries. These specific circumstances are, as we will stress repeatedly, crucial in determining the priorities and the content of national development strategies. Given that agricultural innovations and technologies are by their very nature location-specific, the need to take account of environmental conditions in a particular country, and in its various farming regions, is obvious. But the economic, social, and political circumstances prevailing in a country at a particular moment in its evolution are also crucial. John Sheahan explores the significance of this evolution of local circumstances in his examination of the balance between efficiency and equity considerations. He notes that governments in less developed countries sometimes resort to repression when there is a drastic shift from policies that largely ignore efficiency considerations to policies based on adherence to a dogmatic faith in the price system. Chile is probably the clearest example. Sheahan's final conclusion is that in pursuing policies that reflect a concern with equity and social justice as well as economic efficiency, "the ideal is not maximum possible efficiency but an optimum degree consistent with a particular country's economic structure and capacity for change" (Sheahan 1980, p. 291).

The same need for sensitivity to the local context and environment applies to most of the important issues which must be faced in redesigning strategies for rural development.[22] An especially significant problem, for example, is assessing whether it is feasible and desirable in a particular country and at a particular time to undertake a redistributive land reform program. Our aim is to complement rather than supercede the detailed local analyses required for such assessments.

Energy problems. We have also omitted a deep examination of the implications for rural development of the rising cost and decreasing availability of fossil fuels. Clearly, the energy requirements for food production and distribution must figure prominently on the agenda of both national and global studies of the energy problem.

A recent article by Revelle (1980) provides a concise summary of present and future energy needs in Asia and of the need for greatly expanded research and development activity focused on problems of energy production, conversion, and conservation. Of the fifteen large Asian countries, only China is reasonably well endowed with fossil fuels and potential hydropower, although Malaysia has fairly large energy resources of hydroelectric power and forests relative to its population. Most of the remaining countries, accounting for about 30 percent of the world's population, face acute short-term foreign exchange problems because of the tenfold rise in oil prices since 1972 and extremely formidable long-term problems in developing local energy sources to substitute for imported fuels.[23] Biomass energy from fast-growing trees offers the greatest potential. The competition between food and energy demands for land and other scarce resources will be especially acute in these densely populated countries of Asia. Moreover, the possibility of substantial use of maize for gasohol in the United States may push up world grain prices, with very serious adverse effects on all food-deficit developing countries (Timmer and Mullen 1980).

We note in chapter 3 that the rising cost of petroleum has increased the relative attractiveness of animal draft power. This is particularly significant in relation to the equipment and tillage innovations that should play an increasingly important role in expanding agricultural output under rainfed condi-

---

[22] An analysis by Roger Hansen (1971) of the unique historical and political factors that have shaped and constrained Mexico's development strategy is an admirable example of the sort of understanding that is needed.

[23] Murdoch (1980, pp. 122–28, 273–80) gives a very optimistic view of the prospects for coping with energy problems in the less developed countries.

tions. Furthermore, because of their labor-using, capital-saving bias, animal-powered technologies tend to be better suited to the factor proportions and relative prices that prevail in these developing countries.

Energy requirements for pumping water for irrigation and for the manufacture of fertilizers pose more difficult problems. Traditional devices such as the Persian wheel simply are not a viable substitute for power-driven pumps. Rising energy costs may, however, warrant giving a higher priority to gravity-flow irrigation systems where they are a feasible alternative.

The critical importance of high-yield, fertilizer-responsive crop varieties underscores the importance of energy requirements for fertilizer production. The currently popular notion that developing countries should rely entirely on manure and other organic fertilizers ignores an important fact: supplies of organic fertilizer are very inelastic and simply cannot support the yield levels which are needed and which can be obtained with expanded production and use of inorganic fertilizers.[24]

Our discussion of agricultural development in chapter 3 is based on the assumption that while energy costs will continue to rise, means will be found to prevent shortages or price rises so severe as to cripple otherwise sound production strategies. A pressing and continuing research task, which we do not undertake here, is to discover both the circumstances under which this assumption might not hold and the policy consequences and options open to the late-developing countries if it does not.

Environmental problems. Another important area that we have omitted from our analysis concerns the serious environmental problems which arise when crop lands, forests, and watersheds are abused. Long-term development cannot be sustained if the productive capacity of land and other natural resources is destroyed. To view such problems simply in terms of the need for conservation measures is not an adequate response, however, due to the close relationships between development and conservation. We noted one significant aspect of those relationships earlier in this chapter: rapid in-migration of cultivators to marginal areas where land is still available. Degradation of the land due to soil erosion is being aggravated by farming practices ill-suited to semiarid conditions and by the cutting of trees and shrubs for fuel. It is easy for conservationists to condemn such practices, but there is no easy or even feasible short-term solution, because they are "the result of people acting out of desperate need" (Carter 1980, p. 576). Clearly, these are problems of enormous importance requiring a long-term perspective. The highly publicized "World Conservation Strategy" released in March 1980 signifies an emerging consensus on the importance of these problems and on the need to recognize the interrelationships between development and conservation objectives (IUCN

---

[24] There also have been optimistic expectations that cereal varieties with a capacity to fix atmospheric nitrogen in the manner of soybeans and other legumes can be developed. It remains uncertain, however, whether this expectation is realistic. In any event, new nitrogen-fixing cereals are unlikely to have a significant impact in the next two or three decades.

1980). In our judgment, these very real concerns about the conservation of natural resources underscore the urgency of meeting the objectives of rural development. In particular, they emphasize the need to slow population growth and to attain the higher levels of income and technology which enable a country to curtail the destruction of land and other productive resources. Once again, in the present analysis we do not tackle the conservation-development relationship directly; rather we seek to provide one piece of a strategic policy framework within which the detailed tactical elements of that relationship can be more profitably addressed.[25]

Summary: Constraints and Objectives

In this chapter we have identified the major conditions and constraints affecting people in developing countries where incomes are low and a large percentage of the population continues to rely on agriculture for employment and income. Our analysis has indicated that the problem of overcoming poverty in these "late-developing countries" has four critical dimensions.

1) The existing economic and occupational structure in these countries emphasizes the predominantly rural character of poverty. And because of their structural characteristics, together with the continuation of rapid growth of their population and labor force, they will remain predominantly rural well into the next century.

2) Impressive reductions in mortality have not been paralleled by increases in the health of the survivors. Small children and mothers are especially prone to excessive mortality and morbidity. The contributing factors are complex and synergistic: any marked improvement is likely to require simultaneous advances in nutrition and in access to basic health services.

3) The persistence of high rates of fertility in this subset of developing countries, coupled with falling mortality rates, means that rapid population growth will continue to exacerbate the problems of reducing poverty and transforming the overwhelmingly agrarian character of their economies.

4) Success in accelerating the growth of agricultural production is a necessary but not a sufficient condition for reducing malnutrition and poverty. Agricultural strategies must permit broad participation of the rural population in gains in productivity and income and must be supplemented by programs directed at the distinctive nutritional and health problems of infants and small children and pregnant and lactating women.

The severity of the constraints that these countries face rules out the major resource transfers which would be required to reduce significantly the depriva-

---

[25] See Dasmann, Milton, and Freeman (1973) for a good summary treatment of "ecological principles for economic development." William Clark has worked with a number of other ecologists, including several from the developing world, in a study sponsored by the United Nations Environmental Program to develop a strategy and methodology of environmental management appropriate for use in the developing countries (see Holling 1978).

tions that persist among the large fraction of their populations subject to poverty. Hence there is a need for development strategies which will be effective in attaining the multiple objectives of (1) achieving self-sustaining, cumulative economic growth; (2) expanding opportunities for productive employment (including self-employment in agriculture); (3) reducing poverty (with emphasis on malnutrition and excessive mortality and morbidity); and (4) slowing population growth. The question at issue is not whether those objectives are desirable but how to achieve them. In the chapters that follow we examine the production, consumption, and organization programs which appear to offer the greatest promise for attaining those objectives.

CHAPTER THREE

Production-oriented Programs: Employment Opportunities and Agricultural Development

We noted in chapter 1 that policy analysis resists the temptation to make comprehensive assessments of all relationships. Instead it begins with an examination of what actions can be taken in a particular domain in order to learn from past experience and from analysis of ongoing programs and their outcomes. In this chapter we artificially simplify the picture by focusing on "production."

To further simplify our task, it is useful to define the various types of agricultural strategies that can be pursued in a less developed country. Thorbecke (1979, p. 198) proposes a typology of agricultural development strategies which distinguishes four alternatives: (1) a "unimodal" (or progressive-modernization) strategy; (2) a "bimodal" (or dualistic) strategy; (3) an "industrialization-first" strategy, in which positive actions to promote agricultural development receive scant attention and the agricultural sector is discriminated against; and (4) a strategy for the collectivization, or socialization, of rural areas.

The Choice of an Agricultural Strategy

We shall focus on the fundamental choice between a unimodal and a bimodal strategy. After noting the disadvantages of an "industrialization-first" strategy, we suggest that socialist economies also confront a choice between unimodal and bimodal strategies. We then consider the determinants of the pattern of agricultural development in a mixed economy, which is our principal concern in this chapter.

Unimodal and Bimodal Strategies

The term bimodal was used by Schultz (1964, p. 123) to characterize the contrast between the Soviet Union's large-scale, mechanized collective farms and the very small, highly labor-intensive private plots cultivated as a sideline activity by the members of a collective farm. The term has since been used to characterize contrasting patterns of agricultural development within various developing countries (Johnston and Cownie 1969; Johnston and Kilby 1975). In earlier publications, Johnston (1966, 1969) characterized the unimodal pattern of agricultural development as the "Japanese model," and the bimodal, or dualistic, pattern as the "Mexican model." Japan, Taiwan, Korea, and other countries pursuing a unimodal strategy were able to achieve widespread increases in productivity and income within the existing framework of small-scale farm units. They continued to employ labor-using, capital-saving technologies, relying heavily on divisible innovations, such as the high-yield, fertilizer-responsive crop varieties which recently have figured in the "Green Revolution." In Mexico, on the other hand, the increases in productivity and output, especially commercialized production, were concentrated to a large extent in a subsector of large farms which adopted labor-saving, capital-using technologies. Particularly in the case of cotton, technologies in use in America's Southwest were taken up by Mexican producers; the process was facilitated by the transfer of both capital and technical expertise.[1]

Colombia and a number of other Latin American countries also have been characterized by bimodal patterns of agricultural development. The contrast between the frequency distributions by size class of the number of farm households and of the cultivated area in Colombia and those in Taiwan is, in fact, presented by Johnston and Kilby (1975, p. 15) to illustrate the difference between a bimodal and a unimodal pattern of agricultural development. In Colombia there is a concentration of farm units in the size classes of five to ten hectares and smaller, whereas the large farms of fifty hectares and more account for most of the cultivated area. Because the two frequency distributions are so skewed, fewer than 1 percent of all farm units are within five acres of the average farm size. In Taiwan, however, the distributions of farm units and of farm land are both heavily concentrated near the mean farm size: four fifths of all farms are within one acre of the average farm size.[2] Agricultural development in Asian and African countries generally has been much less bimodal than in Latin America. Nonetheless, in a number of countries, including India and especially Pakistan, the pattern has become more bimodal in the past ten to fifteen years because of the rapid spread among large farmers of tractor-powered technologies, technologies which by their very nature cannot be adopted by the bulk of farm units until considerable structural transformation has taken place.

Although countries with the structural and demographic characteristics

[1] The historical experience of Mexico, the United States, Japan, Taiwan, and the Soviet Union is examined in Johnston and Kilby (1975, chaps. 5 and 6).

[2] Berry and Cline (1979, pp. 38–39) present Gini coefficients as a measure of land concentration for thirty developing countries. Taiwan's Gini coefficient of 0.4 is one of the lowest, although Berry and Cline estimate that Korea's Gini coefficient is only 0.2. Colombia's estimated Gini coefficient is close to 0.9, and the estimates for Venezuela, Brazil, Guatemala, Nicaragua, and other Latin American countries are similarly high. India and Pakistan, with coefficients of close to 0.6, are in an intermediate position.

which typify the late-developing countries confront a choice between the unimodal and bimodal alternatives, often the choice is made by default rather than as a conscious policy choice. Frequently a large-scale, "modern" subsector coexists with the small-scale sector which includes the overwhelming majority of farm families, although the latter may cultivate a relatively small fraction of the agricultural area. Needless to say, the "unimodal" and "bimodal" alternatives that we emphasize represent polar extremes; actual patterns of agricultural development will represent various degrees of emphasis on promoting increases in productivity and output among small-scale and large-scale farm units. Nevertheless, we argue that to a large extent the two alternatives are mutually exclusive: promoting the emergence of a large, highly commercialized subsector tends to preclude the possibility of successfully pursuing a unimodal strategy.

"Industrialization-First" Strategies

The "industrialization-first" strategy in Thorbecke's typology is a highly protectionist import-substitution strategy of industrialization. The effects on agriculture invariably are adverse. Price distortions resulting from high levels of protection, an overvalued exchange rate, and underpricing of capital induce an inappropriately capital-intensive pattern of industrial development within a modern enclave. This "formal sector" typically receives a disproportionate share of investment, while it contributes little to the expansion of job opportunities or to the pervasive process of modernization that is required for a more equitable sharing in the benefits of economic progress (Little, Scitovsky, and Scott 1970; Healey 1972; Morawetz 1974).

Protection of manufactured products and underpricing of capital have been especially pronounced in Latin America; real rates of interest on loans from institutional sources have frequently been negative (Sheahan 1980, p. 270). High levels of protection, overvalued exchange rates, and artificially low rates of interest have also been common in Asian and African countries. In India the antiemployment bias of the pattern of resource allocation seems to have been influenced mainly by a development strategy that assigned a high priority to capital-intensive investments in steel and other basic industries and emphasized import quotas, investment licensing, and other direct controls (Bhagwati and Desai 1970). Both types of policies have tended to stifle the growth of smaller, more decentralized manufacturing firms. Because such firms utilize less capital-intensive technologies and are less dependent on foreign exchange, they are capable of generating a more rapid and more widespread growth in nonfarm employment and a more rapid growth in demand for food. This in turn both permits and requires more rapid growth in agricultural output (Mellor 1976).

Lipton (1977) has been especially eloquent in arguing that in many developing countries a pervasive "urban bias" frequently has contributed to the perpetuation of poverty among the rural population. The existence of such a bias can be explained in part by the vested interests created among industrialists who have come to regard protection from external competition and privileged access to credit "as part of the natural order of the universe" (Sheahan 1980, p. 288). Similarly, workers receiving the relatively high wages paid by modern-sector firms have an interest in maintaining their real wages. Moreover, the decisions of policymakers undoubtedly are influenced strongly by the political pressures generated by a highly visible and frequently vociferous urban population. This means, to cite an important example, that governments in developing countries are under considerable pressure to adopt "cheap food policies," and once those policies are adopted, the pressure to continue them becomes especially strong. More generally, the cost of financing the subsidies to the industrial sector which are implicit in a protectionist import-substitution strategy are borne to a large extent by the de facto taxation of the farm population which results from turning the domestic terms of trade against agriculture.[3]

Government support for activities such as agricultural research and investment in irrigation and other types of rural infrastructure is often inadequate, in part because the agricultural constituencies are not as visible nor as well organized as urban groups. Furthermore, the payoff—political as well as economic—to such investments is fairly long-term. Finally, the measures that governments sometimes adopt to counteract the adverse effects of their economic policies on agriculture usually benefit only the larger farmers and therefore reinforce other polarizing factors which lead to a bimodal pattern of agricultural development. This is especially true of policies such as foreign-exchange allocations and licenses for importing tractors at zero or very low rates of duty. It also applies in large measure to subsidies on inputs and low-interest-rate policies. Because of the excess demand situation that results from holding prices artificially low, some form of administrative rationing of inputs and credit becomes necessary. And the larger and more influential farmers generally receive the lion's share of those scarce resources.

The negative effects on farm income and production incentives of the policies associated with an import-substitution strategy and cheap food policies are the most obvious and probably the most important in the short run.[4] In the

---

[3] For an excellent discussion of these "invisible" intersectoral resources transfers, see Lewis (1973).

[4] A study by Peterson (1979) of fifty-three countries, including thirty developing countries, documents the prevalence of disincentives to farmers in developing countries for the period 1968–70. The average "real prices" (i.e., kilograms of fertilizer that could be bought with 100 kg of wheat or its equivalent) in the top ten countries were nearly four times as high as those in the bottom ten countries, all of which were developing countries. South Korea was the only developing country in the top ten; two others ranked in the top twenty-six. On the basis of his cross-section estimates of supply elasticity for the other twenty-seven developing countries, Peterson concludes that with more favorable farm prices, agricultural output in those countries could have been as much as 40–60 percent greater.

long run, however, the adverse effects on the rate and bias of technical change in agriculture and in the manufacturing sector may be even more important. Clearly, the labor-saving, capital-using bias of the technologies associated with a bimodal pattern of agricultural development will slow the rate of growth of opportunities for productive employment within the agricultural sector. In addition, the pattern of rural demand for purchased inputs and consumer goods associated with a bimodal agricultural strategy provides a relatively weak stimulus to the decentralized growth of nonfarm output and employment in small- and medium-scale firms. In contrast, the widespread increases in productivity and in farm cash income associated with a unimodal strategy provide a strong stimulus to nonfarm enterprises employing relatively labor-intensive technologies.

Unimodal and Bimodal Strategies in Socialist Economies

The fourth alternative in Thorbecke's typology—the "collectivization, or socialization, of rural areas"—really embraces two alternatives, because a socialist strategy confronts a choice between a unimodal and a bimodal pattern. Agricultural development in the Soviet Union clearly has been bimodal, and it has been associated with an "industrialization-first" strategy. China's pattern of agricultural development, however, appears to have been essentially unimodal. The launching of the rural communes in the late 1950s may have been motivated in part by a belief that economies of scale would be realized by creating large operational units; Marx, Kautsky, and Lenin all emphasized the superiority of large-scale agriculture (Wittfogel 1971). Since the early 1960s, however, the decentralization of agricultural decision-making in China has emphasized relatively small production teams of some thirty to forty households as the unit of farm management. This appears to have facilitated a predominantly unimodal pattern of agricultural development based on labor-intensive, yield-increasing innovations associated with expansion and improvements in irrigation and drainage. Thus in terms of the organizational structure for decision-making and especially the choice of technology, China's agricultural strategy contrasts much more sharply with the Soviet Union's bimodal pattern than with the unimodal strategies pursued in Japan and Taiwan.[5]

The progress achieved by the People's Republic of China in the reduction of poverty has depended in large measure on a high degree of social regimentation and control, including a drastic redistribution of land and other productive assets. However, also of major importance has been the pragmatism apparent in the decision to decentralize decision-making in agriculture in order to secure both a workable balance between equity objectives and production

---

[5] The similarity with respect to the technological innovations that have played a major role in China, Japan, and Taiwan is very clear in an analysis by Schran (1980) of agricultural progress in the People's Republic of China between 1952 and 1979.

incentives and an organizational structure compatible with a labor-using, capital-saving pattern of agricultural development (see Timmer 1976; Chinn 1978; and Tang 1980).[6]

Determinants of the Pattern of Agricultural Development in Mixed Economies

We will be concerned mainly with mixed economies in which market forces are a major determinant of the degree of progress achieved in eradicating poverty. In such countries, the most fundamental requirement for ensuring that the mass of a country's population will benefit from development is to achieve a rate of increase in the demand for labor that exceeds the rate of growth of the working-age population seeking employment opportunities. The remarkable success achieved by Taiwan in eliminating poverty and malnutrition between the early 1950s and the late 1960s to early 1970s is an especially clear example of the effectiveness of a tightening of the labor supply/demand situation in leading to widespread increases in returns to labor.

The experience of Taiwan, Japan, South Korea, and a few other countries is especially significant in demonstrating both the feasibility and the desirability of pursuing a unimodal pattern of agricultural development. In a late-developing country, the great majority of farm households inevitably are bypassed when a bimodal pattern of agricultural development is pursued.[7] This appears to be a "hard conclusion." It is a clear implication of the structural and demographic characteristics examined in chapter 2 and is supported by analysis of past experience. When the Japanese and Mexican "models" of unimodal and bimodal agricultural development were compared in the mid-1960s (Johnston 1966), both were commonly regarded as "success stories." There is now general agreement, however, that Mexico's agricultural strategy has made an inadequate contribution to the multiple objectives of development because the great majority of the rural population was by-passed. Even the rate of growth of farm output has declined markedly.

Factors Militating against Unimodal Agricultural Strategies

The fact that absolute poverty is still so widespread, with the number of persons subject to nutritional, health, and other deprivations continuing to increase, is due in large measure to the failure of a great many developing

[6] It appears, however, that there is a good deal of inefficiency in the allocation of resources for agricultural production in China. Most of the major sources of inefficiency are recognized explicitly by the present regime; but it seems unlikely that the reforms that have been announced will have a major impact on the principal sources of inefficiency, viz., external constraints imposed on the individual production team, e.g., the imposition of cropping targets and delivery quotas and reliance on administratively determined prices (Dernberger 1980).

[7] During the past decade a considerable consensus has emerged concerning the importance of fostering a broadly based, unimodal pattern of agricultural development. See, for example, World Bank (1975, 1978); India (1978, chap. 9); Asian Development Bank (1978, 1979).

countries to design and implement effective unimodal strategies for agricultural development. Many will argue that political factors are all-important in accounting for this failure. We certainly do not deny their importance. Our examination of organizational aspects of development and the social techniques of "calculation and control" in chapter 5 gives major attention to the difficult problem of ensuring that program benefits reach the rural poor. Political factors exert their influence, however, in specific problem areas. We focus here on seven such areas, each with a direct bearing on the success or failure of efforts to implement unimodal agricultural strategies:

1. The policy environment and rural development—farm and nonfarm
2. The extent to which unimodal and bimodal strategies represent mutually exclusive alternatives
3. The skewed size distribution of farm operational units
4. Deficiencies in the level and orientation of resources allocated to research activities
5. The special problems of fostering widespread increases in productivity and income among small farmers dependent upon rainfed agriculture
6. The limited effectiveness of organizations serving small farmers
7. Failure to recognize and act upon the enormous importance of the role of women in processes of agricultural and rural development

The Policy Environment and Rural Development— Farm and Nonfarm

Although there is now increased awareness of the need to give a higher priority to rural development, in most of the developing countries this has not been reflected adequately in changes in economic policies and development priorities.[8] The price distortions that characterize the unfavorable environment for unimodal agricultural development will be considered later as important factors leading to a skewed size distribution of farm operational units. We will argue in line with the induced innovation hypothesis of Hayami and Ruttan that the indirect, long-term effects may well be more important than the direct effects leading to inefficiencies in resource allocation. Here we concentrate on the magnitude of the resource requirements for expanding food production and on the failure to exploit the potential for positive interactions between agricultural and industrial development.

In recent years several attempts have been made to estimate the investment requirements for expanding food production in developing countries; all these estimates suggest that the requirements are extremely large relative to the

---

[8] Lele argues persuasively that the failure of governments to give an adequate priority to agricultural development is particularly serious in Sub-Saharan Africa and an important cause of the poor performance of the agricultural sector in most countries in that region during the past ten to fifteen years. The share of the government budget devoted to agriculture is often much less than in Asian countries. In addition, "there is not yet the basic conviction that the smallholder agricultural sector can and will have to be the engine of broad-based economic development and eventual modernization" (Lele 1981, p. 548).

prospects for mobilizing resources in low-income countries and the likely availability of external aid.

Recent estimates of the International Food Policy Research Institute (IFPRI) indicate that an additional investment of nearly $100 billion in 1975 dollars will be required by 1990 in the staple food sectors alone to close the food gap for 36 low-income, food-deficit nations (Mellor 1979, p. 4; Oram et al. 1979). This is for capital investment only and does not include maintenance allowances and other recurrent expenditure. Investment in irrigation accounts for nearly half the total. Such estimates require many assumptions and approximations, but the figures are consistent with earlier estimates by FAO, by the Consultative Group on Food Production and Investment, and by a Japanese-American team that carried out a study on behalf of the Trilateral Commission.[9]

The problems that derive from insufficient resources are compounded in many of the contemporary developing countries by historical and other factors. These factors have made it difficult to mobilize resources within the agricultural sector by land taxes and other efficient means of generating public revenues to finance developmental activities. As we stressed earlier, rural households often have to bear a heavy de facto tax burden because of high tariffs and other import restrictions. However, these resource transfers subsidize profits, relatively high wages, and inefficiency in the "modern" sector. They do not augment governmental revenues for financing development activities, and they are inefficient because they accentuate inequality and tend to maximize disincentive effects. An agricultural land tax is at least proportional to the amount and quality of land owned by the taxpayer. Furthermore, since it is a tax on "economic rent," the disincentive effects are minimized.[10] The

[9] FAO's most recent estimates (for ninety developing countries) focus on the year 2000. According to these projections, gross investment for irrigation for crop production should be at an annual rate of $10.4 billion in 1980 and should rise to $14.8 billion in 2000, adding up to a total investment of $255 billion over the twenty-year period. Gross investment in mechanization would be $31.1 billion in 2000 (more than twice the projected gross investment in irrigation in that year), and gross investment for all categories, including $4.6 billion for working capital, would amount to $59.7 billion for crop production. When investments for livestock production and for storage and marketing are included, the estimated investment requirement rises to $78 billion (all estimates in 1975 prices). These FAO estimates imply an increase in investment at an annual rate of 3.6 percent between 1980 and 2000, a considerably lower rate than is implied by the IFPRI estimates of the incremental requirement for investment to close the food gap for 36 deficit countries by increasing the rate of growth of food production from 2.4 percent to a 4.0 percent growth rate during the 1980s. Although the FAO projections are for their "normative scenario" whereby food production would be increased "to the fullest extent considered feasible," they project that 240 million persons would still be undernourished in 2000 unless new measures to redistribute income or purchasing power are instituted (FAO 1979c, pp. 90–91).

[10] Land revenue taxes in India, Pakistan, and a number of other countries are fixed in money terms, and as a result inflation has eroded their value in real terms. According to an estimate for 1966/67, land revenue in India amounted to only 0.8 percent of the gross value added in agriculture, and the percentage would probably be even less today. In Pakistan, an increase in agricultural income from 7.7 to 15.5 billion rupees between 1959/60 and 1969/70 was associated with an increase of only 11 million rupees in agricultural taxes and a decline from 2.2 percent to only 1.2 percent of agricultural income (Johnston and Kilby 1975, p. 429).

resistance to raising land taxes or even to ensuring that agricultural taxation expands in pace with the rise in agricultural income is unfortunate. Taxation of agricultural land represents an efficient means of mobilizing additional resources while lessening both interfarm and interregional disparities in income.

Our emphasis on the need to give a higher priority to rural development is not an endorsement of a simplistic Food First strategy. Long-term improvements in the well-being of the rural population in late-developing countries require a transformation of the overwhelmingly agricultural structure of their economies. Associated with that transformation is increased specialization and sectoral interdependence, leading to growth in productivity, output, and employment. The dynamic interactions between agriculture and both the rural and urban nonfarm sectors are of crucial importance in achieving the economywide increases in employment, productivity, and output required for self-sustaining, cumulative growth and for the elimination of poverty.

Programs that continue to rely on subsistence production for improving the well-being of rural households are doomed to failure. This important lesson of history is emphasized just as strongly by China's recent experience of socialist transformation as by the experience of market economies such as Japan and Taiwan.[11] Sizable increases in agricultural productivity and output simply are not possible without a steady increase in the use of chemical fertilizers, farm equipment, and other manufactured inputs which complement the on-farm resources of labor, land, and cattle or buffaloes, which provide draft power, manure, and livestock products. Moreover, expansion of nonfarm job opportunities is a necessary condition for the relative and eventually absolute reduction in the size of the agricultural population and labor force. In brief, changes in the occupational composition of the labor force and in the composition of output are crucial: they prevent or eliminate overcrowding on the land and make possible higher levels of productivity and per capita income. The experience of Japan, Taiwan, and China suggests that the growth of rural nonfarm employment can provide a highly significant source of alternative job opportunities. This requires, however, a decentralized pattern of industrial development which fosters growth of rural-based manufacturing firms employing labor-using, capital-saving technologies. We have noted that the pattern of rural demand generated by widespread increases in farm productivity and incomes under a unimodal strategy provides a strong stimulus for expanded local production of simple consumer goods and items of farm and household equipment. These unsophisticated products can be manufactured with reasonable efficiency by small- and medium-scale firms which make maximum use of labor and locally available raw materials while minimizing requirements for capital and for imported raw materials and intermediate products. And being

---

[11] The interrelationships between agricultural and industrial development in market economies are examined in detail in Johnston and Kilby (1975, esp. chaps. 2, 3, 7, and 8). See also Ranis (1979) and Ho (1979). For China's experience, see Perkins et al. (1977) and Rawski (1979).

inexpensive, these products are affordable by small farmers with limited but gradually increasing cash income.

Although industrialization-first strategies have imposed a heavy burden on the farm population, they have failed to induce the investment required for a substantial expansion of nonfarm employment. Even when a development strategy fosters the positive interactions between agricultural and industrial growth, there is a strong presumption that there will be a *net* transfer of capital from agriculture to the more rapidly growing nonfarm sectors.[12] The de facto taxation that results from distorting relative prices and turning the terms of trade against agriculture is likely to frustrate overall development by blunting the incentives needed to achieve satisfactory rates of growth of farm productivity and output. In addition, achieving increases in agricultural productivity and widespread increases in farm income requires substantial investments in infrastructure and also in research and the other supporting services (which we will consider shortly). This makes possible a net outflow of capital—via an agricultural land tax and investment of agricultural savings in rural nonfarm activities, for example—while permitting and even fostering improvement in the well-being of the rural population.

2.   Trade-offs between Unimodal and Bimodal Strategies

Two interrelated factors bear much of the responsibility for the tendency of developing countries to pursue policies that result in a bimodal pattern of agricultural development. First, it is often assumed that the technical superiority of "modern inputs" such as tractors and even combine harvesters means that capital-intensive, mechanized technologies, which are best adapted to large-scale farm units, are superior in terms of economic efficiency as well. Second, large farmers and those who identify with them for personal or political reasons have a vested interest in strategies that continue to concentrate scarce resources in a large-scale, highly commercialized subsector. Coalitions of medium and large farmers are frequently able to block or evade land reform legislation aimed at a more equal distribution of agricultural land. M. S. Randhawa, a former vice-chancellor of the Punjab Agricultural University, provides an unusually good example of the way in which those two factors are linked to demonstrate the "necessity" of tractor mechanization:

> An efficient farmer must have a tractor and tubewell. Without a tractor, multiple-cropping and timely sowing is not a practical possibility. If a farmer has a tractor and a tubewell powered by an electric motor or diesel engine, he must have a minimum economic holding of 20–25 acres of irrigated land. This in itself explodes the myth

---

[12] These intersectoral resource flows are well documented for Taiwan, where the net outflow was very large: 20–25 percent of the net value of agricultural output (marketed and nonmarketed) during the 1920s and 1930s and nearly 15 percent of a greatly increased level of agricultural output during 1966–69 (Lee 1971*a*, 1971*b*; Johnston and Kilby 1975, pp. 315–21). During the latter period, the "invisible" outflow associated with a worsening of the terms of trade between agriculture and nonagriculture accounted for a large fraction of the net outflow.

that the new technology of production is neutral to the size of the holding. Perhaps this cliché was invented by those who wanted to promote a low ceiling for landholdings, ignoring its evil effects on production (in Franda 1979, p. 19).

The linking of tractors and tubewells is especially misleading. Under conditions prevailing in northern India and Pakistan, a tubewell is often an important technical complement to high-yield varieties and increased use of fertilizer. Moreover, by facilitating multiple cropping as well as higher yields, tubewells tend to enlarge employment opportunities in agriculture (Johnston and Kilby 1975, pp. 417–27).[13] In contrast, tractor mechanization is almost entirely labor-displacing in its impact and has very little positive effect on crop yields (Binswanger 1978, pp. 30–42). Moreover, it is only on atypically large farm units that tractors are needed to facilitate multiple cropping. These problems are not confined to market economies where profit maximization provides a clear motive for the beneficiaries to emphasize the large-scale subsector. In socialist Tanzania there are strong interests within the government that seek to expand the role of large-scale, capital-intensive state farms. Indeed, there is reason to be concerned that Tanzania's heavy emphasis on large, capital-intensive state farms may jeopardize the prospects for successfully implementing a unimodal agricultural strategy capable of raising the productivity and incomes of the "village sector," on which the great bulk of the population depends for its livelihood (ILO 1978, pp. 77–79).

This emphasis on state farms may have been influenced by difficulties that the government marketing agencies have encountered in the purchase and collection of maize and other products from several million small-scale producers (Johnston 1978, p. 94). However, Tanzania's food crisis in 1973–75 was also a crisis in food production. Although weather conditions and the low producer prices maintained by the government were contributing factors, many would agree with Lofchie (1978, p. 452) that "there is compelling reason to believe that the programme of collective villagisation was the major cause of a crisis in agricultural production of calamitous proportions." Some observers place major emphasis on the disrupting effects of poor timing and administrative ineptitude in carrying out the villagization program. Others, including Lofchie, emphasize peasant resistance to an unpopular program, resistance which was intensified as the government resorted to coercion from 1971 through 1973. The decision to deemphasize collectivism as a goal of the villagization program and to accept individual farming as a fundamental institution was undoubtedly made with reluctance. According to Lofchie, there are indications that now "the country's highest ranking officials are pessimistic about the possibility of improving agricultural production in the villages and are, instead, turning increasingly to large-scale state and private farms to accomplish that purpose" (p. 475). If preferential allocation of capital and other

---

[13] The employment effects are more pronounced in the Indian Punjab than in Pakistan because of a larger number of small and portable pumps for tubewells and a much higher index of multiple cropping.

scarce resources to the state farm sector deprives the village sector of the resources and support services that are needed to increase farm productivity and output, that pessimistic view is likely to become a self-fulfilling prophecy.

The conscious and unconscious choices that create a bimodal pattern of agricultural development often reflect a failure to recognize the extent to which successful pursuit of unimodal and bimodal strategies represent mutually exclusive alternatives. The trade-off between the two alternatives is more likely to be recognized in land-scarce countries. After all, if most of a country's agricultural land is cultivated by the large-scale subsector, the average farm size of the great majority of households will be even smaller than necessitated by the very large ratio of farm households to the land area suitable for cultivation.

It is sometimes suggested that only in densely populated countries should large-scale mechanization be avoided (see, for example, Wortman and Cummings 1978, p. 239). However, because of the structural and demographic characteristics of late-developing countries, a concentration of resources in a large-scale, relatively capital-intensive subsector will to a large extent preclude the possibility of successfully pursuing a unimodal strategy even if land is available for expanding the area under cultivation. When some 60–80 percent of a country's population is dependent on agriculture, the commercial demand from nonfarm households dependent on purchased food is bound to be small relative to the large number of farm households. Hence the average farm unit can only gradually expand its use of purchased inputs. If a small number of large farms accounts for most of the increase in commercial sales, they escape the sectorwide cash-income constraint and use large amounts of purchased inputs. The inevitable result, however, is that the cash-income constraint for the great majority of farm units is intensified. This consequence of the restricted size of the domestic commercial market may be partly offset by an emphasis on producing export crops.[14] In general, however, the export option qualifies

---

[14] The argument advanced by nutritionists and others against reliance on agricultural export crops receives attention in chapter 6. It is more pertinent to mention here that Malaysia appears to be "the exception that proves the rule" about the substantial tradeoffs between unimodal and bimodal strategies. Because of a virtually unique set of conditions, Malaysia has been able to achieve considerable success in simultaneously expanding production in its large-scale estate sector and in the smallholder sector. An abundance of accessible agricultural land relative to the country's agricultural population has meant that the occupation of large land areas by estates has not significantly limited the scope for expanding the smallholder area. In addition, the estate sector is concentrated mainly on production of rubber and palm oil for export and both products face import demand schedules that are relatively price elastic. Hence, rapid expansion of the estate sector has not aggravated the farm cash income constraint for smallholders. Indeed, increases in productivity and output among smallholders have also been based to a large extent on enlarged production of rubber and oil palm products. It is also noteworthy that the estates have been able to obtain most of their capital for expansion from overseas investors; the funds were therefore largely a net addition to the capital resources available for development. Finally, the special position of the Malay population in agriculture and in the country's political power structure has meant that government policies have been relatively favorable to the smallholder sector. Among African countries, the Ivory Coast probably comes closest to fulfilling the conditions that make it possible to expand successfully both large-scale estate production and smallholder production.

but does not eliminate the cash-income or purchasing-power constraint, which means that the average farm unit can only gradually expand its use of purchased inputs. In land-scarce countries, the growth in productivity and output of small farmers is restricted, of course, by the shortage of land as well as by the purchasing-power constraint.

Thus, because of the cash-income or purchasing-power constraint, there are cogent economic as well as social advantages in pursuing a unimodal agricultural strategy even where land is abundant. Moreover, the structural and demographic characteristics of the low-income and late-developing countries which give rise to this cash-income or purchasing-power constraint can be eased only gradually by the process of structural transformation.

The Skewed Size Distribution of Farm Units

When the political climate is favorable, land redistribution is a very important option for narrowing the inequality in income distribution and ensuring that the expansion of agricultural production is based on capital-saving, labor-using technologies which are appropriate to the factor proportions that prevail. There is substantial evidence of an inverse correlation between farm size and output per hectare, and the proposition that the technologies adopted by small operational units are labor-intensive is well established (Berry and Cline 1979; Bardhan 1973; Lau and Yotopoulos 1971; Johnston and Kilby 1975). Thus it can be asserted with considerable confidence that redistributive land reform programs are likely to have significant economic as well as social advantages, although they may entail some adverse effects on output during a transitional period.[15]

The most difficult questions concerning redistributive land reform programs relate to their political feasibility. One knowledgeable observer sympathetic to land reform programs and fully aware of their potential advantages has recently asserted that "an all out effort to implement land reform in India would undoubtedly fail at this point and would only serve to further exacerbate an already chaotic political situation" (Gotsch 1979, p. 8). Many observers of the Indian scene would endorse that judgment; and in greater or lesser degree it probably applies to many other low-income developing countries. Because of differences between countries, however, it is hazardous to generalize about prospects for land reform. In addition, dramatic changes in political climate can occur within countries even without a change in regime such as that which led to redistribution of land in China or the special circumstances of the post–World War II period that made it possible to implement

---

[15] Schuh (1978) argues that the Chilean land reform under Allende had serious adverse effects on agricultural production. However, the economic structure of Chile, with only 24 percent of its total labor force in agriculture, differs greatly from the circumstances in the late-developing countries. Moreover, the feature of the Chilean land reform which so adversely affected production seems to have been the weakening of incentives because farmers who received land were required to organize their production in collective units (Valdés 1974, pp. 410–13).

effectively redistributive land reforms in Japan and Taiwan.[16] Even if the amount of land that can be made available for redistribution is limited, it may be possible to provide landless laborers with "house-plots" large enough to support a kitchen garden and a cow or a buffalo. This has been done on a fairly substantial scale in India with significant nutritional benefits, and Bell and Duloy (1974, p. 122) make the point that such plots can "go a considerable way toward reducing the dependent status of landless laborers."

Dynamic factors and the size and distribution of resources. Carl Gotsch's characterization of the Rural Production System (shown in figure 3.1) emphasizes that land reform is only one of a number of policies and programs that influence the distribution of land and other resources among farm units of various sizes (Gotsch 1974, p. 137). He rightly emphasizes the central

[16] In Japan, a directive issued by the Supreme Commander for the Allied Powers was of decisive importance in reinforcing groups within Japan sympathetic to land reform. A number of special circumstances influenced the outcome in Taiwan, including the fact that "virtually all of the administrators who took that decision [land reform] and implemented it so effectively were Chinese from the Mainland, whereas the landlords obliged to sell their land were Taiwanese" (Johnston and Kilby 1975, p. 255).

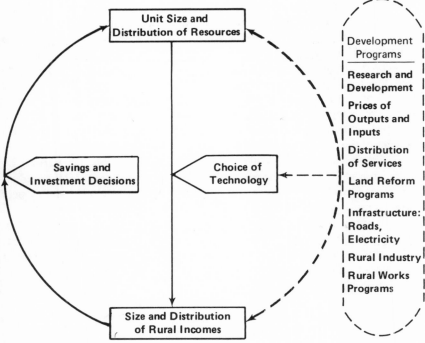

Figure 3.1. The Rural Production System.

Source: Gotsch (1974), p. 137.

importance of technology and that the choice of technology will be affected by the level and orientation of research, price policies, the distribution of credit and other support services, as well as by land reform programs.

The feedbacks shown in figure 3.1 call attention to the way in which an initial size distribution of land and other resources will be affected by the size and distribution of rural incomes in subsequent periods. This is primarily because of the powerful influence of income flows on savings and investment decisions, which in turn are likely to lead to interrelated changes in the size distribution of farm units and in the technology applied. One of the more disturbing consequences of the Green Revolution in India and still more in Pakistan has been the way in which rapid increases in incomes among large landowners, in combination with policies and institutional factors such as an overvalued exchange rate and preferential access to institutional credit, have encouraged premature tractor mechanization. It has sometimes been argued that those tendencies toward an increasingly bimodal pattern of development are an inevitable consequence of the technical innovations underlying the so-called Green Revolution. The vagueness of the term Green Revolution lends itself to such an interpretation.

In fact, however, the high-yield seed-fertilizer combinations that are the core technology of the Green Revolution are highly divisible. Experience in other countries, most notably Japan and Taiwan, demonstrates that in a more appropriate institutional and policy environment those innovations can lead to widespread increases in productivity and income among small-scale farmers. Moreover, the unimodal pattern of agricultural development which characterized Japan and Taiwan was established long before the land reforms of the post–World War II period created an egalitarian distribution of land ownership. According to a land registration survey carried out in Taiwan in 1920, 42.7 percent of the owners had title to only 5.7 percent of the land, and 11.5 percent of the owners possessed 62.1 percent of the land (Thorbecke 1979, p. 137). The size distribution of *ownership units* remained highly skewed until the postwar land reforms in the early 1950s. But the distribution of *operational units* was already unimodal in the prewar period because large landowners found it more profitable to rent out their land to tenants, who cultivated small units intensively, employing labor-using, capital-saving technologies. The combination of strong research programs which generated divisible, yield-increasing innovations suited to the needs of small farmers, plus substantial investments in irrigation and other forms of infrastructure, plus policies that enabled small farmers to have access to credit, fertilizer, and other inputs on the same terms as large farmers led to the progressive modernization of the existing small-scale farm units.

This expansion path for the agricultural sector was economically efficient because the gradually enlarged expenditures for purchased inputs were concentrated on fertilizer and other yield-increasing inputs which enhanced the productivity of the on-farm resources of labor and land. The economic efficiency of a well-designed "unimodal" pattern of agricultural development, so well illustrated by the experience of Japan and Taiwan, is demonstrated by the fact that large increases in *total factor productivity* (that is, increases of output per unit of total inputs) accounted for such a substantial fraction of the increases in farm output (Hayami and Ruttan 1971, chaps. 6 and 7; Johnston and Kilby 1975, chaps. 5 and 6). Furthermore, the unimodal pattern of agricultural development facilitated overall economic growth and structural transformation in many ways. In the period prior to the postwar land reform, which led to an egalitarian distribution of land ownership, a large share of the gains in productivity and income accrued to landowners. But to a very considerable extent those large rental incomes were invested in rural nonfarm industries rather than used to create large and inappropriately capital-intensive farm units.

The direct effects of economic policies and price distortions that lead to underpricing and preferential access to capital and foreign exchange have been among the most important polarizing factors contributing to bimodal patterns of agricultural development. Tractors and tractor-drawn implements often have been highly profitable to large farmers because they have been available at prices well below their social-opportunity cost. According to the induced-innovation hypothesis advanced by Hayami and Ruttan (1971), the longer-term effects of distorted relative prices on the pattern of technical change may be even more significant than their adverse effects on short-term allocative efficiency. Hayami and Ruttan hypothesize that relative factor prices exert a major influence not only on farmers and on firms supplying inputs but also on agricultural administrators and scientists. Their analysis of the contrasting patterns of technical change in Japan and the United States shows that the orientation of research and the contrasting nature of agricultural innovations in those countries was influenced by a dynamic process of factor substitution in response to trends in relative factor prices. Later studies of other countries have provided additional support for their hypothesis (for example, Yamada and Ruttan 1980).

Nevertheless, we believe that Hayami and Ruttan overstate the role of relative prices in shaping government decisions about agricultural research and other programs for supplying "public goods." Elaborating a very similar theory of institutional innovation, Davis and North (1971) recognize that the "primary action group" which perceives the possibility of capturing profits through new institutional arrangements may be motivated by a group interest that does not coincide with society's interest in greater total income or the goal of narrowing inequalities in income distribution. An analysis of research allocations in São Paulo, Brazil, by Ayer and Schuh (1972) provides an interesting example of the powerful influence of such a "primary action group." They conclude that the principal reason why the state of São Paulo invested so heavily in cotton research and so sparingly in research on food crops was the powerful influence of the rural landowners and farmers on the state legislature. Those groups perceived that since cotton was an export crop, technical change leading to increased cotton production would mainly accrue to them (as a producer surplus), whereas productivity gains and increased output of domestic food crops would mean lower prices, so that the benefits of technical change would be realized as a consumer surplus.

It is our contention that the objective of fostering increased agricultural productivity and output by a unimodal strategy should provide the principal guideline for the policy decisions that shape a country's pattern of technical change. We will see in chapter 6, however, that that view is challenged both by those who stress a narrow view of efficiency and by other critics who emphasize equity considerations based on what we regard as an inappropriately narrow and short-term view of technical change.

The economic policies and price distortions associated with industrialization-first strategies have also impeded the growth of small- and medium-scale, rural-based manufacturing firms. This in turn has contributed to a tendency for landowners to concentrate on maximizing their wealth, power, and status within a "closed loop" in which farming is the only economic option that receives serious attention. That tendency has been reinforced in India and Pakistan by the large scope that existed for import substitution. Furthermore, the major impact of the seed-fertilizer innovations was confined to limited areas such as the Punjab, which already had well-controlled water supplies. As a result, the enormous increases in productivity and output in those areas had relatively little impact on agricultural prices; local wheat growers were simply replacing American farmers in the provisioning of India's cities.

Success in fostering more widespread technical progress, together with the investment in irrigation and other infrastructure required to create environmental conditions favorable to the high-yield varieties, should result in a growth of output sufficient to put pressure on grain prices. It should also have more pervasive effects on the demand for labor because of the higher labor requirements associated with the new varieties, even without the increase in multiple cropping which they facilitate through their shorter growth period.[17] In the resulting situation of declining grain prices, the more alert and more aggressive landowners can be expected to turn to new and more rewarding areas of entrepreneurial activity. These tendencies will, of course, be strengthened to the extent that economic policies are modified in the direction of encouraging a more decentralized pattern of industrial development. Under those conditions, the rural elite will be less inclined to concentrate on maximizing wealth and power within farming and will be less motivated to resist changes aimed at improving the income-earning opportunities of small-scale

[17] For a detailed analysis that reaches analogous conclusions see Binswanger and Ryan (1977).

farmers. In fact, there may even be a growing perception of the extent to which rapid, self-sustaining growth of the nonagricultural sectors requires widespread increases in income and purchasing power among the mass of the rural population.

These considerations underscore the importance of viewing policy design for agricultural development as a dynamic, adaptive process. To argue in terms of "absolute priorities" and to assert that a redistributive land reform is a "prerequisite" for achieving a broadly based pattern of agricultural development is likely to be counterproductive. The important need is rather to think in terms of feasible "sequences," as we emphasized in chapter 1.

Land tenure reform and the size of operational units. Land tenure (tenancy) reform aimed at fixing rental ceilings to prevent "rack-renting" is often advocated as a substitute for redistributive land reform. The political resistance to legislation limiting rental rates is generally less determined than the resistance to redistributing land in excess of an acreage ceiling. This, however, is doubtless a consequence of the relative ease with which rental ceilings can be evaded. In situations where the farm labor force is increasing and there is an acute shortage of alternative income-earning opportunities, tenants or those seeking to become tenants have a strong interest in colluding with landlords to ignore rental ceilings in order to have access to a piece of land.

We argued in chapter 1 that it is essential to assess both the feasibility and the desirability of policy options and that "you shouldn't always want what you can get." We believe that land tenure reform promises benefits for the rural poor which are largely illusory and which in practice will usually have the effect of restricting income-earning opportunities in the agricultural sector.[18]

If landlords simply ignore rental ceilings, the main effect of tenure legislation is to increase the tendency to rely on short-term, verbal agreements and, probably, to reduce the already limited bargaining power of tenants. A common outcome, however, is for landlords to evict their tenants and to convert large *ownership* units into large *operational* units (see Lipton 1978, p. 330). This has two advantages for the landowner. First, he retains all of the economic rent accruing to his land, without being bothered by tenancy legislation which seeks to restrict the amount of rent he collects from tenants. Second, he reduces the risk that tenants will establish a claim to land that they may be able

---

[18] There are exceptions. Land reform legislation in the Philippines, for example, has brought about substantial conversion of share tenancy to leasehold tenancy with fixed rental rates. According to a detailed analysis of a rice-producing village some ninety kilometers from Manila, the leaseholders have been able to capture the increase in economic rent accruing to land as a result of growing population pressure and increased land productivity resulting from improvements in irrigation and higher crop yields with the planting of the new semidwarf varieties. For many of the leaseholders, the difference between the new economic rent and their actual rent was retained as part of the mixed income of tenant farmers. In addition, however, many tenants capture the surplus explicitly by subrenting their land. By 1976 close to a fifth of the land in the village was subrented under "subtenancy" even though the practice is illegal (Kikuchi and Hayami 1980, pp. 22–26).

to make effective if the government begins to implement a redistributive land reform.[19]

Tenancy, especially crop-sharing tenancy, is often viewed as an "evil" institution because it is believed to be both inefficient and inequitable. The highly unequal distribution of land ownership is indeed a major source of inequality in income distribution. The notion that crop-sharing tenancy is inefficient has, however, been challenged in a number of important contributions to the development literature during the past decade, from Cheung (1969) to Bardhan and Rudra (1980). Probably the most satisfactory analysis of the fallacies involved in the allegation that share tenancy leads to inefficient resource allocation is offered by Newbery (1975); however, many of the main arguments were advanced by D. G. Johnson (1950) three decades ago. One of the important ways in which allocational inefficiency is avoided under share tenancy is through arrangements whereby landlords and tenants share in the cost of purchased inputs. A recent survey of sharecropping contracts in four states in India—West Bengal, Bihar, Uttar Pradesh, and Orissa—reports that cost-sharing has become widespread and that this is a strikingly new phenomenon in India. Significantly, it has become important with the spread of high-yield varieties and fertilizers, which have markedly increased the returns to purchased inputs (Bardhan and Rudra 1980).

A reasonably uniform size distribution of farm operational units based on tenancy has the important advantage of encouraging reliance on labor-using, capital-saving technologies. It is obviously inferior to land redistribution in its effects on equity because it does not bring about a more equal sharing of the economic rent that accrues to ownership of land. Yet it is consistent with a unimodal pattern of agricultural development and promotes a relatively rapid growth of demand for labor, thereby tending to raise returns to labor. Moreover, there is substantial evidence indicating that the higher productivity which characterizes small farmers applies as much to tenant farmers as to owner-cultivators (see, for example, Berry and Cline 1979, pp. 74–78, 126–127, and *passim*).

In contrast, the creation of large operational units, which is encouraged by fixing legal ceilings on rental payments, encourages the adoption of inappropriately capital-intensive, labor-displacing technologies. This is a consequence of the biological nature of the agricultural production process and the fact that operations are spread out in time and in space. When a big operational unit relies on a large number of hired workers, it encounters problems of supervision in seeking to avoid "shirking" and poor work performance that are much more difficult to solve than those encountered in a factory setting. Because of

[19] Thus Berry and Cline (1979, p. 18) suggest that there is currently a trend toward larger operational units "as land-reform fears encourage large owners to displace tenants and operate the land on their own." It is also reported that those who invest in modern equipment "and who do not employ 'anti-social production systems,' are thought to be fulfilling their social function" and are therefore likely to be exempted from expropriation or permitted to retain more of their land (Eckstein et al. 1978, p. 8). That observation was directed at the situation in Latin America; but it also seems applicable to a number of Asian countries where tenancy is regarded as "antisocial."

the high degree of variability that characterizes farming activities, there are numerous "on-the-spot supervisory decisions" to be made by the individual performing what normally are routine tasks.[20] Because of these characteristics of the agricultural production process, the advantages of decentralized decision-making are very great. Small farmers, whether owner-cultivators or tenants, have an incentive to exercise judgment and initiative because they have a direct interest in the outcome of the farm enterprise. If a large farm operator relies on numerous hired workers, he must either incur excessive costs of supervision or suffer the consequences of poor work performance. Hence, it is often privately profitable to use capital-intensive technologies to minimize the problems of supervising a large work force even though it is socially unprofitable to use scarce capital to displace labor for which alternative employment opportunities are not available. As noted earlier, the private profitability of investing in labor-saving equipment is often enhanced by policies that artificially reduce the price of capital.

Economies of scale are of very limited importance when small-scale owner-cultivators or tenants use divisible, labor-intensive technologies suited to the resource endowment of a late-developing country. When a large operational unit adopts tractor-powered technologies to minimize problems of supervision, however, economies of scale become important: costs are minimized when machinery is used to capacity. Moreover, once an initial investment has been made in a tractor, there is a built-in incentive to adopt increasingly labor-displacing technologies as the owner or manager acquires additional tractor-drawn implements and the knowledge and skill required to mechanize a wider range of farming operations. This increases the probability that land tenure reforms adopted to enhance the welfare of poor rural families will have the effect of exacerbating problems of underemployment and meager incomes by slowing the growth of demand for labor or even reducing it, with adverse effects on returns to labor.

Land reform is only one of the many issues that need to be confronted in the design and implementation of agricultural strategies capable of accelerating the growth of output by means that lead to widespread participation of the rural population in improved income-earning opportunities. The policies and programs that are needed in individual countries are to a large extent location-specific because of the great variation among countries and among farming regions within individual countries. Especially important are the variations in environmental conditions and in socioeconomic and historical factors that determine opportunities and constraints. However, there are other factors, to which we now turn, which are common to many countries.

Deficiencies of Agricultural Research Programs

One of the major advances in economics during the past two decades has been the enhanced awareness of the significance of technological change as a

---

[20] The quoted phrase is from a classic article by John Brewster (1950).

source of economic growth. Studies on economic growth by Kuznets and others have demonstrated that a very large fraction of the growth of economic output can be attributed to increases in "residual productivity" rather than to expanded use of the conventional economic inputs of labor, land, and capital. Analysis of the historical experience of a number of developed countries suggests that the growth of total inputs accounted for only about one fourth of the growth in per capita product, and the balance was due to the growth of productivity (Kuznets 1971, p. 73).

As noted earlier, studies of agricultural development in the United States, Japan, and a number of other countries confirm the great importance of increases in "total factor productivity" to increases in agricultural output.[21] A great many factors account for increases in factor productivity, but the contributions of scientific progress in generating economically useful knowledge and of agricultural research in generating more productive technologies are unquestionably of great importance. During the past two decades there has been a good deal of empirical analysis of the contribution of agricultural research to increased productivity. Evenson, Waggoner, and Ruttan (1979) recently analyzed thirty-two studies of the economic benefits of public research in agriculture; the studies indicate that the annual rates of return on research expenditure commonly fall in the 30–60 percent range, much above the 10–15 percent rates of return realized on more typical investments.

The rapid introduction and spread of high-yield, fertilizer-responsive varieties of rice and wheat provide striking evidence of the potential that exists for creating more favorable input-output relationships and thereby shifting supply functions. The International Rice Research Institute (IRRI), in the Philippines, and the International Center for Maize and Wheat Improvement (CIMMYT), in Mexico, both have contributed greatly to the development of modern varieties of rice and wheat. In both cases advances in plant genetics and related disciplines contributed to the success achieved. The new varieties give a higher increase in yield per kilogram of fertilizer, and at least equally important, they have the capacity to maintain favorable grain/fertilizer response ratios even with very high levels of fertilization. This greater responsiveness was achieved by changes in the plant architecture of the new semidwarf varieties, eliminating a major shortcoming of traditional varieties, which tended to topple over when high levels of fertilizer were applied. In addition, because of success in eliminating photoperiodism, the modern varieties developed at IRRI and CIMMYT typically perform well at a wide range of latitudes. Second and third generations of modern varieties, however, often

---

[21] Given the differences in their factor endowments, Japan and the United States experienced remarkably similar rates of growth in agricultural output and total productivity (output per unit of total inputs) over the extended period from 1880 to 1960. However, the increases in total factor productivity were much more striking in Japan during the first four decades, whereas in the United States virtually all of the increases in total productivity occurred during the 1920–60 period. Johnston and Kilby (1975, pp. 221–26) have examined some of the factors that may account for that contrast.

have reincorporated photoperiodism in order to improve adaptation to local conditions. Although the short maturity period characteristic of varieties such as IR8 (the initial worldwide release by IRRI) has an important advantage in facilitating multiple cropping, longer maturing varieties often have an advantage in avoiding the problems that arise in harvesting rice in the rainy season. Some of the later varieties released by IRRI and selected in national research programs have been of medium stature, with a somewhat lower yield potential but greater tolerance of unfavorable soil-water environments. These have therefore spread rapidly in many situations where conditions are not optimal for the short-stature varieties.

Spread of modern varieties and persistence of a "yield gap." The rate of expansion of modern varieties of rice and wheat in Asian countries has been remarkable. Moreover, small as well as large farmers, tenants as well as owner-cultivators have adopted the new varieties wherever environmental conditions have been suitable (Lipton 1978; Ruttan 1978). The proportion of the total rice area in Asia planted to modern varieties rose from 4 percent in 1967/68 to 25 percent in 1973/74. The increase in India was very similar to the average increase for Asia—and for South Asia and Southeast Asia considered as subregions. By 1973/74 the fraction had reached 43 percent in Pakistan, 55 percent in Sri Lanka, and 63 percent in the Philippines. On the other hand, the 1973/74 fraction was only 5 percent in Burma, about 6 percent in Thailand, and 16 percent in Bangladesh. The limited spread of modern varieties in these and some of the other Asian countries is mainly a reflection of unfavorable environmental conditions. Scientists at IRRI therefore now emphasize that priority must be given to the development of higher-yield varieties suited to a wider range of agroclimatic conditions. For example, in Burma, Thailand, and Bangladesh, varieties are needed that perform well under conditions of uncontrolled flooding and deep water. Elsewhere the need is for greater resistance to salinity or periods of drought. In many Asian countries, however, there is also a great need to expand and improve irrigation so that existing varieties and technology can be adopted (see Anden-Lacsina and Barker 1978, pp. 16, 26, and *passim*).

One urgent research need is to narrow the "yield gap" between the levels of yield that are technically and economically possible and those that are actually realized by the great majority of farmers. The existence of that yield gap points to the need for farm-level surveys to obtain better understanding of the major constraints faced by farmers. It also directs attention to the importance of training programs and improved institutional arrangements to achieve better management and utilization of water and to increase the effectiveness of agricultural extension activities.[22] We return to some of these important manage-

---

[22] For an excellent discussion of these issues, see the "Second Asian Agricultural Survey," carried out under the auspices of the Asian Development Bank (1978, pp. 65–101, 242–55). The *World Development Report, 1978*, prepared by the World Bank (1978), contains (in chaps. 4 and 5) a very concise review of the priority problems of increasing agricultural productivity and output in Asia and in Sub-Saharan Africa.

rial and organizational issues in chapter 5. Methodologies to increase the relevance of research to small farmers are reviewed later in this chapter.

Underinvestment in research. The internal rate of return of the research at IRRI has been estimated to be an astounding 84 percent. Even more significant than its direct impact, however, has been its indirect contribution in making national research programs more productive. The internal rate of return on investments in national research programs in Asia rose from 30 percent in 1965 to 74 percent in 1975 (Evenson 1978, p. 238).[23] These impressive achievements of agricultural research have led to a substantial increase in the allocation of domestic resources for research in a number of countries. There has also been a rapid expansion in the level of support provided for the network of international agricultural research centers. But unfortunately there are indications that the substantial increase in financial and technical assistance for the international centers has been in part a substitution for external support previously provided for strengthening research programs in individual countries. Given the extremely high returns obtained from agricultural research and the limited allocations of funds for research in most developing countries, there is a strong presumption that there is still serious underinvestment in this activity (Evenson 1978, pp. 242–43).

There are many reasons for the underinvestment in agricultural research common in developing countries. Returns to research are by their very nature uncertain as well as fairly long-term in their impact. This makes it difficult to secure adequate allocations of the public resources which are required for the support of most types of agricultural research. Once a high-yield variety or similar innovation has been developed, it becomes part of the public domain; an organization undertaking such research cannot recoup its investment by capturing part of the economic benefits that are generated. There are in fact important spillover effects from country to country and from region to region within a country as innovations spread. Indeed a major contribution of international research centers lies in the facilitating and increasing of this international transmission of knowledge and technologies in an organized and systematic fashion.

The shortcomings of national agricultural research programs are, of course, also related to the fact that government revenues are inadequate in relation to the requirements for investment and recurrent expenditure for education, for infrastructure, and for a host of other activities. The shortcomings of national research programs in developing countries, however, are not to be attributed entirely to a lack of funds. In general, research workers require university and postgraduate training, as well as practical experience, which is best acquired by working in an established and effective research organization. Continuity and the possibility of selecting skillful research workers on the basis of their performance over a period of years is in some respects even more crucial than the size of the research budget. For example, some of the most outstanding work in a very successful maize breeding program in El Salvador was done by Jesus Merino Argueta, a plant breeder with only a high school education working with a very limited budget. However, he had "an innate ability to select promising lines," and continued his efforts over an extended period during which he obtained increasingly impressive results (Walker 1980, chap. 2).

Neglect of research and a consequent lack of feasible and profitable technologies suited to a variety of local conditions appear to be particularly serious in Sub-Saharan Africa. Probably the major conclusion of a recent interdisciplinary study of agricultural change in tropical Africa is that in many areas the lack of a satisfactory "research base" was the principal factor responsible for limited progress in raising agricultural productivity and incomes (Anthony et al. 1979, chaps 5, 8, and 9).

It is not surprising that of the three developing regions, Africa spends the least on agricultural research. Of greater significance is the fact that the percentage increase in expenditure on research in Africa between 1959 and 1974 was only about half that of the other developing regions (Boyce and Evenson 1975, p. 3). We have suggested that the success of the new varieties of rice and wheat generated increased support for research in Asia. Research programs in Africa can claim relatively few successes. This can probably be attributed in part to Africa's later and more limited investment in institutions. This is in especially marked contrast with India, where the agricultural universities established in the 1950s and 1960s have already trained many agricultural scientists to staff expanded research programs. The shortcomings in Africa are also due to the special difficulty of carrying out useful research in relatively small countries, especially in terms of population and GNP, which have extremely varied farming conditions because of the diversity of their agroclimatic environment. Even in Asia there has been relatively little research carried out that is relevant to the less favorable rainfed farming areas, where a large fraction of the region's agricultural population is located.[24]

5   The Special Problems of Rainfed Agriculture

Although a methodology of proven effectiveness exists for developing biological and chemical innovations for conditions of controlled water supply, the scientific knowledge and research methodologies that would permit similar progress in rainfed areas are highly deficient. In a number of countries, especially in Asia, huge investments in expanding and improving irrigation and

---

[24] An important area of research ignored in our summary account concerns techniques for reducing storage losses. Some of the claims that are made of the potential for reducing postharvest losses are exaggerated and ignore cost and other constraints. Nevertheless, significant improvements appear to be possible by practices that can be used by small farmers (see, for example, ..indmarsh, Tyler, and Webley 1978).

drainage facilities represent a central feature of programs to expand production, to intensify agriculture through expanding multiple cropping, and thereby to enlarge the capacity of the agricultural sector to absorb labor into productive employment. However, because of technical and economic constraints on extending the area under irrigation, the bulk of the agricultural land in many developing countries, including most of Sub-Saharan Africa, will continue to depend on rainfed production. The task of generating a sequence of feasible and profitable innovations adapted to farming conditions in those areas poses special problems.

There are a number of examples of success in developing high-yield varieties of maize that perform well when the rainfall is reasonably ample and well distributed. In Kenya and El Salvador, for example, experiment stations have developed high-yield, hybrid varieties of maize which have spread rapidly among small farmers (Gerhardt 1975; Walker 1980). In both countries, however, the adoption of improved varieties has been distinctly limited in areas where the environmental conditions are relatively unfavorable.

The general fact is that in many areas the level of rainfall, its year-to-year variability, and its seasonal distribution limit significantly the yield increases that can be obtained simply by the introduction of improved seed-fertilizer combinations.[25] The challenge is especially great in the semiarid tropical regions, such as Kenya's "medium potential" zone, discussed in chapter 2. In these semiarid tropical regions "more than 500 million of the poorest people in the world eke out a livelihood from the meager resources of land and capital in an unfriendly climate" (Ghodake, Ryan, and Sarin 1978, p. 1). Biological and chemical innovations need to be supplemented by equipment and tillage innovations to improve land and water management before their yield potential can be realized. Unfortunately, the research efforts devoted to such problems have been so limited that the research base for increasing productivity and output in semiarid areas is grossly inadequate.

One of the principal conclusions of a recent study of "the political economy of rice in West Africa" by Pearson, Stryker, and Humphreys (1981) is that neither labor-intensive, manual techniques nor highly mechanized, capital-intensive techniques are economically profitable for rice production in West

---

[25] The difference in yield potential between irrigated and rainfed production is illustrated by the following estimates (in tons per hectare) of present and potential yields for rice in eight Asian countries (IRRI 1979, p. 12):

	Present yield	Present potential yield
Irrigated (wet season)	2.6	3.6
Irrigated (dry season)	3.1	4.2
Upland	1.1	1.7

The substantial difference between wet- and dry-season yields for irrigated rice reflects mainly the greater availability of sunlight during the dry season. The lower yields for upland rice are influenced strongly by water stress when crop growth depends on rainfall rather than controlled irrigation and by lower levels of fertilizer application related to yield variability. The estimates were made by rice scientists from Bangladesh, Burma, India, Indonesia, Nepal, the Philippines, Sri Lanka, and Thailand attending an IRRI conference in 1977.

Africa. It is therefore argued that a high priority should be given to identifying and evaluating intermediate technologies such as animal-powered implements and power tillers to reduce costs of production and increase output per worker.

Farm-equipment and tillage innovations. Until recently, IRRI was the only international agricultural research center with a substantial program aimed at testing and designing improved equipment for small farmers. The IRRI program appears to have had a considerable impact in fostering local manufacture and expanded use by farmers of items such as small threshers and a simplified version of the power tillers that spread rapidly in Japan beginning in the mid-1950s and in Taiwan some ten to fifteen years later. The work at IRRI has benefited considerably from the long experience in Japan and Taiwan in developing a widening range of farm implements suited to the needs of small-scale farmers. The direct relevance of the work at IRRI, like that of the earlier experience in Japan and Taiwan, is pretty much limited to irrigated rice production.

The IRRI experience is nevertheless very important in demonstrating that a well-conceived research and development (R&D) program for promoting farm-equipment innovations in developing countries can achieve significant results. It also demonstrates, however, the need for a sustained effort and a systematic methodology for evaluating promising areas for product development and for establishing design parameters based on analysis of the potential market and of the technical and economic environment in which the equipment will be produced and operated. Another important lesson derived from that program is that promotion of backward linkages through local manufacturing should become an explicit goal (Duff 1980). This evidence from the IRRI experience is significant for two reasons. Some economists and agricultural engineers have argued that the scarce resources available for research should not be allocated to farm-equipment programs. It is noted, for example, that in the United States local blacksmiths and machine shops spontaneously designed and manufactured farm equipment in response to the growth of an effective demand among farmers. And the frequent failure of ad hoc poorly conceived and understaffed programs is cited as evidence that publicly supported research on equipment innovations is inefficient as compared with "induced innovation" in the private sector. In our opinion, which seems to be supported by the IRRI program, the valid conclusion is that R&D on farm equipment faces special difficulties because of the need to take account of factors influencing both the demand for and the supply of items of improved equipment. We believe, however, that it is important to learn how to overcome those difficulties, because R&D carried out by international and national agricultural centers can yield substantial returns both in accelerating the growth of agricultural output and in fostering widespread growth of rural-based manufacturing firms (Johnston and Kilby 1975, chap. 8). The advantages of achieving more widespread and more efficient use of animal-powered equipment have been enhanced by the sharp increases in the price of petroleum imports.

The establishment of the International Crops Research Institute for the Semi-Arid Tropics (ICRISAT) is of particular importance because of the attention that it is giving to equipment and tillage innovations, as well as to improvement programs for sorghum, chickpeas, and other crops adapted to areas of limited and unreliable rainfall. Research already carried out at ICRISAT demonstrates that improved systems of land and water management utilizing animal draft power and a well-designed tool carrier can lead to large increases in output and in net farm income. The results obtained vary greatly, however, depending on the type of soil (Ryan, Sarin, and Pereira 1980; Binswanger, Virmani, and Kampen 1980).

The need to stress location-specific research programs which include an emphasis on equipment and tillage innovations appears to be especially urgent in rainfed farming regions because of the great heterogeneity of their environmental and socioeconomic conditions. It therefore seems unfortunate that CIMMYT has concentrated exclusively on biological and chemical innovations. The National Agricultural Research Institute in Mexico (INIA), however, has recently initiated research on equipment and tillage innovations. A simplified and less expensive version of the animal-powered tool carrier used at ICRISAT has recently been designed by the National Institute of Agricultural Engineering in the United Kingdom. A prototype was imported by INIA in 1981, and manufacturers in Mexico have produced a limited number of the tool carriers. Trials are being carried out by local farmers to test the value of this wheeled tool carrier in implementing tillage systems which will improve soil and water management under rainfed conditions.[26]

By and large, the R&D activity on inexpensive farm equipment adapted to upland conditions has had only limited impact on farming in developing countries. The principal exceptions appear to be certain areas in India and some of the francophone areas of West Africa (Johnston 1978). Mazubuka District in Zambia is also an interesting example of an area where there has been widespread adoption by small farmers of a considerable range of improved animal-drawn equipment, including moldboard plows, interrow cultivators, and carts (Anthony and Uchendu 1970).

The IRRI experience cited above emphasizes the importance of an effective methodology for undertaking R&D activities to generate and diffuse mechanical innovations. This appears to be especially important in rainfed regions, where the need is for improved implements that will fit into improved farming systems. It is not surprising that engineers working on their own to develop and test new equipment have not had much impact. This seems to be an obvious case of a need for a "systems approach" by engineers, agronomists, and other scientists which takes account of the interacting effects on crop yields of equipment design, tillage methods, soil characteristics, moisture conditions, and varietal improvement and fertilizer use (Johnston 1980).

---

[26] Dr. Antonio Turrent Fernandez, Colegio de Postgraduados, Chapingo, and INIA, personal communication, June 1980 and July 1981.

Risk attitudes and perceptions. Risk associated with unpredictable natural hazards is always present in agriculture, but it obviously poses more acute problems under rainfed conditions. Much of the literature has concentrated on problems believed to be associated with risk *attitudes*, on the assumption that small farmers with limited resources are excessively averse to risk. It is noteworthy, for example, that the one chapter in the influential volume *Redistribution with Growth* (Chenery et al. 1974) which focuses explicitly on rural development gives major attention to a scheme aimed primarily at offsetting the effects of small farmers' attitudes toward risk. Bell and Duloy (1974, p. 129) advocate a "package approach" that "requires an Agency for Small Farmers (ASF) which conducts a combined credit, extension, crop insurance, and input supply operation." The crop-insurance component of the package is stressed because the authors assume that the critical factor limiting the adoption of new, yield-enhancing technologies by small farmers is their exceptional averseness to risk. The proposed ASF would enter into a contract with a small farmer stipulating a guaranteed yield, and the farmer would be "allowed a remission of his debt to the ASF equal to the shortfall in yield." The administrative and financial requirements for implementing such a scheme would obviously be formidable.

There is, however, evidence that suggests that the risk *attitudes* of small farmers are not nearly as significant in affecting their adoption decisions as are their risk *perceptions*.[27] This evidence seems to indicate that small farmers are not significantly more averse to risk than are larger farmers. It is differences in risk perception which are important; and the significant variations in risk perception are interregional, not interfarm differences. Therefore government programs need to concentrate on ways of modifying the objective conditions that give rise to perceptions of high risk. Plant breeding programs aimed at improving drought resistance or enhancing the drought-evading potential of crops clearly are of considerable importance in modifying the objective conditions that lead to perceptions of high risk.[28] The same applies to tillage meth-

[27] Thomas Walker (1980) presents a valuable review of the sizable literature on risk factors affecting agricultural development, plus a very interesting empirical analysis based on fieldwork in El Salvador. See also Binswanger, Jodha, and Barah (1980); Gladwin (1976); O'Mara (1971); and Roumasset (1977).

[28] In some areas, such as the semiarid region in eastern Kenya, a sorghum research program probably would have yielded higher returns than has the investment that has been made to develop short-maturity varieties of maize. Sorghum has a considerably higher potential for drought resistance than maize. But a successful sorghum program would have to give attention to problems of palatability, bird damage, and milling.

It is also argued that intercropping is important in lowering risk, but evidence is mixed. Intercropping does, however, have advantages, such as reducing seasonal peaks in labor requirements and obtaining early ground cover to reduce soil erosion (Norman 1974). It is also noteworthy that intercropping is often especially prevalent on small farms (Ryan and Binswanger 1979, p. 16). The common emphasis in extension programs on promoting planting in pure stand because this is equated with "good farming" seems highly questionable. But it also seems doubtful whether national research programs should give a high priority to research on intercropping. There are so many permutations of crop combinations and spacing to be studied that it is difficult to obtain useful results. Trial-and-error experimentation by farmers probably has a comparative advantage over research at experiment stations.

ods which result in more efficient utilization of available moisture. Timely planting and weeding are often very important; and more precise seed and fertilizer placement may also have a significant effect on yield, (Binswanger, Virmani, and Kampen 1980, p. 17).

There is also a need for programs that enhance the capacity of small and marginal farmers to cope with crop failure. For example, Jodha has shown that rural work programs that provide supplementary employment and income during periods of drought in India represent virtually the only coping mechanism available to small farmers which does not have serious detrimental effects on the human and physical capital of poor rural households (see Jodha 1978; and Binswanger, Jodha, and Barah 1980).

Limited Effectiveness of Organizations for Reaching the Small Farmer

The shortcomings of agricultural research organizations are intimately related to deficiencies in diffusing innovations among small farmers. One response to the problem has been the recent emphasis on the ex ante evaluation of agricultural research priorities and programs (Binswanger and Ryan 1977). The ex post evaluations we discussed earlier have demonstrated that the economic returns to expenditures on agricultural research *can* be very high indeed. Still, a good deal of the research that is carried out has very little impact on productivity and output at the farm level. One important function of ex ante evaluations is to increase the probability that the scarce resources of funds and manpower available for research will be directed at problems of high priority. Ex ante evaluations can also facilitate interactions of biological and physical scientists with economists and other social scientists in evaluating the relevance and appropriateness of alternative research objectives.

Linkages between research, extension, and farmers. A closely related problem concerns techniques for improving the two-way interactions between research workers and farmers. In the conventional model of agricultural extension, one of the important functions of extension field staff is to facilitate communication between farmers and research workers. For a variety of reasons, that conventional model has not worked at all well in developing countries. Even the linkage between research workers and extension staff typically has been extremely weak. Key features of the Training and Visit system (Benor approach) to agricultural extension, discussed in Chapter 5, have been the creation of organizational structures and institutional procedures that provide tighter linkages between research and extension staff and the identification and promotion of innovations that are feasible and worthwhile at the farm level.[29] Three international agricultural research centers—IRRI, CIMMYT,

---

[29] A study of farmers in the Hooghly District of West Bengal before and after the introduction of the Training and Visit system indicated that the new approach had a considerable impact on productivity and cropping intensity—and that the favorable effects were more pronounced among small (with less than five acres) than among large farmers (Ray et al. 1979).

and ICRISAT—are currently very active in attempts to increase the relevance of research to small farmers. IRRI has particularly emphasized factors responsible for the previously mentioned "yield gap" between experiment stations' and farmers' yields (see, for example, Herdt and Wickham 1975). Studies of the yield gap problem, carried out mainly in the Philippines, have been paralleled by field surveys in thirty-six villages in six Asian countries carried out by research workers in the various countries (IRRI 1978, 1979).

CIMMYT's economics program was not established until the 1970s. However, the center played a major role in initiating the Puebla Project in Mexico, aimed at achieving "a breakthrough in ways of efficiently channeling knowledge, credit, and modern production inputs to a vast number of farmers" (Myren 1968, p. 10). In recent years, CIMMYT economists responsible for regional programs in eastern Africa, southern Asia, and the Andes have emphasized a variety of cooperative projects. These have included collaborative efforts with research workers in individual countries to carry out farm-level surveys of farmers' practices and attitudes to provide information for agricultural scientists and policymakers. A manual has been prepared to assist both biological and social scientists in increasing the relevance of research programs to the needs of small-scale farmers (International Maize and Wheat Improvement Center 1978, p. 3; 1980).

ICRISAT was only established in 1972, but from its inception it has done pioneer work in evolving a multidisciplinary approach to monitoring prospective technologies for their potential value to small farmers (Ryan and Binswanger 1979). This has included serious attention to their effects on risk, equity, and the demand for labor (Ghodake, Ryan, and Sarin 1978). As noted earlier, the multidisciplinary farming systems program has concentrated on developing and testing bullock-powered equipment and tillage innovations because it was recognized that it will be many years before a significant fraction of the 100 million farm households in the tropical semiarid areas of developing countries can afford to rely on tractors. In fact, even the animal-powered "bullock tractor" which is being used at ICRISAT is too large and costly for small farmers unless several of them can share its use through joint ownership or by contract plowing (Binswanger, Ghodake, and Thierstein 1980).

In order to acquire knowledge of conditions at the farm level and to create "learning laboratories" for facilitating better understanding of a wide range of problems at the farm level, ICRISAT has evolved an interesting and innovative Village-Level Studies program (Binswanger and Ryan 1979). ICRISAT's Village-Level Studies were designed initially by the Economics Program primarily for its own objectives, although in close consultation with technical scientists. Two "typical" villages were selected in each of three agroclimatic regions within semiarid tropical India. A sample of thirty cultivators and ten landless laborers was randomly selected to be monitored continuously over a period of years. The substantial output of India's agricultural universities made it possible to post an investigator with a degree in agricultural economics in each village to collect data and also to act informally as a participant observer. It is also noteworthy that the investigator selected came from a rural background and spoke the local language. Almost from the beginning the Village-Level Studies program was used by technical scientists at ICRISAT to obtain information on existing farming techniques and on problems such as the prevalence of pests, diseases, and weeds. Some of ICRISAT's entomology research has been transferred to farmers' fields, where it can be carried out under more realistic conditions than can be replicated at an experiment station.

Selected village sites are being used increasingly as an essential element in ICRISAT's technology development and adaptation activities. Binswanger and Ryan (1979, p. 15) stress that "they provide a locus for multidisciplinary effort on what may be the most difficult research problem of the semiarid tropics: generating improved soil-, crop-, and water-management techniques which are adaptable to different agroclimatic, economic, and sociocultural environments."

There also have been some encouraging organizational developments in national programs which offer promise of more effective generation and diffusion of knowledge and technologies to small farmers. An approach evolved at the Instituto de Ciencia y Tecnología Agrícolas (ICTA) in Guatemala emphasizes agrotechnical and socioeconomic reconnaissance surveys of existing farming systems. The approach focuses on identifying constraints confronting farmers in regions selected on the basis of similarities in their production problems and opportunities. The surveys provide the basis for determining research objectives and priorities. Trials carried out by research staff on farmers' fields help to verify the suitability of the innovations under the conditions faced by small farmers. Subsequent "tests" of the more promising innovations by representative farmers provide further verification of the profitability and feasibility of innovations. These are then promoted through coordinated action by regional research stations and extension workers (Hildebrand 1976).

Reaching large numbers of small farmers. We have emphasized the linkages between research and extension because we are persuaded that it is the lack of feasible and profitable technologies that has been mainly responsible for the inadequate spread of agricultural innovations. There is now a vast experience from Asian, African, and Latin American countries which indicates that attractive and divisible innovations such as high-yield seed-fertilizer combinations can be diffused quite rapidly among small as well as large farmers. Nevertheless, it is a major challenge to build programs that can reach the bulk of small farmers on a routine basis.

Where crops have a high value this has been accomplished with specialized and well-funded crop administrations. Kenya's success in fostering rapid expansion of tea production among small holders is an interesting example of accomplishing that type of training and extension by the use of a relatively large number of specialist extension agents. An effective institutional innovation, the Kenya Tea Development Authority (KTDA), set up as a semi-independent government organization, has recruited, trained, and supervised field staff responsible for tea extension activities. The KTDA also has built factories and "tea roads." It has organized the collection of tea leaf from small farmers and the prompt delivery to factories which is necessary in order to meet quality standards and to compete successfully in export markets. Similar organizational arrangements have been instituted in Malawi and a few other African countries. This has permitted a substantial expansion of small-holder production of tea, which long had been regarded as a plantation crop *par excellence* because of the need for close coordination between production and processing operations.

Special institutional arrangements are feasible for a high-value crop such as tea, and they are justified because of the need for coordination and for maintaining quality standards. For most crops, however, the need is to raise the level of performance of the general agricultural extension service. Studies by Chambers (1974), Leonard (1977), and others have demonstrated that deficiencies in organizational structure and procedure are often responsible for the unsatisfactory performance of extension field staff in reaching the bulk of the small-farmer population. One of the interesting reforms that has been recommended and tested is the use of a group approach aimed at increasing the effectiveness of extension work and also achieving more equitable access to knowledge. This innovation derives in part from questioning the effectiveness of traditional efforts to diffuse innovations from progressive farmers to the majority of cultivators. Schönherr and Mbugua (1974, p. 8) argue that

> the most progressive have little time or interest for explaining to others in detail the problems and tasks of new cultivation methods. The others do not readily call upon the most progressive farmers because of the social distance between them. Lastly, the average farmers . . . believe that the most progressive ones are in a position to adopt innovations because they understand all about these things, they have the necessary contacts and are financially secure . . . so that the agricultural innovations adopted by the progressive farmers are irrelevant for them.

The first alternative tested in Kenya involved concentrating on farmers somewhat below average in their adoption of innovations. The results of that pilot project, carried out as part of the Special Rural Development Program in Tetu Division of Nyeri District, showed it to be an effective means of diffusing innovations widely. Groups of about fifty farmers were selected on the basis of not having planted hybrid maize or not having kept exotic cattle. They were brought to a Farmer Training Centre for a three-day course designed to persuade them to plant hybrid maize and to teach them how to do so successfully. The success of that project led to a decision to carry out another pilot project in selected areas of Kisii and South Nyanza districts based on training groups of farmers in their own sublocation. Clusters of farmers in a particular locality were selected on the assumption that a group of neighboring farmers would be fairly representative of the average farmers in that area. Concentrating on a cluster of farmers eased transportation problems and facilitated supervision by the instructors who were specially trained in a one- or two-week preparation course at a local Farmer Training Centre (Schönherr and Mbugua 1974; Leonard 1977, pp. 203–7; Anthony et al., 1979 pp. 243–44).

The problem of reaching the majority of small farmers is not confined to agricultural extension. There is a long history of attempts to organize farmers into cooperatives, farmers' associations, and other types of local organizations in order to facilitate the distribution of credit, the purchase and distribution of farm inputs, and the marketing of agricultural products.

The difficulties that have been encountered in enabling small farmers to have access to credit are an important example. These problems have been due in part to the special difficulties that arise with low-interest-rate policies. As noted earlier, the administrative rationing of the subsidized credit available from institutional sources invariably favors the larger and more powerful farmers. In addition, however, the administrative costs of investigating loan applications are inevitably high when an effort is made to reach large numbers of small farmers. In principle, there are cost-saving and other advantages when a local organization of farmers can assume responsibility for reviewing loan applications of members, for making decisions on loan applications, and for insuring that loans are repaid. The performance of credit cooperatives and similar organizations in less developed countries has been very uneven, and in a great many instances the expected advantages have not been realized. The analysis of organizational and managerial issues in chapter 5 seeks to throw light on the problems that arise in organizing farmers and in providing effective support services.

Neglect of the Role of Women in Rural Development

In many developing countries women play a major role in crop production and other agricultural activities in addition to the food preparation, child rearing, and other functions they perform in the household. Efforts to raise the productivity, income, and well-being of rural families clearly call for increased attention to both sets of activities. In addition, women sometimes make a significant contribution to the cash income of farm households through wage employment, trading, and nonfarm services (Ho 1980). The focus here, however, is on their agricultural and household activities. Particular attention is given to conditions in Africa. To some extent, similar conditions and problems prevail in other developing countries, but there is great variation in the roles that women play. In the Philippines and elsewhere in southeast Asia, women often earn supplementary income by operating a store in the family residence, and in West Africa women are prominent as traders in agricultural commodities.

Increased involvement of women in income-earning opportunities may, of course, have negative consequences for the family. Especially when women work outside the home, there are likely to be undesirable effects on family nutrition and child care. Poverty is an important cause of inadequate infant and child care, however, and "women of lower income groups have no option but to seek ways and means of increasing family revenues" (UNICEF 1980, p. 8). This directs attention to the importance of alternative arrangements for child care, a problem that also arises as older siblings are enrolled in school and therefore are less available for their traditional role of taking care of younger children. The discussion in chapter 5 of opportunities for organizing the rural poor is of course highly pertinent to such needs of women as establishing childcare centers.

Our focus here is on women's agricultural and household activities. In most societies there is a traditional sexual division of labor in the activities performed by men and women. Given the regional and ethnic diversity that exists, it is difficult to generalize about the sexual division of labor even in the countries of tropical Africa. Moreover, evidence from many areas suggests that there is increasing flexibility and even a breaking down of the traditional sexually based division of labor (Cleave 1974, pp. 170–73). However, women usually are responsible for the production of food crops and for lighter tasks such as weeding. In tropical Africa, women typically devote considerably more time than men to productive work, because of the demands of their agricultural and household activities. Furthermore, women often play a major role as decision-makers and managers. In fact, a large percentage of rural households are headed by women—estimated at 45 percent in Kenya and 35 percent in Malawi and an estimated 18 percent as a global average (UNICEF 1980, p. 8). Nevertheless, most agricultural extension agents are men, and farmer training and extension programs have given relatively little attention to reaching women. There is inadequate recognition that women have the right and the capability to participate in decision-making; efforts to increase farm productivity will become more effective as that is recognized. Lele (1975, p. 77) has concluded that "the neglect of women's role in agriculture may act as a drag on economic growth and contribute to imbalances in the distribution of the benefits of the growth that does occur."

Extension programs concerned with women frequently have been oriented exclusively toward domestic science and the care of children. Too often the foreign advisers who have influenced these programs have ignored the significant involvement of women in subsistence production and in cash income-earning activities, and in some cases the practices demonstrated have been ludicrously beyond the reach of the great majority of rural women in developing countries.

Some of the most promising opportunities lie in reducing the time-consuming drudgery of tasks such as hauling water and firewood. Innovations for supplying water at the village level have had widespread and significant impacts. In some areas simple dug wells have provided a convenient source of water, but it is often necessary to resort to schemes for bringing piped water from a river or spring. This entails substantial capital and recurrent costs and maintenance problems, especially if a motorized pump is required. Low-cost methods of storing water also offer promise. Catchment tanks are not uncommon in relatively prosperous areas where metal roofs have been introduced. The use of wheelbarrows or carts for hauling water also has been advocated.[30]

Hand-operated gristmills and small motorized mills for grinding maize, other cereals, and dried cassava have been particularly important innovations. Hand-operated maize shellers and groundnut (peanut) decorticators are additional examples of inexpensive items that permit a considerable saving of labor time. Community development programs in India as well as Africa have sometimes promoted stoves of improved design as a means of reducing requirements for firewood or dung for fuel, although it is reported that an "improved" stove introduced in Sierra Leone reduced the amount of smoke inside the house but used more firewood (Carr 1979, p. 26). For many years there has been considerable interest in methane generators using manure and other types of organic matter. These generators can provide gas for cooking without reducing the nutrient value of the residue, which is then used for fertilizer.[31] The spread of biogas generators has been rather slow in India, but an even simpler and cheaper design which reportedly has been spreading rapidly in parts of China arouses new hope (Dosik and Falcon 1978; Darrow and Pam 1978, p. 183).

Understanding is still inadequate of both the range of problems related to the role of women in rural areas and of the possibilities of raising their status. More equal access to education is clearly of great importance (World Bank 1980a, p. 50). Priority must also be given to reducing drudgery and increasing the productivity of women in household and agricultural activities. Apart from a few examples such as the gristmills mentioned above, expanded use and local manufacture of various items of improved household equipment appear to be quite limited. This no doubt partly reflects the severe cash-income constraint faced by rural households in low-income countries; but it probably also reflects to a considerable extent a failure to recognize that women's time has a high opportunity cost and that the welfare of the entire family, as well as

---

[30] According to an estimate by D. J. Vail, the introduction of a ten-dollar wheelbarrow would reduce the time required for hauling water to Tanzania villages from an average of over three hundred hours per family per year to about one hundred hours (Lele 1975, p. 27n). Wheelbarrows, handcarts, and animal-drawn carts can, of course, also reduce the labor time for many other hauling activities, including the hauling of manure to fields. The latter practice often increases yields considerably because it both increases the water-holding capacity of the soil and provides additional nutrients.

[31] DaSilva (1979) provides a concise review of the technology of biogas generation, the potential benefits, and problems in achieving wider use of methane generators in rural areas. See also Parikh and Parikh (1977).

the well-being and status of women, suffers from viewing it as a "free good."[32]
Rural progress will benefit greatly as women come to be viewed as full partners
in the activities of the farm household.

One observer who has studied the role of women in African rural households asserts that "schemes which aim at improving conditions by teaching
rural women better nutrition and primary health care constantly fail because
the women at whom they are aimed are just too busy to attend classes on a
regular basis or put the fruits of their learning into practice" (Carr 1979, p. 9). It
is difficult to assess the validity of this generalization on the basis of evidence
now available. But clearly in designing rural health schemes it is important to
consider the competing demands on women's time. It also seems pertinent that
success in promoting better child spacing and smaller families can help reduce
the time burden associated with the care and feeding of small children, as well
as directly benefit the health of mothers and their children. In many traditional
societies the status of women has depended almost entirely on their childbearing role. It is therefore often stressed that changes that enhance the status of
women and provide new opportunities to achieve recognition are of major
importance in facilitating the spread of family planning.

"Looking Backward" and "Looking Forward": Some Observations on Research and Population Growth

The complementary activities of looking backward and looking forward
were emphasized in chapter 1 as essential elements of a policy-analysis perspective. One especially important illustration of their importance concerns
the priority to be given to strengthening agricultural research. The ex post analyses of the economic returns to research and of the significance of the potential for increasing total factor productivity demonstrate that agricultural research programs aimed at generating innovations suited to the needs of small
farmers should be given an extremely high priority. Analysis of past experience and projections of future growth of the total and rural population and
labor force in late-developing countries also are of special importance because
of their implications concerning the success of efforts to raise per capita
incomes.

Underinvestment in Agricultural Research

Government decision-making processes tend to neglect activities such as
research, which yield returns only in the longer term.[33] We have noted that this

---

[32] This is part of a broader pattern. We argue in chapter 5 that programs for rural
organization often have failed because policymakers and planners have undervalued the time both
of the rural poor and of implementing organizations' field staff.

[33] A recent analysis by Lele (1981, p. 548) emphasizes that "the short time perspective" of
policymakers in Africa has had serious adverse effects on agricultural development, including
inadequate support for agricultural research.

problem is exacerbated in developing countries because of the pervasive problem of urban bias and the limited ability of small farmers to articulate their needs and bring pressure to bear on the political authorities.[34] In the newly independent countries of tropical Africa, there also appears to be a tendency for policymakers (and farmers as well) to be more preoccupied with political and distributional problems than with factors affecting productivity.

These problems are well illustrated by experience in Kenya, even though agricultural research programs in Kenya are relatively strong as compared with most other countries in Sub-Saharan Africa. Leonard (1977, p. 247) notes that during the colonial period, Kenya's European farmers exerted pressure on the government to support a strong agricultural research program. The share of the development budget devoted to such research declined from 17 percent in 1963–64, just prior to independence, to 6 percent in 1970–71. Leonard suggests that the Africans who replaced Europeans as the administrators and architects of Kenya's development programs have responded to pressures for rural development in a significantly different way. African leaders have tended to view development primarily as a matter of access to resources and a political problem. Issues such as research and the efficient use of resources have received much less attention. Inasmuch as successful pursuit of a unimodal strategy requires a sequence of profitable innovations suited to the needs of small farmers, this tendency to assign a low priority to agricultural research is indeed unfortunate.

Rapid Growth of Population and Labor Force in Late-developing Countries

The consequences of rapid growth of a country's rural population represents another problem area in which looking backward and looking forward are especially important concerns. We noted in chapter 2 that because of their structural and demographic characteristics, the late-developing countries will have to contend with a substantial increase in the size of their farm population and their farm labor force. According to the four hypothetical scenarios summarized in table 2.2, the increase in the farm labor force over the next fifty years could range from a minimum of 75 percent, assuming a rapid decline in fertility and a very large increase in the rate of rural urban migration, to a maximum of 475 percent, with fertility and migration unchanged.

India: a retrospective analysis. A retrospective analysis by Vyas (1979) of changes in the number and size distribution of farm households in India offers a concrete illustration of how the arithmetic of population growth and structural transformation influences the problem of rural poverty in a country that is still predominantly agricultural. In spite of the very considerable industrial growth that has taken place in India, there has been only a slight decline in the proportion of the labor force in agriculture: from 72 percent in 1951 to 69

---

[34] See also chapter 5.

percent in 1970.[35] India's population growth has not been as rapid as that in most of the developing countries, but nevertheless there has already been an enormous increase in the number of rural households.

It is estimated that between 1953–54 and 1971–72 a 66-percent increase in the number of rural households was associated with a 2-percent increase in the cultivated area, from 305 million acres to 311 million. As a result, the average size of farm holdings in India declined from 6.3 acres to 3.8 acres.[36] Of greater significance for the prevalence of poverty, the number of marginal holdings of less than one acre increased from 15.4 million to 35.6 million, and the average size of those marginal holdings declined from .27 acre to .14 acre. To some extent the increases in the number of marginal holdings and in the degree of landlessness were a result of large landowners' evicting their tenants in order to create large, mechanized operational units. However, the increase in the number of farm households and the resulting subdivision of holdings appears to have been the dominant factor. The number of "big" landowners (with fifteen to fifty acres) declined moderately, from 4.3 million units to less than 4.1 million units, between 1953–54 and 1971–72, and the fraction of the total cultivated area owned by these "big" farmers declined from 35 percent to 31 percent of the total. For "large" holdings (of fifty acres and over), there was a sharp decline from 604,000 to 350,000 holdings, and the share of land in these "large" holdings dropped from 18 percent of the total to 8 percent.

IRRI projections of rice production and population in Asia. In many developing countries continuation of rapid population growth will lead to or accentuate the problems of declining farm size illustrated by Vyas's retrospective analysis of changes in India. The first forward-looking study to be considered examines the problem of expanding rice supplies in South and Southeast Asia to keep pace with the growth of population. This study, carried out by economists at IRRI, estimates the investment requirements related to projected increases in rice production in South and Southeast Asia during the period 1974–85. Their projections imply that in the absence of technological change, it will be impossible for production to grow fast enough to match population growth even if the level of annual investment is twice as high as that of the preceding decade (Herdt, Te, and Barker 1977, p. 201). The increase in the level of investment required for the projected expansion of rice production is influenced considerably by an approximate doubling of the cost per hectare for expanding irrigation. This increase in the cost per hectare (which is independent of the effects of inflation) is due to the fact that most of the lower cost sites for irrigation schemes have already been developed.

---

[35] See Krishna (1978); World Bank (1978, p. 102); and Johnston and Kilby (1975, appendix table 5). According to a recent World Bank publication (1980a, p. 146), the share of the labor force in agriculture was 74 percent in both 1960 and 1978.

[36] The estimates by Vyas (1979) on which this discussion is based were derived from various rounds of the National Sample Survey, and the breakdown by size group refers to land holdings *owned* by households. This presidential address by Vyas to the Indian Society of Agricultural Economics also includes an analysis of changes in individual states.

Their analysis also directs attention to the fact that the scope for future fertilizer-related increases in rice production in South and Southeast Asia will be more limited than during the past decade and a half. During the five-year period 1963–67, an extraordinarily rapid rate of increase in fertilizer use—18.5 percent per annum—made a very significant contribution to the expansion of rice output. Because the initial levels of fertilizer use were so low, the effect on rice yields during that period is probably fairly well approximated by a linear response function using the rule of thumb that 1 kg of fertilizer yields 10 kg of additional paddy output. The IRRI projections for 1974–85, however, take account of the influence of the type of rice variety (modern, fertilizer-responsive vs. traditional); whether production is under irrigated or rainfed conditions; and the projected levels of fertilizer application. A number of scenarios were explored in which it was assumed that fertilizer use would continue to expand rapidly during the 1974–85 period, at an initial rate of 12 percent per year in 1974, declining gradually to 8 percent per year by 1985. A projection which assumed a more gradual decline in the growth rate, so that the expansion of fertilizer use was still growing at a 9.5-percent rate in 1985, implies a greater decline in the marginal returns to investing in fertilizer. In fact, because of the considerable reduction in the grain-to-fertilizer response ratio, a large subsidy would be required to induce farmers to apply the level of fertilizer assumed in that scenario.

These IRRI projections are, of course, dependent on assumptions that are somewhat arbitrary. However, the general implications of the analysis seem to be valid and important. One implication stressed by Herdt, Te, and Barker (1977) is the urgent need for intensified efforts to strengthen agricultural research, extension, and other training and institution-building activities required to increase the productivity of conventional inputs such as irrigation and fertilizers.

Assessing the implications of such projections on the well-being of rural populations is not a simple undertaking, and the IRRI study does not examine those issues. Failure of rice production to keep pace with the growth of effective demand obviously will tend to result in sharp increases in the price of rice and of substitutes for rice because demand for staple foods is so inelastic. Although this implies an increase in income for the more commercially oriented farm households, higher prices for food staples obviously would have serious adverse effects on the food intake and nutritional status of many low-income families. These effects would be particularly serious for marginal farmers and landless agricultural workers, whose dependence on purchased food may be nearly as great as that of urban households (Mellor 1978). The increased cost of expanded irrigation and the diminishing returns from further increases in fertilizer use have additional implications for the per capita and per household income of rural families. Subdivision of farm holdings is inevitable in countries where land is scarce and the farm population is continuing to increase in absolute size, due to the structural-demographic characteristics that we have emphasized repeatedly and illustrated by the Indian experience.

Experience in Taiwan. An upsurge in population growth began in Taiwan in the 1920s, and the average farm size declined from about 5 acres in 1930 to approximately 2.5 acres in 1960. However, Taiwan's experience illustrates that with effective investments in research, irrigation, and drainage, and with expanded multiple cropping, increases in per capita farm income are possible even with rapid population growth. In the 1960s, a "structural transformation turning point" was reached and the farm population and labor force began to decline in absolute size. By the 1960s and the early 1970s a considerable tightening of the labor supply/demand situation led to the substantial increases in returns to labor and the reduction of poverty which we mentioned in the first section of this chapter.

The initial tightening of the labor supply/demand situation was mainly a consequence of the rapid expansion of employment opportunities, especially in the nonfarm sectors of the economy.[37] However, the remarkably rapid reduction in fertility and in Taiwan's rate of natural increase, which we noted in chapter 2 and will consider in more detail in chapter 4, also has been highly significant. The decline in fertility very quickly reduced the dependency burden and the magnitude of investment requirements for the expansion of primary schools. The reduced rate of natural increase is being reflected now in slower growth of the population of working age, thereby easing the task of expanding employment opportunities to absorb a growing labor force into productive employment.

Growth of agricultural production and employment in China. The operation of diminishing returns is emphasized strongly in a retrospective and prospective analysis by Rawski (1979) of agricultural development and employment issues in the People's Republic of China (PRC). China's total labor force increased by a little over 50 percent between 1957 and 1975—from 282 million to 430 million. Even though nonagricultural employment increased at a rapid rate—nearly 5 percent annually (from 42 million in 1957 to 100 million in 1975)—two thirds of the increase in the labor force was absorbed by agriculture: the agricultural labor force rose from about 230 million in 1957 to 330 million in 1975 (Rawski 1979, p. 133).[38]

With the intensification of agricultural production, labor inputs in terms of man-days per worker for farming activities and for construction and maintenance of agricultural infrastructure (land improvement, water control, and irrigation) seem to have increased: from an average of about 160 workdays in 1957 to between 215 and 280 workdays in 1975. This increased rate of utilization of the "stock" of farm labor occurred despite the large increase in the rural

---

[37] From 1952 to 1962 nonfarm employment in Taiwan expanded at the rapid annual rate of 4.7 percent, and from 1963 to 1973 the rate of increase was a phenomenal 7.1 percent per year (Little 1979, p. 491).

[38] There is considerable controversy and uncertainty with regard to estimates of China's population and labor force. These estimates are based on John Aird's relatively high estimates of China's population, which "appear to provide the most realistic picture of current demographic conditions" (Rawski 1979, p. 123).

labor force. Moreover, the intensification of production allowed a modest increase in the average product per worker in agriculture even though the land base was virtually fixed: sown area increased by only 5 percent between 1957 and 1975. This was possible, Rawski argues, only because of the large increase in the average number of workdays, a sizable increase in the use of chemical and organic fertilizers, and a very large increase in capital inputs. Because the rate of increase in total inputs was considerably more rapid than the rate of growth of agricultural output, this meant a substantial decline in total factor productivity (Rawski 1979, p. 120). The estimated decline of some 15–35 percent in the gross value of output *per man-day* (as the number of man-days of work was increased) is cited by Rawski (1979, p. 128) as "clear-cut evidence of Malthusian diminishing returns."[39] Moreover, given the time lag before declines in fertility affect the rate of increase in the population of working age, China's agricultural labor force probably will not reach a peak and begin to decline until after 1990. With an annual average growth rate of nonfarm employment of 5 percent between 1975 and 1990, agriculture would still be absorbing some 40 percent of the annual increase in the labor force in 1990. But if nonagricultural employment were to expand at an extraordinarily rapid rate of 7.5 percent, the agricultural labor force would begin to decline before 1990 (Rawski 1979, p. 133).[40] The vigorous steps being taken to reduce fertility in the PRC, which are examined in the next chapter, may well have been influenced by concern with the growth of population pressure in the countryside.

Population growth and rural poverty in Africa—projections for Kenya. The prospects for reducing rural poverty in most of the contemporary low-income countries, however, appear still to be jeopardized by the persistence of high rates of fertility. The implications of continued rapid growth of a country's population and labor force become more dramatic as the time horizon is extended, because of the awesome power of compound interest. In a longer-term perspective the problems of rural overpopulation and of absorbing a rapidly growing labor force into productive employment appear to be especially formidable in the countries of tropical Africa, even though the potential for expanding the area under cultivation is greater than in Asian countries. The rates of natural increase are exceptionally high, and the prospects for an early and rapid reduction of population growth are not good.

In Kenya, for example, the current rate of population growth appears to be approximately 3.9 percent, compared with 2.1 percent in India. Reducing fertility will be especially difficult because some 80 percent of the population is

---

[39] A recent paper suggests that there was probably a small decline in per capita availability of grain in China between 1957 and 1977 and that as of January 1980 perhaps one third of the peasants living in communes remained below a poverty line (defined as 200 kg of grain per person per year in the double-cropping rice areas and 150 kg of grain elsewhere) (Dernberger 1980, pp. 51–52).

[40] It was noted above that nonfarm employment in Taiwan increased at a phenomenal rate of 7.1 percent annually between 1963 and 1973. Such rapid growth in nonfarm employment was facilitated greatly by remarkably rapid expansion of exports of manufactured products.

still dependent on agriculture, and the traditional attitudes which reinforce the large family norm are strong. Although Kenya was one of the first African countries to adopt a population policy, the efforts to promote family planning have not yet had much impact. The Development Plan for 1979–83 (Kenya 1979a, p. 130) expresses the hope that sufficient progress has been made in building up an infrastructure for providing family planning services to make it possible to begin to reduce the rate of population growth during the current plan period. However, because many of those who will be added to the labor force by the year 2000 have already been born or will be born before family planning will begin to have any significant effect, the 118-percent increase in the potential labor force between 1978 and 2000 which is projected on the basis of a declining birth rate is only a little less than the 125-percent increase anticipated with a constant birth rate (Kenya 1979a, p. 63).

Another set of projections for Kenya traces the effects on population and labor-force growth until the year 2024 of six scenarios of possible changes in fertility and mortality that might take place between 1969 and 1999 (Shah and Willekens 1978). The most likely estimate, according to these projections, is for a nearly sixfold increase in Kenya's population, from approximately 11 million in 1969 to 64 million in 2024. The projections are broken down by rural-urban location as well as by age and therefore direct attention to the problems resulting from the arithmetic of population growth and structural transformation and the daunting challenge of absorbing a growing labor force into productive employment. On the basis of rather optimistic assumptions about the growth of nonfarm employment, it is projected that the rural labor force would decline from 87 percent of the total labor force in 1969 to 65 percent in 2024. This change would be associated with a *sixteenfold* increase in the active age population in urban areas; but even so, the rural labor force would increase fourfold (Shah and Willekens 1978, pp. 29, 38).

Many of the differential effects of slow and rapid population growth do not become manifest for some years. As just noted, success in Kenya in slowing population growth is expected to have only a very modest effect in slowing the expansion of the labor force between 1978 and 2000—a 118-percent increase instead of a 125-percent one. This is, of course, because of the time lag before a decline in fertility begins to affect the annual additions to the population of working age.

The effects of rapid population growth on the prospects for raising per capita consumption of essential goods and services become apparent more quickly. According to the same population projections for Kenya, the anticipated increase in the number of children of primary-school age between 1978 and the year 2000 would be a relatively manageable 75 percent with a declining birth rate, compared with a 141-percent increase with a constant birth rate (Kenya 1979a, p. 63). A similar marked contrast applies to resource requirements for achieving more adequate coverage of rural areas in the provision of health services, especially if priority is given to the needs of infants and small children. A closely related implication concerns the prospects for improving the food intake and nutritional status of children generally. If Kenya attains its goal of reducing the birth rate, the population under age fifteen will increase by 63 percent between 1978 and 2000, compared with a 140-percent increase with constant fertility. Clearly, Kenya's parents will confront a considerably more formidable challenge in meeting the food needs of their children if fertility remains at its present high level.

Concluding Observations

It has been noted that "when a country is developed to the point where the opportunity cost of labor is relatively high, the special efficiency advantages of small farmers tend to disappear" (Berry and Cline 1979, p. 134). A major reason for emphasizing the need both to accelerate the expansion of employment opportunities and to slow the growth of population and labor force is, of course, to speed up the process of raising the opportunity cost of labor.

Throughout this chapter we have emphasized the need for a pattern of development which ensures that the demand for labor, within agriculture and in the nonfarm sectors, increases more rapidly than the growth of the labor force seeking employment.[41] The development literature has tended to divert attention away from the fundamental importance of the labor supply-demand situation in determining returns to labor by its emphasis on models that have assumed a rigid "institutional wage" or "subsistence wage." The historical experience of Japan and Taiwan which we have emphasized provides persuasive evidence that a tightening of the labor supply-demand situation is indeed a powerful force leading to widespread increases in returns to labor. Given the emphasis on wage rigidities, however, recent empirical evidence on this issue from the Philippines and from India is worth noting.

Detailed analysis of changes in a rice-producing village in central Luzon, in the Philippines, offers particularly clear evidence of the influence of the pressure of population on limited land resources in holding down returns to labor. We mentioned in chapter 2 that the population grew at a rate of 5.3 percent between 1966 and 1976 because a high rate of natural increase was augmented by net migration into this village, where employment opportunities were *relatively* favorable as a result of improved irrigation which permitted double cropping, rapid spread of high-yield varieties of rice, and the adoption of improved cultural practices, including intensive weeding. A 170-percent increase in the number of households of landless workers accounted for a large part of a 65-percent increase in the total number of households. By 1976 landless-

---

[41] This is an important point of convergence between our essay and Keith Griffin's *Political Economy of Agrarian Reform* (1979). Thus, in the preface to the second edition, he states: "One of the most alarming things about the pattern of agrarian growth in many underdeveloped countries is the failure of the demand for rural labour to grow as fast as the supply. As a consequence, real wages have been falling in a number of countries" (p. xii).

worker households accounted for half of the households in the village, compared with 30 percent in 1966 (Kikuchi and Hayami 1980, p. 24). In discussing land-tenure changes earlier in this chapter, we noted that one consequence of this growing pressure of population on the land was a remarkable increase in subtenancy. The impact of these economic forces on the hiring of agricultural labor is especially relevant to the effects of supply-demand conditions on returns to labor. An element of institutional rigidity is evident because workers hired for harvesting, a principal source of income for landless laborers, have continued to receive the traditional one-sixth share of paddy output. Because productivity of rice farming had increased with the new varieties, and because the labor supply had become more abundant due to the growing population pressure, this one-sixth share was larger than the marginal product of labor for harvesting. The response to this situation was the rapid adoption by farmers of an institutional innovation whereby employment for harvesting is limited to workers who have previously weeded the fields to be harvested *without receiving wages*. Moreover, data from large-scale surveys indicate that this so-called *Gama* system, in which weeding labor is a service performed by workers in exchange for the right to participate in harvesting and receive one-sixth of the crop, has spread widely throughout this rice-growing region of the Philippines (Kikuchi and Hayami 1980, p. 32).

The evidence from India is derived from analysis of data for about eighty-five hundred rural workers in five hundred villages. Bardhan (1977, p. 3) concludes from his analysis of these data that "contrary to the constant wage hypothesis, the wage rate seems to be quite sensitive to demand and productivity factors." He further emphasizes that in a situation characterized by extremely unequal access to land, severe unemployment or underemployment, and a lack of alternative employment opportunities, employers are frequently in a position to exert monopsonistic or oligopsonistic power in fixing wages and terms of employment (Bardhan 1977, pp. 8, 25). It is precisely the prevalence of such conditions which underscores the fundamental importance of development strategies that expand employment opportunities as rapidly as possible and also foster the spread of family planning to slow the growth of the population of working age seeking employment opportunities.

Historically, the substantial increases in returns to labor have occurred when sufficient structural change has taken place to enable growth of nonfarm employment to absorb a large fraction of the annual additions to a country's labor force. The significance of the "structural-transformation turning point" discussed in chapter 2 is, of course, that it marks the end of the period in which the agricultural sector must provide employment opportunities for a growing farm labor force. We have seen, however, that because of the structural and demographic characteristics of most of today's late-developing countries, it will be two or three decades at least before they reach that turning point. Hence, the economic and social advantages associated with the pursuit of unimodal agricultural strategies fostering increased productivity among a large and growing fraction of their small-scale farm units will become even more important during the next twenty to thirty years.

"The juncture of agrarian evolution at which countries such as India and Pakistan find themselves is," as Berry and Cline emphasize, "a particularly delicate one." They conclude their monograph *Agrarian Structure and Productivity Growth in Developing Countries* by stressing the need for "sophisticated analysis of the forces at work for change to steer a wise course that neither discourages large farmers from raising their productivity nor permits them to encroach on the future of the usually more productive small farmers" (Berry and Cline 1979, p. 140). Governments in such countries confront a dilemma. Given a status quo in which large farms account for a substantial fraction of the area under cultivation, there are obvious short-term advantages in continued expansion of tractor cultivation. Tractor cultivation makes it easier for large farms to expand output through multiple cropping and otherwise increasing their intensity of cultivation, thereby narrowing the productivity differential between small and large farm units. Hence, the policy debate commonly focuses on a choice between tractors and bullock cultivation.

Our emphasis on the critical importance of the choice between unimodal and bimodal strategies suggests, however, that from society's point of view, the more fundamental issue is the balance between the allocation of scarce resources of capital and foreign exchange to the large-scale, relatively capital-intensive subsector versus the allocation of funds, manpower, and the attention of policymakers to programs that will promote widespread increases in productivity and output among small farmers. Moreover, as we pointed out earlier in this chapter, strong emphasis on promoting expanded output by a large-scale, highly commercialized subsector is likely to foreclose the option of pursuing successfully a unimodal strategy. The cash-income, or purchasing-power, constraint that inevitably conditions the progressive modernization of small-scale farm units is accentuated if the domestic market is largely preempted by the modern subsector.

Redistributive land reform suggests itself as an especially appropriate policy instrument for countering the tendency for large landowners, responding to the increased profitability of farming with the advent of the seed-fertilizer revolution, to evict their tenants and purchase additional land for direct cultivation. But inasmuch as "large-scale redistribution of land usually has severely limited political likelihood," it is important "that government policies toward land rental should encourage large landowners to rent out their land in small operational units" (Berry and Cline 1979, p. 137). It seems probable that raising land taxes so as to reduce the large gains in economic rent resulting from the increased productivity of land would also curb the tendency for landowners to create large operational units. Nor should the possibility of an effective redistributive land reform be ruled out because circumstances can change. Few would have predicted, for example, that the pace of land reform in Mexico would be as abruptly and enormously accelerated as it was under

President Cárdenas between 1934 and 1940 (Hansen 1971, p. 33; Eckstein, et al. 1978, p. 19).

Important though it may be, land reform is neither a necessary nor a sufficient condition for successful implementation of a unimodal strategy. It creates a favorable environment for the progressive modernization of the millions of small-scale farm units that inevitably predominate in late-developing countries, but whether widespread increases in productivity and income occur depends on effective action related to the "details" which we discussed at length above.[42] The seven problem areas that we singled out for consideration are all important. None of them is a prerequisite, with perhaps one exception: we find it difficult to conceive of successful implementation of a unimodal strategy in the absence of agricultural research programs that generate a flow of profitable and feasible innovations adapted to the needs of small farmers in a variety of local agroclimatic environments.

In brief, the short-term advantages of encouraging expanded output by the large-scale, modern subsector should be assessed in relation to the need to spread the impact of divisible, yield-increasing innovations by strengthening research and extension programs and by expanding investments in irrigation and other types of infrastructure. Especially in India, the private profitability of investments in labor-displacing farm equipment has remained high because the significant increases in productivity and output have been confined to limited areas such as the Punjab; the rapid increase in commercial sales has had little effect on prices because its main consequences have been to substitute for imports and to enable the government to build up substantial grain reserves. Action to reduce the underpricing of capital and foreign exchange could influence the choice of technology directly and also indirectly, by inducing landowners to rent their land out for cultivation in small, labor-intensive holdings.

The desirability and feasibility of various policies will, of course, depend on specific local circumstances. However, the issues related to "organizing the rural poor" and "organizing the facilitators" which we examine in chapter 5 are always crucial to the success of unimodal agricultural strategies, as well as the consumption-oriented programs to which we now turn.

[42] In a passage that we quote in chapter 5, A. K. Sen argues that in developing countries a "shift in focus to technical and institutional details is long overdue" (quoted in Hunter 1978a, p. 37).

CHAPTER FOUR

Consumption-oriented Programs: Nutrition, Health, and Family Planning

In chapter 3 we concentrated on certain production-oriented programs that merit attention in the design of rural development strategies. In this chapter our simplification is even more drastic. We focus on programs aimed directly at improving the nutritional status and health of the rural population and at slowing their rapid rate of population growth. The ultimate problem, of course, is to determine an "appropriate" balance between production- and consumption-oriented activities. We examine this difficult but critically important issue in chapter 6, emphasizing that there are important complementarities as well as competitive trade-offs between the two sets of activities.

Consumption and Basic Needs

In the last decade, the international development community has expressed considerable enthusiasm for what has become known as the "basic needs approach" (ILO 1976; Streeten and Burki 1978). An obvious but significant implication of this is that some needs are more "basic" than others. It is therefore important to focus on the *composition* of the goods and services produced and consumed in a country, as well as on the *growth* and *distribution* of output. An interesting demonstration of the significance of the composition, or content, of the goods and services that are made available is provided by Preston (1978, p. 14) in his analysis of factors associated with declines in mortality. He demonstrates that "unstructured" economic development is generally less efficient in lowering mortality levels than more "structured" development, in which a larger fraction of income is directed toward education expenditure and preventive health measures. That example also emphasizes the operational significance of giving explicit attention to the composition of output in designing rural development strategies. That is, various social services, such as education and preventive health activities, offer opportunities for modifying a society's pattern of consumption. Moreover, they merit special attention as "public goods" which have significant effects on human capital formation and economic growth as well as on individual well-being.

116

Education and Welfare

At the present time the earlier view that health and even education programs should be viewed essentially as welfare activities to be subordinated to the goal of expanding production until a country has achieved a substantial increase in the level of per capita income has been pretty much discredited. Thus T. W. Schultz, in his Nobel lecture, declares that "since schooling is primarily an investment, it is a serious error to treat all schooling outlays as current consumption" (Schultz 1980, p. 648). He also asserts that it is misleading to treat public expenditures on health as well as on schooling as "welfare" expenditures.

The basic needs concept is invoked to justify a host of interventions aimed at directly raising consumption levels by providing certain social services and by increasing private consumption. There is virtually unanimous agreement concerning the fundamental importance of education, nutritional status, and health in determining the level of well-being of individuals. In addition, there is now considerable agreement that public schools and certain types of interventions directed at improving nutritional status and health should be regarded as public goods which merit government support because such actions improve the "quality" of a society's human resources and contribute to national goals of economic and social development.

Among those "consumption-oriented activities," the importance of giving a high priority to expanding and strengthening educational programs is most widely accepted. That is the principal justification for our very summary treatment of education. There is now general acceptance of the proposition that expenditures on education are an investment that contributes to economic growth in addition to conferring benefits on those receiving education (see, for example, World Bank 1980*a*, pp. 46–53). It is also widely recognized that education, especially of women, contributes to the changes in attitudes and behavior required for reduction of fertility. And there are also positive relationships between education and health.

Most of the developing countries are in fact allocating a substantial fraction of the government budget to the support of primary and secondary schools and institutions of higher education. Indeed, the expansion of outlays for education in some developing countries may have been too rapid. This is one problem area that receives particular attention in an excellent review by Blaug (1979) of educational problems and issues in developing countries.[1] Neglect of primary education and disproportionate investment in higher education,

[1] A comment by Tanzania's President Nyerere, quoted with approval by Blaug (1979, pp. 376–77), is pertinent: "It is essential that we face the facts of our present economic situation. Every penny spent on education is money taken away from some other needed activity—whether it is an investment in the future, better medical services, or just more food, clothing and comfort for our citizens at present. And the truth is that there is no possibility of Tanzania being able to increase the proportion of the national income which is spent on education; it ought to be decreased."

which in Sub-Saharan Africa yearly costs about one hundred times as much as a year of primary education, has received much attention (Blaug 1979, p. 377; Pyatt and Thorbecke 1976, pp. 71–72; World Bank 1980a, p. 46). It is obviously essential for a fraction of a country's population to obtain secondary and higher education in order to meet the needs for skilled and professional manpower; but returns to education often appear to be highest for investments in primary education, which is so much less expensive. Especially in tropical Africa, however, rapid expansion of primary and secondary education has given rise to an acute and growing "school-leaver problem" because of the failure of job opportunities to expand in pace with the output of the educational system.[2]

Another set of controversial issues concerns the balance between formal schooling and nonformal education. Agricultural extension and health and nutrition education are important examples of nonformal education and training activities which receive attention in chapter 5. But aside from these specific components of a rural development strategy, we have chosen not to discuss the important and complex issues related to the design and reform of educational policies.

Nutrition, Health Services, and Family Planning

Although it is generally recognized that nutritional deprivation and the interrelated problems of ill health are two of the most serious manifestations of poverty, there is little agreement on the specific programs which merit priority attention in responding to those problems. There is also an increasing tendency for policymakers in developing countries to accept the view that rapid population growth is a serious obstacle to achieving national goals of economic and social development. This is coupled with increased awareness of the significant interrelationships between changes in fertility and changes in socioeconomic variables. Once again, however, there has been considerable uncertainty and controversy over the measures that are likely to be most effective in lowering fertility and slowing the rate of population growth.

The themes of "feasibility and desirability" and "ineffectiveness and consensus," which we discussed in chapter 1, apply with special force to the design of programs related to nutrition, health, and population. Because reducing malnutrition and improving health are such desirable objectives, a great variety of interventions are advocated. Inevitably, these exceed the range of programs that is feasible within the resource constraints that prevail in a low-income country. The problems of choice among alternative options are difficult because the determinants of nutritional status and health are complex. The cost-

---

[2] An analysis of the school-leaver problem in Nigeria by McQueen (1979, p. 96) notes that in spite of the country's ambitious development plan and the increase in income and government revenue resulting from rapid expansion of petroleum exports, the school-leaver problem "may grow in magnitude and seriousness, especially in light of very high population growth rates and explosive growth of cities from continuing rural to urban migration."

effectiveness of a particular intervention is difficult to assess, and the problems that arise in seeking to quantify the benefits of alternative nutritional and health actions are enormous and largely insuperable.[3] Moreover, the difficulties in comparing the benefits of alternative interventions are compounded by the likelihood that the beneficiaries are different groups.

Complications with respect to population policy also are severe, even though a growing number of countries are undertaking programs to reduce fertility. As of 1970, fifteen developing countries had adopted official antinatalist policies, and another six countries were providing public support for family planning, but without a specific antinatalist policy. By 1977 the number of countries with an official antinatalist policy had doubled. An additional twenty-two countries were providing public support for family planning related to health and similar considerations rather than an antinatalist policy (Ness 1979, p. 625). Inasmuch as most of the larger developing countries are included in one of those two categories, countries providing public support for family planning account for more than 90 percent of the total population in developing nations. In some countries, the allocation of funds for family planning is now large in relation to the total allocation of resources for the health ministry (Nortman and Hofstatter 1980, p. 35).

Given the problems of reaching a workable consensus, it is not surprising that the "let's get on with it" point of view has considerable appeal. The results obtained by "orthodox" family planning programs have certainly been disappointing in many countries. Nevertheless, there is a strong case for going ahead with such programs and trying to increase their effectiveness by better management and increased community participation.

We argue later, however, that often it may be desirable to enhance the effectiveness of family planning activities, and to further other development objectives as well, by linking family planning and health programs. The shortcomings of conventional family planning programs appear to be especially great in many of the low-income countries in tropical Africa, where the "environment" is so unfavorable that the cost-effectiveness of conventional programs is very low. In these countries, efforts to improve the survival prospects for infants and small children may be very effective in improving the context in which attitudes and motivations with respect to family planning are shaped.

Interventions concerned exclusively with nutrition, such as school lunch programs, have usually had limited impact, especially in reaching the rural poor. We stress the fundamental importance of strategies that simultaneously expand food supplies and improve *access* to those supplies because of broad participation and income-earning opportunities. But we also argue that the especially significant interactions between nutritional status and health among

---

[3] Johnston (1977, pp. 884–85) argues that there is no satisfactory way to quantify the benefits associated with an intervention that, for example, avoids blindness by the prevention of xerophthalmia. He notes, however, that some have argued for a major research effort to find ways to overcome the special difficulties of quantifying such benefits (See also chapter 6).

infants and small children provide a strong justification for interventions linking those two sets of activities.

In this chapter we deal in turn with nutrition programs, health programs, and population programs. Our emphasis is on access to services in those three areas. As noted earlier, these are essentially "public goods" which can be provided more effectively and with greater benefits to society when they are handled as social-service programs. We argue that relying on services supplied in response to private demand represents a slow and ineffective approach to promoting improvements in health and nutrition and the spread of family planning. In a final section we review the arguments that have been advanced for administratively integrating the three sets of consumption-oriented activities.

Consumption-oriented programs which seek to influence the satisfaction of nutritional and other basic needs by measures for the redistribution of current flows of income also have been advocated. Schemes for free or subsidized distribution of food are an important example. We prefer, however, to consider such options as part of the problem of determining an appropriate balance between production- and consumption-oriented programs (chapter 6).

Nutrition Policies and Programs

The debate on nutrition policy epitomizes the problems of arriving at the consensus required for effective action. It is therefore not surprising to find a large gap between the rhetoric calling for prompt action to eliminate malnutrition and the results that have actually been achieved. The World Food Conference of 1974, which adopted a "universal declaration" calling for the eradication of hunger and malnutrition by 1985, also called for a strong emphasis on nutrition planning (United Nations 1975). This has given rise to what Chafkin (1978, p. 806) refers to as "a modest growth industry" giving attention to nutrition problems.

Nutrition Planning and Its Limitations

The various views on nutrition planning that have emerged can be usefully categorized as representing either an "intellectual-establishment view" or a "bureaucratic view" (Field 1977, p. 229). Field's description of the intellectual-establishment view is worth quoting at length because as he rightly suggests, it is widely shared:

> The conception is deliberately broad. Nutrition planning covers anything and everything that is thought to impinge upon nutritional status. There may be certain discrete interventions which, by common consensus, are nutrition interventions . . . but nutrition planning . . . covers much more: from micro-level activities to macro-level planning designed to influence the production, distribution, consumption, and absorption of nutrients. One's purview is sweeping, embracing food policies in their entirety, also much in the realm of public health, environmental sanita-

tion and the like, and extending all the way to export-import policies and a country's overall development strategy. . . . One's professional gaze spans virtually the entire range of public policies, resources, and constraints that might apply.

In contrast, the bureaucratic view is "quite restricted: supplementary feeding, child-care education of mothers, and food fortification especially and perhaps exclusively" (Field 1977, p. 230).

In its assumption that such a vast range of socioeconomic policies and programs could be subsumed under "nutrition planning," the intellectual-establishment view is advocating an approach that is neither politically feasible nor administratively workable. It is indeed a clear example of the tendency to equate the feasible with the desirable.

The bureaucratic view is feasible in the sense that food fortification, supplementary feeding, and similar schemes can be and are undertaken. However, they rarely if ever have much impact on malnutrition, which is such a pervasive problem in developing countries. In particular, there is little evidence of any significant progress in reducing malnutrition in the villages of the low-income developing countries.[4] For example, given the strong correlation between poverty and malnutrition, the presumption is strong that the large increase in the number of marginal rural households in India that we discussed in chapter 3 has been paralleled by a similar increase in the number of individuals subject to malnutrition.

Project Poshak, a major nutrition project in India initiated in 1971 by the state government of Madhya Pradesh and CARE, is an important example of the failure of ad hoc nutrition interventions to lead to sustained progress in reducing malnutrition. A considerable number of children benefited from the take-home food supplies that were provided during the four-year life of the scheme, and some lessons were learned from the experience. Nonetheless, an analysis by Pyle (1980) of the failure of that major pilot project to become an operational program points up two especially significant lessons. First, Pyle demonstrates how precarious it is for a pilot scheme to be dependent upon foreign assistance—in this case both the key operational role of CARE-India staff in administering the project and the reliance on instant corn-soya-milk supplied by CARE and AID. Second, Pyle demonstrates that there is little hope for a successful transition from pilot project to operational program unless the scheme is a "part of the government's normal operations and not

[4] *Malnutrition* is used in this essay to refer to "an impairment of the state of health due to nutritional causes" (Margen 1978, p. 103). Sometimes a distinction is made between *malnutrition* and *undernutrition*, the latter referring to an insufficiency of energy intake. However, the body's requirement for energy tends to take precedence; if energy intake is inadequate, a part of the dietary protein will be "burned" for energy and therefore will not be available to perform its distinctive functions in supporting growth, tissue repair, and so on (FAO/WHO, 1973). Thus *malnutrition* and *Protein-Energy Malnutrition* (PEM) are commonly used to describe quantitative as well as qualitative deficiencies. *Malnutrition* in this sense of "bad nutrition" also embraces "overnutrition" leading to obesity, which may contribute to diabetes, heart disease, and other health problems.

merely an appendage to it" (Pyle 1980, p. 45). Programs that are essentially "appendages" typically fail to survive beyond the period of external assistance. They almost certainly fail to be replicated and to achieve broader coverage.

Both the intellectual-establishment view and the bureaucratic view of nutrition planning are based on "the working premise . . . that a few resources plus good planning and programming inputs" can have a significant impact on malnutrition (Field 1977, p. 238). That view is valid in a few instances. In regions where goiter is a serious problem, allocating "a few resources" and providing the good programming required to ensure that the inhabitants use iodized salt is remarkably cost-effective. Similar possibilities may exist for vitamin A and iron deficiencies. Promoting expanded local production and consumption of leafy green and yellow vegetables and green leaves is of fundamental importance because those items are such valuable sources of vitamin A, iron, and other essential nutrients. But this tends to be a slow process and certainly does not preclude the possibility of direct distribution of vitamin A capsules or iron tablets to groups identified as "at risk."

The view that specific nutrition interventions could have a significant impact had some plausibility during the years in which it was widely believed that a "protein gap" represented the principal nutritional problem in developing countries. However, the earlier enthusiasm for high-protein foods such as fish protein concentrate or Vitasoy now seems to have been misplaced. The present consensus is that in most situations Protein-Energy Malnutrition (PEM) is associated with inadequate intake of *food*, even though the nutritional problem may manifest itself as protein malnutrition (FAO/WHO 1976, p. 33n).

Agricultural Development and Nutrition

One of the most significant complementarities between production- and consumption-oriented measures concerns the fundamental role of a unimodal agricultural strategy in achieving those increases in food intake that are essential for improving nutritional status and health. Agricultural development affects food intake through its influence on the availability and price of food products. It also determines *access* to food, either through expanded home production for subsistence consumption or by generating income that enables households to augment their food purchases. Although the direct effects of the pattern of agricultural development on farm households are especially important, the indirect effects on the growth of employment opportunities outside agriculture are also highly significant.

In recent years a good deal of attention has been given to "the role of agriculture in improving nutrition" (FAO 1979*b*, p. 3). Given the concentration of malnutrition among poor families, it is especially important to ensure that they benefit as much as possible from agricultural development programs. The factors which determine the rate and pattern of agricultural development (examined in chapter 3)—and the rate and bias of technological change—are of central importance in enhancing the ability of low-income families to raise their level of food intake. We noted in chapter 3 that Taiwan's broadly based and remarkably rapid development led to a very substantial increase in returns to labor—subsistence as well as monetary income. One consequence was an increase between 1953 and 1970 of over 15 percent in the average per capita availability of calories—from 2300 to 2700—and larger increases in intake of other nutrients. These increases seem to have virtually eliminated problems of malnutrition (Galenson 1979, pp. 436–37; Chiu 1976). They doubtless contributed to an increased work effort as well, since underemployment was reduced.

Increases in productivity and output of basic staple foods such as rice and wheat are especially important because these foods are so often the principal sources of energy, protein, and a number of other essential nutrients. In low-income countries, starchy staple foods—cereals, root crops, and tubers—frequently account for some 60–80 percent of total energy intake and nearly as large a fraction of the dietary protein. Increases in productivity and output of beans and other pulses are also of special significance: not only are they a cheap source of protein but they complement cereal proteins effectively because they are relatively well supplied with the essential amino acids that are limiting in cereals and are therefore effective in enhancing the nutritional quality of the diets of low-income families. As noted earlier, promoting the production and consumption of leafy green and yellow vegetables is also important because vitamin A and iron deficiencies are often widespread and serious.

In a number of developing countries, maize, sorghum, cassava, sweet potatoes, or other "inferior" staple foods are a major component of the diet of poor families. Research, extension, and marketing programs that expand the supply and reduce the price of such products represent an opportunity for what Timmer (1979) has described as "self-targeting food programs"; they are especially effective in raising the energy intake of the poor. Although those staple foods are all "inferior" in the usual hierarchy of consumer preferences, only cassava and bananas/plantains are significantly inferior to rice and wheat in nutritional quality (Johnston 1958, p. 160).

Nutrition scientists and others who are acutely conscious of the extent and seriousness of malnutrition in developing countries often disparage "development" as a means of eliminating nutritional deprivation. Our first response to their concern is to emphasize the differential impact on nutritional status of alternative agricultural programs. Under a bimodal strategy of agricultural development there is indeed reason to suspect that the many rural households by-passed by development will confront declining levels of food intake and nutritional status, exacerbated by increased pressure of population on the land. In the context of a unimodal strategy, however, accelerating the increase in agricultural production can lead to widespread and fairly rapid increases in income.

There is abundant evidence that poor families allocate a very large fraction of increments in their income to increases in food consumption. But because low-income families devote such a large fraction of their total income to food, increases in food prices have extremely serious adverse effects on their nutritional status and well-being.[5] Higher-income groups can adjust to even sharp increases in food prices by increasing the share of their income devoted to food and by shifting from more to less expensive sources of energy and other nutrients. However, the poor typically devote some 50–70 percent of their income to food and already depend heavily on cheap starchy staples. They are therefore exceedingly vulnerable to increases in food prices which result when food supplies fail to expand in pace with the growth of demand.

The distinctive nutritional problems of small children and mothers. Our second response is to affirm that there is indeed a need for specific actions related to the distinctive nutritional problems of infants, small children, and pregnant and lactating women. Increasing the availability of food at the household level by broad-based, employment-oriented development strategies obviously facilitates efforts to improve the nutritional status of those vulnerable groups; but increasing availability is *not* by itself a sufficient measure—for reasons related only in part to the question of intra-family distribution of food.

We emphasized in chapter 2 that a disproportionate fraction of the mortality and morbidity in developing countries is concentrated among young children. In India, for example, the zero-to-five age group accounts for 40–50 percent of all deaths even though it constitutes less than 20 percent of the population. We also emphasized that the two-way interactions between malnutrition and infection are particularly significant causes of not only this high mortality and high morbidity but also retarded physical and mental development characteristic of so many small children in developing countries. In many societies these symptoms are also related to faulty child-feeding practices. Sometimes this takes the form of mothers' not feeding their newborns the colostrum secreted at the onset of lactation. A report from Indonesia, for example, states that colostrum is believed to be "dirty" and to cause illness, and that many women expelled and discarded it (Hull 1979, p. 317). But colostrum contains antibodies that confer considerable immunity against infection during the critical first weeks and months of an infant's life.

A problem that is becoming serious in developing countries where there is

---

[5] For a particularly good analysis of the interrelationships between food prices, income distribution, and changes in consumption, see Mellor (1978). Mellor's evidence is drawn almost entirely from Indian survey data, but estimates of the income elasticity of demand for "all food" and for energy based on food consumption surveys in many other countries tend to confirm his conclusions. A recent study of protein-energy intakes in a malnourished population in Guatemala provides especially interesting evidence of the tendency for low-income families to increase their intake of energy and protein when the income constraint is relaxed. In this experimental intervention the purchasing-power constraint was removed by distributing a substantial supplement of free maize and beans during a two-month period. For all adults there was a significant increase in food intake of about 400 calories and 15 grams of protein per person per day. Moreover, for the tercile with the lowest intake during the base period, the increase averaged 694 calories and about 23 grams of protein, whereas for the top tercile the increase amounted to only 227 calories and 9.8 grams of protein per person per day (Martorell et al. 1979, p. 165).

vigorous promotion of infant formula foods is the rejection or shortening of breast-feeding. Under the conditions that prevail in poor households, bottle-feeding almost invariably leads to malnutrition because the costly formula is stretched by excessive dilution with water. Infections are also multiplied because of the extreme difficulty of maintaining a high standard of hygiene in the cleaning of bottles and nipples. Another problem is that supplementary feeding is often delayed. Perhaps even more frequently the energy intake of small children is inadequate because of the low "calorie density" of the staple foods that are used when supplementary feeding is begun.[6] Because of lack of knowledge and competing demands on mothers' time, infants may not be fed frequently enough to enable them to ingest sufficient food to satisfy their energy requirements. Even though breast milk needs to be supplemented from about four to six months of age, prolonged nursing is important in maintaining the quality of the diet. In addition, in many communities the postpartum amenorrhea that is associated with frequent and prolonged breast-feeding remains a very important form of contraception and helps to minimize the health problems caused by closely spaced births.

It will also be recalled that malnutrition in infants and small children impairs many of the body's defense mechanisms against infection and thereby accentuates the frequency and seriousness of illness (Chandra 1979; Reddy and Srikantia 1978). At the same time, frequent bouts of diarrhea and other infections often precipitate severe malnutrition. They result in reduced food intake because of loss of appetite and the tendency to withhold food when a child is sick. Vomiting and impaired absorption of nutrients further aggravate the nutritional problems of small children.

In many cultures there is insufficient recognition of the special nutritional requirements of women during pregnancy and lactation. Failure to increase food intake to cover those additional nutritional requirements frequently impairs the health of mothers. It also results in reduced stores of nutrients available to the newborn and therefore increases infant mortality and morbidity rates.

For all these reasons, to rely only on production-oriented measures is an inefficient means of reducing the especially serious health problems of infants,

[6] The experience in Guatemala described in note 5 provides tentative but interesting support for the view that the energy and protein intake of preschool children may often be limited because of the relatively low energy density of the traditional staple foods. In this instance a substantial free supplement of maize and beans led to an average increase in energy intake among small children of about 200 calories and 6 grams of protein daily (Martorell et al. 1979, p. 168). Those increases were nutritionally highly significant; but the additional energy intake may have covered less than 60 percent of the estimated energy deficit for that group. That estimate of the "energy deficit" was based, however, on the ideal rather than the actual body weight of the children in order to allow for "catch-up growth." In another recent paper Martorell, Yarbrough, Klein, and Lechtig (1979, p. 388) conclude "that catch-up growth in chronically malnourished children is limited and related to maturity delays," so that estimates based on ideal rather than actual body weights may overstate the energy deficit. This raises an important issue concerning the interpretation of estimates of the prevalence of malnutrition among children based on weight-for-age or height-for-age data; but that issue is too complex (and controversial) to be pursued here.

small children, and pregnant and lactating women. The counter-argument is sometimes advanced that the nutritional status of adults is even more critical because the survival of the family depends on the productivity and income of the working members of the household. The availability of food for the entire family is clearly of crucial importance. However, the benefits to be expected from nutritional interventions aimed at adults and older children are much less significant relative to their cost than interventions concentrated on the more vulnerable groups. Among young children, small increases in food intake can make a highly significant difference in their nutritional status; and better nutrition for pregnant and lactating women yields major benefits for their health as well as that of their children. Furthermore, as we emphasize in the next section, a strategic combination of nutritional and health activities can result in a dramatic reduction in infant and child mortality and morbidity. Similarly cost-effective techniques for improving the health and nutritional status of adults are simply not available.

Health Programs

In virtually all of the developing countries there has been support for a limited range of public health measures and for mass campaigns such as those that have led to a dramatic decline in malaria and the virtual elimination of smallpox as a world health problem. These actions have enabled the developing countries "to vastly improve the morbidity and mortality rates with only a minor expenditure of resources" (Myrdal 1968, p. 1575). The substantial reductions in crude death rates and increases in life expectancy that we noted in chapter 2 have of course been influenced strongly by such measures. Indeed Myrdal, writing in the late 1960s, found it "rather surprising that health programs have not so far been given a higher priority," considering the success achieved by the mass campaigns (Myrdal 1968, p. 1577).

The Problem of Coverage and Alternative Strategies

Only one of the low-income countries and a small number of middle-income countries have progressed beyond the initial phase of mortality reduction obtained by mass campaigns and a limited range of public health measures. Until fairly recently the "Western model" of health care, with its emphasis on the role of physicians, individual curative care, and urban hospitals, tended to be viewed as the relevant means for achieving further improvements. But given the characteristics of the low-income countries—their poverty and limited government revenues, a predominantly rural population, and a rapid rate of natural increase—broad coverage of their populations by reliance on the "Western model" of health care is impossible. One consequence of the quest for such infeasible "solutions" is that access to health services for the rural population in these countries has been totally inadequate—and highly inequitable. An analysis of health expenditures in sixteen less developed countries indicates that in nine of the countries, between 74 percent and 86 percent of the budget of the ministry of health was concentrated on hospitals and individual curative care (World Bank 1975, p. 418). A knowledgeable health specialist with extensive experience in less developed countries suggests that "typically health coverage reaches only 10 to 15 percent of rural populations" (C. E. Taylor 1977, p. 79). C. Gopalan (1979, p. 17), until recently director-general of the Indian Council of Medical Research, states that "it is now widely recognized that our present health services do not reach 80 percent of our population living in rural areas."

Another consequence was a tendency for many external agencies and a number of developing countries to concentrate on population programs. This emphasis was undoubtedly related to the hope and expectation that the spread of family planning would slow the rate of natural increase and thereby make the achievement of health as well as other development objectives more manageable. In some countries the increases in financial and manpower allocations for population programs were very rapid. By the mid-1970s on the order of one third of the health ministry budgets in Indonesia and Bangladesh were being allocated to family planning; but this amounted to an expenditure of less than twenty cents in U.S. currency per capita in Bangladesh, and only about thirty cents in Indonesia, because their total health budgets were so small. In India family planning expenditure reached a peak of about thirty cents per capita in 1976, when it was 17 percent of the health budget (Nortman and Hofstatter 1980, pp. 35, 37). There has been a widespread feeling among public health specialists that a priority has been given to family planning, with adverse effects on efforts to strengthen health programs.[7]

Finally, the growing awareness of the problem of health coverage, and of the inappropriateness of the Western model of health care, has led to an intensification of efforts to evolve alternative health strategies. The first important contribution to the literature in Western countries that emphasized the need to face up to the trade-off between meeting conventional medical standards and achieving broad coverage appears to have been the 1966 book *Medical Care in Developing Countries*, by Maurice King and an interdisciplinary group of associates. The volume was preceded by several village-level projects in Nigeria and other developing countries which demonstrated the potential for rapidly reducing infant and child mortality by programs that emphasized preventive activities and the use of health auxiliaries.

Largely as a result of the various demonstration projects which we describe below, a considerable consensus has emerged concerning the essential features of health programs capable of achieving wide coverage of the population in low-income countries. The following appear to be especially important: (1) an emphasis on infants, small children, and their mothers because of recognition

[7] In 1973 the director-general of WHO, Halfdan Mahler, expressed the view that the promotion of ambitious population projects by external donors was tantamount to a "rape of the health structure" (Finkle and Crane 1976, p. 386).

that the most serious health problems are concentrated in those vulnerable groups; (2) emphasis on selected health and nutrition interventions (such as child-feeding practices) based on improved understanding of the significant interactions between health and nutrition; (3) a priority for highly cost-effective measures such as immunizations and other preventive measures and a few simple but effective curative measures, such as oral rehydration; (4) major reliance on health auxiliaries and community-level health workers given limited but appropriate initial training and continuing in-service training through supportive supervision; and (5) active community participation through a village health committee or similar local organization.

Demonstration projects. A project initiated in the Nigerian village of Imesi in the late 1950s as an outreach effort of the Wesley Guild Mission Hospital is notable as an early example of a successful demonstration project. The "under-fives" clinic concept and the use of regular weighing of young children and the well-known Morley growth chart were originated there. Morley (1966, p. 2) reports that between 1957 and 1962 infant mortality declined from 295 deaths per thousand live births to 72 per thousand, and the annual number of deaths of children between the ages of one and four declined from 69 per thousand to 43 per thousand. An effective measles vaccine has become available since 1962, which means that the reduction of mortality among small children could have been considerably greater, because more than one third of the deaths among small children were due to measles.

A project initiated in 1959 by the Institute of Nutrition for Central America and Panama (INCAP) was the first of two major village-level studies undertaken by INCAP involving a combination of health and nutrition interventions. That project generated some of the first evidence documenting the great importance of the two-way interactions between nutrition and infection.

In the late 1960s and early 1970s a number of noteworthy projects were initiated in India, including the Narangwal Project in the Punjab, carried out by the Johns Hopkins School of Hygiene and Public Health in collaboration with the Indian Council of Medical Research.[8] The Jamkhed and Kasa projects in the state of Maharashtra were initiated by Indian physicians concerned with achieving broader and more effective health coverage of village communities. Two of the most interesting and best documented of the Maharashtra projects provide evidence of the effectiveness of community-oriented health projects that place major emphasis on preventive and promotive activities. In the Jamkhed Project, infant mortality was reduced from 97 per thousand in

---

[8] A recent report to the World Bank prepared by Gwatkin, Wilcox, and Wray (1979) presents an interesting description of ten reasonably well-documented projects, including the two INCAP projects and the Imesi and Narangwal projects mentioned in the text. The earliest of the projects examined was carried out in a Navajo reservation in the United States (Arizona) by the Cornell University Medical School. The major significance of that project was that it "gave rise to the concept of a 'technologic misfit' between Western medical care concepts and the nutrition and health situations of the Third World" (Gwatkin, Wilcox, and Wray 1979, p. 31). All the other projects were located in developing countries.

1971 to 39 per thousand in 1976; infant mortality in a nearby control area was still 96 per thousand in 1976. An integrated health-services project in Miraj achieved a reduction in infant mortality from approximately 68 per thousand in 1974 to 23 per thousand in 1977.[9]

Estimates of child mortality are not available, but a substantial reduction can be inferred from the dramatic increase in the percentage of "under fives" that now receive immunizations. According to the base-line survey in Jamkhed only 1 percent of that age group had been immunized in 1971, but some 98 percent by 1978. For Miraj, there are separate estimates for different types of immunization. The percentage immunized against smallpox increased only from 85 percent in 1974 to 99.7 percent in 1977; but in the case of DPT (diphtheria, pertussis, i.e., whooping cough, and typhoid) and polio the increase was from about 2 percent to close to 85 percent. The increase in BCG vaccination against tuberculosis was more limited: from 6 percent to 55 percent (Pyle 1979, attachment II).

A recent analysis of ten health projects, including the Jamkhed and Imesi projects, reports that all of the projects achieved declines in infant and child mortality and that "most of the declines were large: on the order of one-third to one-half, sometimes more" (Gwatkin, Wilcox, and Wray 1979, p. 16). Moreover, these were achieved within one to five years of the projects' initiation.

National programs. China's "barefoot doctor" program has received a great deal of attention because of its apparent success in providing access to basic health services for the great mass of the country's rural population in spite of severe resource constraints. Cuba's health program also has attracted a good deal of attention, but the level of income and availability of medical personnel was considerably higher there than in the late-developing countries.

The same caveat applies to Costa Rica, although the rural health program initiated there in 1971 demonstrates the feasibility of implementing a low-cost but effective health program in the rural areas of a country with a mixed rather than a socialist economy. The program was targeted toward the small rural communities (with a population generally less than five hundred) that had been most neglected by earlier health programs. By 1975 some 60 percent of the target population was being reached by "health workers with shoes," who had responsibility for controlling communicable diseases such as malaria, for immunizations against infectious diseases, and for promoting hygiene and environmental sanitation. There has been a marked decrease in deaths preventable by immunization since the program was initiated (Mata and Mohs 1978, pp. 262–63).

---

[9] This project, which was based on the Miraj Medical Centre in Sangli District of Maharashtra and covered a population of over two hundred thousand, was one of several operated jointly by the Government of Maharashtra and a voluntary agency. The impressive results achieved in that project area were obtained by adding only 35 percent to the government's normal appropriation for a primary health center. The agreement for a joint project covered only the period 1973–77; health operations then reverted to the status quo ante, although with certain residual effects (Pyle 1979, pp. 2, 42).

The Rural Health Scheme and Community Health Worker Program initiated in India in 1977 represents a notable effort to move toward nationwide coverage in a country with a mixed economy and a very low level of income. We note later that serious problems are being encountered in the implementation of this program, but the experience offers enormously important opportunities to derive lessons about the design and implementation of rural health programs capable of achieving broad coverage.

Characteristics of Successful Community Health-Care Systems
It is difficult to generalize about the distinctive characteristics of the successful rural health programs because of differences in the health and socioeconomic conditions which prevail in different countries and in different areas within a country.[10] One important generalization, however, is that "effective projects seem to have featured a judicious mix of both nutrition and health components" (Gwatkin, Wilcox, and Wray 1979, p. 28). Measures to improve maternal nutrition and to monitor the nutritional status of small children by periodic weighing appear to have been especially significant. Weighing has been a useful tool for alerting mothers to their children's retarded growth—a sensitive indicator of nutritional and health problems—thereby encouraging improved child-feeding practices.

Immunization against tetanus, whooping cough, diphtheria, typhoid, smallpox, measles, tuberculosis, and poliomyelitis are highly cost-effective interventions, especially as a critical threshold of immunity is reached within a community. Improvements in personal and household hygiene, environmental sanitation and fly control, and provision of a safer and more ample water supply can make an important contribution to the reduction of diarrhea and

---

[10] A recent article by Walsh and Warren (1979) is especially interesting as an attempt to define the most cost-effective interventions to be included in "selective primary health care." It offers a priority ranking for a number of health problems on the basis of their prevalence, the mortality and morbidity rates associated with various diseases, and the cost and efficacy of the interventions that are available. This priority ranking is based in part on estimates of prevalence, mortality, morbidity, and costs, estimates which Walsh and Warren present for the major health problems and interventions. They stress, however, the importance of local variations and the need to modify priorities on the basis of experience and accumulating evidence. Their recommended program would concentrate on children up to three years of age and on women of childbearing age. It would include immunization against measles and diphtheria, pertussis, and tetanus (DPT) for children over six months, tetanus toxoid to women of childbearing age, encouragement of long-term breast-feeding, chloroquine for treating fever (where malaria is prevalent), and oral-rehydration packages and instruction. Letters by Henderson and Keja (1980) and others comment on these priorities. Henderson and Keja, who are WHO staff members, criticize mainly the omission of poliomyelitis vaccines and BCG immunization against tuberculosis. They emphasize that the marginal cost of these additions, of immunizing against six rather than four diseases, would be small. In their reply, Walsh and Warren (1980) stress the importance of being truly selective and also cite evidence that casts doubt on the efficacy of BCG. It is also noted by one critic that promotion of family planning should be included in even a highly selective program of health care.

A highly interesting attempt to apply policy analysis, including the use of both simulation and optimization models, to determine the components of an integrated and cost-effective health program is presented in Barnum et al. (1980). That approach and its main conclusions are described briefly below.

other gastrointestinal diseases, which are such an important cause of m̶o̶ and morbidity among infants and small children. However, these latter me̶ sures are relatively difficult to implement because they require behavioral change and in varying degree are dependent on community action. Furthermore, improving a community's water supply may be fairly costly, although chlorination of wells is cheap and simple. Reducing the adverse consequences of gastrointestinal infection is relatively easy because of the results that can be obtained from teaching mothers the simple technique of oral rehydration— spoon-feeding of water with added sugar and salt.[11] Improving resistance to infection through better nutrition can reduce the incidence and especially the severity of gastrointestinal and many other types of disease problems.

The successful projects have managed to emphasize highly cost-effective preventive activities and have kept the distribution of medicines to a minimum. However, in many areas lower-respiratory infections are a major cause of morbidity and mortality. Oral administration of an antibiotic is effective and safe. Simple drugs such as aspirin tablets relieve discomfort and help a village health worker to gain the confidence of the community by responding to the felt need for curative services. In areas where malaria continues to be or is again becoming a serious health problem, chloroquine tablets are valuable, especially if their distribution is timed to coincide with the seasonal cycle of prevalence of malaria in a particular area. Where vitamin A deficiency is a serious problem, high-potency vitamin A capsules can be a cost-effective means of reducing the incidence of xerophthalmia and blindness among children. And in some areas where anemia is a major problem, iron/folic acid capsules can have highly beneficial effects on pregnant and lactating women and their infants. Finally, virtually all of the successful health schemes include the promotion of family planning because of the favorable effects of child spacing on the health of mothers and infants, as well as the more general objective of slowing population growth.

Program management. It is obvious that village health workers face an impossible task unless priorities are established and various components of the health program are introduced in sequence. That alone emphasizes the fact that the quality of management of rural health schemes is a critical factor. Pyle

[11] The death rate from diarrheal diseases rose to 30 percent in Bangladesh refugee camps in 1971, but oral therapy administered by family members played a key role in reducing the mortality rate to about 1 percent (Hirschhorn 1980, p. 653). This excellent survey article by Hirschhorn also points out that understanding of the scientific basis of the effectiveness of oral therapy for treatment of diarrhea dates only from the 1960s. Hence it is not surprising that its practice is not nearly as widespread as would be desirable. A further problem concerns the choice of procedure. A sucrose/electrolyte solution prepared in the home by adding sugar and salt to water eliminates the cost and logistic problems of using a special rehydration mixture. However, the "pinch and scoop" method for measuring the amount of salt and sugar to be added can easily result in a dangerously high sodium level. But that problem can be minimized and perhaps avoided by using a double-ended plastic spoon being promoted by the Institute of Child Health in London (Levine et al., in press). The advantages of a special rehydration mixture are most significant in the treatment of severe cases of diarrhea (C. Taylor, October 1980: personal communication).

1ap. 2) has stressed, for example, that the successful
a are all characterized by a style of management which
:ientation" rather than "procedures-orientation." This
on outcomes rather than on activities or inputs, on a
n a disciplinary approach to supervision, on training that
1roblem-solving, and on organization that emphasizes a

>st critical and difficult problems in implementing a
commu... ed health strategy is the reorientation of medical doctors.
Broad coverage of the rural population in a low-income country clearly depends on major reliance on paramedical personnel and village-level health
workers. This means that a considerable number of physicians must acquire
the skills and commitment to perform the role of leader of a health team and to
give a high priority to training and supervisory activities, a range of responsibilities that is very different from the more familiar role of providing curative
care in a medical facility. In fact, Korten (1975, p. 26) argues that this requirement for very different orientations and skills on the part of medical personnel
represents "the internal contradiction" that makes it doubtful whether national programs can replicate the success of demonstration or pilot projects, which
often have had unusually dedicated leadership.[12] It is reported that even the
"barefoot doctor" program in China required strong personal intervention—
by Chairman Mao—to counter the biases of the medical profession towards
curative care and towards maintaining standards rather than achieving broad
coverage. Because of those difficulties, effective implementation of the program dates from only about 1965 (Maru 1977). We will explore problems of
program management further below.

Community participation. Another important characteristic of successful programs relates to active participation and involvement of a local
community. To speak of "delivering services" within an effective, community-
oriented health program is misleading. Mass campaigns against malaria, and
to some extent immunization programs, can be carried out by procedures that
treat the local population as passive recipients of program benefits. But the
behavioral changes that are essential in order for community health programs
to have significant and lasting benefits require a "partnership" between
members of both the health team and the local community. Although the need

---

[12] A study by Pyle (1981) provides a valuable analysis of the difficulties encountered in
implementing a government Community Health Worker Program (CHWP) in the Indian state of
Maharashtra patterned after some highly successful small demonstration projects. In the small
projects it was possible "to reorient and sensitize their doctors" so that they performed effectively
as leaders of a rural health team. Pyle's analysis is based on a field study of seven demonstration
projects and randomly selected villages in all five of the state districts included in the CHWP.
Separate chapters examine the performance of the program from three different perspectives—a
rational-actor analysis, an organizational analysis, and a political analysis. The advantages of
employing that threefold perspective are well illustrated in a classic study of the Cuban missile
crisis by Allison (1971).

for local participation is easy to assert, in practice it is very difficult to achieve. Demonstration projects have the important advantage of being able to ensure that a village community agrees to certain conditions and accepts responsibilities. The project can even withdraw its services if the villagers do not live up to the conditions (Pyle 1979, p. 34; 1981, chap. 5). Moreover, it is relatively easy for those undertaking a demonstration project to take the time required to explain the objectives of the health program, including the role of the village member who is to be selected and trained to work in the village to serve its health-related needs.

We discuss the means for securing effective community participation at greater length in chapter 5. It is important to emphasize at this point, however, that meaningful and effective community participation is difficult to achieve and should often be viewed as a long-term objective rather than as a requirement. Promoting active involvement of the local community—for example, by requiring a village council and individual families to cover a part of the cost of a local health program—is probably more realistic as an immediate objective.

One problem that has bedeviled the Community Health Worker Program initiated in India in 1977 is that insufficient time and effort were devoted to preliminary discussion with local leaders and others in the village community. As one consequence, there has been a tendency to view the selection of village health workers essentially as an employment scheme, and partly for that reason, mainly young men have been selected as village health workers, whereas women are likely to be more effective (Bose et al. 1978; Pyle 1981, chaps. 2 and 3). The greater effectiveness of women derives in part from the advantages of giving priority to the health needs of infants and small children and their mothers. Women also have a chance to discuss family planning at appropriate "entry points," emphasizing the advantages of better birth spacing and limiting the number of children. In addition, experience in a number of demonstration projects suggests that the most effective training strategy is one that emphasizes a short initial period of training of two or three weeks followed by frequent in-service training. There tends to be greater continuity with women health workers, which naturally facilitates the process of gradually upgrading the competence and the range of skills of the village-level workers.

We note below that a community orientation appears to be an effective means of securing an emphasis on the highly cost-effective preventive activities rather than on individual curative care. Important objectives of India's Community Health Worker scheme were to introduce a community orientation and to bring about a shift in priorities in rural health activities away from individual curative care toward an emphasis on preventive and educational tasks such as personal and environmental hygiene, immunization, and family planning. According to an excellent analysis of the implementation of the scheme, those objectives have not been realized (Maru 1981, pp. 40–43). Recent experience with population programs suggests that active local participation has been a key factor in the success of some of the population programs which have had a considerable impact on fertility in spite of an unfavorable socioeconomic environment.

Costs and the Mobilization of Local Resources

Most community-based health projects appear to have been able to hold their costs to a modest level through their emphasis on preventive and promotive activities. Gwatkin, Wilcox, and Wray (1979, pp. 18–19) report an annual per capita cost ranging from $1.50 to $7.50, including both capital and recurrent expenditure. This represented from 0.5 percent to 2 percent of annual per capita GNP in the countries where the projects were located. In its 1980 health-sector policy paper, the World Bank (1980b, pp. 37–38, 75–78) reports estimates of government health expenditure for eighty-six developing countries. In almost half of the countries government health outlays in the mid-1970s were less than two dollars per capita. However, even in many of the low-income countries, 1–2 percent of GNP was devoted to public expenditure on health. Inasmuch as health expenditures in most countries are concentrated in urban areas and serve a small fraction of the total population, the community-oriented programs appear to have a lower cost per person actually served.

Even though the costs of health programs that stress preventive measures are relatively modest, it is difficult in late-developing countries to obtain the government funds required for broad coverage of the rural population. This resource constraint militates against expensive components such as supplementary distribution of food or a strong emphasis on dispensing drugs. There are also advantages in designing projects in such a way that some of the costs are covered by charges for a particular service.[13] Charging fees to cover the cost of drugs, except to families that would otherwise be unable to benefit from the simple drugs dispensed by a community health worker, is a promising means of holding down costs.[14] Moreover, by easing the problem of excess demand which arises when drugs are fully subsidized and in very short supply, a policy of charging for drugs seems likely to reduce the risk that drug supplies will be sold illegally.

Since donated food is often available from external sources, it is a temptation to include distribution of supplementary food in rural health programs. It

[13] The Jamkhed Project, for example, includes a thirty-bed hospital which is more than self-supporting. It caters mainly to the needs of higher-income groups who can afford to pay for more sophisticated curative services, and the charges provide income that subsidizes some of the cost of the village outreach activities (Pyle 1979, p. 29).

[14] Pyle (1981, pp. 231–32) reports that opposition of local officials to imposing charges on the village community is the principal barrier to mobilizing local resources to cover part of the cost of the Community Health Worker Program in India. These leaders assert that the local people would not be willing to pay even small charges for health services; but Pyle reports that virtually all of the villagers that he interviewed stated that they would be willing to pay a small fee to cover their share of the stipend of the village health worker. Pyle further emphasizes that this would have the advantage of increasing the villagers' sense of involvement in the program and of increasing the accountability of the village-level worker to the local community.

is dangerous, however, for such programs to rely on food donations that are almost certain to be temporary; and reliance on local commodities has greater educational value. The point has also been made that "community concern and understanding of undernutrition are heightened if the supplementary foods are provided by the community"—for example, produced on village land set aside for the purpose (Pyle 1979, p. 38). Especially in promoting supplementary feeding of infants and small children, it is important to emphasize cereal-pulse mixtures which the mother can prepare from locally available foods. It is likely to be desirable to increase the calorie density of the mixture by adding a little sugar or oil.

Population Policies and Programs

Attitudes toward population policy differ greatly among countries and over time within individual countries. These differences are reflected both in the priority given to population programs and in the nature of those programs.

Population Programs and Evolving Attitudes
Towards Population Policy
The World Population Conference held at Bucharest in 1974 saw a reaction against "orthodox" family planning programs and a strong emphasis on the interrelationships between population growth and socioeconomic development. Carmen Miró (1977) has written an extremely valuable analysis and interpretation of the Bucharest Conference and of the World Population Plan of Action, which was its main final product.

At about the same time as the Bucharest Conference, the earlier optimism about the prospects for rapidly reducing birth rates through family planning programs was giving way to considerable pessimism. It was emphasized that reducing fertility depends on changes in attitudes, motivation, and ideas about ideal family size, and it was often argued that "the mere act of launching a family planning programme cannot be expected to have a significant impact on those determinants of fertility" (FAO/WHO 1976, p. 24).

Recent experience in a few low-income countries, most notably in Indonesia, has reinforced the competing viewpoint that vigorous, well-managed family planning programs with strong political support can bring about rapid declines in fertility even when the level of living is very low (Clinton and Baker 1980; Hull, Hull, and Singarimbun 1977). Furthermore, a monograph by Tsui and Bogue (1978, p. 4) has attracted a good deal of attention because of its assertion that a "turning point" was reached between 1970 and 1975 and that the decline in fertility that became evident during that period "appears to be progressing at an accelerating rate." A major conclusion of their monograph is that "the substantial negative impact" of family planning programs has augmented considerably the fertility-reducing effects of changes in socioeconomic variables such as infant mortality and literacy. Tsui and Bogue also present projections that indicate that the future growth of population in the less developed countries will be much lower than indicated by alternative projections (Tsui and Bogue 1978, p. 38). However, some of their estimates of Total Fertility Rates (TFRs) indicate declines that seem too large to be plausible for such a short period (1968–75) and conflict with other evidence.[15]

Demeny (1979) has vigorously criticized Tsui and Bogue's analysis. In addition to noting that earlier projections by Bogue of a marked slowing of population growth in developing countries have proved to be exceedingly optimistic, Demeny has challenged their emphasis on the influence of family planning programs. He argues that there are no cogent reasons for inferring causation from a statistical correlation between declines in fertility and family planning efforts. He believes it is more plausible to argue that in countries where there is relatively strong demand for fertility control because of the effects of socioeconomic change on attitudes toward family size, there will also be a strong demand for family planning programs.

The major study "Conditions of Fertility Decline in Developing Countries, 1965–1975," by Mauldin and Berelson (1978a), is more cautious in claiming an independent effect of family planning programs on declines in fertility. Nevertheless, they conclude that "countries with both significant program effort and high social setting had an average CBR decline of about 30 percent; those with only significant program effort, a decline of about 20 percent; those with high social setting alone, a drop of 5 percent; and those with neither, a zero change" (Mauldin and Berelson 1978a, p. 127).

The concept of "program effort" is, as Mauldin and Berelson acknowledge, a vague concept, and difficult to quantify satisfactorily. Their approach is to adopt a procedure, originally developed by Lapham and Mauldin, for assigning scores to countries for each of fifteen "programmatic criteria"—such as whether there is an adequate family-planning administrative structure, whether political leaders publicly support family planning, and whether contraception is readily and easily available throughout the country. All fifteen criteria are weighted equally in arriving at an aggregate score, and countries are then divided into four categories of "program effort": strong, moderate, weak, or no program (Mauldin and Berelson 1978a, pp. 102–3).

Given the limited understanding of the effectiveness of the various elements of a family planning program, it is clearly impossible to assign differential weights to Mauldin and Berelson's criteria—it is even difficult to judge whether their list is too short or too long. The list includes items that generally were not included in the early family planning programs, such as "full-time home visiting field workers" and "use of mass media on a substantial basis."

Large-scale statistical studies will always remain imperfect and controver-

---

[15] For example, they report a decline in Kenya's TFR of nearly 15 percent between 1968 and 1975, whereas Kenya's National Demographic Survey and the survey carried out in conjunction with the World Fertility Survey both indicate that the (adjusted) TFR *increased* between the 1969 census and 1977/78 (Kenya 1980, p. 89).

sial tools for assessing the effectiveness of complex social policies. Even whe unambiguous correlations can be drawn from a mass of incomplete and unreliable data, causative linkages and prescriptive conclusions will largely reflect predilections of the investigator. Our own predilection is to find it difficult to reject the view that family planning programs have a "causal" effect on population growth rates. Certainly, the effective spread of information and easy access to reliable contraceptives will, *ceteris paribus*, facilitate a more rapid decline in fertility. Furthermore, the rather abrupt changes in government policy and programs in Mexico and Indonesia appear to have had favorable effects on fertility reduction which cannot be explained solely in terms of the influence of socioeconomic change on the demand for family planning. We remain skeptical, however, of some of the more extreme claims of those who would reduce the policy problem to one of statistically "proving" the need for more investment in more of something defined merely as "family planning." In fact, the policy problem is a good deal more complicated and needs a good deal more focused advice. Experience suggests that the key to effective policy design is not so much the amount as it is the kind of family-planning activity.

From the "Clinic Era" to the "Field Era." Rogers (1973, pp. 84–93) describes the period from the early 1950s to the mid-1960s as the "Clinic Era" of family planning. It was only from the mid-1960s that a "Field Era" began, which relied on field motivators and gave more attention to actively seeking out potential adopters and reaching them with family planning "messages."

The early, clinic approach was adopted when there was very little experience with organized family planning programs and little understanding of alternative approaches. Moreover, there was also a prevailing assumption that a large latent demand for family planning services existed and that providing access to services through clinics would suffice. Although the clinic programs had some impact on the small fraction of the population which constituted a receptive audience, they had little impact on the overall population growth rate. J. Mayone Stycos has emphasized that "the early programs of several countries tended to copy the administrative, technical, and philosophical orientation of the Planned Parenthood movements in the United States and England, where, for historical reasons, they have been dominated by feminist, medical, and middle-class thinking." This meant, of course, that family planning activities were characterized by problems of limited coverage similar to those which characterized health programs based on the "Western model" (quoted in Rogers 1973, pp. 84–85).

Dissatisfaction with the limited results obtained during the Clinic Era led to a shift towards the diffusion approach that characterized the Field Era. In some countries financial incentives in the form of payments, either to those adopting family planning or as a bonus to field staff for enlisting acceptors, were also adopted. Incentives have been paid in India since 1956; and in the early 1970s such incentive payments, mainly for male or female sterilization, became a large budget item (Rogers 1973, p. 154). There is considerable evi-

.e incentive programs have increased the rate of adoption perhaps mainly because they "are a way to boost interper-.tion about family planning ideas" (Rogers 1973, p. 170).[16] ad, some incentive schemes have had the undesirable effect of ligible couples to postpone birth regulation until an incentive reinstated or made more attractive. Incentive programs are also and therefore have a high opportunity cost.

ocal community organizations. In recent years increased attention has been given to the role of local organizations in promoting acceptance of family planning and other innovations. It has long been recognized that changes in attitudes are more readily achieved when individuals are organized in groups, so that there is reinforcement for those adopting the change. Etzioni (1979, p. 556) has argued that formal communication "is a weak agent of social change" but that "means of education which seek to mobilize the emotive and normative power of small groups" can be more powerful.

There seems to be general agreement that in South Korea some twenty thousand women's clubs organized to provide reinforcement for family planning adopters have played an important role in the rapid decline of fertility in that country. The role of local community organizations appears to have been especially significant in China and Indonesia. An analysis of Indonesia's family planning program by Korten (1975, pp. 29–30) suggests some important similarities with the Chinese experience, which we shall discuss in a moment. Among these similarities are a heavy reliance on local community organizations, a focus on bringing about changes in community norms, effective use of paramedical personnel (in inserting IUDs, for example), making the distribution of birth control pills a community function, presenting family planning messages in many different contexts (including youth organizations and schools), and moving the service to the community and the people instead of expecting them to come to a clinic.[17]

In spite of these similarities, obviously there are fundamental differences between China's and Indonesia's approach to population problems. China looms so large in the total world population that it is of considerable interest, if only for that reason, to review the very comprehensive population program now being implemented.

Recent policies in the People's Republic of China. A recent article by Chen Muhua, a vice-premier of the PRC and director of the State Council

[16] Rogers also makes the point that incentive payments may be a way of redistributing income, because the poorest are most likely to respond to incentives, especially vasectomy bonuses (Rogers 1973, pp. 165–66).

[17] The important role of the village community in Indonesia's family planning program is also stressed by Surjaningrat et al. (1980, p. 321). Ness (1979, pp. 36–37) argues that the success of the Chinese and Indonesian programs indicates that "new forms of normative support, involving both national level legitimacy and small group level actions, are probably of greater importance than material rewards alone in promoting fertility decline." And Freedman (1979, p. 76) has also stressed the role of village-level groups in bringing to bear peer pressure for acceptance of family planning.

Birth Planning Leading Group, published in *Renmin Ribao* [The People's Daily] in August 1979 is of exceptional interest in describing the comprehensive and vigorous effort currently under way to bring the rate of natural increase down to 0.5 percent by 1985 and to zero by the year 2000.[18]

In a candid reference to population policies in the PRC in an earlier period, Chen Muhua (1979, p. 353) notes that "in our previous critiques of the Malthusian theory of population we one-sidedly stressed man's role as producer, even going so far as to assert that the more people the better, and that the more producers, the quicker, the better and the more economical would be socialist construction." She states emphatically that the view that "a large population is not something to be afraid of . . . is erroneous." Her article emphasizes that "development of production *is* the favored way to solve many problems"; but she stresses a number of reasons why it is essential that efforts to expand production be accompanied by policies and programs to control growth of population. She concludes that "controlling excessive population growth via a well-run planned-birth program will vastly reduce the population pressure on employment, facilitate the accumulation of capital on the part of the state and the collective, and improve the people's standard of living" (Chen Muhua 1979, p. 354). And she begins her article by recalling that a June 1979 report by Premier Hua Guofeng to the National People's Congress designated "firm control" of population increase as one of ten important tasks confronting the nation (Chen Muhua 1979, p. 349).

We have noted that lack of accurate information concerning births and deaths is a problem in virtually all developing countries, and acute in the PRC. At least until recently a low priority was given to assembling vital statistics on a national basis, even though service statistics for many municipalities and even individual communes apparently are quite good. Therefore the statement by Chen Muhua (1979, p. 351) that the rate of natural increase was reduced from 2.3 percent in 1971 to 1.2 percent in 1978 must be treated with reserve, although it is the rate implied by the CBR and CDR figures now adopted by the World Bank.

There is currently strong emphasis on limiting births to one child per family because it is recognized that high fertility in the recent past has resulted in a young population with large numbers of women entering their childbearing period, thereby imparting a considerable momentum to population growth. In addition to the peer pressure exerted through small groups and other factors mentioned earlier, there is now a strong emphasis on both incentives and sanctions. Policies already in operation in a number of provinces, and being extended rapidly throughout the country, reward parents of a single child who pledge to have no more with a monthly cash stipend (in urban areas) or extra work points, which are an entitlement to supplementary income (in rural

[18] The English translation of the Chen Muhua article is accompanied by an interesting introduction and explanatory notes by Pi-chao Chen (1979), professor of political science at Wayne State University.

communes). In addition, such couples are entitled to living space equal to that given to two-child families, and their children are to be given priority in admission to schools and in job placement. The incomes of parents with three or more children are subject to a deduction for "welfare expenditures"; an exception is made, however, in the case of multiple births.

China's program includes the full range of measures for lowering the birth rate, including sterilizations and abortions. There is also explicit recognition that "the task of controlling population increase in rural villages is more difficult than in cities," and strong efforts are made to reach and influence the 80 percent of the country's population residing in rural areas (Chen Muhua 1979, p. 351). The broad coverage achieved by China's rural health program of "barefoot doctors" is clearly an important factor; and Chen Muhua explicitly emphasizes that "it is necessary to manage maternal-and-child-health-care work well, thereby further reducing neonatal and infant mortality, so that when one baby is born, he or she will survive" (1979, p. 353).

This account of recent population policies in the PRC seems especially interesting in relation to earlier interpretations that accepted quite literally Mao's aphorism, "Take care of the people, and the population [problem] will take care of itself." We have serious reservations about both the desirability and the feasibility of transferring the Chinese model, although we believe that there is much to be learned from that experience. It is noteworthy that Taiwan and South Korea also experienced dramatic declines in fertility between 1960 and 1978, without the extremely intrusive and even coercive techniques that have been relied upon in the PRC. In the next section, we examine their experience and that of some other countries that have achieved significant declines in their rate of natural increase.

Understanding the Determinants of Fertility Change: "Thinking Through" and "Acting Out"

The determinants of changes in fertility are exceedingly complex. As we stressed in chapter 2, they include a number of biological factors, as well as the social and attitudinal factors that determine both the motivation to practice family planning and access to contraceptives and knowledge about them. It is therefore not surprising that Cassen (1978, p. 332), reviewing "Current Trends in Population Change and Their Causes," reports that "despite the great intensification of research in the last decade, the factors influencing levels of and changes in fertility remain elusive."

We are persuaded that interactive experience derived from "acting out" various strategies for slowing population growth provides more valuable guidance to policymakers than does reliance primarily on intellectual cogitation. Efforts to achieve better understanding of the determinants of fertility change by analysis of evidence on the effects of various socioeconomic variables have been of value. We suspect, however, that the large investments made in the collection and analysis of survey data for that purpose have reached a point of sharply diminishing returns. We will suggest, however, that a simple analytical framework for "thinking through" the interacting effects of various factors influencing changes in fertility is useful in assessing the feasibility and probable effectiveness of alternative policies for slowing population growth.

A decade ago, Kirk (1971) assessed the evidence of rapid population decline in a small but growing number of developing countries. He advanced the conclusion that once the contemporary developing countries enter the phase of the demographic transition when birth rates begin to decline, the rate of decline in fertility is "enormously speeded up," as compared with Europe and other areas that experienced the demographic transition in an earlier period.[19] We will see that there is now substantial evidence to support Kirk's conclusion (1971, p. 125) that the unprecedentedly rapid reduction in mortality in today's developing countries can be followed by a similarly rapid reduction in birth rates if a country can reach "a certain threshold and 'mix' of socioeconomic development."

A great many studies have been carried out in an effort to assess the relative importance of various socioeconomic variables that appear to be correlated with changes in fertility. Mauldin and Berelson (1978a, pp. 91–93, 133–38) provide a useful summary of twenty-four studies published between 1962 and 1977. Ridker (1976) includes papers which review the available evidence concerning the influence of education, nutrition, health, and many other factors and which put forth numerous proposals for further research. We will turn shortly to an examination of the characteristics of countries that have experienced significant declines in fertility; and our choice of variables will reflect the findings of these various studies of the socioeconomic correlates of fertility change.

There have also been a number of attempts to develop theories of fertility which go beyond the theory of the demographic transition. Some economists are even pursuing the Holy Grail of an "endogenous" theory that would adequately explain fertility change. That the goal of reaching satisfactory and agreed understanding of the major determinants of fertility change and of their relative importance remains elusive is, if anything, an understatement.

A provocative review article by Leibenstein (1974) and a critical comment on it by Keeley (1975) emphasize that there is sharp disagreement even with respect to the most promising approaches to research. Keeley deplores, for example, attempts to consider "threshold effects" and changes in tastes. He makes a plea for more and better data, "not an abandonment of the economic approach" (p. 466). The "economic approach" that Keeley is defending is "the new household economics" that derived from work by Gary Becker and others who have extended the microeconomic theory of demand to include an emphasis on the family as a decision-making unit. Their approach also stresses

---

[19] The quoted phrase is from Oechsli and Kirk (1975), an article which examined evidence on fertility change and modernization in Latin America and the Carribean.

the concepts of "household production" and "full income," concepts which emphasize the importance of considering not only wage employment and other conventional economic activities but also household activities such as producing and rearing children. The economic calculus is applied to decisions about the allocation of available *time* within the household as well as in economic pursuits outside the home.[20]

In an early paper emphasizing the "new household economics approach" to analyzing the determinants of fertility, T. P. Schultz (1971, p. 151) acknowledged the importance of "nonpecuniary factors." His treatment, however, concentrated on the pecuniary benefits and costs of children because they are not as "difficult to observe, conceptualize, and evaluate." But in the later paper which we quoted in chapter 1, Schultz calls for a much more ambitious approach. He raises the important policy issue of comparing the social returns from direct-incentive payments to parents who avoid births with the benefits of programs such as "promoting the health and nutrition of mothers and young children, accelerating the growth of educational opportunities . . . , facilitating the entrance of women into the labor force, and strengthening the economic and legal status of women." He recognizes that the latter programs have benefits that go beyond the slowing of population growth but notes that they may be resisted because they "could absorb large resources per prevented birth." He argues that in order to resolve that issue, there must be "two advances in the social sciences": agreement "on how to characterize a society's intergenerational goals and their trade-offs" and "improved understanding . . . of how economic and demographic variables influence and are influenced by reproductive behavior" (Schultz 1976, p. 111).

Seeking such advances in the social sciences may well be laudable in terms of the academic and disciplinary concerns of scholars. But as long as research objectives are defined in such ambitious and academic terms, the results can hardly be expected to be of much practical value to those concerned with the design and implementation of rural development strategies.

A simple analytical framework. In our opinion, a much more modest effort by Easterlin (1975, 1977) to provide a synthesis of "the economics and sociology of fertility" is more useful than the more elegant efforts to develop a theory based on the new household economics.[21] Easterlin's conceptualization

[20] A long essay by Birdsall, Fei, Kuznets, Ranis, and T. P. Schultz (1979) provides a recent statement of that approach which is characteristic in its emphasis on the need for further refinements of theory and for gathering additional and highly disaggregated data that will permit additional testing of various linkages postulated by the theory.

[21] The models based on the new household economics focus on a demand analysis, i.e., parents' desires concerning the number and "quality" of children wanted. Easterlin (1973) has also presented a demand analysis of fertility which emphasizes different variables (Kocher 1979, pp. 8–10). In spite of lively controversy concerning the two "schools," there has been a progressive blurring of differences, so that they can now be merged into a single model (Sanderson 1976). In fact, both appear to be of limited relevance in developing countries because of their neglect of supply factors, as discussed in the text.

is not a theory but merely an "analytical framework." Nevertheless, it is of considerable heuristic value in a "thinking-through" approach to seeking better understanding of the enormously complex determinants of fertility change and to assessing the probable effects of alternative policies.[22] It seems fairly obvious that in less developed countries reductions in infant and child mortality which change the number of surviving children will be an important influence on attitudes and behavior affecting fertility. Thus a significant feature of Easterlin's framework is that it focuses on changing relationships between the supply of children who survive and parents' demand for children.

In brief, Easterlin proposes to view parents' motivation to restrict family size in terms of a relationship between the potential supply and the demand for children. Particularly pertinent to the demographic situation in the low-income countries is that before a country has begun the demographic transition there is no "problem" of unwanted children. That is, because of high infant and child mortality the "potential supply" of children falls short of the number that is desired. Traditional practices, such as an intercourse taboo during lactation, may hold expressed fertility well below the biological maximum, but there is no conscious desire or action to limit fertility. In fact, traditional values and attitudes, such as the importance of childbearing as a source of status for women, serve to reinforce a large-family norm in the premodern situation that exists prior to the demographic transition.

As child-survival prospects are improved, argues Easterlin, a threshold is reached as parents become aware of a new situation in which the potential supply exceeds the desired number of children. Reaching that threshold marks the transition from premodern to modern fertility determination, the latter being characterized by a situation in which it is usual for family size to reflect conscious decisions by parents. The emergence of a situation of "excess supply" will of course be influenced by changes that reduce the desired number of children, such as changes in perceptions concerning the economic benefits and costs of rearing children which occur as child labor is reduced and more children attend school. It is important to emphasize that there may well be a significant discrepancy between the private and the social calculus of costs and returns from having children. For example, among landless laborers the individual family may well perceive an advantage in having many children to contribute to family income by working as wage laborers. But for the group as a whole, rapid growth in the supply of landless laborers will be a powerful factor depressing returns to labor. Finally, it should be noted that the amount of deliberate birth prevention will also be influenced by the costs of fertility regulation, including psychic costs.

---

[22] When the supply/demand perspective on children is taken too seriously, certain difficulties ensue. One sober and determined effort to deal with this complexity includes the following passage: "Analysis of both demand and supply for children is further complicated by pregnancy and sexual pleasure being joint products of sexual intercourse and possibly having very different demand functions" (Kocher 1979, p. 19n). Now there's a challenge for econometricians!

Various aspects of "development" or "modernization" will have important effects in determining how soon Easterlin's "fertility threshold" will be reached. Urbanization, which has historically been a key factor in the process, will be considerably less significant for the contemporary late-developing countries. Their structural and demographic characteristics make it inevitable that their rural population will continue to weigh heavily in their total population for several decades at least. Other aspects of modernization, such as increases in per capita income, expansion of education, and exposure to mass media, will have positive as well as negative effects, so there is no simple relationship between those variables and changes in fertility.

Characteristics of countries with "significant" declines in fertility. We noted in chapter 2 that in recent years there has been great variation even within the relatively homogeneous group of late-developing countries in the extent to which fertility has begun to decline. Parental decisions and actions that determine family size are obviously influenced by a great many interacting factors. We have just noted, however, that in late-developing countries, some of the most critical questions pertain to the factors that determine when the threshold is reached, so that it becomes usual for family size to depend on conscious decisions by individual parents.

Table 4.1 summarizes some of the relevant data on changes in Crude Birth Rates (CBRs), Crude Death Rates (CDRs), and rates of natural increase for thirty-eight low-income countries, fifty-two middle-income countries, twelve centrally planned countries, and a dozen developing countries which achieved "significant" declines in population growth between 1960 and 1978. Table 4.1 also includes information about five characteristics of the three groups of countries and the twelve countries where between 1960 and 1978 the decline in the CBR exceeded the decline in the CDR by more than six per thousand.[23] Our choice of variables was somewhat arbitrary; they are, however, variables which have been included in many of the studies that have examined relationships between socioeconomic change and fertility. In China the government policies and programs reviewed earlier are probably the dominant factors; but to the extent that data are available, we also comment here on changes in these socioeconomic variables in China.

What conclusions are suggested by the data in Table 4.1 concerning changes in CBRs, CDRs, and their socioeconomic correlates? The variation among the twelve countries with respect to the socioeconomic variables that we have included is so great that no firm conclusions are supported. We believe, however, that some of the relationships have interesting implications for policy.

There is enormous variation in annual per capita income (column 8), which ranges from $190 in Sri Lanka and $230 in China to $2910 in Trinidad and

[23] Hong Kong and Singapore also qualified by our test of "significance," but they are of less interest and are omitted from the table because their populations are so overwhelmingly urban.

Significant Declines in Natural-Increase Rates[a]

Country/Group	1960 CBR (per 1,000)	1960 CDR (per 1,000)	1978 CBR (per 1,000)	1978 CDR (per 1,000)	Change in Natural Increase, 1960-78 (%)	Rate of Natural Increase, 1978 (%)	Per Capita GNP, 1978 (U.S. Dollars)	Adult Literacy Rate, 1975 (%)	Agriculture's Share in Labor Force, 1960 (%)	Child Death Rate (Ages 1-4), 1978 (per 1,000)	Family Planning Effort[b]
	(1)	(2)	(3)	(4)	(5)	(6)	(7)	(8)	(9)	(10)	(11)
Average for 38 low-income countries[c]	48	24	39	15	0.0	2.4	200	38	77	20	
Average for 52 middle-income countries	40	14	35	11	-0.2	2.4	1,250	71	58	10	
Average for 12 centrally planned economies	32	13	18	7	-0.7	1.1	1,190	—	64	1	
Average for 12 countries with significant declines	40	11	25	7	-1.1	1.8	1,137	82	50		
Chile	37	12	22	7	-1.0	1.5	1,410	38	30	5	M
China	36	15	18	6	-0.9	1.2	230	—	75	1	S
Colombia	46	14	31	8	-0.9	2.3	850	81	52	9	M
Costa Rica	47	10	28	5	-1.4	2.3	1,540	90	51	3	S
Cuba	32	9	19	6	-1.0	1.3	810	96	39	1	M
Jamaica	39	9	29	6	-0.7	2.3	1,110	86	39	3	S
Korea, Republic of	41	13	21	8	-1.5	1.3	1,160	93	66	5	S
Malaysia	39	9	29	6	-0.7	2.3	1,090	60	63	3	M
Sri Lanka	36	9	26	6	-0.7	2.0	190	78	56	3	M
Taiwan	39	7	21	5	-1.6	1.6	1,400	82	56	2	S
Trinidad and Tobago	37	7	22	6	-1.4	1.6	2,910	95	22	1	M
Tunisia	49	21	32	12	-0.8	2.0	950	55	56	5	M
										15	M

Source: World Bank (1980a), pp. 110-11, 144-47, 154-65; and Mauldin and Berelson (1978a), p. 103.

[a] A CBR decline that exceeded the CDR decline by more than 6 per thousand is arbitrarily defined as "significant."

[b] Based on a classification of countries by Lapham and Mauldin (1972), where S = strong, M= medium, W = weak.

[c] As in other tables, these group averages are weighted by population. We noted in chapter 2 that the decline in the average CBR for low-income countries from 48 per thousand in 1960 to 39 per thousand in 1978 was influenced strongly by the changes in India and Indonesia. It was noted that the very small reduction in the unweighted average, from 47 per thousand to 45 per thousand, emphasizes the fact that very few of the low-income countries had experienced an appreciable reduction in fertility by 1978.

Tobago. In fact, Sri Lanka and China are the only countries where the per capita income is less than $800; and the $230 figure for China may be too low.[24]

In the case of adult literacy, Sri Lanka is far above the group average for low-income countries, and no doubt China's literacy rate is also high, although no estimate is available. Only Tunisia and Malaysia among the middle-income countries had an adult literacy rate below the average for their category. All the other countries had a literacy rate well above the fairly high average rate for the middle-income countries.

A recent analysis by Potter, Ordóñez, and Measham (1976) of the fairly rapid decline in fertility in Colombia illustrates the difficulty of reaching agreement on an interpretation of the causal factors involved in such a decline. The authors report that "Colombia has been cited as an exception to the general rule that major declines in fertility are preceded by major developmental changes" (p. 509). Their analysis demonstrates conclusively, however, that the rapid decline in fertility has in fact been associated with significant socioeconomic change, most notably in rapid changes in urbanization and in the occupational composition of the labor force and in education. Between 1964 and 1973, the percentage of Colombia's total labor force engaged in agriculture declined rapidly from 47 percent to 30 percent. And over the same period, the percentage of the female population that had received some formal education rose from 72 percent to 85 percent, while the proportion of women who had received some secondary education increased sharply from 15 to 28 percent. Sizable differences in fertility between subgroups of women classified by education and by rural or urban residence confirm the causal significance of those changes.

Colombia's experience does appear to be "an important counter example to the thesis that income redistribution is a prerequisite to fertility decline" (Potter, Ordóñez, and Measham 1976, p. 519). The distribution of income has been and continues to be highly unequal in Colombia, and the country is one of the more extreme examples of a bimodal pattern of agricultural development (Johnston and Kilby 1975, pp. 14–18).[25] It seems doubtful whether the substantial decline in fertility from 46 per thousand in 1960 to 31 per thousand in 1978 would have been possible without the economic and structural conditions that made possible the fairly rapid industrialization and urbanization that took place during that period. Because of the arithmetic of population growth and structural transformation, such a rapid increase in urbanization is not a feasible option for countries where some 60–80 percent of the labor force is still engaged in agriculture.

The degree of structural transformation as reflected in the occupational

[24] This recent official estimate of "net material product" plus an allowance for depreciation and services is considerably lower than alternative estimates and may not be comparable with the estimates of per capita GNP for the other countries (World Bank 1980a, p. 158).

[25] It is estimated, however, that between 1964 and 1974 there was a modest reduction in the inequality of income distribution in Colombia (Chenery 1980, p. 29).

composition of a country's labor force appears to be one of the variables most highly correlated with declines in fertility. Sri Lanka is unusual among the low-income countries in the extent to which structural change had already occurred by 1960: only 56 percent of the country's labor force was still dependent on agriculture in that year; the group average was 77 percent. In 1960 agriculture's share in the labor force still exceeded 50 percent in five other countries with "significant" declines in fertiity: China, Costa Rica, Korea, Malaysia, and Taiwan. With the partial exception of Malaysia, it is noteworthy that the "pattern" of agricultural development in all of those countries permitted unusually widespread participation of their rural population in processes of economic, technical, and social change, including broad access to rural health services.

A fair amount of evidence suggests that reaching a particular level of per capita income is more likely to induce a substantial decline in fertility when income distribution is relatively equal (Yotopoulos 1977, p. 19; Bhattacharyya 1975; Kocher 1973). In the case of Taiwan, a detailed study of fertility change among rural households by Mueller (1971) led to the conclusion that "where agricultural improvement is confined to a minority of cultivators . . . the expansion of economic horizons will be more limited than in Taiwan. Only a minority will then experience the rising aspirations that in Taiwan seem to be contributing so importantly to acceptance of family planning in rural areas" (pp. 37–38).

We noted in chapter 2 that in spite of their great significance as indicators of the "physical quality of life" in a country, the available statistics on infant and child mortality in developing countries are only rough approximations. Many of the estimates of child death rates summarized in column (10) of table 4.1 are indirectly derived from the Coale-Demeny model life tables. Nevertheless, they probably give a fairly good indication of the relative success achieved in various countries and groups of countries in reducing mortality among this vulnerable one-to-four-year-old age group. It therefore seems noteworthy that with the exception of Colombia and Tunisia, the countries with "significant" declines in fertility had exceptionally low child death rates. Indeed the estimated rates of one per thousand for China and two per thousand for Sri Lanka are not only below the average of twenty per thousand for the low-income countries but also much below the group average of ten per thousand for the middle-income countries. If the estimates of child mortality in table 4.1 are reasonably good approximations of reality, then those correlations provide crude but nonetheless persuasive support for the "child mortality hypothesis" which we discuss in the following section.

Finally, it will be noted that all of the countries had family planning programs rated as "strong" or "moderate." In contrast, among ninety-four countries classified according to their family planning effort, over 70 percent had weak programs or no programs at all (Mauldin and Berelson 1978a, p. 103).

Concluding observations. A critique by Dixon (1978) of the major study by Mauldin and Berelson mentioned earlier (1978a) raised some challenging questions about formal attempts to reach conclusions concerning the relative importance of various factors influencing changes in fertility. Most of her questions are related to the difficulty, which we noted earlier, of drawing conclusions about causative linkages or policy prescriptions on the basis of correlation analysis or similar statistical techniques. The thoughtful replies by Mauldin and Berelson (1978b) to two more general questions raised by Dixon provide a fitting conclusion to this section.

To the question whether family planning effort is more important than socioeconomic conditions in inducing fertility decline, Mauldin and Berelson's answer is "probably not." They reiterate their belief that family planning programs have a significant, independent effect additional to the effect of socioeconomic factors; but they particularly stress that the best results are obtained when the two are combined.

In response to Dixon's question concerning the type of social setting that is most conducive to fertility decline, Mauldin and Berelson emphasize that "health and education seem to be of particular importance" (1978b, p. 288). They go on, however, to suggest that "better questions are: what 'restructuring' of development would achieve the developmental goal and at the same time achieve more fertility reduction in the process, and how is it to be brought about given the political, economic, and cultural realities of the matter?"

It will be clear from chapter 3 that in our view, a unimodal pattern of agricultural development is of special importance in achieving the multiple objectives of development, including the objective of slowing population growth. We argue in the following section that wide coverage of a country's rural areas with a "package" of nutritional, health, and family planning services also offers great promise in improving the well-being of the rural population.

The Case for an Integrated Approach to Nutrition, Health, and Family Planning

In this final section, we consider the possibility of linking the nutrition, health, and population programs considered in the preceding sections. While noting that there may be advantages in linking these activities administratively, we emphasize the need for additional experience and learning to better understand whether, and under what circumstances, the advantages of integrating this set of activities outweigh the disadvantages of administering a more complex program.

The Potential Advantages of Integration
The discussion of nutrition, health, and population in the preceding sections suggests that there are highly significant *potential* advantages in linking the three sets of activities in an integrated rural health or "family welfare" program. But the design and implementation of programs capable of realizing

that potential is an exceedingly formidable undertaking. Experience in China (and perhaps Costa Rica and Sri Lanka) and demonstration projects in a number of countries show that the task is not impossible. However, it will require strong political and organizational support. Also needed is a willingness to learn from both successes and failures in order to increase the efficacy of such programs. This is only one of the reasons why the range of services and geographical coverage should be expanded gradually in a sequential fashion. It will be difficult to mobilize the political and administrative support required for a sustained effort without a considerable consensus among nutritional, health, and population specialists.

Hard decisions must be made with respect to the objectives and components of such programs. One of the important lessons of the community development programs of the 1960s is that when village-level workers are given a range of responsibilities that exceed their capabilities, most of them will be ineffective and accomplish very little. An important step in making rural health programs feasible is to give priority in the initial phase to infants and small children and their mothers. That priority is justified in the first instance by the disproportionate concentration of mortality and morbidity among those vulnerable groups. It is also reinforced by the evidence, reviewed above, that interventions aimed at the health and nutritional problems of those groups can be exceptionally cost-effective. Finally, integrated nutrition, health, and family planning programs have the potential for achieving further reduction in infant and child mortality *and* also for promoting increased awareness that the risk of child loss has been reduced significantly.

Thus a rural health program that achieves broad coverage can simultaneously increase the "demand" for family planning and reduce both the psychic and objective costs of fertility regulation. Providing convenient and inexpensive access to reliable methods of contraception can greatly reduce the objective cost of regulating fertility. It might seem obvious that improving the prospects for infants and small children to survive to maturity would have the effect both of increasing the demand for fertility regulation as parents begin to perceive an "excess supply" of surviving children and of reducing the psychic cost of practicing family planning. This so-called child survival hypothesis has, however, been highly controversial and even a source of resistance to the concept of an integrated approach to health, nutrition, and family planning. Some of the earlier statements advocating a higher priority for programs to improve nutrition and health made extravagant claims about the more or less automatic reduction in fertility that would result from reducing infant and child mortality. It was suggested that individual parents would tend to expect that the mortality risk for their children would be even higher than the high average child death rate, so that parents would "overcompensate" by having a large number of "insurance births." A reduction in child mortality would therefore, so it was claimed, lead directly to a more than proportionate reduction in the number of births. This controversial view has given rise to a huge literature.

The not very surprising conclusions are that reduced child mortality will not "automatically change child-bearing attitudes or levels of fertility" and that the rate of natural increase will rise because "the fertility reduction will be smaller in magnitude than the mortality reduction" (Madigan 1975, p. 278; Preston 1975, p. 191). The rapid rates of population growth that now prevail are, of course, a result of the slow and limited declines in fertility that have been associated with rapid declines in mortality levels. However, the reductions in mortality that have occurred cannot be ignored. Thus the relevant question is, How best complete the half-completed demographic transition?

Cogitation and Interaction: The Special Importance of "Acting Out"

In our discussion of a policy-analysis perspective in chapter 1 we emphasized that "thinking-through" solutions to problems through intellectual cogitation and "acting-out" solutions through social interaction represent complementary approaches. We believe that the most persuasive reasons for emphasizing an integrated approach to family welfare derive from the evidence provided by demonstration and pilot projects and a few national programs, not from a priori reasoning. The remarkable effectiveness of well-designed rural health programs in reducing infant and child mortality was documented above. A number of the demonstration projects also achieved notable success in promoting the acceptance of family planning. In the Jamkhed Project in India the percentage of eligible couples practicing family planning rose sharply from 2.5 percent in 1971 to just over 50 percent in 1976. Some increase undoubtedly would have occurred without the integrated health project. But in a control area, the percentage of couples practicing family planning was still only 10 percent in 1976. In the Miraj Project, also in the state of Maharashtra, the emphasis was on "target families," with three children or more. At the beginning of the project, in January 1974, coverage of that group had already reached 30.6 percent. But by January 1977 the proportion had increased to 89 percent, and in all cases sterilization was the method of contraception (Pyle 1979, attachment II; and personal communication). In the case of the Narangwal Project in the Punjab, it is claimed (mainly on the basis of estimated changes in "continuing-use rates" and "effective-use rates") that there was approximately a threefold increase in the number of births prevented under the integrated program as compared with the standard family planning program (Taylor, Singh, et al. 1975, pp. IV.A.4–7 and table IV.A.2).

Thinking-through and acting-out approaches seem to converge in emphasizing several features of integrated programs which appear to enhance the effectiveness of efforts to foster family planning. There are cogent reasons for expecting that the effects of general attitudinal changes associated with improved health and a less fatalistic view can be reinforced by establishing routines for integrated programs whereby family planning information is introduced at strategic "entry points," when parents are likely to be receptive to the idea of family planning. There is also some evidence that reinforces the expectation that integration of nutrition, health, and population activities will have favorable effects on the motivation of both field staff and the potential acceptors of family planning. The Narangwal Project included a test of an intensified family planning program without supporting health services, and it is reported that the family planning educators participating in that program placed "great pressure on their superiors to give them something more to discuss with village women than just family planning" (Taylor, Singh, et al. 1975, pp. IV.A.1–2). A recent report from Indonesia also emphasizes that family planning field workers express "their desire to provide services other than family planning" and "frequently ask for advice or medicine for sick children, and some have begun supplying simple medicines on their own" (Hull 1979, p. 323). Moreover, the involvement of field workers in activities to improve family health is likely to increase their credibility in promoting family planning.[26]

The significance of a more favorable "environment," or "context," for the attitudes and motivation of potential adopters of family planning is brought out by two reports from tropical Africa. A study by Kocher (1977) of four rural areas in Tanzania led to the conclusion that changes in the "supply" and "demand" variables (of Easterlin's analytical framework) have not yet led to the threshold that marks the transition from premodern to modern fertility determination. In fact, he suggests that "family-planning programs introduced into rural areas which have experienced little or no socioeconomic transition will probably find little demand for their services. Because their purposes run counter to traditional values, they may generate an adverse response and perhaps make it more difficult to promote birth control successfully at a later, more suitable time" (p. 73). A similar conclusion is suggested by an evaluation report on an intensified family planning effort in Kenya's Kakamega District. This report indicates that the program's impact on the birth rate has been very limited, and "there is a strong local feeling, which is perfectly understandable, that family planning facilities should not be considered a priority in an area in which basic medical facilities are still lacking. This may itself engender a negative attitude toward family planning" (Livingstone and Pala 1975, chap. 17, p. 17).

A valuable review article by Watson, Rosenfield, Viravaidya, and Chanawongse (1979) provides a useful summary of "the imposing arguments for integration." Their wise conclusion, however, is that "the ultimate answers will derive from empirical experience rather than eloquent arguments or counterarguments" (p. 162).

Although the potential advantages of an integrated approach appear to be very significant, we emphasize once again that they are only potential advantages. The multiple objectives served by an integrated program offer the possibility of enlisting the support of both those concerned with basic needs and

[26] See also chapter 5.

those concerned with rapid population growth. But such coalitions are only a possibility, difficult if not impossible to mobilize in practice. As previously noted, there is considerable resistance within the medical profession to a health strategy that emphasizes broad coverage and preventive and promotive activities. In addition, many nutrition and population specialists are either opposed to such programs or provide only grudging support. Some population specialists, for example, have expressed concern that family planning activities may be "neglected, weakened, or rendered inefficient by too much dilution with other programs" (Bogue and Tsui 1979, p. 113). Finkle and Crane (1976) provide a more explicit description of that viewpoint, noting that "many population specialists take the view that fertility limitation is too urgent a task to leave to health organizations and that there are alternative ways of implementing programs to reduce fertility that require little, if any, involvement of health services and medical personnel" (p. 368). Although the resistance of population and nutrition specialists can be attributed in part to a normal bureaucratic preference for emphasizing one's own particular program, there are more serious reasons for concern about integrated programs.

It can certainly be argued that single-service programs are less likely to encounter the "channel overload" problems which may arise when a community-health worker is concerned with a range of activities embracing nutrition, health, and family planning. It has been suggested, for example, that "integrated programs require stronger management to maintain the same level of performance as a comparable vertical program" and that "family planning tends to get crowded out of a busy integrated program" (Korten 1975, pp. 25, 26). In analogous fashion, many nutrition specialists are concerned that the medical personnel responsible for an integrated program will have little appreciation of the fundamental importance of nutritional status and of the significance of the two-way interactions between nutritional status and infection.

These are legitimate concerns. In the early phases of implementing India's Community Health Worker Program, for example, there has been a tendency for village health workers and health personnel at higher levels to emphasize individual curative care rather than preventive and promotive activities (Maru 1981; Pyle 1981). Clearly, one of the key problems in the design and implementation of rural health programs is to secure a concentration of limited resources on priority problems, such as the health of infants and small children, and on the most cost-effective activities, such as nutrition and hygiene education, immunizations, and family planning.[27]

[27] The major study by Barnum, Barlow, Fajardo, and Pradilla (1980) mentioned earlier appears to be one of the few serious efforts to identify the most cost-effective activities to be included in an integrated health program. The results are broadly consistent with those discussed in this chapter, with four exceptions: the activities (interventions) considered in the study do not include oral rehydration, BCG immunization against tuberculosis, chloroquine for treatment of malaria, and family planning. The first three omissions may be explained by the fact that the analysis is based on subjective estimates of the impact of various interventions on morbidity and mortality among infants and small children derived from experience with urban health programs

There is great danger that preventive and promotive activities will be neglected. They are more difficult than passive activities such as dispensing a few drugs. Moreover, local people as well as medical personnel are likely to be more concerned with individual curative care. It is reported, however, that active participation of local groups, such as village health committees, promotes a community orientation and greater recognition of the fact that preventive and promotive activities are most cost-effective.[28] Even more clearly, local participation is essential to the success of efforts to improve the water supply and environmental sanitation in a village community (World Bank 1980c, chap. 3). We have seen that active participation of local organizations has been a key factor in the success of some of the population programs that have had a considerable impact on fertility in spite of an unfavorable socio-economic environment. We believe that it is important to acquire better understanding of the relative advantages and disadvantages of efforts to induce local participation in relation to integrated health, nutrition, and family planning programs as compared with a single-service program such as nutrition or family planning.

Little is known about the means or even the possibility of overcoming the formidable problems that arise in the design and management of integrated health programs. Moreover, a good deal of the relevant experience and knowledge derives from demonstration projects and therefore cannot be generalized confidently to programs aimed at broad coverage. Hence in designing and implementing programs such as India's Community Health Worker Program, there is a particular need to emphasize adaptive learning which makes use of the inevitable and indeed expected failures in an iterative process of trial-and-error improvement. That learning process must embrace a concern for questions of organizational choice as well as of policy design because of "the need for consistency between policy, program design, and organization" (Korten 1979d, p. 13).

In concluding this chapter, it is well to reiterate the potential advantages of a composite-package approach to providing a country's rural population with access to nutrition, health, and family planning services. Because of the important complementarities among these activities, they can be mutually reinforcing if combined within a single program. Those complementarities and certain possibilities for savings in cost in comparison with single-service programs mean that an integrated approach can be more cost-effective in realizing the interrelated objectives of improving nutritional status and health and slowing

---

in Colombia, a middle-income country. The principal interest of the study for low-income countries seems to lie in the possibility of applying a modified and probably simplified version of the methodology. Two especially interesting results are estimates of the cost per additional life saved as resource constraints are relaxed. The marginal cost per life saved is just under two hundred dollars at a low level of resource allocation; and it rises to close to five hundred dollars for an additional life saved at a higher level of resource allocation (Barnum et al. 1980, p. 167).

    [28] C. E. Taylor and V. K. Tatochenko both made this point in presentations at a July 1979 meeting in Laxenburg, Austria (IIASA, 1979).

population growth. In principle, and perhaps in practice, the prospects for obtaining sufficient political, financial, and administrative support for achieving broad coverage are enhanced. The analysis by Pyle (1981) emphasizes that the implementation of India's Community Health Worker Program has indeed encountered formidable organizational and political problems. In fact, Pyle is not at all optimistic about the prospects for overcoming those difficulties within government programs because of the problems they encounter that are not present in a small demonstration project carried out by a nongovernmental organization. We believe, however, that the prospects for bringing about the major changes in organizational structure that are required and of mobilizing sufficient political support are probably somewhat better in the case of a program embracing health, nutrition, and population activities than in the case of a single-service program. Because of the multiple objectives being promoted, there is at least the possibility of organizing a relatively broad coalition of support groups. Finally, there would appear to be a better prospect for enlisting the active participation of local village communities and of creating effective problem-solving organizations: improving "health and family welfare" represents a felt need around which popular interest can be aroused (C. E. Taylor 1977; Johnston and Meyer 1977). We have underscored the practical difficulties of realizing those potential advantages. Indeed we believe that there is little prospect of success unless determined and sustained efforts are made to cope with the difficult problems of organizational design and management that we examine in chapter 5.

CHAPTER FIVE

Organization Programs: Institutional Structures and Managerial Procedures

Organization and Development

The preceding chapters focused on programs designed to influence production- and consumption-related aspects of rural well-being. We now consider a third element of development strategy: the organization of people for policy design and implementation.[1]

Organization, as we use it, concerns the institutional, managerial, and administrative linkages among actors in the policymaking process. Studies of policymaking in other fields show that organization is a central element of successful strategy: attempts to change *what* things are done must be accompanied by appropriate changes in *how* things are done.[2] Studies in the developing world suggest the same conclusion: "Those cases in which there was more organization reaching down to the local level, accountable to the local people, and involved with rural development functions . . . have accomplished rural development objectives more successfully . . . than have those with less rural organization" (Uphoff and Esman 1974, p. xi). The analyses of development organization which we present in this chapter illuminate and extend this view.

The Tasks of Development Organization

No single person acting alone can accomplish much to accelerate rural development. This is obviously true for the poor: they need knowledge, material, protection, and other resources which lie beyond their grasp as individuals. It is equally true, however, for policymakers and administrators: the boldest decree has no effect until it is acted upon by those whose behavior it seeks to change.

In brief, effective development requires organization. Brewster has de-

---

[1] Esman and Montgomery's (1980) review "The Administration of Rural Development" appeared after we had completed this chapter, and we regret that we have been unable to benefit from and pursue some of the relevant points it raises. While we do not agree fully with all their conclusions, their essay should provide excellent counterpoint to ours.

[2] See Chandler (1962) and Bower (1970).

scribed this as "the capacity for concerting reciprocally helpful behaviors into a continually widening network of larger, specialized units of collective action necessary for enabling people to . . . transform their physical and biological world into a place of ever increasing goods and services" (Brewster 1967, p. 69). In this essay, we will be concerned with organization policies as means for enhancing a nation's capacities to undertake collective actions which improve the well-being of the rural poor. We view organization as a framework for calculation and control through which collections of individuals determine what each should do and ensure that each does what is expected of him.[3] We noted some of the specific tasks of organization in our earlier discussions of agricultural extension and health-care delivery. It will be useful, however, to outline more systematically the full range of calculation and control tasks that development organization is called upon to perform.[4]

Making claims and choices. Organization must provide a means for people to choose among the various claims they might make on the larger social system and to signal the responses desired from that system. If concerted claims are to be advanced by the rural poor, organization must also include means of surfacing and settling local conflicts.[5] Planners, administrators, and other actors in the development process require effective claim-making at the local level if they are to have any hope of responding to or even recognizing the actual needs of the rural poor.

Distribution of resources among claims. Not all of everyone's claims can be satisfied at once. Organization must provide a means of determining whose claims have how much priority, and of reconciling available resources with those priorities. The contemporary development debate tends to slight these tasks. This is a mistake, and a dangerous one. The failure to set priorities among objectives—the failure to include among those priorities only such objectives as can be obtained with the resources available—remains the surest way for a national government to destroy the prospects for improved well-being among the rural poor.

Allocating resources. Organization must provide both the incentives to induce and the channels to permit appropriate responses to those claims which have been made. Developing the institutional infrastructure and the managerial capacity for linking resource owners with resource users is one important aspect of this task. In addition, an effective system of rewards and penalties is needed to ensure that resources are actually put to the uses called for. The required control may be exerted through a variety of techniques ranging from

---

[3] The view of organization as a means of calculation and control is developed at length by Dahl and Lindblom (1953).

[4] A wide range of analyses suggest categories similar to those adopted here. See, for example, Uphoff and Esman (1974, pp. 16–18) for a perspective on Asia; Chambers (1974, pp. 85–86) for East Africa; and Dahl and Lindblom (1953, pp. 129–31) for a parallel treatment of organization functions in modern Western democracies.

[5] A useful discussion of the problem of conflict resolution is provided by Powelson (1972).

price systems to bureaucracies. More important than the specific form is that the rural poor have *some* effective means of ensuring that "appropriate" quantities of the resources on which they have made claims are in fact allocated to them at the appropriate time, place, and cost.

Resource mobilization. Effective social action requires means for increasing the quantity of available resources. This is true whether the resource in question is financial capital, technical knowledge, trained staff, or political power. Organization must therefore promote investment, discovery, and education appropriate to the needs of rural development.

Resource productivity. Securing high productivity of resources in their assigned allocations is a further task of development organization.[6] Productivity is generally thought of in terms of the output-increasing capabilities of capital investment or technological change. Perhaps even more important is the human element: the "intelligence, skill, industry, precision, and speed" with which managers, workers, and others in an organization discharge their activities (Dahl and Lindblom 1953, pp. 130–31). Increasing resource productivity is often the orphaned task of organization efforts, primarily because it lacks an established constituency (Leonard 1977). Policies for redesigning organizations must therefore make increased productivity one of their foremost objectives.

Techniques of Development Organization

How can policymakers improve the capacity of organizations to perform the tasks of choice, allocation, distribution, mobilization, and productive use of resources? The development debate has remained silent on such questions, at least relative to the verbiage expended on agricultural production, foreign trade, population growth, and health. Moreover, of the little debate that is conducted on organization, most is preoccupied with what might be called the great isms, grand alternatives, and fundamental ideologies of development (Dahl and Lindblom 1953, pp. 3–6). Disembodied polemics abound on the relative virtues of capitalist versus socialist economics, synoptic versus incremental planning, top-down versus bottom-up management, paternalist versus populist attitudes, mechanistic versus organic administration, and so on and on.[7]

The resulting picture of mutually exclusive, monolithic alternatives—with its implication that assigning proper labels is the true challenge of organizational redesign—typifies the immaturity of the development debate to which

[6] This argument is distinct from the formal economic one concerning efficient resource allocation, in that it takes allocation as given.

[7] We do not for a moment doubt that the basic values and beliefs—in short, the culture— held by a society are fundamental determinants of how that society performs the tasks of calculation and control. Strong and broad commitment to a common set of values may even provide a means of achieving otherwise unobtainable consensus on particular social-action programs. Powelson (1972, p. 26), for example, hypothesizes that some degree of national consensus on economic and political ideology is a *sine qua non* of "institutional effectiveness." He also suggests that

we referred in chapter 1. The tendency to focus on matters of form rather than substance has discouraged competition among different types of organization and therefore has failed to exploit the great potential for organizational pluralism (Lele 1975, p. 187; Uphoff and Esman 1974, pp. 7–11 and ff.). Most important from the policymakers' perspective, ideological wrangles over organizational alternatives have remained empty as guides to practical action. Even a quarter of a century ago, Dahl and Lindblom could begin their tract *Politics, Economics, and Welfare* by observing:

> In economic organization and reform, the "great issues" are no longer the great issues, if ever they were. It has become increasingly difficult for thoughtful men to find meaningful alternatives posed in the traditional choices . . . for they find their actual choices neither so simple nor so grand. . . . The possibilities for rational social action, for planning, for reform—in short, for solving problems—depend not upon our choice among mythical grand alternatives but largely upon choices among particular social techniques (Dahl and Lindblom 1953, pp. 3, 6).

More recently, this view has been reconfirmed by A. K. Sen, one of the outstanding economic theorists to deal with development problems: "For developing countries the shift in focus to technological and institutional details is long overdue. . . . The most serious problems lie, not in the grand design, but in what has the superficial appearance of 'details' " (Sen 1975, as quoted in Hunter 1978*a*, p. 37).

The "details" of Sen and the "techniques" of Dahl and Lindblom are the fundamental relationships on which social organization is built—the basic processes through which various actors in development are linked with one another in units of collective action. Reduced to sufficiently abstract elements, the same basic organizational techniques are available in both developed and developing societies. These are enumerated below.[8]

Hierarchical techniques are means of organization through which services, orders, information, and other resources are distributed. Hierarchies are usually bureaucratic in structure, and unilateral in the control relationships they seek to impose. One of the great contemporary challenges for organization designers is to build into hierarchies the capacity for a two-way flow of resources, particularly information.

Exchange techniques reflect some degree of mutual adjustment among the

---

the kinds of institutions that will be most effective will depend on the particular ideology on which consensus is formed. We wish we were able to utilize such ideas more effectively in the present analysis of rural organization. But we must confess that we simply do not understand these relationships between politics and culture sufficiently to apply them as analytic tools. We therefore ignore the effects of culture and ideology on organization out of necessity rather than choice. While we would welcome positive descriptions of this relationship as it affects specific rural development situations, we remain convinced that little is to be gained from normative debates over which ideology is "best."

[8] See Dahl and Lindblom (1953) and Uphoff and Esman (1974), for example.

actors in an organization. Markets are one common form of exchange, but so are feudal and traditional patronage systems.[9]

Polyarchical techniques, to the extent that they differ from other means of organization in more than name, embody some degree of accountability to choice endurers. Elective, representative local councils are only one such form of organization; commune arrangements and single-party structures are others.

Bargaining techniques provide a means through which sovereign individuals with common or complementary goals can join together to enhance their capacities for collective action. Often these include an ability to better make and enforce claims on other actors through the formation of interest groups. Agricultural cooperatives, irrigation associations, and the like are common examples.

Each of these basic organizational techniques can help in the performance of the tasks of calculation and control required for effective social action. As figure 5.1 suggests, the techniques differ primarily in terms of the leadership function: who is calculating and controlling whom. The figure is also useful in emphasizing how one kind of organizational technique merges and combines with others in actual practice. For example, small groups of sovereign individuals may be linked primarily through bargaining techniques. As the number of individuals increases, the rising difficulty of one-on-one calculation and control may well encourage emergence of a leadership function. Depending on the relationship of the leaders to the led, the resulting organization will look more hierarchical or more polyarchical. As another example, exchange techniques (in the pure form suggested here and in economics textbooks) are distinguished by relative reciprocity among members and the absence of a leadership function. But the figure suggests the ease with which exchange systems are captured by an emergent leadership and turned into de facto hierarchies. We shall explore the implications of this and other relationships suggested by figure 5.1 throughout this chapter.

[9] Leonard (1977) explores a somewhat broader view of exchange in the context of development organization.

		Calculation and Control of	
		Nonleaders	Leaders
Calculation and Control by	Nonleaders	Exchange techniques (eg. markets)	Polyarchy techniques (eg. local council)
	Leaders	Hierarchy techniques (eg. civil service)	Bargaining techniques (eg. interest groups)

Figure 5.1. Basic Techniques of Calculation and Control.

Each of the basic techniques of organization has structural and behavioral aspects. Thus the institutional framework of, say, a market is of little use without complementary human skills of entrepreneurship. An agricultural extension service provides little help to the farmer unless the procedures governing agent activities are appropriately designed and are supported by research that generates feasible and profitable innovations. Interest groups are likely to be crippled by corruption (or the suspicion of it) unless satisfactory rules governing accountability can be created. In general, the institutional channels provide only the potential for linkages among actors. Whether, and how efficiently, that potential is realized depends on complementary skills, rules, and procedures to shape the actions that actors actually take.

In contrast to the stereotypes we have discussed so far, any real-world organization links people, actions, and resources through some combination of basic social techniques, representing some combination of institutions and procedures. *Which* techniques are to be used in a particular instance and *how* these are to be combined in and adapted to local circumstances are the fundamental choices of organization policy. The view that such organizational choices are somehow unimportant—that they are less subject to manipulation and experimentation than the conventional choices among production and consumption options—is fundamentally mistaken. As Uphoff and Esman conclude, organization is "amenable to public policy choices and intervention, to governmentally sponsored experimentation and action. . . . Organization for rural development is a subject that governments can do something about" (Uphoff and Esman 1974, pp. 5–6). The question remains of what policy analysis has to offer such governments.

The Role of Policy Analysis

The ultimate choices among techniques of organization must be made by national, regional, and local authorities. More than in any other area of development, the role of foreign advisors and advice is restricted. Sensitivity regarding the involvement of external actors in matters affecting the basic power structure of society is one source of these restrictions. The vast range and subtlety of existing organizational relationships is another. Nonetheless, national governments are increasingly aware of the need for designing more effective organization as part of their rural development strategies. Here, as elsewhere, there *is* a need for good policy analysis—for systematic efforts to build a perspective from which the broader implications, constraints, and opportunities associated with particular organizational choices can be better understood.

One of the most important things which a policy analysis perspective can do is to emphasize the historical dimension of social organization. Effective organization does not spring full-blown from the brows of policymakers or analysts. Rather, it is an organic entity, growing and developing over time. The development of organization involves the obvious growth in infrastructure and administrative skills, plus a less evident change in cultural values and expectations. The result is a complex, dynamic system of linkages which is only partially understood at any given time by the people it unites in programs of social action.

Even in the least developed societies, some such linkage structure exists, employing various organizational techniques to one degree or another and performing the various tasks of organization more or less badly. One of the most significant contributions of basic survey research such as that reported by Uphoff and Esman (1974) is that it documents the richness and variety of organizational structures presently in place throughout the developing world. In the wake of such evidence, no argument needs to be taken seriously which presumes that policymakers and analysts have a history-free clean slate upon which to write their organizational prescriptions.

The real business of policy analysis, as we have said before, is to improve the capacity for effective social action by redesigning and reorganizing existing patterns of linkage. Viewed from this perspective, reorganization is obviously a risky endeavor: in tinkering with an existing organization in hopes of making it work better, there is always the possibility of making it worse.

Unfortunately, people who would never dream of dismantling a recalcitrant wristwatch have too often been ready to recommend the dismantling and comprehensive reconstruction of societies. The resulting utopian reorganization schemes have wasted appalling amounts of time, spirit, and talent throughout human history.

> We trained hard—but it seemed that every time we were beginning to form up into teams we would be reorganized. I was to learn later in life that we tend to meet any new situation by reorganizing, and a wonderful method it can be for creating the illusion of progress while producing confusion, inefficiency, and demoralization.

That familiar lament is from the Roman courtier Petronius, writing in the first century A.D. Nearly two thousand years later, things have not changed very much. The keynote paper at a recent meeting of the major Third World management institutes evoked a response almost identical to that of Petronius:

> I see problems with the new organization model being proposed. . . . We are reaching a point here . . . and in other countries where we are questioning the capacity of our clearly structured vertical organizations to achieve congruence with the needs of our people. Yet this is the model with which our people have experience and within which they are finally learning to function. Now we are proposing a completely different model of organization, which will require our people to develop new skills and learn how to move within new structures (Bustillo 1979, p. 54).

We do not mean to suggest that reorganization is undesirable. We *do* mean to argue that any substantive reorganization necessarily wrenches the social fabric upon which the existing capacity for collective action depends. This wrenching results, at the very least, in a period of inefficiency while people learn to function with new roles and rules. The more drastic the reorganization, the greater the wrench and the more likely that serious, even permanent, damage will be done to the historically evolved capacity to resolve social problems. The clear implication, well confirmed by policy analysis in other fields, is that reorganization policy should almost always forsake comprehensive utopian reforms in favor of more piecemeal, less heroic ones. Modest policies will not solve all the problems of development organization at once, but they may provide a beginning for that "sequence of steps" on which Hirschman and others assure us that most progressive improvement depends.

Where should this sequence of modest, incomplete programs of social reorganization begin? How should the policymaker select from among all tasks of organization clamoring for his attention and all those techniques of organization available for his use? A growing number of development analysts are addressing these questions; an authoritative treatment of their views is beyond both our wit and ambition.[10] As elsewhere in this essay, we proceed by focusing on some of the most serious failures of existing organizations, and on some of the most feasible and desirable opportunities for mitigating those failures. We seek not to supersede other perspectives on these questions but rather to add a complementary viewpoint from which certain ambiguities and disputes of the current debate can be more clearly perceived, and a certain amount of unremarked consensus more clearly discerned.

Failures and Opportunities

The failures of contemporary development organization are many. Four, however, are both serious and ubiquitous, appearing again and again across a range of ideological, national, and sectoral settings.[11] We alluded to some of these in chapter 1, but they will bear reiteration as foci for our analysis of reorganization policy.

Most obvious are the failures of implementation. Time after time, in country after country, there is little correspondence between policy plans and what actually happens to the poor. Sometimes implementation fails because of the limited technical knowledge and resources we discussed in chapters 3 and 4. All too often, however, the administrative systems used and the manpower they require constitute the dominant constraints (Lele 1975, pp. 183–84). Perhaps most frequently, policymakers fail to mobilize the political support necessary to guide their initiatives through the maze of competing and conflicting interests which lie between intention and successful implementation (Leys 1971). Implementation failures may surface as unfunded projects and unspent allocations. Or as directives from above saddling village-level workers with impossible tasks and reporting responsibilities. Or as seed that reaches the

---

[10] Notable efforts to redress this imbalance include works by Korten (1979a, 1980a), Chambers (1974), and the Rural Development Committee at Cornell (e.g., Uphoff and Esman 1974). Other recent works that deal with organization and development are Lele (1975), Leonard (1977), Hunter (1978a, 1978b), and Caiden and Wildavsky (1974).
[11] See, for example, Chambers (1974), Lele (1975, pp. 176–77), and Korten (1979a).

farmer only after the planting season is over.[12] The prevalence of such failures—their virtual acceptance as the norm—must not obscure their consequences. Politicians, bureaucrats, and consultants can benefit from unimplemented development plans almost as much as they benefit from implemented ones. The poor cannot.

A second common failure of development organization is its inability to channel benefits to the poorest members of society rather than to those who are already relatively well-off. Even when programs seem to have solved their implementation problems, even when governments are truly concerned about the plight of the rural poor, the bulk of development's benefits do not accrue to those who need them most. Cooperatives end up excluding the poor or exploiting them (UNRISD 1975, pp. ix–x; Korten 1980a; Chambers 1974, pp. 108–9). Village workers and extension agents align themselves with the relatively more aggressive and articulate local elites, perpetuating or even intensifying income differentials (Leonard 1977). Human and material resources gravitate to urban centers, where careers must be made and where politically potent demands successfully clamor for priority (Chambers 1974, p. 28). Graft and corruption siphon off resources nominally destined for the poor. Again, the triteness of the observation must not obscure its truth: many rural development programs make the relatively rich richer, and the poor at least relatively poorer.

A third failure of development organization is that it seldom increases the problem-solving capacity of the rural poor. International declarations, national plans, and academic treatises have argued that further increases in rural well-being will require that the poor themselves play an active role in shaping and supporting development programs. Nonetheless, organization of the rural poor often remains dominated by traditional kinship and patronage systems which militate against the formation of problem-oriented "units of collective action" (Brewster 1967; Leys 1971). External initiatives to organize the rural poor generally have failed to take these traditional structures into account, with predictable results. Often, and with good reason, the new cooperative or committee is viewed as something for "others"—something that is probably useless and most likely a means of enhancing existing authority and exploitation (Hunter 1971, p. 2).

Even when development organization does reach the poor, it too often functions as a one-way conduit of implementation through which services, solutions, and prescriptions invented somewhere else are imposed on the rural community. This situation is not helped by the tendency of international donors and national planners to prefer capital projects with tangible products in lieu of programs with recurrent expenditures (Chambers 1974, p. 29). There is

---

[12] Merely a problem of coordination? As Pressman and Wildavsky rightly remark in their study of efforts to implement American poverty programs (1973, p. 128), "Coordination . . . is a term not for solving problems but for renaming them so that they emerge at the end the same as they were at the beginning."

always a great deal of pressure to maximize the chances that such high-profile demonstration projects will succeed in solving a particular problem. As a result, expert-ridden, well-financed organizations are established on an ad hoc basis, with little attention to how they will perform as the experts leave for home and the problems evolve (Lele 1975, p. 189). An ever-expanding flock of itinerant consultants have just enough time to lecture, but never quite enough to learn the local problems of local organization, during the interval between air flights (Leonard 1977, p. 168). Organization remains a means of doing development to the poor.

Finally, a significant failure of development organization is its inability to sustain a long-term perspective in its problem-solving activities. Development programs often require continuing support of complex functions over time spans that exceed those of annual budgets, staff appointments, or even particular governments.[13] Many entail an explicit sacrifice of present consumption in favor of long-term production gains. The short-term bias of most organizational arrangements typically undercuts such programs even when other factors do not.[14] The tendency of many organizational frameworks to degenerate into (or to recapitulate) patronage-dependency relationships is well known. What is less appreciated is that patronage is almost always based on the expenditure of scarce resources for immediate consumption goods, to the exclusion of longer-term, later-maturing benefits. Sadly, the participatory electoral organizations so desirable on other grounds seem more likely than most to enforce such distortions (Chambers 1974, p. 86; Lele 1975, p. 159).

These shortcomings of existing institutions and administrative systems could be addressed through a variety of specific techniques of social organization. We shall focus on two specific areas of development reorganization in which we believe that feasible and desirable interventions are competing for the attention of real-world policymakers: programs for organizing the rural poor and programs for organizing the facilitators. In each case our goal is to identify the constraints responsible for past and present program failures and to explore the prospects for removing or mitigating these constraints through specific policy interventions.[15]

Organizing the Rural Poor

We have noted the tendency of development to be done to the poor, and we have emphasized the poor's failure to benefit from much of the doing. Of the remedies which have been proposed, none have been so hotly debated as those

---

[13] Frequent shifting of field staff, and the destructive effects this had on program continuity, contributed importantly to the ineffectiveness of development programs in Dharampur, where the Indian Institute of Management, Ahmedabad, carried out a major study (Gupta 1981).

[14] Thus, notwithstanding the many substantive difficulties of the community-development movement, its "failure" may have been as much a result of its not being given the time to accomplish its objectives as of any fundamental inability to do so (Uphoff, Cohen, and Goldsmith 1979, p. 19).

[15] See Lele (1975, p. 177) for a similar approach.

dealing with organization of the poor themselves.[16] The basic notion is simple enough: link the poor into Brewster's "continually widening network of larger, specialized units of collection action," thus helping them better to solve local problems, to make demands on the broader system, and generally to become involved in the choice and execution of development programs. A great variety of organizational techniques have been adopted in pursuit of these goals. Interest-group organizations have linked the poor "horizontally" with other people to form units of collective action; cooperatives, self-help groups, political unions, farmers' associations, and the like are obvious examples. Numerous "vertically" linked organizations have tied poor people directly into the larger socioeconomic structure, with little emphasis on the formation of local groups: some agricultural extension efforts, health clinic and paramedic programs, and attempts to reach the poor with credit and market opportunities suggest the range of those vertically oriented activities.

In this section, we adopt a broad view encompassing both styles of organization and, indeed, including any linkage system in which poor people themselves constitute at least one end of the link.[17] Our goal is to analyze the performance of past efforts to organize the rural poor, and from that analysis to shape practical guidelines for the design of more effective organization policies.

The Social Context

We have argued that the perspectives of academics, analysts, and planners are often distorted by the presumption that they have a clean slate on which to write their policy recommendations. This is particularly evident in studies on organization of the rural poor: "Thus, many scholars . . . tend to treat the existing peasantries as some exotic social type characterised by a basic benevolence and by being relatively undifferentiated. But these assumptions do not obtain in actuality. Socio-economic differentiation and kinship loyalties emerge into prominence among factors affecting differential participation by individuals in . . . organization" (Migot-Adholla, as quoted in Hunter 1971, pp. 2–3). In addition, even the least developed community is likely to possess

---

[16] This and the following section draw heavily on recent work by David Korten. We are deeply indebted to him for his critical comments on our ideas and for letting us see a number of his unpublished papers. Among the published works we have drawn upon are Korten (1979a, 1979c, 1980a, and 1981). In retrospect, we wish that we had also drawn on Mancur Olson's (1971) *Logic of Collective Action*. It has much to say that is relevant to organization of the rural poor; our work is the poorer for not having utilized it.

[17] This is the criterion by which we separate the subject matter of this section from that of the section on "Organizing the Facilitators" (beginning on p. 199). The latter section deals with linkages relevant to the organization of staff activities within the broader context of development administration. Although (it is hoped) these staff activities are ultimately concerned with reaching the poor, the organizational problems of staffing and controlling a large marketing board or extension service are radically different from those of mobilizing a score of peasants into "reciprocally helpful behaviors." The distinction blurs, of course, at the interface where staff meets the poor, and we will discuss this critical area explicitly.

some external linkages through the activities of priests, traders, tax collectors, or agents of civil administrations (Uphoff and Esman 1974).

Efforts to organize the rural poor are in reality efforts to reorganize, to create new patterns of linkage different from the old ones which already bind them. Effective policies for reorganization begin with a recognition of what the existing linkages are, and how they affect the well-being of the rural poor. We shall not attempt to review the extensive sociological and anthropological literature on the structure of rural communities.[18] Restating some central themes of that literature will be appropriate, however, if for no other reason than that they are so commonly overlooked in efforts to formulate policy for rural organization.

The phrase "traditional community structure" covers such a range of specific realities that we hesitate to use it even in the strategic context of the present essay. Nonetheless, for some common organizational features of rural communities in the late-developing countries the term "traditional" remains a practical shorthand. The most important such feature for our present discussion is the dominance of immediate personal ties as a form of organizational linkage. Aid, protection, cooperation, and reciprocal obligations are looked for primarily within groups defined by extended family and kinship ties. Such groups are entered by birth, and given up, if at all, only through drastic wrenching of the social fabric. They thus stand in radical contrast to "modern" groups linked together through specific (but transient and limited) common interests.

In the early days of the cooperative and community-development movements, many argued that the traditional forms of cooperation could be smoothly taken over by cooperation within modern interest groups. Experience has been unkind to this hope. A wide consensus has emerged that interest-group organization "involves different kinds of action, for different purposes, by people in different relationships with each other, from the kinds of action, purpose and relationship enshrined in traditional co-operative activity."[19] The relevant questions for policy have become, When is a transition from traditional modes of organization desirable and feasible? and, How, and to what extent, is that transition to be affected?

Such questions cannot be answered, however, without reference to a second important feature of rural organization: its socioeconomic differentiation. "The rural poor" are not a homogeneous group. In this respect rural communities in the late-developing world are much like communities everywhere: a few individuals, by birth or luck or labor, are much better situated than anyone else. They have accumulated sufficient wealth, power, and skill that these re-

---

[18] Brewster (1967) and Hunter (1969) provide useful reviews of that literature. See also Friedland (1969), Epstein (1973), Migdal (1974), Scott (1976), and Victor Uchendu's discussion of "Social Determinants of Agricultural Change" in Anthony et al. (1979, chap. 6).

[19] See Hunter (1972, p. 193) summarizing papers by Hyden, Migot-Adholla, and others in the Uppsala seminar on "Cooperatives and Rural Development in East Africa"; Widstrand (1970); Crocombe (1971, pp. 161–98).

sources feed on one another, creating more of each. Such privileged positions nearly always come to entail disproportionate ownership of land and other scarce productive assets. Differentiation of a small group distinguished by accumulated assets virtually guarantees differentiation of a much larger group distinguished by the relative lack of such assets—in our case the small farmer and the landless laborers. Between these two extremes lie a variety of other socioeconomic strata with a range of assets, objectives, and organizational connections. The most significant for rural development are those with ties to vigorous outside structures, be they religious, economic, or political in character (Hyden 1970, pp. 61–80).

The problem of elites. Traditional group structures and strong patterns of social differentiation often combine to create a system of organization dominated by a few powerful local elites. The elites are linked to the poor through a variety of patronage/dependency relationships. As we noted earlier, because of the traditional group attitudes ingrained in most members of the community, people look for help to kinfolk, or at most to individuals whom they know personally. But the locally acknowledged stratification ensures that only individuals with wealth or contacts are seen as able to offer such help, especially in situations dealing with the "outside." The poor then tender support of various kinds in exchange for, and expectation of, such patronage. In general, the exchange reinforces the stratification on which it is based. Patronage further secures the privileged position of the elite, while the reciprocal dependency further undermines the position of the poor (Hunter 1969, pp. 38, 70).

Viewed through the glasses of egalitarian ideology, the power of local elites appears to be just one more unmitigated evil visited on the long-suffering rural poor. Such a perspective, however, is both narrow and distorted. The emergence of a local elite can mean many things, among them the beginning of the rural community's ability to impose itself on the outside world. As we shall see later in this chapter, local elites are also an important if imperfect source of home-grown, grass-roots leadership—a resource both scarce and invaluable for promoting the transition from traditional kin-group to modern interest-group forms of local organization.

Political and entrepreneurial elites have performed similar linkage functions throughout Western history, as well as in many of the developing countries. That they have also, and simultaneously, exploited the people they were leading constitutes one of those moral ambiguities of action which make serious debate about organizational issues so difficult and so rare.

About the exploitation itself there can be no question. The evidence from the developing countries is monotonous and depressing. Most attempts to organize the rural poor, if they survive at all, are "captured" by the local elites, who use them to enhance position, power, and wealth more effectively than before. This was the case in early efforts to build political organization at the local level (Leys 1971; Chambers 1974, p. 86). It is the fate of most functioning cooperatives (Inayatullah 1972; Hunter 1971, p. 2) and community-development programs (Holdcroft 1978, p. 15). It almost certainly is the future of most of today's New Directions programs, cast as they are in the old community-development mold (Korten 1980a, pp. 482–85).

Experience with such exploitation has led prudent development workers to conclude that chances for effective local reorganization along interest-group lines will be greatly enhanced wherever social conditions provide a relatively unstratified population, a relatively equitable distribution of assets, or a means of holding elites at least partially accountable in their leadership. This is undoubtedly true as far as it goes; impressive quantitative support is provided by the Asian survey data of Uphoff and Esman (1974). There has been a tendency, however, for some analysts to take the argument a step further. They then suggest that "deparochialization" of the masses, radical land reform, and popular control or removal of the local elite are necessary *preconditions* for effective rural reorganization.

This is a very serious claim. A precondition, in common usage, is something you can't do anything about. Accepting the notion of preconditions therefore means abandoning as untouchable some of the most important goals of rural development, for instance, social modernization, increased equity, and greater popular control. More precisely, it means declaring that these goals are things that incremental policies of local reorganization can't do anything about; it means admitting that people wishing to obtain them should consult revolutionaries, not policymakers. As we argued in chapter 1, revolution may indeed be necessary to improve conditions of the rural poor when social conditions render incremental improvements infeasible. The historical fact that revolutions usually devastate the lives of many people (especially the poor), and that they seldom fulfill their promises, merely emphasizes the sadness and the seriousness of the choice.

In this light, it seems to us that the responsibility of the analyst—indeed his greatest challenge—is to discover and promote programs of incremental improvements which *are* feasible, within the constraints of the social context that the poor actually face. In much of the developing world, this context does include tradition, stratification, and patronage—all of which indeed make it likely that most efforts to reorganize the poor will fail. But for analysts to demand a clean slate, uncluttered by such historical constraints, as a precondition for analysis is a failure of another sort, one which we are tempted to call a failure of nerve.

Adopting a perspective that views considerations of social context as constraints on, rather than preconditions for, reorganization makes a great practical difference. Constraints, we argued in chapter 1, need not be taken as fixed but instead may be slowly relaxed through carefully implemented policies of reform and redesign. The relevant question for policymakers is how to do this gradual relaxing. In general, we concur with those development workers who see this as a two-part problem. First, it is necessary to design local organizations that link rural poor people with one another and with the larger social system. Second, it is necessary to design higher-order support organizations that protect the local groups, help them perform their problem-solving functions, and integrate their needs with those of society at large. We discuss these two facets of the organization-design problem in the remainder of this chapter.

Participation As Investment

Why have efforts to reorganize the poor into nontraditional linkage patterns so often failed to improve rural well-being? The vested interests of local elites doubtless constitute one reason. Another is the hostility or apathy to meaningful reorganization so often displayed by central government administrations. We argued in chapter 1, however, that analysts commonly overrate the contribution of venality to policy failures and underrate the contribution of self-delusion. This is almost certainly true in the contemporary debate on rural reorganization.

There have been numerous sincere efforts to discover more effective ways of organizing the rural poor. These, however, have produced an array of apparently contradictory findings which may confuse policymakers as much as help them. Thus, some analysts conclude that a major obstacle to greater participation by the poor is the existence of strong, antiegalitarian local elites; others conclude that effective participation requires strong, grass-roots leadership, which when present at all usually emerges from the ranks of the elite. Some argue that the appropriate size of the "primary group" of local organization is the village or an even larger unit; others are adamant that only small, relatively homogeneous and "like-minded" groups work well in practice. Cogent analyses are advanced that the most successful local organizations serve multiple functions; yet single-industry institutions like the Indian National Dairy Development Board, the Kenya Tea Development Authority, and the Colombia Coffee Association are widely acknowledged to be among the brightest achievements of development. Many stress that local groups need a multiplicity of linkages with the larger socioeconomic system if they are to be effective; other respected students of local organization argue that the most important goals of local organization often are achieved as soon as a small, primary grouping has been forged. Moreover, they argue, these primary achievements are jeopardized by efforts to build larger, more efficient, more tightly integrated structures. The list of apparent contradictions could be extended indefinitely.

Planning participation. The sad fact is that analysts, planners, and politicians simply *do not know* what kind of local organization is actually in the poor's interests. The delusion that sufficient cogitation can overcome this ignorance—that the "newest direction" will finally be the right direction—may be a greater obstacle than ignorance itself to designing better reorganization programs.

The self-delusion of analysts and advisors manifests itself in many ways. Most obvious is the continued commitment to programs on the basis of their professed form rather than their revealed function. Thus development planners continued to advocate cooperatives modeled on a strict English-Scandinavian Rochdale pattern long after actual performance had demonstrated that this was inappropriate for most developing countries. Why? Because everyone knew that the Rochdale plan was designed with the express intent of ensuring that maximum benefits would flow to coop members (Hunter 1971).

The policy-analysis perspective discussed in chapter 1 suggests that where intellectual cogitation has proved delusory as a problem-resolving technique, greater provision should be made for social interaction—for acting out those parts of the problem most resistant to thinking-through solutions. In particular, to avoid the pitfall of self-delusion the planner needs to supplement intellectual cogitation with interactive signals or feedback through which he can learn when a program is actually benefiting the poor. Many interactive mechanisms suggest themselves once reorganization is perceived as a problem of choosing and learning rather than one of discovering and knowing.[20] We shall focus on one such mechanism, somewhat akin to the concept of induced institutional innovation developed by Davis, North, Hayami, and Ruttan.[21] In essence, we shall propose that the poor themselves signal what is in their interests, by means of *their* decision to invest *their* scarce resource of active participation in a particular local reorganization. Let us consider the implications of this shift in perspective.

The term "participation" appears with great frequency, emotion, and looseness in the development debate. This imprecision may have rhetorical value in certain political contexts, but for purposes of analysis it serves merely to cover up fuzzy or nonexistent thinking. We shall follow Uphoff and Esman (1974, p. 81), using "participation" in its ex ante sense of "before-the-fact involvement in the choices and efforts producing benefits."[22] When we intend the economists' ex post sense of after-the-fact distribution of benefits, we shall say so explicitly.

Ex ante participation in effective organizations can greatly increase the ability of the rural poor to solve local problems and to make demands on the larger social system. In many circumstances, participation in "units of collective action" may be poor people's only organizational alternative to continued dependency on traditional or state patrons. In fact, a consensus approaching dogma has emerged throughout the development community that effective

---

[20] This is a theme that we will return to throughout the present chapter: how to design organizations not as answers to problems of calculation and control but as means of learning, through interaction, how collective social action can be more effectively promoted.

[21] A "theory of institutional innovation" is set forth by Davis and North (1971). This is expanded and applied to the development context in Hayami and Ruttan (1971), Ruttan (1978), and Hayami (1978). Most of this latter work has emphasized the technological component of the innovation opportunity; we stress the personal perspective of the rural "investor." The two views, we believe, are complementary.

[22] Additional useful perspectives on the treatment of "participation" are given in Chambers (1974, pp. 84–88); Lodge (1970); and Huntington and Nelson (1976).

participation by the poor is a *sine qua non* for development strategies seeking major improvements in rural well-being.

The costs of participation. Both political rhetoric and academic arguments on development strategy have tended to treat participation in local organization as a free good, desirable in unlimited quantities. This is particularly evident in the credo of New Directions planning, one of the more recent schools to hold forth on the development stage. The World Bank's sector paper on rural development policy typifies the trend, unreservedly endorsing more "participation by the rural poor in the planning and implementation processes through local government, project advisory committees, cooperatives and other forms of group organization" (World Bank 1975). Nor is the enthusiasm confined to official agencies with political clientele. A thoughtful academic review concludes that "participation should *not* be viewed as a separate program or sector for rural development, but rather as an approach to be integrated as *feasible* in all development activities" (Uphoff, Cohen, and Goldsmith 1979, p. 28; emphasis added).

There is much to support in such sentiments. Nonetheless, the policy-analysis perspective warns us that feasible participation is not necessarily useful or desirable participation. Chambers decries the pernicious influence of "those who, for ideological reasons, or because they are simple-minded, or more commonly from a combination of these causes, reify 'the people' and 'participation' and push them beyond the reach of empirical analysis" (1974, p. 109).

Whatever its cause, the "more is better" view of participation flies in the face of both experience and common sense. Anyone who has been active in a local government council, a committee of concerned citizens, or a community cooperative knows a truth virtually ignored in the current development debate: effective local organization is expensive to those who choose to participate in it.

Concerting reciprocally helpful behaviors requires that individuals join together in social problem-solving efforts. Through some combination of intellectual cogitation and social interaction, these individuals must perform all those tasks of calculation and control we discussed earlier. Linkages of understanding, mutual expectation, and trust must be built and nurtured. Goals must be agreed upon, conflicts settled, and tasks allocated, all within a shifting context of incomplete information, personal rivalries, and individual motivations. Whatever else is involved, organization therefore requires substantial and continuing investments of time, energy, and personal freedom of action on the part of participants.[23] This is surely one reason why, even in modernized

---

[23] There is nothing novel about our emphasis on time and energy as scarce resources (see especially March and Olsen [1976, p. 14 and passim] and also Becker [1965]). There has, however, been remarkably little attention given to this constraint in the burgeoning literature on community participation.

Western societies with multiple opportunities for local organization, studies show that most people choose not to participate at all.[24] It should not be surprising to find even lower rates of participation within the traditional societies of the developing world.

Time, energy, and freedom from unproductive obligations are among the very few resources that the rural poor possess. The notion that investment of these scarce resources in local organization is always or often a rational choice reflects the same peculiar view of reality which can't understand why rural women don't spend more time at home-economics lectures. The behavior of the poor themselves suggests that they suffer from no such delusion. On the contrary, the actual choices that poor people make concerning which local organizations to participate in, and how much participation to offer them, have much the look of rational investment decisions. In short, poor people invest their participation when they believe it will secure them valuable benefits not otherwise available at comparable cost, time, and risk.

We shall see that many of the historical failures and successes of local organization efforts begin to make sense, and many of the apparent contradictions mentioned earlier can be resolved, when viewed from this investment perspective. Moreover, the notion that the poor are investing participation in organization suggests the relevance of questions familiar from capital-investment situations: What are the opportunity costs of committing this scarce resource to a particular use? What risks do they run and what returns do they expect from the contemplated commitment? What other means do they have for achieving comparable returns? Above all, the investment perspective emphasizes that it is poor people themselves who make the investment choice, who decide whether a proposed program of local organization offers sufficient incentives to attract their personal resources of time, energy, and freedom of action away from other urgent and competing tasks.

The poor as investors. Our perspective of participation as investment does not "reify the people," nor is its admitted simplicity altogether simple-minded. We do not assume that the poor make smart investments. We do not argue that participation is always in everyone's—or even anyone's—best interests. We argue only that it is poor people's choices of which organizations they will participate in, not the analysts' discoveries of "correct" organizational designs, which result in action on the social front. Moreover, though the choices made by the poor may not turn out well, they can be and are made on the basis of available perceptions. The analysts' discoveries, in contrast, require data and understanding that do not exist now and are unlikely to become

[24] The present infatuation with participation is such that many will doubt this statement. Consider, however, that comparative studies show the United States to be among the most participatory of modernized societies (Almond and Verba 1965, chaps. 5, 10). Even in America, however, less than half the people bother to vote in local elections, less than a third are active in a single organization dealing with community problems, less than one in five has even contacted a local government official about an issue, less than one in seven has ever formed a group to resolve a local problem (Verba and Nie 1972, p. 31).

available in the foreseeable future. Moreover, what policymakers want—what they believe to be in the poor's interests, what they perceive as "meaningful" organization—is largely irrelevant. Participation is "owned" by the poor. Experience shows that the investment of effective participation cannot be commanded by policymakers but must instead be induced. The requirement of effective policymaking for local organizations is therefore not omniscience but entrepreneurship: the ability to recognize and design programs capable of mobilizing participation; the ability to abandon as unviable and ill-advised programs unable to attract that investment.

"Entrepreneurial" policymaking will be imperfect, like all its alternatives. But in a world of inevitable trial and error, it provides a relatively efficient way of learning when you have guessed wrong. As in the capital-investment analog, the self-proclaimed (or self-deluded) "goodness" of the entrepreneur's proposal is immaterial. What counts is how attractive the proposal appears to the investors, and how able and willing they are to mobilize sufficient resources for its effective support.

We next propose some entrepreneurial guidelines for the design of local organizations which should be better able to attract investment of participation from the rural poor.

Attractiveness of Benefits

One of the most obvious lessons of past experience is that the rural poor will invest active participation only in an organization that is responsive to their most intensely felt needs (Hunter 1971). More specifically, they will invest only in organizations that offer highly desirable and tangible benefits not otherwise obtainable at similar cost, time, and risk. In part this is due to the opportunity costs of participation discussed earlier. In part it is because only such needs and benefits provide sufficient force to overcome the bonds and habits of traditional organization (Lodge 1970, pp. 146–47).

Available evidence suggests that the "needs" that most readily induce the active participation of the rural poor are related to production, in particular capital formation and income enhancement. For example, the justifiably famous Anand Milk Producers' Union (later the Indian National Dairy Development Board) grew from acute dissatisfaction of local producers with low and fluctuating prices offered by existing commercial markets (Korten 1980a).

Nonetheless, sufficiently urgent consumption-related needs can also serve the mobilization function. An excellent example is Thailand's Community Based Family Planning Cooperative, another of the successful organizations cited by Korten (1980a). In this case, a centrally organized operation identified a strongly felt need—the desire of rural women for a reliable means of birth control—and set out to help provide access to the required technology. Little "selling" of the benefits was necessary, though innovative means of enhancing the acceptability of those benefits obviously enhanced the program's success. That success has been substantial: by 1979 women from more than sixteen thousand villages were participating through the regular purchase and use of birth control pills.

The requirement for intensely felt local needs to mobilize active participation is all the more evident when we consider the many experiments in organization where local perceptions of need (or changes in those perceptions) have been ignored. The latter situation occurred in many previously colonial countries during their time of independence. Active local groups had been organized around intensely felt needs to be rid of colonial administration. Once independence was obtained, participation in these groups waned or fractured into smaller conflicting factions built around new, less unifying priorities. Another example is the cooperatives that have failed to attract the active participation of landless laborers or subsistence farmers because the services they offered were confined to production loans and marketing aid (Korten 1980a, p. 481). Many "cooperatives" have not even pretended a concern with responding to local needs, seeking instead to exercise control over distribution and sale of goods and to promote government directives. The pitfalls of such organizational designs appear obvious but are nonetheless still widely ignored. Korten summarizes a number of critical studies when he decries New Directions programs for their continued "reliance for the planning and implementation of 'participative' development on centralized bureaucratic organizations which have little capacity to respond to diverse community-defined needs" (1980a, p. 483).

Ironically, a consequence of the emphasis in U.S. aid programs on New Directions and "basic human needs" has been a tendency to restrict allocations for irrigation, roads, bridges, and other infrastructure projects that often rank high among the felt needs of people in rural areas. Moreover, a very significant role of local organizations or other participatory mechanisms is to enable local groups to influence decisions about the design and location of roads, irrigation works, and other infrastructure projects in the light of local knowledge and priorities.[25]

Planning benefits. Many analysts have come to identify the problem of designing participative organizations in terms of "bottom-up" versus "top-down" initiatives. Needless to say, "bottom-up" is good, reflecting the needs of the people, while "top-down" is bad, reflecting the needs of the bureaucrats. There is just enough truth in this view to make it rhetorically attractive. Once again, however, the willingness to let ideology masquerade as analysis has hindered rather than helped the policy debate.

Organizing from below, as we shall see later on, often results in both ineffi-

---

[25] Two recent papers by Tendler are pertinent to these issues. One of the papers notes that "New-Directions critics say that infrastructure projects do not have a direct impact on the rural poor, in comparison to projects in the areas of rural health, nutrition and agriculture" (Tendler 1979b, p. v). The other paper emphasizes that an additional advantage of decentralized management of rural roads projects is that it facilitates the adoption of labor-using construction methods (Tendler 1979a, pp. 42–59).

ciencies and grave inequities; the organizers, after all, are more likely to be the local elite than the poor. Conversely, initiatives from above have produced some of the most successful and participative local organizations in development history.

To return to a theme we broached at the beginning of this chapter, effective design of organizations is more complex than the dichotomous isms of popular debate allow. The critical issue is not from where the initiative comes but whether it in fact promotes the "fit" of locally felt needs, available technology, and organizational means. Sometimes, as in our dairy example, that initiative will come from "below" as a spontaneous outpouring of realized need and recognized potential. Other times, as Chambers (1974) has emphasized, a community-development or other "top-down" initiative will be required to help local groups identify and articulate their needs.

Our earlier discussion of means-ends relationships in action programs puts this particular experience of development into a larger perspective. The "intensely felt needs" we refer to in this chapter, like the general "preferences" we referred to in chapter 1, are not tangible and immutable entities waiting to serve as passive guides to action. Rather, they are the product of a continuing interaction between what people believe they want and what they believe they can get. Belief and perception are key elements here. The high-yield varieties of wheat and rice made available in the Green Revolution powerfully altered farmers' perceptions of what they might get from research and from their fields. In this context, it has become fashionable among certain analysts to bemoan the conservatism of the rural poor and the aversity to risk of the peasant farmer. In other words, poor people have been known to act as though when things get worse you starve or lose your land or get shaken down by the big men, while when things get better it is only a matter of time until they get worse again.[26] It is in this context that the notion of "an intensely felt need" must be perceived. If the poor do not look on an organization proposal or a new technological gadget with great enthusiasm, their "conservatism" may well have some justification. At a minimum, it is a reality with which a successful effort to induce the poor's participation must cope. The challenge of designing local organization—from top *or* bottom—is to understand how risks and uncertainties color perceptions of needs and how opportunities can be made more tangible. Thus we shall emphasize shortly the important role that convincing and realistic demonstration projects have to play in mobilizing participation in all manner of local organizations. More generally, the changing and relative nature of "intensely felt needs" suggests that perceptions of feasibility as well as desirability are relevant to the individual investing in participation, and therefore to the design of organizations seeking to call forth that participa-

---

[26] This view of life is not unique to poor people in today's developing countries. Leys reminds us of Stendhal's view that an average Frenchman's hierarchy of needs in the days before the Revolution was "(a) not to be killed; and (b) for a good warm coat" (Leys 1971, p. 110).

tion from the rural poor. One of the most important of these feasibility considerations turns out to involve the creation of harmony concerning the objectives the proposed organization will pursue.

Harmony of Objectives

Organizations of the rural poor promote collective social action by, among other things, surfacing and settling conflicts among potential participants. When this capability is lacking or underdeveloped, as is too often the case, "local organizations can become overpoliticized, immobilized by factionalism, with rural development objectives displaced by struggles for local power and control" (Uphoff and Esman 1974, p. 82). Our investment perspective emphasizes the costs that the surfacing and settling of conflicts imposes on an organization's prospective participants: if too much conflict requires too much time, energy, or commitment to resolve, then active participation is unlikely to be mobilized. In this section, we argue that the rural poor are more inclined to make sustained investments of participation in organizations that embody a relative harmony of objectives, that is, organizations in which most participants agree on what the organization should be doing. We focus on the specific choices of organization design which promote this harmony through effective and efficient resolution of potential conflicts.

A first step towards understanding the nature of conflict and harmony in rural organizations is to recognize that different people have different needs and priorities. We noted earlier how often this truism is rejected by a rhetoric of development planning which portrays the rural poor as a homogeneous group with undifferentiated objectives.[27] Even within the broad socioeconomic groups we described in our discussion of social conduct, however, the reality is that individual people will share some interests but not others. Two landless laborers, to take a common developing-world example, may agree on goals of land reform but support different political factions. Two small farmers may agree on matters of access to credit but disagree over access to water because one has it and the other needs it. Two women may stand united on the need for markets in which to sell their household produce but, especially if they belong to different age groups, may have radically different views on the need for family-planning support. The list obviously could be continued. In general, any effort to link people into units of collective action will carry with it the potential for conflict as individual members seek to bend the organization to their own interests and to resist the corresponding activities of other members.

Choice of membership and function. Two design choices are particu-

[27] One of the most important and obvious differences, of course, is that between elites and nonelites. We will defer consideration of the role played by elites in the creation and resolution of conflict until later (p. 193). This is not because we underestimate the significance of that role; rather, we wish to emphasize that the problems and costs of conflict resolution must be borne by an organization even when there are no elites complicating the local picture. The ubiquitous need to build harmony of objectives among participants who differ in their interests, if not their socioeconomic status, is often overlooked when elites are viewed as the essence of the conflict problem.

larly important determinants of the kind and degree of conflict which actually arises over a particular organization's activities. The first is the choice of membership: Who will be included in, and who excluded from, the organization? The second is the choice of function: What benefits will be pursued by the organization, and what benefits will be left to other organizations or to individual pursuit? These choices are interrelated. Effective conflict resolution does not require that all members of a particular organization share a common view of what should be done in the world at large. Rather, members need only to reach reasonably harmonious agreement on who should do what within the limited range of activities which the organization that links them chooses to pursue. If the who and the what of organization design are carefully matched, the amount of conflict with which participants must contend can be kept within tolerable bounds. This relationship is sketched as a hypothetical example in figure 5.2, which can be used to follow the historical evidence that follows.

		Function (What is done)					
		i	ii	iii	iv	v	. . .
Membership (Who belongs)	A	+	+	+	+	−	. . .
	B	+	+	+	−	−	. . .
	C	+	−	+	+	+	. . .
	D	+	−	−	−	−	. . .
	:	:	:	:	:	:	. : .

Figure 5.2. Harmony of Objectives.

Note: This portrays the range of people (or of relatively homogeneous groups) present in a given community, and in range of activities, functions, or benefits about which at least one of them feels sufficiently strongly to invest participation in an organization committed to its attainment. In a particular instance the "people," who we have labeled "A, B, C, D, . . . " might include (groups of) small farmers, landless laborers, local merchants, unmarried women, and so on. The "functions," which we have labeled "i, ii, iii, iv, v, . . . " might include building a tubewell, providing family planning services, providing access to markets, and so forth. In this simple illustration, the entries in the matrix indicate merely whether a particular person (or group) does (+), or does not (−), desire the benefits sought through a potential function sufficiently intensely to consider investing participation in an organization that adopted that function. A particular organization can be described (or designed) in terms of which rows and which columns—which members and which functions—it includes. This in turn defines the organization in terms of which cells of the matrix it encompasses. Where functions and members are chosen so that all cells encompassed by the organization contain "+" marks, everyone in the organization wants it to do exactly the same things and total harmony over the organization's objectives will prevail. On the other hand, where functions and members are chosen so that some cells encompassed by the organization contain "−" marks, at least some members may be asked to support the pursuit of benefits they do not particularly desire. Other things being equal, we would expect the latter kind of organization to embody more conflict and less harmony over its objectives, to require more onerous investments in calculation and control of its collective actions, and to be a less effective mobilizer of sustained participation by the rural poor.

Conflict problems can arise, as we have said, when more different kinds of people and more different kinds of functions are encompassed within the same organization. Not surprisingly, organizations that are successful in attracting the participation of the rural poor have often limited conflicts over objectives by limiting membership to relatively homogeneous groups sharing both common identity and common needs.[28] The limited internal conflict of such homogeneous groups was a key characteristic of the few successful organizations identified by a United Nations survey of cooperative efforts in Asia (UNRISD 1975; see also Hunter 1978b, chap. 4). The Cornell Committee on Rural Development reached a similar conclusion from its broader survey of a variety of Asian organizations (Uphoff and Esman 1974, p. 68); evidence from East Africa points in the same direction (Hunter 1971, p. 10).

A particularly illuminating example is that of the Bangladesh Rural Advancement Committee (BRAC).[29] Initial attempts to include both the landed and the landless poor within one organization were counterproductive; efforts to create a single community center foundered on underlying factionalisms unperceived by program designers. Having learned from these mistakes, BRAC changed its approach and is now enjoying heightened success with organization policies which restrict membership to specific target groups defined in terms of common needs.[30]

Conflict can also be limited by restriction of the organization's functions to pursuit of a single, narrowly defined benefit. This in fact has been the design strategy in some of the most spectacularly successful local organizations in the history of development: the single-industry, vertically integrated cooperatives. The Malaysian Rubber Association, the Kenya Tea Development Authority, the Colombia Coffee Association, and the Indian National Dairy Development Board are illustrative of the range of locations and activities to which the single-function design has been successfully applied. Significantly, Korten (1980a) points out in his analysis of the Indian dairy cooperatives that the membership of such organizations often includes individuals from different social (caste) and economic backgrounds who represent a variety of different, even conflicting interests. Their cooperative organization operates effectively precisely because members have agreed that it shall function only in pursuit of that one benefit they all desire (good, steady prices for their milk) and shall not attempt the difficult calculations and controls which would be required to resolve conflicts on other matters.[31] The large single-industry organizations are only the most obvious example of this phenomenon; as Hunter (1971) reminds us, there are undoubtedly thousands of less well-known or unreported instances of a few community members banding together through informal

---

[28] In table 5.2, this means confining membership to a single row, such as A.

[29] This account of BRAC is from Korten (1980a).

[30] For example, those who sell their labor to third parties.

[31] In table 5.2, an example of such an organization would be one including groups A, B, and C in its membership, and function iii as its only activity.

bargaining to install a tubewell or to build a cattle dip, despite their inability to agree on a wider range of community issues.

Two caveats. Adopting a single function or a homogeneous membership admittedly represents an extreme (and extremely successful) solution to the problem of harmonious organization design. Indeed, Uphoff and Esman conclude from their survey of Asian experience that the adoption of multiple functions often can help organizations "to insure their viability and capacity to integrate diverse services" (1974, p. xix).[32] Moreover, Uphoff and Esman suggest that if circumstances temporarily stop the organization from performing one of these functions, it might persist by continuing to attract participation through its continuing performance of its other functions. These arguments do not necessarily conflict with our view of the importance of harmony in organizational objectives. Again, it is not limitation of membership or function per se which is needed to reduce conflict. What is needed is a "fit" between the two that produces no more conflict than the organization is currently able to resolve in an efficient manner.

Two caveats should be borne in mind when considering the evidence cited to demonstrate the feasibility of multiple-function organizations. First, on closer inspection many such organizations turn out to be composed of relatively small "suborganizations" of restricted membership and function. It is within these latter classically harmonious designs that most of the actual collective activity takes place. To cite just one example, in the Sarvodaya Shramadana Movement of Sri Lanka, "the preferred village level organization includes individual groups for youth, mothers, farmers, children, pre-school, elders, and for persons with special education and skills" (Korten 1980a, p. 486). Only at higher levels—with access to professional administrative support for the required calculation and control—are these groups integrated into a multiple-function, relatively open-membership organization.

The second caveat is an essentially methodological one. Scholars who, like Uphoff and Esman, conduct large-scale, "cross-sectional" surveys necessarily sacrifice a temporal perspective on the dynamics of specific organizations for a comparative perspective on the many different kinds of organization that exist at the time of the survey. The two perspectives can be complementary. But it is important to realize that most of the organizations observed in a cross-sectional analysis will be relatively mature and established ones rather than those that have lost (or are still fighting) their battles to attract and hold participants. We will argue later on that many mature organizations have sensibly and naturally diversified their functional base after getting started and gaining experience from a narrow—and often single-function—beginning. In contrast, scholars who follow the birth, evolution, and survival or demise of par-

---

[32] In terms of table 5.2, they are suggesting that the individuals or groups represented by A and C could build an organization around functions iii and iv without, in principle, producing any conflict at all.

ticular local organizations are often able to identify the design features responsible for early failures, which the cross-sectional-survey people hardly ever see.

There seems little doubt that one of the most common causes of such early demise is too much unresolved conflict caused by too many different groups trying to accomplish too many different things under a single organizational roof. On the other hand, detailed studies which are able to observe particular local organizations in their infancy are not likely to know what kind of functional diversification is eventually undertaken by the few that grow to maturity. Those who study the evolutionary dynamics of particular organizations are therefore least likely to observe the "facts" that the cross-sectional scholars are most likely to observe, and vice versa. No wonder they seem to disagree.

Common to both sorts of scholarship, however, is the basic finding that pursuit of multiple functions carries potential benefits *and* potential liabilities for an organization. Although historical experience with local organizations does not let us resolve the implied trade-off unambiguously, it strongly suggests that the success of multiple-function organizations depends on their relative sophistication or experience in resolving conflict *and* on their ability to restrict membership sufficiently that the total conflict encompassed by the organization does not overly tax whatever conflict-resolving capability it has been able to build.

The design of harmonious organizations. The view we have just advanced suggests that attempts to start local organizations that simultaneously encompass a broad base of membership and a wide variety of functions are likely to fail. This expectation is confirmed by, and sheds light on, the previously mentioned failures of the community-development movement. Many factors were surely at work in this failure, but community development was precisely an attempt to build an organization that included all members of the community, and functioned in pursuit of all of their needs. It is hardly surprising that the organizations were unable to perform the monumental tasks of calculation and control which their choice of membership and function forced on them, or that so many of them disintegrated in the face of conflicts they were unable to resolve. That so much was expected of community-development organizations and that so little time was allowed for them to build up the necessary organizational skills and attitudes no doubt also contributed to the movement's demise.[33]

The need for time to learn conflict-resolving (and other) skills and attitudes is a theme which we will consider at the end of this chapter. The difficulty—the virtual impossibility—of moving the rural poor away from their traditional kin-group organizations by means of open membership, multiple-function designs is clearest, however, when we consider the history of local political organ-

---

[33] In fact, many of the activities have continued with new labels. In the Philippines a Department of Local Government and Community Development continues to operate. In addition, many of the rural trainers and community organizers who are performing effectively in other programs in the Philippines acquired their skills as community-development field workers.

izations in the developing world. Here, the ideological commitment to open membership and comprehensive functions runs directly counter to the practical need for effective and efficient conflict resolution. Local political organizations did indeed enjoy a certain amount of success in the previously colonial developing countries during their transitions to independence. In these cases, however, it was precisely because a single, universally desired function (replacing foreign rule) temporarily dominated all others that the organizations could temporarily function.[34] Typically, once this function was no longer necessary, its unifying influence dissipated, and the latent conflicts of an open-membership, multiple-function organization began to surface. Factions broke away, ineffectiveness was rampant, and the local political organization declined in importance as a technique of collective social action throughout much of the previously colonial developing world (Chambers 1974, pp. 86–88).[35]

Simplicity of Technique

However harmonious the objectives of an organization, there remains the problem of designing means by which those objectives can be realized. Marx saw this as a problem of taking "from each according to his abilities" and giving "to each according to his needs." Others, from the author of Psalm 62 to Adam Smith to Mao Tse-tung, saw it in much the same way but substituted *work* for *needs*.

Regardless of ideology, resolving questions of who gives and who gets what in a social group requires effective organizational techniques for calculation and control. The specific techniques employed may involve exchange, hierarchy, polyarchy, or bargaining, combined to provide all manner of mixes of social interaction and intellectual cogitation. Once again, however, our perspective of participation as investment suggests that calculation and control—whatever their form—will be more or less expensive activities for an organization's members. We therefore expect—and find—that people are more inclined to invest their participation in organizations with relatively simple demands for calculation and control.

Two related features of organization militate against simplicity of calculation and control. The first and more obvious is large size: the more people

[34] For example, function i in table 5.2.
[35] We shall have more to say on the reasons for this decline in subsequent sections. The Tanzanian *ujamaa* movement is frequently cited as an exception or even a counter-example to the kind of argument we have advanced here. We hope this is true, though if so, it will be the exception which proves the rule. The planners of *ujamaa* explicitly staked its hopes for success on (1) an ability to redistribute access to basic resources and benefits in such a way that all members of the village "family" *do* have identical interests and minimal occasion for conflict over the *ujamaa's* objectives, and (2) a gradual process through which individual villagers learn the admittedly difficult tasks of calculating and controlling communal activities in a manner satisfactory to all participants (Tanzania 1969). No one will disagree that achieving these goals, if possible at all, has been an exceedingly difficult, time-consuming, risky, and expensive endeavor. Whether *ujamaa's* highly politicized and ambitious attempt at reorganization has actually succeeded in bringing increased benefits to a large fraction of the rural poor is a question we leave to others.

engaged in a social enterprise, the more complex is the problem of assigning, coordinating, monitoring, and legitimating their individual responsibilities and rewards. The second is what might be called "communality": when participants contribute their labor and other resources to a common productive activity, calculation and control are more complex than when each individual's contribution is immediately and directly reflected in his own individual reward. Different techniques of organization impose different costs on, and yield different benefits to, participants as size and communality increase. The challenge for designers of reorganization programs is to design combinations of techniques which fit effectively with the size, communality, and other requirements of a particular local situation.

Small and selfish organizations. Calculation and control obviously pose their simplest demands within the simplest form of organization: the individual acting alone and in his own self-interest. Whole philosophies have been based on this theme, and some improvements in rural well-being can indeed be accomplished with such minimal formal organization. This, of course, is the great practical advantage of the family farm. We noted in chapter 3 that because of the distinctive characteristics of the agricultural production process, hard work, initiative, and the "on-the-spot supervisory decisions" so pervasive in farming are generally performed better when the farm unit's work force has a direct interest in the outcome. It has also been emphasized that in agriculture "the small proprietary or family firm" tends to promote more efficient and more rapid capital formation and technological change (Raup 1967, pp. 273–77, 293–97).

Frequently, however, the gadgets and activities that can improve the well-being of the rural poor exhibit some degree of increasing returns to scale; agricultural research, crop processing, irrigation systems, and political power are only a few of the benefits not accessible to the individual acting alone.[36] The challenge of organization design is to balance the benefits that can be obtained through larger, more complicated organizations against the costs of calculation and control which such complexity tends to impose.

Organizations comprising only a few members have in fact been reasonably successful when they have designed their function to require little communal activity. Joint use of a small tubewell or a low-lift pump is a good example. Even in such cases, however, problems arise, especially with respect to ensuring satisfactory maintenance.

When participants' contributions and benefits take on a significant communal character, even small groups face serious problems in seeking to form and sustain an effective organization. There are instances in which a few people have organized for the communal purchase and use of a tractor, a boat, or

---

[36] We do not imply that potential benefits continue to increase with increasing scale of social enterprise; in most cases, there is in fact a size above which further growth yields little but trouble. This does not change the fact that technical and other factors militate in favor of groups large enough to incur significant costs of calculation and control.

a thresher and thereby radically improved their own well-being. Our impression, however, is that for every such success there have been many failures— many instances in which the available techniques for calculating and controlling proved inadequate to the task at hand. This does not suggest that small communal organizations should be discouraged in the future, but only that such organizations are in general marginally viable and more likely than not to fail. Less organizationally expensive means of improving rural well-being should also be considered. The emergence of commercial tractor contractors in many developing countries is a notable example of a simple commercial solution to sharing the use of a "lumpy" piece of equipment.

Large and selfish organizations. Tractor contractors typically remain small, but frequently the commercial operations carried out by private firms are characterized by significant economies of scale. We note shortly that large-scale public enterprises created to perform essentially commercial functions such as marketing of agricultural products or the distribution of credit or inputs commonly resort to a "multi-tier" form of organization. In many countries, however, this type of commercial operation is often performed by large private firms engaged in the marketing and processing of agricultural products or the manufacture and distribution of farm inputs. In these instances, calculation and control are accomplished by exchange techniques, specifically market and price mechanisms. The internal control and management of these private firms is hierarchical, thus simplifying problems of coordination. Private profit-maximizing firms of this nature have significant advantages in being relatively flexible and capable of making decisions promptly in response to changing conditions affecting costs of inputs or product prices.

In discussing the role of markets and prices in chapter 6, we note that the results obtained by relying on a market system as a means of calculation and control are often criticized, especially in relation to the equity goal of social policy. A major justification offered for promoting some of the "multi-tier" cooperative and public organizations discussed in later sections is that they protect small farmers from exploitation by large private organizations. There are, however, some important practical arguments for utilizing the organizational capacity and technical and entrepreneurial skills that are often available in private firms. Even in late-developing countries, competition among private firms frequently limits their monopoly power. Lele reports, for example, that "most price exploitation that has been observed in Ethiopian markets is covert, through false weights and measures, rather than overt"; and this implies that farmers "have the potential to enjoy real bargaining power" (1975, p. 114).[37] Therefore, the most appropriate government action may be to facilitate more effective performance of a market system and to reduce the scope for

[37] Lele (1974, p. 430) cites 15 marketing studies carried out in Africa, Asia, and Latin America "which indicate that, contrary to general belief, the private marketing systems in L.D.C.s are, by and large, highly competitive and operate efficiently given the conditions in which they function."

exploitation by measures such as the introduction of standard weights and measures, dissemination of adequate and reliable price information at all levels of the marketing system, and improving means of communication and transportation. There are two cogent arguments for governments to emphasize facilitative and regulatory actions rather than to attempt to replace private firms in carrying out essentially commercial operations. First, government organizations such as a grain marketing board tend to be relatively inefficient, in part because of the need for bureaucratic regulations to limit graft and corruption. Such regulations increase administrative costs and reduce flexibility. The second and more general argument is that in a situation in which administrative manpower is in short supply, government programs should be concentrated on those types of activities "which are not likely to be undertaken without public intervention" (Lele 1975, p. 191).

Most controversial of all is the role of large transnational (multinational) corporations (TNCs). Such corporations are, of course, very large. They possess significant economies of scale because of the resources that they can devote to R&D, their market connections and experience in advertising and other techniques of market promotion, and their easy access to international capital markets. In the case of technologies that are inherently large-scale and complex, such as the manufacture of nitrogen fertilizers, TNCs can play a very useful role in the design and construction of efficient, low-cost plants.[38] Particularly in the case of a perishable commodity such as bananas, TNCs have been highly successful in organizing the assembly, packaging, transportation, marketing, and quality-control functions involved in exporting to overseas markets. (We defer consideration of the advantages and disadvantages of agricultural exports for developing countries until chapter 6.)

Several significant arguments against the role of TNCs need to be emphasized. Such firms often transfer technologies that are inappropriate to the factor proportions prevailing in less developed countries. However, this is often in response to economic policies and price distortions which also encourage domestic firms to choose inappropriately capital-intensive technologies. Perhaps equally important is the tendency on the part of a number of TNCs to promote inappropriate products.[39] Finally, the sheer size and "multinationality" of many TNCs poses problems because of their economic and political power.[40]

---

[38] It is noteworthy that in recent years the People's Republic of China has contracted with several TNCs to build very large nitrogen-fertilizer factories to take advantage of the dramatic cost-reducing developments that have occurred since 1963, when the centrifugal compressor was introduced. There are, of course, instances in which companies have persuaded governments to contract for the construction of relatively small, inefficient factories. For example, a 50-percent subsidy on fertilizer in Tanzania simply offsets the high cost of producing fertilizer in the uneconomic plant built to supply the country's limited market for nitrogen fertilizer (ILO 1978, p. 70).

[39] A favorite example is the virtually worldwide spread of Coca Cola. The most unfortunate example, however, is the vigorous promotion of infant formulas for bottle-feeding, which has contributed to the decline of breast-feeding in many areas, with the adverse consequences that we noted in chapter 4.

[40] For more extended discussion of transnational corporations, see Vernon (1977) and Lall and Streeten (1977).

Large and communal organizations. What happens to local organizations which are not only large but also communal? We would expect such organizations to impose even higher costs of calculation and control on potential participants and to run even higher risks of failure. From the few hard data available, this indeed seems to be the case. Uphoff and Esman, for example, point out that successful communal organizations in Asia comprise few enough people that an informal "bargaining" through shared knowledge of performance and special circumstances suffices as a technique for calculation and control. Their survey data suggest that within groups of thirty to fifty families there is often an effective trade-off between the increasing returns to scale of organized communal action and the rising costs of organization which larger groups entail (Uphoff and Esman 1974, p. 68).

A similar result emerges from China's experiments with different scales of farm organization. Early efforts to build communal groups at the commune and brigade level experienced crippling problems of performance and incentive. This experience led to the present, apparently more satisfactory design, in which production teams of thirty to forty families carry most of the burden of calculating and controlling who gets and gives what.[41] Above this scale, organizational functions are carried out by more formal arrangements which do not impose direct costs on local participants.

Additional relevant evidence comes from a survey of successful irrigation communes in the Philippines conducted by de los Reyes and her colleagues (1979, as cited in Bagadion and Korten 1980). Communal organizations of water users have existed for centuries in the Philippines, uniting people in complex social functions which serve from less than ten to as many as four thousand hectares. Most organizations, however, cover an area of less than one hundred hectares and involve fewer than fifty families. The studies show that irrigation organizations in this small size range often prosper without much in the way of formal administrative structure; again, informal personal knowledge of individual performance and circumstance appears sufficient to perform the relatively simple tasks of calculation and control required. This was not the case for groups with an area of more than one hundred hectares or involving more than fifty families. These groups generally had to subdivide into smaller local groups and to develop formal hierarchical structures in order to perform their more complex tasks of calculation and control without imposing an unacceptable burden of organization on participants.[42]

The examples just cited suggest that one practical means of making and

---

[41] For a masterful account of the theory and practice of rural organization by China's Communist party, see Schurmann (1968, chap. 7 and esp. pp. 471–92). For more recent summary accounts, see Timmer (1976), Chinn (1978), and Schran (1980).

[42] Of successful irrigation organizations covering more than one hundred hectares, 90 percent have formal organization structures and 60 percent have also subdivided into smaller groups; of organizations covering fewer than fifty hectares, less than 25 percent have formal structures and less than 5 percent have subdivided (Bagadion and Korten 1980, table 2, citing de los Reyes et al 1979).

keeping organizations attractive to potential investors is to keep them small. This is not as academic a notion as it may at first appear. Hunter (1972), for example, argues that the greatest return *to the poor* on their participation investment often comes as a result of forming interest groups of a few cooperating individuals, linked through informal bargaining procedures. Further increases in size beyond the initial primary group often benefit leaders and administrators performing support functions more than they benefit the poor themselves.

It remains true, however, that technological or political factors often force an organization to grow beyond the size at which calculation and control can be handled by techniques relying on shared knowledge and bilateral bargaining between individual participants. What design alternatives then remain?

Design alternatives: polyarchy and hierarchy. One common response to this situation has been to adopt polyarchical techniques of organization, in which formal leadership by a few accountable individuals is used to simplify participants' problems of calculation and control. Though this approach has worked on a limited scale, we noted earlier that in much of the developing world, local political organizations have not provided a particularly effective means of organizing the interests of the poor. Almost everywhere that local political organizations have survived, their original polyarchical relationships have drifted towards exchange, hierarchy, and thinly disguised recapitulation of the patronage/dependency design of traditional organization (Chambers 1974, pp. 86–88). Such techniques work to the extent that relatively inexpensive participation—for instance in the form of voting—can be exchanged for benefits desired by the individual participants, and available to the local elite. But the superficiality of the resulting "organization" is clearly revealed when the political leadership can no longer provide the accustomed benefits—perhaps because a centrally administered aid program no longer provides the resources that had been used for this purpose. Time after time, in country after country, as the dole dries up, the "participation" in the local organization disappears, leaving little but dependency in its wake.

A more commonly effective design for large-scale enterprises invokes "multi-tier" organization (Uphoff and Esman 1974, p. 69; Korten 1979a). The lowest tier comprises the same like-minded groups of poor people to which we have been referring. These "primary" groups are characterized by members' predominant commitment to activities other than organizing and by their consequent preference for those techniques of calculation and control which entail a minimum investment of their time and effort: informal shared knowledge and bilateral bargaining. Above this primary level, one or more hierarchical tiers may be added to handle inter-group tasks of calculation and control. The design and management of these upper-tier organizations is discussed at length in the last section of this chapter (p. 199ff.). The upper tiers are distinguished from the primary, or lowest, tier by their participants' commitment to careers as professional organizers and their (consequent?) preference for efficient and effective techniques of organizing large numbers of people. Hierarchical and, more rarely, political techniques are their preferred means of calculation and control.

The problems of multi-tier support structures are many, and we will discuss them in a moment. Nonetheless, multi-tier support structures can perform important functions, not the least of which is relieving participants in the primary groups of the burden of directly negotiating responsibilities, rights, and obligations with all other members of the organization. When the multi-tier, hierarchical structure can also actually deliver attractive benefits to the primary-group members, and when it can achieve a suitable harmony of objectives, it therefore has real attractions as a means of inducing participation of the poor in inherently large and potentially complex organizations.

Design alternatives: limited communal obligations. The costs of participation in local organization can be mitigated not only by limiting the size of the primary group but also by adopting functions and designs which reduce the amount of explicit calculation and control required for allocating communal tasks and benefits. Once again, this is an area in which ideologically grounded self-delusion of advisors and planners has often clashed with the practical self-interest of the poor themselves. Reporting on another aspect of the Philippine irrigation studies referred to earlier, Alfonso (1981) describes a typical example of such a futile misunderstanding. Engineers working with the local farmer group knew that one irrigation turnout from the main system per every forty to fifty hectares was the most efficient design in a resource-scarce world. They were therefore bewildered and unsympathetic to the "wasteful" farmers' demands for a much more expensive design providing one turnout per farmer. The engineers did not recognize that for the farmers the most significant costs were not those of construction. Rather they were the costs of calculation and control which would be incurred if each individual had to negotiate with one or two dozen neighbors over access to, and control of, a single communal turnout. Neither we nor Alfonso suggests whether the engineers or the farmers are right in this particular instance. Our general point is that the poor often attach great significance to limiting the communal content of local organizations. So long as advisors remain unaware of and insensitive to such concerns, they will continue to design technically efficient, elegant, and otherwise admirable organizations which fail to produce the anticipated benefits because the poor inexplicably refuse to participate in them.

It is worth pointing out that some of the most successful local organizations *have* recognized the importance of limiting communal obligations. The cooperatives of the Indian National Dairy Development Board, to which we referred earlier, are a case in point. In his summary of the conditions that led to the outstanding performance of this organization, Korten emphasizes that "the basic functions of the village milk cooperatives . . . plac[e] few demands . . . for communal labor, or for complex decisions that might favor one group over another" (1980a, p. 485). The same story could be repeated for a number of the single-industry cooperatives we have mentioned elsewhere in this essay.

The design feature that makes possible organization with limited communal obligation was spelled out long ago by Chayanov (1966) in his concept of "vertical" cooperation: local outputs and needs are handled by major commercial (exchange) or administrative (hierarchical) organizations at a regional or higher level, without requiring any "horizontal" grouping of the poor with each other.[43] Individual poor people thus can obtain many of the benefits of organization without incurring substantially more costs than they would by remaining in their tradition-bound, individualist state.

Vertical organization of this extreme form is anathema to many advisors and policymakers. These people are correct in recognizing that vertical organization does little, at least in any direct way, to develop the indigenous problem-solving capabilities of the rural poor. They are mistaken, however, in letting this lack of comprehensive intent blind them to the limited but important practical accomplishments of vertical organization, especially when it is employed in the context of a pluralistic approach to organizational design. Health-related activities such as malaria control are built on an essentially vertical pattern of organization, as are the single-industry cooperatives noted above. Perhaps most impressive, however, is the performance of certain agricultural extension efforts which we discussed in chapter 3. These efforts typically do not involve much in the way of horizontal organization and communal problem-solving.[44] The essential need is for organizational techniques that tap the local knowledge, experience, and judgment of individual farmers in order to ensure that the technologies recommended by extension workers are feasible and rewarding for those farmers, given the constraints and opportunities that they face. Equally important is that agricultural research workers should be linked with these information flows so that their decisions concerning research priorities take account of conditions and perceptions at the farm level. How such techniques can be structured and administered will be discussed below.

In summarizing this argument, we must again emphasize that we have not recommended forsaking horizontally structured groups employing bargaining or polyarchical techniques in favor of organizations emphasizing vertically structured, hierarchical or exchange techniques. We have only suggested that—measured by poor people's willingness to invest participation rather than policymakers' preconceived biases—more local problem-solving obligations are not always what the poor want; furthermore they are sometimes not

[43] In the terminology of figure 5.1, hierarchical and exchange techniques have been substituted for those of bargaining. In the process, the individual poor people have lost their status as co-leaders.

[44] Korten (1981) argues that this is an interesting aspect of the methodology evolved in Guatemala for making research and extension more useful for small farmers, a methodology which we discussed in chapter 3 (see Hildebrand 1976).

even what the poor need. Problem-solving is expensive to problem-solvers, who are often acting with good appreciation of their own limited abilities for calculation and control when they opt for a smaller problem and simpler techniques than their advisors might have them adopt. The proper goal of analysis is to understand the trade-offs involved in this behavior, to articulate the alternative organizational techniques available, and so to help design pluralistic patterns of linkage which can better serve the needs of the rural poor. We next advance some thoughts on how such designs can be promoted.

Guidelines for Design

Our argument and evidence to this point are summarized in figure 5.3, which portrays the three design features that we have identified as major determinants of local participation: attractiveness of benefits, harmony of objectives, and simplicity of technique. Each feature is shown as one axis of a three-dimensional volume. Note that each axis is oriented such that low values occur at the periphery of the figure, and high values towards the center. Within this volume, we have suggested relative "locations" of some specific organiza-

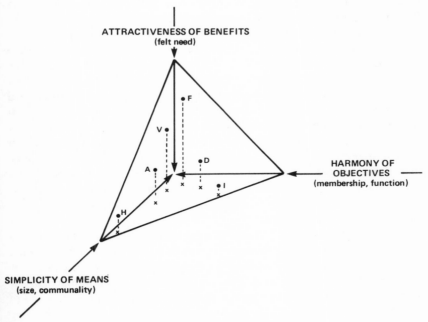

Figure 5.3. Design Features of Participatory Organizations.

Note: Some specific organizational programs that have been historically successful in attracting the participation of the rural poor are given: *F* represents family planning organizations; *A*, agricultural extension; *I*, irrigation projects at the community level; *V*, vaccination programs; *D*, dairy cooperatives; and *H*, household task allocation.

tional programs which historically have been successful in attracting the participation of the rural poor. The assigned locations are highly impressionistic—it is not by accident that no scales are given on the axes.

It would be silly to take any such figure too literally: we intend only to suggest certain qualitative relationships between design and historical performance in organizations of the rural poor. The figure reflects our finding that such organizations have tended to attract and retain active participation to the extent that they score "high" on the three design features portrayed. Such organizations lie towards the figure's center. Conversely, the rural poor have generally been less willing to invest participation in organizations scoring low on these design features and therefore lying towards the periphery of the figure.

Figure 5.3 also reflects the limited trade-offs of organization design implicit in our argument. Organizations with sufficiently high ratings on any two of the three design features have often competed successfully for the poor's participation, even when their rating on the third was relatively low. We have not, however, found a single instance of successful participation in an organization that rated low on more than one of the design features.[45] The implied constraint leads to the "organizational opportunity" surface we have sketched in the figure. Historically speaking, locations lying inside this surface have represented the most feasible designs for participatory local organization, in the narrow but operational sense that the rural poor have been more willing to invest participation in them.

It remains to be seen whether the historical relationships suggested in figure 5.3 can help to prescribe specific interventions for future programs of local reorganization. If they can, it will be by functioning not as a finished blueprint but rather as an incomplete guide to what must ultimately be an interactive process of trial-and-error learning. Put somewhat differently, though our analysis does not say how to build a particular organization in a specific context, it may suggest some good ways to start the sequence of construction. Equally important, our analysis highlights some major pitfalls of past experience in a way that should help contemporary development workers to avoid them.

Local field studies. Our analysis suggests that the most important interventions are local field studies to support reorganization efforts. Effective designs for reorganization require intimate knowledge of certain local conditions: what the poor want, where potential conflicts lie, and how much capacity for calculation and control exists. This knowledge cannot be deduced by planners, analysts, or ideologues sitting in central offices. Instead, it requires the creation of trained assessment teams and their placement in the local community. There they can tap "common" knowledge and observe for them-

---

[45] Such organizations surely exist; we suggest only that they are relatively rare and that their design is relatively risky.

selves the particular circumstances which set the constraints and opportunities for specific organizational interventions. We will have more to say on the conduct and management of such field assessments below. Suffice it for the moment to note that neither the one-day, hit-and-run visits so popular with some development agencies nor the exquisitely detailed surveys of some academic analysts are what is needed.[46] Later, we shall cite studies which lead us to suspect that a couple of weeks' work by an experienced team, focused on a few specific questions, will often be sufficient to get the interactive design process off to a good start.

    The first and most important job of the local field study is to identify one or more intensely felt local needs which can serve as the core of a reorganization program. Unless such a need is identified, the program will almost certainly fail to attract any meaningful participation from the local people. It cannot be overemphasized that local perceptions, not national priorities or overall efficiencies, are of ultimate importance here. Local desirability lies at the heart of organizational feasibility and thus is an essential component of any effective development program. Some development workers have recognized this explicitly.[47] More frequently, however, the debate on development priorities proceeds with blithe disregard for whether the programs that planners select are programs in which the poor will participate. This sort of mismatch helps no one; and it is one of the reasons why we insist upon the interdependence of production, consumption, *and* organization programs throughout our discussion of development strategies in chapter 6.

    The next important issue for study by the local field team concerns the interaction of benefits, membership, and organization function. The goal, we have argued, is to achieve sufficient harmony of objectives that the organization can cope with its tasks of surfacing and settling conflicts. Although good sociological analysis probably can be of some help here, the chances of arriving at a "correct" answer through cogitation alone are bleak. We suspect that the best bet is for a reorganization program to start with a relatively narrow function and membership in order to maximize the chances that it will survive at all. If it does survive, additional functions and member groups can be added as necessary or appropriate.

    We are equally skeptical that even the best of field studies can identify in advance the optimal means of calculation and control for a particular organi-

---

[46] Recent discussions of "rapid rural appraisal" are relevant (see, for example, Chambers [1980]).

    [47] Korten, for example, advances the "radical proposition" that "having the local people identify a need around which popular interest can be aroused may be more important than selecting a program that will deliver the most units of service at the lowest cost" (1979a, p. 27). And a foreign advisor working with the UNICEF Village Technology Unit in Kenya provides a refreshing view: "Our approach to the generation of interest in technologies which may be appropriate for use at village level amongst very poor people, is based on the fact that *we* do not know what is, or is not, appropriate, and neither do our government counterparts. The only people who can really decide what is, or is not, appropriate are the people, themselves" (McDowell 1978, p. 75).

zational situation. Our analysis has identified some of the factors that such a study might profitably consider, but a good deal of subsequent trial-and-error learning will almost certainly be necessary. Again, we will explore how this learning might be carried out and supported in a later section (beginning on p. 199). Our general recommendation, however, is that a first attempt to redesign a traditional organization should begin with one of the simpler techniques we discussed in the last section. Communal efforts should generally be avoided, and the opportunities for shedding some of the required calculation and control onto existing commercial or support organizations should be seriously considered.

Inadequacies of local participation. In the preceding pages we have discussed the design of basic starting points from which a trial-and-error process of local reorganization might profitably begin. We have been reasonably explicit about what we think such designs will offer the rural poor. It remains to be equally explicit about what they will not.

Nothing we have said in our discussion of local reorganization should be taken as an endorsement of the naive, ideologically distorted view that the poor are uniformly wise and goodly people, thwarted in their development efforts only by evil elites and callous bureaucrats. Rather, we believe that although effective local participation is a necessary component of development organization, it is rarely sufficient to handle all the organizational tasks on which effective programs of social action depend. These tasks, to recapitulate our argument in the first section of this chapter, include choice, allocation, mobilization, distribution, and productive utilization of resources. The dimensions of local organization's insufficiencies are well known, if for no other reason than that they have been displayed so frequently in past efforts at local reorganization. It should be sufficient to recall some of the most serious.

An obvious problem is the inability of autonomous local groups to obtain high productivity from their local resources. The common sight of two cattle dips built next to each other by rival clans is representative of a great number of similarly inefficient practices (Oyugi 1973).

An ability to mobilize local resources of knowledge, material, and labor has justifiably been hailed as one of the strong points of participative local organization. Even here, however, the frequent failure to link local resource mobilization to a broader social perspective leads to wasted effort and disillusionment. For example, local initiatives started under the ill-informed belief that the central government would supply operating budgets and staffing have left a trail of unused schools and clinic buildings throughout the developing world (Chambers 1974, p. 102).

A further shortcoming of local organization is its inability to cope with the tasks of resource distribution among competing objectives. A bias for short-term programs over long-term programs is understandable in rural communities, but it clearly blocks access to many important benefits. We mentioned earlier the predilection of local governments for consumption-oriented rather than production-oriented programs (see also Chambers 1974, p. 86; Lele 1975, p. 159).

At a more fundamental level, the widespread advocacy of local autonomy has been counterproductive in terms of local groups' abilities to perform the organizational tasks of surfacing and settling conflicts, signaling group choices, and securing allocation of resources appropriate to those choices. The community-development movement failed in part because it treated the traditional village as a self-contained development unit which would carry out most organizational tasks without the aid of external intervention (Heginbotham 1975; Sussman 1980). We showed above why this rarely works, and outlined conditions under which smaller, more specialized local groups linked through broader support structures were more likely to perform the required tasks.

In general, an informal group offering attractive benefits to a few like-minded individuals is a good point from which to start a program for redesigning local organizations. It is only a start, however, and a very imperfect one at that. To realize its potential—perhaps even to survive—the initial local group will almost always have to begin reaching out to form linkages with the broader social system. There are dangers in such linkages, especially if attempts are made to forge them too ambitiously or too soon. Nonetheless, the dangers of pursuing a mythical local autonomy are even greater; the goal is not isolation but rather an ability to build *reciprocally* helpful linkages with the national, regional, and local communities which form each local group's social environment. The need for resolutely pursuing this goal is particularly clear when we consider the special design problems posed by rural elites.

Coping with the Elite

Skilled assessment teams often will be able to identify more than one design around which a local reorganization program might be built. We have argued that one of the central failings of past efforts to build local organizations is that so frequently the design chosen is one which could be bent to the benefit of the relatively well-off local elite. There is no sure way to avoid such failures. Nonetheless, a growing body of practical experience suggests that a few fundamental design choices each reflecting detailed knowledge of local circumstances can substantially improve the chances for success. We shall outline four such choices, proceeding from simpler to more complex organizational designs and following the general design framework we developed in figure 5.2.[48]

Passive exclusion. The most direct way to keep the local elite from taking over or unduly influencing an organization is to define the function of the organization in such a way that the elite do not want to participate at all. In our general discussion of harmony and conflict, we showed how choice of

---

[48] Discussions with David Leonard have contributed substantially to this section. Throughout the remainder of this section, we will frequently use the succinct term "elites" as an admittedly approximate shorthand for the more awkward but more inclusive phrase "relatively well-off and influential."

organizational function can influence membership. A typical constructive use of this influence was gradually evolved by the Bangladesh Rural Advancement Committee (BRAC), described earlier. By defining their organization's function in a manner that simultaneously required inputs of manual labor from participants and eliminated handouts to them, the BRAC organizers discovered that they could lose the interest of the relatively well-off villagers and restrict the willingness to invest active participation to their target group of the very poor (Korten 1980a, pp. 488–90).

The benefits of this approach to organizational design are obvious. The potential disadvantages, however, are not insignificant. First of all, restricting an organization to functions that are *not* attractive to the local elite means forgoing a large number of functions that *are* attractive to the poor. In addition, as we have already pointed out (and will discuss in more detail below), local skills of leadership and management tend to reside disproportionately with the elite members of the community. A local organization explicitly cutting itself off from those skills must either seek comparable skills from outside (for example, from a professionalized supporting organization, as was the case in BRAC) or adopt techniques of linkage which do not require them. As noted earlier, one solution is to build around existing commercial institutions, if suitable ones exist. More likely, the solution will be to remain sufficiently small or noncommunal that informal bargaining techniques are sufficient for the required tasks of calculation and control. This small-group solution should not be lightly dismissed. As Hunter has so frequently pointed out (1969, 1970, 1978a), such groups can accomplish many of the primary goals of local reorganization. Moreover, they have frequently provided the initial experience in interest-group cooperation from which more ambitious programs later grow.

Active exclusion. When the benefits of local organization desired by the poor are also desired by the elite, several design alternatives remain. The most extreme is explicitly to exclude the elite from membership in the organization. But this is at best a risky choice. Competent, committed external organization will be required to support and protect the poor people's organization if it is to have any chance of success. A good example of the potential and limitations of such a design is India's Small Farmer Development Administration as described by Hunter (1976). We discuss some of the substantial problems of organizing the required external support in a later section. Nothing we say there, however, gives us reason to believe that efforts to exclude the elite from organizational benefits which they strongly desire can be successful in any but the most exceptional circumstances. More often, if the interests of the poor are to be protected, organization redesigners will have to look beyond the choice of membership to the character of the benefits pursued and the choice of particular techniques for calculation and control.

Willingly shared benefits. One class of organizational designs which has been particularly effective in advancing the interests of the poor is that which pursues benefits that the elite desire for themselves but cannot—or do not want to—keep the poor from sharing with them. Somewhat surprisingly, at least for those who see the world as a constant struggle between the haves and have-nots, a number of such benefits are of great importance to poor people in the developing world.

For one thing, elites have been known to be more altruistic than rapacious. Cynicism and habit should not blind social reorganizers to the opportunities inherent in altruistic circumstances such as those exemplified by the previously mentioned Sarvodaya Shramadana Movement of Sri Lanka. In another group of programs accrual of benefits to the elite is in part contingent on the program's effectiveness in reaching the poor members of the community. Sanitation and immunization programs are typical examples. Only slightly different are programs such as family planning, in which little is to be gained by the elite in denying or controlling access to an organization's benefits.

Consumption-related benefits are generally more likely than are production-oriented ones to be willingly shared by elites. Nonetheless, when productive benefits are characterized by substantial externalities, the elite may not be able to limit use by the poor whether they want to or not. The road-building programs we remarked on earlier provide one example of how production-related benefits with high externalities can be successfully pursued by organizations including both elite and poor segments of a rural community.

Obviously, only a small proportion of the benefits desired by both poor and elite will be shared due to altruism, common interest, or externalities. But the few benefits which are conducive to such willing sharing constitute an invaluable resource for social reorganizers trying to design programs which will reach the poor in an elite-ridden world.

Zero-sum contests. If some program benefits are willingly shared by the elite and the poor, others are essentially the prizes of a contest in which winners take from losers. Land, water, and local political power are only the most obvious benefits which may be at stake in such "zero-sum" situations. Conditions precipitating head-on battles between the poor and the elite over these benefits are not nearly so ubiquitous as some writers suggest. They are nonetheless latent and significant in many rural-development situations. And the chances of the poor emerging as victors in such battles are virtually nil. We therefore cannot overemphasize the desirability of discovering policies and organizational designs which mitigate the need for fighting them at all. One reason why we have emphasized our preference for unimodal production programs is the organizational difficulty of securing benefits for the poor within the structure of directly conflicting interests so often encountered in bimodally structured societies.

Frequently, however, bimodal or other conflict-laden social structures will be the reality with which the social organizer must work. In some such cases it may be feasible to design an organization that provides alternative benefits more attractive for the elite, thus moving them out of competition with the poor. We discussed one such case in chapter 3 while reviewing the prospects of providing nonagricultural sources of income and status for the most well-to-do and progressive members of rural communities, thus mitigating the contest for scarce land and related assets. Realistically speaking, however, in most cases of direct conflict between the poor and the elite, there are few direct and effective cures to be had through mere tactical modifications of existing organizational structures. The tricks we have suggested may be worth a try, but it would be naive to pretend that revolutionary change or strong and sustained intervention from outside will not usually be required before the poor have much hope of bettering their condition.

Getting a fairer share. Between the extremes of willingly shared benefits and zero-sum conflict, there exists a large, fertile, and relatively unexplored ground for innovative organizational designs which help the poor to obtain some share, if not always a fair share, of development's benefits. Here we are concerned with the variety of programs that are capable of providing more benefits for everyone. The question is not whether the poor will receive any share of these benefits but rather how close they can come to receiving a fair share. How can specific techniques of organization be used to increase the magnitude of the benefits which the poor actually receive? Of the basic organizational techniques which we discussed in the first section of this chapter, bargaining is unlikely to play a dominant role in such designs: neither the size constraint nor the implicit requirement of negotiation among equals is likely to be met. Polyarchical techniques, in contrast, have often been applied to such situations. They have not met with outstanding success. In fact, experience suggests that it will usually be most useful to the poor if reorganization programs designed to effect immediate improvements in their well-being are kept entirely separate from local organizational structures dealing in political power. This is neither defeatism nor a contradiction in terms. First of all, political forms of organization are particularly ill-suited to attaining benefits for the rural poor. A principal goal of elective and even single-party political organizations is to achieve as large a membership as possible. Typically, this is done by providing (or at least promising) something for everyone. Indeed, the very legitimacy of the political organization often rests on its commitment to open membership and its pledge to pursue the interests of all its members. As we argued earlier, however, this sort of open-membership, multiple-function design almost guarantees a dangerous amount of conflict over organizational goals. Moreover, where local political organizations have survived at all in the developing world, they have done so largely in terms of traditional patronage/dependency linkages functioning to enhance the status of the local elite. New social functions, when added to such organizations, are likely either to threaten the status of the elite or to be taken over by them. In either case, the poor will fail to benefit. Lele (1974, p. 74) describes such a situation in the context of East African agricultural development. Pyle (1979, p. 17) provides a similar story from his work on Indian health programs. In the latter case, the popular village health workers were explicitly instructed to avoid any political involvement because this might alienate an otherwise cooperative or indifferent elite.

Exchange techniques, especially when embodied in a well-developed commercial structure which is relatively immune to the pressures of local elites, are often more effective than political organizations in promoting fairer shares for the poor. We noted in chapter 3, for example, that small farmers are more likely to have access to credit and inputs if these benefits are provided at competitive, market-clearing prices. When artificially low prices create an excess demand and necessitate reliance on bureaucratic or political rationing, the local elites generally can be expected to capture a greater share of the benefits.

How great that share will be may be influenced by auditing and other regulatory controls imposed through specific (and usually hierarchical) techniques of organization. In cases like that of the Indian dairy cooperatives, this control derives in part from a heavy reliance on publicly visible techniques of exchange: justice is seen to be done. Elsewhere, periodic elections may conceivably keep elites accountable for their excesses. In general, however, the need is for what Dore (1971) has called "institutionalized suspicion": a formal, probably hierarchical auditing system visibly insulated from the traditional kin and patronage obligations of the local community. Such auditing systems cannot, of course, guarantee equitable distribution of benefits among poor and elite participants. To be even reasonably effective they require a truly extraordinary commitment of senior officials in supporting organizations. Nonetheless, it remains one of the truisms of development that in organizations of the sort we describe here, a failure to provide and to diligently pursue such institutionalized suspicion virtually guarantees that the poor will suffer.

Prospects for progress. What can the poor realistically expect to gain from the various technical reorganizations we have discussed here? Not everything they need, not a fair share of benefits, and quite possibly nothing but increased exploitation. Nonetheless, it is important to emphasize that the poor *can* and have extracted substantial improvements in their well-being from organizations that include members of the elite.

By joining with the elite in local organizations such as those we have described here, poor people gain leadership talents and initiative which they would be less likely to find within their own ranks. They also gain the tangible benefits of effective organizations. Furthermore, the opportunity for some small amount of mutually beneficial interaction between different strata of society is also an opportunity for initiating more ambitious organization-building programs.

The potential for coincident interests of poor and elite, and for beneficial interaction between them, seems to require that elite and poor members of the community both have access to the resources or assets on which the functions of the organization are based. This condition of common access has been identified as one of the key factors underlying the success of single-industry, vertically integrated organizations such as the Indian National Dairy Development Board, described earlier. A similar case can be made for some of the more prosperous East African cooperatives described by Hyden (1970). More broadly, it is a condition intimately associated with a unimodal rather than a bimodal approach to rural development. In contrast, failures of programs like the much-touted CADU Project, in Ethiopia, can be ascribed in large part to the mistake of trying to join landed elites and landless tenants together under an organizational design which can actually benefit only those with access to land.[49] The operative word is *access*. As we noted in chapter 3, the patterns of agricultural development in Japan and Taiwan were unimodal long before the post–World War II land reforms. But because landlords rented out their land in small operational units, tenants had access to land; owners and tenants had a shared interest in yield-increasing innovations even though a large fraction of the incremental output accrued to the landlord. It is therefore not surprising that the prewar agricultural associations in both countries functioned reasonably well even though typically they were dominated by elite landlords.

Even when the poor have access to the basic resources required for participation in the benefits of an organization, even when a credible auditing system exists, it remains true that the elite will more than likely sequester the greater share of an organization's benefits for themselves. This is regrettable, unjust, and inevitable. We believe, however, that it will be in poor people's best interest to accept even substantial disparities in benefits. In order to get on with the urgent job of securing absolute improvements, even substantial disparities in benefits should not, in general, disqualify development programs which can secure absolute improvements in the well-being of the rural poor. One important exception to this general recommendation has been pointed out to us by David Leonard. This exception applies under conditions where allowing a disproportionate share of benefits to accrue to the elite will increase their ability to exploit the poor in the future. It may be particularly relevant to programs dealing with agricultural and other productive enterprises. In such cases an increase in the relative productivity of the elite could, unless otherwise controlled, bring them into a position where they were increasingly able to purchase the productive assets of the poor. If at all possible, social reorganizers should avoid designs with this sort of potential.

In summary. We have argued that programs to reorganize the rural poor must be based upon intimate knowledge of local conditions obtained by firsthand, village-level assessments. Such assessments should seek to discover what benefits of organization are desired by the poor, what sorts of potential conflict exist in the community, and what techniques and experience relevant to organization are available. Knowledge of these factors as they pertain at a particular place and time should help substantially in identifying those initial interventions most likely to lead to a sequence of reorganization programs which actually benefit the poor. Other things being equal, it would seem best to start with an intensely desired benefit which can be shared with (or is not desired by) the elite, a combination of membership criteria and organizational functions which assures a reasonable harmony of objectives among partici-

---

[49] The CADU (Chilalo Agricultural Development Unit) Project, its ostensible goals, and its actual impact are discussed in Cohen and Uphoff (1977).

pants, and a commitment to extremely simple techniques of calculation and control. The evidence we have reviewed suggests that more difficult or complex organizations should be undertaken very cautiously—if at all—in the early stages of the reorganization effort. In particular, it seems unwise to pressure small informal groups to include more members or more functions, at least until they have evolved a substantial amount of confidence and experience. Even then, designers should always ask what interest *of the poor* will be served by expanding a small organization and thereby incurring the risks of overextension and overexposure.

Our analysis also suggests that social-service and productive programs should be separately pursued in the early stages of an organization's growth. The risks and liabilities of organizing productive functions are so different from, and generally so much greater than, those of organizing service activities, that combinations will succeed only rarely. It is much more likely that organizationally feasible social-service programs will become the pawns and victims of a much rougher contest over control of productive activities.

Finally, every effort should be made to separate all other organizational activities from those which unavoidably involve a conflict of interest between poor and elite. Such halting progress as can be made in social reorganization may even require a willingness to set aside irresolvable equity issues in order to get on with the many beneficial activities which can be pursued within the existing social context. Trite but true: the poor do not benefit when social reformers let an ideological or personal predilection for the best stand in the way of the good.

Organizing the Facilitators

In chapters 3 and 4 we considered some of the development initiatives which a national or regional government might wish to pursue. So far in chapter 5 we have considered prospects for reorganizing the rural poor to better recognize and exploit their own opportunities for development. There remains the problem of linking the two levels, of fusing national plans and unique local opportunities into effective programs of rural development.

The Needs for Facilitation

The missing links in this framework of development organization are the "facilitator" people: the administrators and field staff, managers and entrepreneurs who are neither villagers nor policymakers but nonetheless serve an essential organizational function by facilitating reciprocally helpful interactions between those two groups.

Any attempt to redesign the functions and functioning of facilitator organizations must be based on an appreciation of their inherently schizoid nature. Facilitator organizations are constantly and simultaneously called upon to serve the needs of three radically different clients: the rural poor and their local organizations, the national policymakers and their planning organizations, and—as is too often forgotten—the facilitator people themselves. Let us briefly consider what each of these needs entails.

The needs of poor people. For groups of rural people, facilitator organizations are the major links with the larger social system. Earlier we discussed in some detail the weaknesses of autonomous local organizations and their consequent requirements for outside linkages.[50] Most obviously, local organizations need facilitator organizations to perform an allocation task: to provide them with reliable access to the range of goods and services required for increasing production and rural well-being. More broadly, local groups need to be given access to a range of knowledge resources, both technical and managerial. They need to be trained in ways of doing things, helped to settle local conflicts, and helped to learn more effectively from their trial-and-error experiments. One function of effective facilitator organizations is to meet these needs.

Continuing with the themes we developed above, local groups may also need some sort of facilitator organization to link them with other local groups. In some cases, this will be necessary in order to achieve economies of scale, for example, a dairy cooperative for efficient processing and handling of milk. In other cases, the primary need will be for an outside organization to take on some tasks of calculation and control in order that these will not overwhelm the local groups.

Finally, many local groups need facilitator organizations to provide them with protection. This may be protection from external forces, for example, where attempts have been made to exclude an elite group from the local organization. More frequently it will be protection from internal forces of corruption and graft, and will be provided through an auditing function relatively independent of local politics, kinship, and social pressures.[51]

The needs of policy people. Facilitator organizations are also called upon to serve some of the needs of national and regional policymakers. Those needs are many and varied, but their essence is captured in the word *implementation.* As we stress in chapter 6, the one organizational task which absolutely must be performed by national policymakers is that of setting priorities for the distribution of scarce national resources among competing programs. In the field of rural development, however, policymakers have "made" nothing until those priorities are reflected in actual changes in the lives of the poor. For virtually every one of the development programs we have discussed, such changes require that individual villagers themselves adopt new technologies and behavior patterns. We have already argued that policy initiatives imposed from above without consideration of local needs and circumstances seldom accomplish such changes. Policymakers need a great deal of help from facilita-

---

[50] See also Lodge (1970, pp. 148–49) and Korten (1979a, 1980a).

[51] Dore (1971) argues convincingly that the required auditing functions can seldom be performed in a sufficiently convincing manner from within the local group.

tor organizations if they are to translate their wishes into meaningful change at the village level.

Good implementation help has been notoriously difficult to come by in both developed and developing countries. Even when the programs to be implemented are relatively routine (such as delivery of vaccines or tax collection), implementation commonly fails entirely, or distorts the implemented program beyond recognition.[52] This may be due to corruption, apathy, or infighting on the part of the facilitators. It is at least as likely, however, that the policymakers have never faced up to the "mere details" of who will do what with which resources. Implementation and facilitation "fail" because only at this stage of the policy design process do planners' failures to balance resources and objectives collide with reality. The policymaker will need good facilitator organizations to help him interactively adjust means (resources) and ends (objectives) if this sort of failure is to become less common.

Implementation problems become even more difficult when programs require substantial flexibility in the face of unforeseen and often changing local circumstances. We noted earlier how the need for on-site decisions in agricultural extension posed this sort of difficulty. In such cases, the policymaker needs facilitators able both to exert control and to promote the local adaptability necessary for fitting local circumstances. This is almost a contradiction in terms, which is why facilitating program implementation is such a difficult art.

The needs of facilitator people. Each of the general failures of development organization which we described at the beginning of this chapter has at one time or another been blamed on the inadequate performance of facilitator people. The diagnoses are monotonously similar. The people on whom development organization relies for facilitation are said to be undertrained, to have poor work attitudes, to lack integration in their activities, to have no structure to their work, to be callous in their disregard for the poor, or to engage in empty procedural ritual.

There is sometimes some truth in each of these observations. Each, however, is based on a perspective that treats the "human capital" of facilitator organizations as something very like the capital stock of a factory: a piece of machinery performing inadequately and therefore in need of repair or replacement. What this perspective misses is that facilitator people seek from the facilitator organization professional satisfaction, stable employment, and career advancement. Facilitator organizations will be able to attract good facilitator people, to motivate their activity, and to channel their energies in a manner that helps others only to the extent that the organization can satisfy the needs of its staff and management people. This perspective raises the possibility that the popular diagnoses cited above may have mistaken the symptoms of inadequate facilitator organization for the disease itself. Do facilitator

---

[52] See Lindblom (1979) for a useful summary of the implementation problem. Pressman and Wildavsky (1973) provide an insightful and entertaining case study of implementation problems in a North American context; Bardach (1977) treats the subject more systematically.

organizations in the developing countries in fact provide the career opportunities and the prospects for significant work that good facilitator people need? Once this question is asked, the answer is an obvious and resounding "No." Facilitator people need from facilitator organizations the management procedures and institutional structures which will change the answer to "Yes."[53]

Organizational alternatives. A variety of organizational techniques have been employed to meet different people's needs for facilitation: co-op federations grown from below, civil administrations imposed from above, special project groups supported by foreign aid and advisors, commercial networks emerging from the self-interested actions of individuals, and so on. The facilitator linkages which emerge from these individual endeavors are inevitably redundant and inefficient, since policymakers, villagers, and facilitator people will seek sometimes conflicting, sometimes complementary, and sometimes merely different goals.[54]

There exists a vast literature on the design of facilitator (administrative, managerial, implementing) organizations, much of it relevant to development problems.[55] Nonetheless, the schizoid nature of development facilitation raises certain questions on which the standard literature is either mute or misleading (Korten 1979a). Three of these questions are especially critical for efforts to redesign facilitator organizations.

First, how can facilitator organizations respond to both the local needs perceived by innumerable groups of poor people and the national needs defined as priorities by policymakers? In other words, how can pressures to decentralize so as to be more sensitive to local issues be balanced against pressures to centralize so as to be more effective in implementing national goals?

Second, how can facilitator organizations remain the servants of changing local and national needs but still provide an environment that gives facilitator personnel opportunities for job security, predictable career advancement, and reasonable exercise of authority? Put somewhat differently, how can facilitator organizations be designed to provide high-quality, well-motivated civil service rather than retrenched, territorial, and autonomous bureaucracy?

Third, how can facilitator organizations provide both the tightly structured

---

[53] This view is argued forcefully by Chambers (1974) and Leonard (1977).

[54] Very plausible arguments for the benefits of redundancy (institutional pluralism) have been made. Redundancy provides alternative channels for the flow of resources and information, making the system less susceptible to intentional or accidental blockage and therefore more effective (Uphoff and Esman 1974, pp. 70–72; Lele 1975, p. 187; Caiden and Wildavsky 1974, pp. 49–63; Landau 1969). Caiden and Wildavsky point out, however, that redundancy can also be viewed as a luxury good—a superfluity of linkages and organizational alternatives—which the poor could certainly use but lack because they are poor. This raises the possibility that high redundancy may be effect rather than cause of development success, effectively reversing the implied causality in Uphoff and Esman's empirical correlation. The matter needs more research and less theorizing. We believe that policymakers cannot gain much practical guidance on organizational design from the present evidence and debate on the redundancy issue. Other considerations we have addressed in this essay are far more relevant.

[55] See Leonard (1977) and Korten (1979a, 1980a) for extensive bibliographies.

work programs necessary for effective implementation and the flexible, "error-embracing" adaptiveness necessary for effective learning?

Anyone pretending to have general answers to such questions is either a fool or a fraud. In the last decade, however, development workers have begun to explore these and related organizational questions explicitly, and to experiment with specific techniques for resolving them more satisfactorily. Much remains to be done, but some exciting beginnings have been made. We find these beginnings to be particularly well documented in the writings of Guy Hunter, Deryke Belshaw, Robert Chambers, David Leonard, Daniel Benor, and David and Frances Korten.[56] The disagreements among these authors are many, as is to be expected from the range of countries, stages of development, and types of programs which they have addressed. More remarkable, in our view, are the large areas of overlap and convergence which are apparent in their work. For the strategic purposes of this essay, we shall focus on three such areas of agreement where the implications for specific reorganization interventions are particularly clear. We cover these in the next three sections, under the headings "Structuring Implementation," "Managing People," and "Managing Programs." Throughout, we draw extensively on the work of the authors cited above. Our aim is neither to provide a comprehensive review of facilitator organization nor to resolve the conflicts latent in the multiple demands placed upon those organizations. Rather, we hope to clarify the roles of the major actors in the facilitation process and to suggest how those roles might sometimes be played more effectively. More ambitiously, we hope to sketch the outlines of an organizational framework within which poor people, facilitator people, and policy people might better learn what they should want out of the facilitation process and better recognize how joining in reciprocally helpful behaviors could help them realize their goals. If this preliminary sketch can help to focus subsequent debate, it will have served our purpose.

Structuring Implementation

Institutional structures establish the channels of resource distribution and flow of information within an organization (Uphoff and Esman 1974, p. 63). They constitute opportunities for action which can be exploited only through the accompanying management of people and programs, subjects discussed later in this chapter. We concentrate next on the structures that channel responsibility and authority, two resources which have played a central role in the performance of organizations designed to facilitate rural development.

Authority and responsibility. Lack of fit between an individual's authorities and responsibilities is a problem as old as organizations themselves. In late-developing countries, however, misfits and their consequences are particularly widespread and acute.

---

[56] We draw heavily on the following publications: Hunter (1978*a*), Chambers (1974), Leonard (1977), Benor and Harrison (1977), Korten (1979*a*, 1980*a*), Korten and Alfonso (1981), and Korten and Korten (1977).

Several development analysts have argued that the most pressing need is to devise organizational structures which permit feasible and efficient distribution of workloads—that is, responsibilities—among field, national, and intermediate-level personnel. Efficiency of workload distribution amounts to assigning people responsibility for the specific tasks they are best suited and best situated to perform. For facilitator organizations throughout the developing world, however, chronic underloads or overloads of work seem more rule than exception (Chambers 1974, chap. 3).

Even when facilitators are assigned an efficient and feasible set of responsibilities, they often lack the authority required to perform their work in a timely and effective manner. Such mismatches are frequently the result of half-hearted or ill-conceived decentralization efforts which fail to match new district-level responsibilities with the spending authority necessary for action.[57]

Bureaucratic Balkanization (not to be confused with well-conceived decentralization) poses a related problem. National policymakers find that they have given away so much power and budgetary discretion to their myriad implementation bureaucracies that they now lack any means of control. Stuck with yesterday's organizations, policymakers can only continue to address yesterday's problems. They thereby fail in their own responsibilities to shape and direct the continuing redesign of national development strategy.[58] The bureaucracies, with insufficient central authority to hold them in check, commonly fall into various competitive and territorial behaviors all of which bode ill for the facilitation of development. Sometimes the resulting battles carry right through to the village level, where one field worker ends up pushing nutrition supplements, another malaria programs, another family planning, and all each other. Alternatively, to put on a show of "integration" while leaving each bureaucracy's authority and autonomy undiminished, the same "multipurpose" village worker or district "coordinating" committee is simply assigned all the village-level responsibilities of all the bureaucracies combined. The result—overloaded impotence—facilitates nothing.

The challenge of designing a more effective distribution of responsibility and authority has called forth a variety of decentralization schemes and other

---

[57] Alfonso (1981) reports that this occurred even in the generally successful Laur Project of the Philippines National Irrigation Administration. The admirable desire to keep responsibility and authority together at the regional level had to compromise with the sad fact that the region simply couldn't command the necessary resources. The project was reluctantly (but successfully) reassigned upward in the national administrative structure.

[58] They are stuck with inappropriate organizations because too often foreign aid donors have encouraged the formation of semiautonomous special-project administrations as a blanket "solution" to organizational difficulties. The "solution," of course, is to the donors' problems of achieving visible results within the short time frame of prevailing funding cycles. Seldom are the special projects later amalgamated into the existing bureaucracy. Rather, they become another fiefdom—a part of the labyrinth which justifies the next special project. National policymakers, who must live with the resulting mess, may be opposed by the donor agencies themselves when attempting to impose some control or unification (see Lele 1975, chap. 8. We thank Carl Taylor for some illuminating remarks on this subject [May 1980: personal communication]).

institutional reforms throughout the developing world. We focus in the remainder of this chapter on one class of structural reorganizations which has met the challenge with notable success. These organizations may be grouped under Leonard's term "development bureaucracy," broadened sufficiently to cover complementary ideas associated with Chambers's (1974) Programming and Implementation Management System (PIM), Benor and Harrison's (1977) Training and Visit System, the Kortens' (e.g., Korten 1980a) Learning Process Approach, and many of Hunter's (1978a) proposed administrative reforms.[59]

Ⅺ *Starting at the bottom.* The defining characteristic of the organizational style which we will call development bureaucracy is a bottom-up concept of structure. This stems from the hard-won lesson that programs seeking to make positive contributions to rural development must above all else reach and change the lives of individual poor people. Many years of experience have shown that such changes are unlikely to occur so long as program "implementation" consists largely in trying to force "the poor" and "the field staff" into their assigned locations in national planners' social blueprints. Development bureaucracy works the other way around, starting with a specific package of benefits or services which is desired by specific poor people and which a specific resource-holding segment of the larger society is willing and able to allocate for the desired use.[60]

Having defined a specific product as the goal of facilitation efforts, the structural-design question becomes, How many poor families can be reached with the benefits package by each individual field worker at the lowest level of the facilitator organization? Answers to this question will obviously depend upon a variety of factors, including the density of settlement, availability of transport, degree of social organization, and most of all, the type of package envisioned. Nonetheless, by analyzing some of the poor-to-facilitator ratios which have characterized successful development bureaucracies, we can secure some guidance on the feasibility of future structural designs.[61]

Reviewing agricultural extension programs in Asia, Benor and Harrison (1977) report effective results when between three hundred and five hundred families are covered by each facilitator person at the lowest field level. They suggest a working mean of around five hundred families, about the same

---

[59] Besides the material reported in the cited publications, particularly interesting case-study evaluations of the approaches are to be found in Pyle (1979) and Kingshotte (1980a, 1980b).

[60] At risk of repeating ourselves too often, we reemphasize that the composition of such "benefit packages" is not decreed by the Almighty. Rather, it is a product of mutual adjustment between the various actors, acted out within the framework of constraints that each perceives. One of the jobs of local organizations and, as we shall see, of facilitators, is to facilitate those adjustments. As we discussed in chapter 1, successive iterations of the interaction serve to modify initial perceptions and to help each actor learn what he should want and what he can get out of the envisioned package.

[61] The terminology used by different authors in describing the various levels of facilitator organizations can be very confusing. The table below may help to relate our usage to that of others. We attach some very rough representative numerical values in order to help make the

number reported for Kenya by Leonard (1977, table 2). It should be noted that in both cases, the facilitators "reach" such large numbers, not directly, but rather by focusing on a smaller number of individuals (usually about fifty) who serve as local leaders or examples.[62] Meaningful numbers are less readily available and more variable for health, nutrition, or family planning programs, but a ratio of some two hundred families per village-level health worker is not uncommon for effective facilitation efforts (for example, Pyle 1979). As benefit packages become more complex, and the tasks of building local organizations to support them become more acute, the number of families that can be effectively aided by a single village-level facilitator predictably declines. Experimental irrigation projects in the Philippines, for example, have used one "community organizer" for about every eighty families covered. (This ra-

---

definitions clearer. It should be obvious that these numbers and the "levels" they define are intended as a heuristic convenience, not a prescription for design. We believe, however, that other discussions of organization structure could benefit from an equally explicit if equally arbitrary definition of terms.

Representative Structure for a Facilitator Organization

Operational level		Representative designation of facilitator at this level[a]	Representative number of households per facilitator at this level	Representative number of facilitators at this level for a district of 300,000 families
Local	0°	Family head	(1)	(300,000)
	1°	Local leader	50	(30,000)
Field	2°	*Lower-level field facilitator* village worker; junior field staff	500	4,000
	3°	*Upper-level field facilitator* field extension officer; field assistant; local assistant	4,000	500
District	4°	*Lower-level district facilitator* subdivision extension officer; assistant officer	30,000	50
	5°	*Upper-level district facilitator* district extension officer	300,000	1
	(6°, . . . , as needed)	Zonal extension officer; regional coordinator	(2 million, . . .)	
Central	(N-2°, . . . , as needed) N-1° N°	Various central bureaucrats	(Region, state, nation)	(. . .)

Note: Entries in parentheses are listed for completeness but are not justified or used in the text.

[a] Our usage appears in italics.

[62] We discussed the topic of local organization generally earlier in this chapter. The special problems of grouping farmers to facilitate extension and of selecting the appropriate farmers to serve as local targets were discussed in chapter 3. For the sake of clarity, in this section we will continue to refer to the family as the basic unit of rural organization, implicitly assuming the existence of appropriate local groupings.

tio is not directly comparable to those given for agriculture and health, since after the irrigation agent has spent six to nine months organizing one small group, he moves on to another group [see Bagadion and Korten 1980; Alfonso 1981].)

Supervision and support. As we shall see shortly, the lowest-level field workers, who do the ultimate reaching to the poor, have little training, often are illiterate, and cannot be expected to build work plans and enforce priorities on their own. Experience shows that careful structuring of supervision and support functions is necessary if these workers are to perform effectively their crucial facilitation functions.

Continuing development bureaucracy's bottom-up concept of structure, the next design question is, How many of the lowest-level field facilitators can one individual effectively supervise and support? Again, the answers depend on several factors, but the key requirement is to achieve a span narrow enough that direct, personal, and frequent contact is possible. Experience in a variety of development programs and settings consistently turns up numbers in the range of four to twelve low-level field workers per immediate supervisor. Attempts to include more usually have proved infeasible, leading to inefficient workload distribution and job dissatisfaction.

Close supervision and support are required at each successive level of the development bureaucracy. The same general design question remains relevant, and since the same basic issues of human relations are involved at all levels of the development bureaucracy, the number of people who can be directly supervised and supported by each supervisor does not seem to be drastically different at the different levels. The one major difference is that at high levels it often is worthwhile to include technical specialists—doctors, agronomists, economists—who serve no immediate supervisory role but who can be called upon to support the lower level when appropriate.

Successive levels of supervision and support can be added in a similar manner until a formal hierarchy reaches to the national level. This has been done successfully for cooperatives working with high-value, centrally processed crops—for example, the Kenya Tea Development Authority, discussed in chapter 3, and the Indian National Dairy Development Board, mentioned earlier in this chapter. For most successful reorganization efforts, however, the typical development bureaucracy is one in which the supervision-and-support structure reaches up from the village to some intermediate "district" level, where it is met by various national administrations, commercial institutions, and special-project authorities reaching down from above (Leonard 1977, pp. 211–13). The result is a relationship of mutual coexistence between strong national organizations and semiautonomous operations groups at the district level (Chambers 1974, chap. 4).

In such a relationship, authority is exercised more through mutual adjustment than through unilateral control. Ministries, authorities, and parastatals (quasi-governmental organizations) at the national level set forth an array of programs that they would like to see adopted and would be willing to support.

District-level facilitator organizations counter with proposals for benefit packages which they believe are feasible and desirable from the perspective of villagers and field staff. Both parties recognize that they need the cooperation, resources, and "distinctive organizational competence" of the other to achieve significant results.[63] The mixed structure of hierarchy and bargaining which emerges looks horrible on organizational charts, is rarely peaceful, and requires the constant support and attention of the most senior national planners and policymakers if it is not to lose its balance and slip into the adjoining abysses of local autonomy or centrist control. Nonetheless, this form of development bureaucracy, when complemented with appropriate management procedures of the sort discussed later in this chapter, has provided a framework for the negotiation of implementable policies in areas as different as agricultural extension and family planning, and in countries as different as the Philippines and Kenya. We believe it deserves increased attention from both policymakers and scholars throughout the development community.

Policy implications. Three structural features suggested by the development-bureaucracy perspective are particularly relevant for policymakers seeking guidance in the design of facilitator organizations. The first feature is the people ratios. The number of villagers per lower-level field person, the number of lower-level field people per field supervisor, and so forth, set constraints on the size of area or population which can be covered effectively with a given staff of facilitators. Sometimes the limiting factor will be a shortage of low-level field staff, at other times a shortage of experienced supervisor-supporters at the district level. Whatever the level, these human constraints are no less binding than those of technology or biology. To relax them requires time, coupled with appropriate recruitment and training efforts. Attempts to cover larger areas and populations with structures that spread existing facilitators too thinly are likely to result in serious shortcomings. The lesson for policy design is the same that we encountered in our analysis of local organizations: start by concentrating existing resources on a small and feasible program, expanding only as success, experience, and relaxed constraints warrant.

The second feature is scale. The different scales of facilitator support required by different benefit packages affect the feasibility of integrating those packages into single rural-development programs. The issue is clearest at the field level. In short, except at a great loss of efficiency and concentration, a single lower-level field facilitator cannot "integrate" one set of responsibilities best performed at a scale of, say, five hundred families (such as agricultural extension) with another set of responsibilities best performed at a scale of two hundred families (such as primary health care). On the other hand, we might

---

[63] There is a growing recognition by development bureaucrats and politicians that center-periphery power relationships need not constitute a zero-sum game (Uphoff and Esman 1974, pp. 79–81). The "distinctive competence" of an organization "relates to the structures, routines, and norms which govern the organization's functioning and the technical and social capabilities it brings to bear in providing the program" (Korten 1980a, p. 496).

expect tuberculosis and malaria programs to require similar scales of coverage and therefore to be good candidates for integration at the field level.[64] Much more analysis needs to be done before considerations of organizational scale are refined enough to provide detailed guidance on the feasibility of alternative integration proposals. Nonetheless, it is only when integration issues begin to be treated in such pragmatic organizational terms, rather than as the ideological pawns of present practice, that progressive improvements in policy design can seriously be contemplated.

The third feature is authority. Development bureaucracy's conceptual commitment to bottom-up structural design has implications for the distribution of authority as well as responsibility. The people ratios and benefit-delivery scales we have discussed are obviously meaningless if the facilitator organization structures itself around one kind of benefit package but is then required by other authorities to deliver additional or entirely different ones. Such an add-on mentality is common to many central governments, despite the unambiguous lesson of past experience that nobody gains from imposing multiple lines of vertical authority on the operational level. Reaching the rural poor with effective facilitation is difficult enough under the best of circumstances. Where such efforts have succeeded at all, facilitator organizations have usually enjoyed a single, clear line of vertical authority reaching from at least the district down to the lowest field-staff level. *What* the organization does is often a matter for debate with, or even determination by, national authorities. But once the what has been decided upon, the operational part of the organization needs to be authorized to determine the how, to build its staff structure accordingly, and to resist outside efforts to impose additional responsibilities (see especially Benor and Harrison 1977, p. 11).[65]

Proper attention to questions of people ratios, scale of integration, and lines of authority is in no sense sufficient to guarantee success in the design of facilitator organizations. Successful resolution of such questions, however, probably is a necessary condition for successful development. We believe that students and practitioners of organization design will find substantial potential for better understanding and performance in all three areas.

Managing People

The best institutional structure is only inert opportunity. To contribute to rural development, structures must be vitalized through the ambitions and activities of people. We argued at the beginning of this chapter that the ability

[64] This example suggests a related theme we have not touched on here: similarity of task requirements. To expect the same facilitator to help women with birth control and men with irrigation is to expect a great deal.

[65] What about "matrix" structures of authority, in which a "vertical" line of functional authority is combined with a "horizontal" line of area-management authority? We agree with Korten (1979a) that in many development situations, such structures are a fact of life—a pragmatic adaptation to the reality of task interdependence. We merely wish to emphasize the primary importance, especially in new organizations, of resisting the common tendency of organizations to acquire multiple, relatively unrelated masters far removed from the field realities.

of any organization to perform its fundamental tasks depends as much as anything on the intelligence, skill, industry, precision, and speed with which its members execute their responsibilities. In organizations as large and far-flung as those needed to facilitate development, however, the productive performance of people can be neither commanded from above nor left to emerge from the unguided initiatives of individuals. Building feasible and effective alternatives to these organizational extremes is the challenge of development management.

Recent work in the developing countries has emphasized that a necessary component of people management is the design of rules and procedures which "institutionalize" individuals' behaviors and expectations.[66] Formal procedures alone are not sufficient, however. Effective management also requires an intangible that might be called morale: a common vision, a sense of commitment, motivation, and confidence shared among the people who make an organization work.[67]

Effective people management is a burgeoning subject about which more is written than known. We shall confine our remarks to a few issues particularly relevant to management of the development bureaucracies we described in the previous section. Again, Chambers (1974), Leonard (1977) and Benor and Harrison (1977) provide much of our material and should be consulted for more extended discussions.

Careers for facilitators. There is no question that without a sufficient number of appropriately trained people, facilitator organizations cannot fulfill their responsibilities for rural development. Early recognition of this constraint and of its seriousness led to an era of "manpower planning" programs designed to promote widespread educational advances at primary, secondary, and university levels. By the mid-1970s, although absolute shortages of trained manpower still existed, these programs had made substantial progress in accomplishing what they had set out to do. As a result, the "manpower problem" throughout the developing world came to be viewed as less a problem of numbers and credentials, and more one of inadequate job performance.

Many diagnoses of this poor performance have been offered; some were reviewed earlier in this chapter. The significant contribution of the "development-bureaucracy" school has been to analyze the performance problem from the perspective of facilitator people themselves. From this perspective, the problem of providing manpower for facilitation is more naturally perceived as a problem of designing career structures for facilitators.

This change in perspective has important implications for policymakers. Practical and tested approaches to people management built from the career

---

[66] The term is from Uphoff and Esman (1974, pp. 92–96). Leonard (1977, chap. 10) calls essentially the same thing "depersonalization."

[67] Mosher (1957, p. 268) uses the term "self-generating resources" to describe the cumulative effects of a process in which the morale and effectiveness of members of a facilitator organization are increased. They are "self-generating" because they are "augmented rather than consumed by use."

perspective have just begun to take shape over the last five years, but some useful policy guidelines are already emerging. It is now recognized, for example, that traditional programs aimed at creating more formal education for more people do not solve the problem of performance difficulties, and often contribute to it. It is well established that formal education of facilitator staff, especially when carried into the secondary level, can often raise career expectations higher than the facilitator organization can or should fulfill. The resulting disappointment frequently results in loss of highly trained facilitators to the private sector or parastatals, and contributes to the urban bias observed in those who stay with the organization. More generally, it leads to a deterioration of commitment and performance.[68]

This experience has led to the emergence of recruitment policies for facilitator organizations which not only seek a better fit of educational background to job requirements and prospects but also place a much higher value on practical experience and motivation. Thus, the best field-level facilitators in some of India's integrated health programs have been illiterate middle-aged women with a strong personal desire to help (Pyle 1979, pp. 19–21). For agricultural extension work secondary-school graduates are often preferred, though selected "master farmers" have successfully served as low-level facilitators in countries as different as Nepal, Thailand, and Turkey (Benor and Harrison 1977, p. 36). Good, job-focused training programs carried out after recruitment, coupled with continuing on-the-job training, have proved to be more important than formal schooling per se. Upper-level field facilitators may benefit from prerecruitment training at universities. Even here, however, some of the most successful have come up through the ranks, gaining extensive practical experience and cumulative on-the-job training as lower-level field workers. More generally, David Leonard (November 1980: personal communication) has argued that effective performance of facilitators requires a good fit between prospects for upward mobility and status on the one hand and expectations of someone with a given educational background on the other. Where both the status of facilitator work and the prospects for career advancement are high, excellent village-level work can be expected from secondary-school or even university graduates. Where the status and career prospects of such work are low, the most effective village-level workers may well be those who are illiterate or have no more than a primary-school education.

The prospect of upward mobility is a key element in the incentive schemes which have begun to replace traditional satisfaction-motivation notions at the conceptual core of people-management programs in development bureaucracies (Leonard 1977, p. 126). A general finding of recent field studies in this area has been that staff performance responds well to career-related incentives rewarded through fair evaluation of actual work performance (e.g., Har-

---

[68] Leonard's statistical studies in Kenya showed that "secondary education has a uniformly detrimental effect on the work performance" of agricultural extension staff (1977, chap. 6). A similar relationship has been reported for low-level health staff in India (Pyle 1979, p. 20).

rison 1969, cited in Chambers 1974, p. 61). Merit promotions are one obvious incentive; every effort should be made to fill available vacancies in this manner.[69]

Except in periods of rapid expansion, promotions are too few to serve as a credible incentive to the majority of facilitator staff. Moreover, the majority of low-level field workers, especially those recruited with minimal formal education, will never have the qualifications to move into supervisory roles requiring extended interactions with the center. It is therefore also desirable to establish very long salary scales *within* each facilitator level, providing an opportunity for pay increments throughout the career of the unpromoted facilitator. Obstacles to the introduction of such organizational innovations have come less frequently from budgetary officials (the upper salary brackets are for the most part future expenses) than from established civil-service administrators intent on defending their own jurisdictional authority.

Opportunities for providing promotion or salary incentives will always be limited, particularly in the late-developing countries. Building of morale and career commitment in facilitator staff must finally rely on innovative management of the organizational environment. Prospects of increased status within a respected peer group, of treatment as a professional colleague by higher-level staff, of expanded responsibility within one's sphere of action—these and other intangibles represent invaluable but largely untapped resources for incentive-based management of facilitator people. Whether the potential inherent in those resources can be realized is largely a question of how communication among supervisors, support personnel, and field staff is handled by the facilitator organization.

Communication for facilitators. Facilitator organizations, when operating successfully, are essentially communications devices through which people interact in a mutual teaching-learning exercise. Historically, however, the communication in most development organizations has been one-way: orders and answers flow out from the center towards the periphery. In contrast, the development-bureaucracy experiments we are considering here have emphasized the need for two-way communication: each level of the organization is assumed to possess unique skills and knowledge needed by the other levels. This perspective has led to less authoritarian management and to more mutual negotiation of task schedules and performance criteria. In particular, it has emphasized that upper-level facilitators should serve support as well as supervisory functions, acting as sources of expertise and guidance on which lower-level facilitators are encouraged to draw. Let us review what this means for facilitator personnel at each of the principal levels.[70]

---

[69] This should not be interpreted as a sanction of frequent staff transfers between different geographic areas, however. Each of the development-bureaucracy studies on which we base this section has identified such transfers as generally counterproductive, emphasizing instead the importance of staff's building a deep understanding of, and links with, a particular area.

[70] See above, n. 61, for definition of the various levels.

The lower-level field facilitators of development bureaucracy engage in three essential communications functions. First, they are continuously trained in relevant techniques and methods by people higher in the organizational framework; they then teach what they have learned to individuals and groups in rural communities. Second, in the course of their training they communicate upwards through the organization their firsthand knowledge of what is needed in the villages and how the recent innovations are faring. Third, they provide immediate, on-the-spot diagnoses and prescriptions for many of the more common local problems, calling on their supervisor-supporters only in cases of more difficult problems which require higher-level expertise and attention.

People at the next level of development bureaucracy—the upper-level field facilitators—spend most of their time in the field, supervising and supporting the activities of their lower-level colleagues. They are responsible for negotiating work schedules and performance criteria. In addition, they conduct training and refresher sessions on many of the more common techniques and methods which lower-level staff will be teaching in the villages. One of their important communications functions is to elicit feedback from the lower-level facilitators on the problems and potential of ongoing development-program activities as seen from the village level. In addition, these facilitators should be capable of resolving the vast majority of problems referred to them by their subordinates. Experience suggests that if the first two (field) levels of a facilitator organization are competently staffed, they should be able to deal with 90 percent or more of the specific health or agricultural problems encountered by villagers. Paradoxically, a delicate management problem has been to keep this "solution rate" from becoming 100 percent. Upper-level field facilitators, often lacking either formal education or extensive experience, seem particularly prone to the insecurities of what is known elsewhere as the "first-year intern syndrome": if you don't know the answer, dazzle them with many long words and hope no one will notice your ignorance. One of the foremost communications challenges of district-level supervision-and-support personnel is to help such field staff distinguish between when it is best to ask for help and when it is best to proceed on one's own.

Third-level facilitators—the lower-level district staff—often stand on a social and organizational watershed in the development bureaucracies. On one side are the various field-staff levels, people who spend most of their time in the field and whose professional and social lives are rooted "below," in the rural community (see especially Leonard 1977, chap. 3). On the other side are upper-level district facilitators, who spend most of their time in offices and whose professional and social lives tend to be rooted "above," in the civil-service and power elite. By and large, this two-way orientation of the overall facilitator organization is probably as advantageous as it is inevitable. It does, however, place particular strains on those at the lower district levels, whose responsibility is to communicate across the boundary.

In many ways the supervision and support services performed by district facilitators for upper-level field staff are like those performed by upper-level field staff for their junior colleagues. Negotiation of work schedules, review of work in the field, and conduct of training and refresher exercises occupy a central place in the district activities of most of the development bureaucracies. In addition, a more or less informal liason is maintained with other organizations facilitating other programs. These may include government administrations, parastatals, and commercial organizations.

District-level support usually also includes a variety of subject-matter specialists: the doctors, agronomists, engineers, and other highly trained professionals on whom the facilitator organization's ability to resolve difficult problems and propose innovative solutions so often depends. Good subject-matter specialists, with both experience and sound education, remain one of the most pressing resource constraints in many of the late-developing countries. Everywhere, it is essential that this resource be used efficiently and not squandered in low-priority tasks.

In particular, district-level managers must guard against the tendency of specialists to immerse themselves in the curing of individual patients, in the yield increases of individual fields, or in the construction details of individual irrigation canals. It cannot be overemphasized that the cumulative effect of such misdirected enthusiasm is seriously detrimental to the performance of the overall organization. Its opportunity costs are obvious. More important, however, may be the subtle demoralizing effect which such activities have on the field staff, whose responsibilities and authority the specialists unwittingly undermine. The most valuable specialist is one who has learned to guide field staff towards their own diagnoses and prescriptions, in such a manner that not only is the problem resolved but the self-esteem and community status of the field staff is enhanced as well.

Finally, it may be useful to state explicitly two obvious but often neglected realities concerning the logistics of communication. Meetings, paperwork, and the printed word are often assumed to be the essentials of communication in large organizations. But the development-bureaucracy experiments have shown that the fewer those "essentials" and the simpler the role, the more effectively a facilitator organization is likely to perform. We assume that there must be a lower limit to this trend. Nonetheless, it is remarkable how often various architects of reorganization have thought they had reached the absolute minimum, only to find, upon careful analysis, that one more "essential" report was never read by anyone, one more "key" meeting never resolved anything, or one more "significant" datum was being faked by the form-fillers. As in so many other aspects of development, the hard lesson has been to simplify, simplify, and simplify again.

In practice, the essence of effective communication in facilitator organizations is not paperwork. It is transport. We suspect that there would be enormous returns on an investment providing sturdy, simple bicycles or—where necessary—motorcycles for every field staff member of a facilitator organization. The finance ministries' tradition of turning down requests for such "luxuries" reflects an ignorance of, or indifference towards, the realities of time and distance with which facilitators must contend.[71] It cannot be overemphasized that effective transport is not a luxury but an essential component of development organization.

Leadership.   Formal structures and procedures are necessary components of effective development organizations. Experience has shown, however, that for many of the tasks those organizations must perform, an additional requirement is strong and sustained leadership. The following conclusion of Ickis (1981) is based on work in Central America, but it is supported by experience in Africa (Leonard 1977, chap. 5) and Asia (Korten 1980*a*) as well:

> The basis of more effective action will not be found either in the application of more sophisticated methods for the preplanning of development action or in conventional management training to build implementation skills. The need is to build the capacity of action agencies to work in a supportive interactive mode with their client populations. Effective leadership by individuals who understand the nature of the problem and are willing to make strong personal commitments to its resolution is perhaps the key input to this capacity building process. It is to the problem of facilitating the emergence of such leadership that both planners and management specialists must be addressing themselves.

The facilitation of leadership for development organization has received very little constructive attention in the literature for three interrelated reasons. First of all, leadership in any form is largely irrelevant to those visions of development based on what we have called the intellectual-cogitation theory of policy design. Leaders are not necessary—indeed, their initiatives are a positive hindrance—in a world that sees local villagers and facilitator staff as the obedient implementors of preprogrammed solutions. We have argued, however, that the pure cogitation view of policy is rarely if ever appropriate to the real world of development. Instead, we have suggested that development organizations normally function under highly politicized conditions where formal sanctions and authority are seldom sufficient to ensure successful program implementation. Social interaction must therefore complement intellectual cogitation as a means of calculation and control. And unlike cogitation, interactive problem-solving requires leadership—leadership to build consensus and negotiate compromises where values conflict, leadership to shape the common vision which coordinates individual actors in the absence of formal

---

[71] Chambers (1974, p. 60) addresses this issue, and provides some specific examples. This planners' presumption that other people's time is a free good pervades development; we encountered it earlier in our discussion of why the rural poor don't participate in time-consuming organizational activities which the planners have prescribed for them.

plans, leadership to prod and cajole and guide an action program through the unpredictable maze of what Bardach (1977) has called the "implementation game." Leadership will not get much serious attention in the development debate until the present infatuation with "thinking-through" approaches to policy design is replaced with a more balanced cogitation-plus-interaction perspective.

A second reason for the neglect of leadership issues is ideological. Leaders are by definition members of an elite. Moreover, it is well known and hardly surprising that effective leaders at all levels of development organization tend to be drawn from the more progressive, better educated, and often relatively better-off strata of rural society (see, for example, Korten 1980a). We have already called attention to foreign advisors' often uncritical advocacy of superficially democratic and egalitarian forms of organization. In the present context, this advocacy often amounts to a hostility towards the emergence of forceful, innovative leadership. It emphasizes instead a vague blend of local (leaderless) autonomy and "professional" (central or imported) program management. Such a simplistic attitude is precisely the opposite of what is needed to achieve practical results.

Effective leadership does not require democratic selection, and its emergence may be squelched if a popularity contest is insisted upon. Programs do benefit from leaders whose roots in the local community give them a deep knowledge of its structure and a long-term commitment to improving its well-being (Uphoff and Esman 1974, p. 87). Uncontrolled leaders are likely to abuse their powers, as we discussed in our review of the local-elite issue. Some of this abuse may be inevitable and regrettable but still a cheap price to pay for the benefits of productive and dynamic development programs. Some of it can be mitigated through the design of appropriate auditing and accountability controls on leaders at all levels (see, for example, Pyle 1979, p. 39; Uphoff and Esman 1974, p. 20). Rather than discarding the benefits of effective leadership in order to maintain an ideological purity, development planners and managers would better spend their time and effort seeking to strike a productive, delicate balance between the facilitation and the control of leadership behavior.

A third hindrance to the facilitation of effective leadership in development organizations is in a sense the converse of that just discussed. Of the few writers who have recognized the importance of dynamic leadership to development programs, most have tended to place it beyond the reach of systematic analysis. Indefinable "charisma," personal character traits, and hereditary influences are put forth as the qualities of which effective leadership is made. Fortunately, serious scholarship has begun to replace this superficial and misleading folk wisdom by defining "relevant skills, behaviors, and role definitions, all of which can be encouraged and developed as conscious acts of (policy) choice" (Korten 1981). Particularly important are the abilities to engage in supportive, nonauthoritarian guidance of other actors in the development process, to articulate unifying themes and values, and to facilitate a general learning-process approach to program implementation.[72] We review ways in which effective leaders can utilize these skills for program management in the next and final section of this chapter.

Managing Programs

We have discussed the structural framework and human content of facilitator organizations. The question remains of how the organizations are to be managed.

Progress in the design of effective, efficient, and transferable approaches to program management has been hindered by the dominance of two extreme and opposing biases. One has been the quest for "standard solutions": if only the right variables could be identified, the right prescriptions agreed upon, the appropriate organizational design discovered, then development would leap forward throughout the world. The other has been the cult of "unique solutions": no problem is ever encountered twice, all cases are special cases, and any effort to generalize or transfer experience is naive.

Neither extreme is realistic, and neither has been productive. In fact, all successful development programs involve some degree of trial-and-error learning, if only in their need to be implemented at particular times and places. It is, however, a rare program indeed in which learning cannot be accelerated and some of the more disastrous trials cannot be avoided through judicious use of proven—that is, "standardized"—biological or technical innovations, institutional structures, or managerial procedures. The challenge of program management is to steer an intermediate course between the extremes of the "standard" and the "unique," making tentative use of what is relatively well known to learn more effectively about what is relatively unknown.

Managing the predictable. The appropriate management style depends on the "predictability" of program activities.[73] Where little prior experience exists, where success depends more on building local problem-solving organizations than on implementing or delivering known solutions, then management is best oriented towards exploration and learning. We will have more to say regarding such situations later. At the other extreme, many similar programs have been previously implemented, recurrent pitfalls have been identi-

---

[72] Leonard (1977, chap. 5) provides a systematic analysis of leadership skills in an East African context; he links his findings—which we have drawn on here—to the formal organizational exchange theory of Blau (1964). Complementary findings are reported by Tanco (1981) and de Jesus (1981).

[73] Those determined to misunderstand our usage of *predictable* will do so even if we employ a more awkward expression. A development program can be predictable in the same way that driving a car on a major highway can be predictable. Constant attention to changing local circumstances is required to avoid disaster, which may occur anyway. Nonetheless, a trained driver can usually perform the job reasonably well. His pragmatic predictions that the road will behave in certain ways, that it will not suddenly end up in a lake or plunge off a cliff, are generally upheld by experience. When bad weather, poor roads, a lack of maps, or the car's need for repairs makes driving less predictable, the rational driver changes his procedures accordingly.

fied, and a variety of procedures for avoiding or recovering from errors have been evolved and tested. The managerial challenge is therefore not so much to explore new territory as to guide a larger number of programs along a difficult but fairly well-charted course, and to do so in an increasingly effective and efficient manner. This guidance function is most evident in agricultural extension programs, an area with more cumulative management experience than any other in development.

Especially in regions with relatively favorable growing conditions, extension has become in many of its broader aspects a "predictable" activity. A variety of managerial guidelines for performing this activity have been proposed by the various "development bureaucracies" referred to earlier. Belshaw and Chambers's Programming and Implementation Management System (PIM) and Benor and Harrison's Training and Visit System, for example, differ in many respects but share managerial emphasis on explicit specification of the what, how, who, and when of program implementation. *What* are the priority objectives? *How* are these to be reconciled with available resources? *Who* is to perform each task required for meeting the objectives? *When* is each task to be initiated and completed? Each of these questions is asked for all program activities and at each level of the facilitator organization. Flexibility is maintained through a periodic renegotiation of the resulting plan as actual program experience unfolds. Two-way communication is supported by a schedule of in-service training and site visits, parsimonious use of reports and meetings, and simple visual aids to planning and decision-making.[74] Institutional structure and staff management procedures are organized along lines discussed earlier.

The more or less independent evolution of such similar management strategies by different workers in different countries is an encouraging sign. So is the insistence of each group that its approach is not a blueprint to be slavishly copied but rather a core of managerial components from which locally adapted extension programs can be designed. Experience indicates that such local adaptations can be quite successful.[75]

Management approaches resembling those just described for extension have emerged in other development areas as well.[76] Invariably, however, this has happened where the requirements for local organization are relatively undemanding and only after an extended period of experimentation and failure,

---

[74] The programming charts described by Chambers (1974, p. 186) and the Morley growth chart for monitoring child development are good examples of such visual aids (see Morley 1966, chap. 16: 7)

[75] In chapter 3 we cited a study of the impact of the Training and Visit system in West Bengal (Ray et al. 1979); and Kingshotte (1980b, esp. pp. 320–22) has reported on the successful implementation of an extension management system in Botswana, which has some striking similarities and certain differences. For an evaluation of the Programming and Implementation Management System (PIM) in Kenya, see David, Oyugi, and Wallis (1975).

[76] See Korten's (1980a) description of the Indian National Dairy Development Board and Thailand's Community Based Family Planning Services.

during which the management system was evolved. It is essential to keep in mind that the highly sophisticated and structured systems of managerial guidance typified by agricultural extension are the end result, not the starting point, of a long sequence of exploratory learning activities. Management in the latter, less sophisticated exploratory mode is still required for most development programs.

Managing a learning sequence. Planners and academics, we have argued, have long been infatuated with the "intellectual-cogitation" approach to development programs. Their goal apparently has been to perfect a blueprint specification of the "correct" development design, which can then be implemented by obedient cadres of development managers. This approach has been totally and repeatedly discredited by experience; yet despite much rhetoric to the contrary, it persists at the conceptual core of much development activity (Chambers 1974; Caiden and Wildavsky 1974; Korten 1979a, 1980a). It will doubtless continue to do so until the accomplishments of alternative "social-interaction" approaches begin to get a better press in the professional development community.

Hunter (1970, 1978a), Hirschman (1971), and more recently Korten (1980a) have been articulate spokesmen for sequential, learning-oriented approaches to program management. Their basic theme is that programs which lack a well-developed foundation of demonstrably replicable experience should start with simple, informally organized activities built around small groups at the local level. Based on lessons learned in the actual doing of the program at that level, new tasks, linkages, and management procedures then can be tentatively adopted. Those that work are retained. Those that cause too much conflict or overload field staff or are otherwise counterproductive are abandoned. The organization will grow gradually and dynamically towards Brewster's "continually widening network of large, specialized units of collective action."

Korten (1980a) reviews the experience of five such "learning organizations," all of which grew from small local teams into larger-scale programs with notable accomplishments: the Indian National Dairy Development Board, the Sarvodaya Shramadana Movement of Sri Lanka, the Bangladesh Rural Advancement Committees, Thailand's Community Based Family Planning Services, and the Philippine National Irrigation Administration's Communal Irrigation Program. He suggests that despite the lack of any "key variables" or "standard designs," a three-stage "learning sequence" was common to all the program successes.

First, each program had to learn to be effective. As we argued earlier in our discussions of production, consumption, and local organization programs, this means focusing on some benefit package that is desirable to the local poor and feasible in terms of the existing resource, organizational, and political constraints. This stage of the sequence often requires substantial outside support and encouragement. It involves many false starts and requires much trial-and-error learning to discover local desires, capabilities, and power cleavages.

Its ultimate aim is to achieve a dynamic fit between the needs of the poor, the benefits of the program, and the capabilities of the supporting organization.[77]

Second, each program had to learn to be efficient. The resource limitations are too great, and the needs too acute, for effectiveness to be the only criterion for program management. Once effectiveness is firmly established, the organization should begin to seek ways of increasing efficiency by reducing the input requirements per unit of output. This is one of the accomplishments of the highly structured extension organizations we referred to earlier: time and tasks of facilitator staff are carefully programmed in order to serve the maximum number of poor people in the most efficient manner. Once again, such programming is not some planner's daydream but the end result of a learning process in which various schemes to make the programs' organization more efficient are evaluated through trial and error.

Third, each program had to learn to expand. Development needs are too urgent to let every local community reinvent all of the necessary building blocks. The goal of program management is to transfer the fruits of one learning sequence to other people and other areas. This is a tricky subject, in which too much is often attempted too quickly, resulting in loss of both efficiency and effectiveness. Like it or not, each program must often recapitulate the entire effectiveness-efficiency-expansion learning sequence at each new location simply because the new groups must go through a good deal of the learning themselves. Management must seek to use previous experience to facilitate and accelerate this learning, without pushing it too fast.

Attempts to plot in advance the detailed course of such learning exercises are naive and counterproductive. The need, in the previously quoted phrase of Hirschman, is to "think in terms of sequences in the course of which a forward step in one direction will induce others." This means that a program must be thought of, not as the implementation of a static blueprint, but rather as the guidance—the facilitation—of an organic design process. Above all else, it means recognizing that learning how to organize development takes time— time to develop trust and commitment among individuals; time to learn new skills; time to try, and fail, and try again. The Thailand family planning program described above took seven years to grow from its first trials to its coverage of 16,000 villages in 1979. The Bangladesh Rural Advancement Commit-

---

[77] There has been a good deal of dogmatic argument, even among supporters of the "learning-sequence" notion, over what specific benefit package is the "right" one to start with. This is particularly true for consumption programs, where too much has been made of a rigorous progression from simple curative health measures through more complicated nutritional activities to the wholesale changes of behavior required for family planning and improved sanitation. The inherent logic to this progression is attractive, and it responds to the previously mentioned lament of family-planning workers: "Give us something else we can talk about." Nonetheless, the reverse sequence sometimes works as well. The family planning program in Indonesia started with birth control and is only now beginning to include health and nutrition activities. We articulated our position earlier in this chapter: find out what the local groups desire by working with them, not by coming to them with preconceived notions; then organize around whatever benefits the local groups most want and the support groups are most capable of furnishing.

tees are active in 800 villages eight years after their inception. In twenty-two years the Sarvodaya Shramadana Movement has established effective organizations in 240 villages. Even the cooperative effort which became the Indian National Dairy Development Board spent ten years in trial-and-error learning before seeking to expand beyond the state in which it originated.[78] The Philippines irrigation work we have discussed will take, under optimistic assumptions, at least seven years to go from its initial pilot project to an effectively implemented means of managing the overall organization.

Why learning takes so long and how it can be accelerated are fundamentally important questions deserving more research attention than they now receive. One thing is already clear, however: the funding cycles of both national and international development administrations are much shorter than the time typically required for a development organization to learn its trade. Until and unless these ostensible "managers" can take a more realistic, longer-range perspective in their program-development efforts, the historical record of overhasty expansions and premature terminations can be expected to continue.

Evaluation and adaptive management. Learning from social interactions requires continuous monitoring and evaluation of experience. Asking Where are we? and How are we doing? should become integral to managerial operating procedure. But although trials and errors are inevitable components of interactive development, learning is not. Michael (1973) describes two basic organizational responses to error: to reject it or to embrace it. Error rejection is much the more common response; organizations bury their mistakes, refuse to admit they are wrong, or seek to pass the blame for failure elsewhere. Since no error is admitted, no learning occurs. The same non-errors are repeated over and over in the pattern we have emphasized throughout this essay. In contrast, error-embracing organizations accept error as inevitable. They are therefore committed to seeking it out, diagnosing it, and thereby avoiding its repetition.[79] Error-embracing behavior is rare because of the costs it usually imposes on the people and organizations that attempt it. When the admission of error is taken as a sign of incompetence, an opportunity for attack, an excuse for withdrawal of funds or the withholding of promotion, it is only rational to hide or deny errors whenever possible. The challenge of program management is to reverse these relationships and make the timely, aggressive identification and correction of error a highly respected and well-rewarded activity.

We have already noted that facilitator staff at all levels generally respond best to supportive, nonauthoritarian management styles. Chambers (1974), Benor and Harrison (1977), and Korten (1980a) all have emphasized the im-

---

[78] For a brief account of how the original Anand pattern evolved and led to the creation of the National Dairy Development Board, see Halse (1980).

[79] Korten (1980a), drawing on Michael (1973), discusses these alternatives in a development context. Wildavsky (1978), using the term "self-evaluating organization," discusses error-embracing behavior from an institutional viewpoint.

portance of designing performance evaluations around a mutually negotiated set of targets or criteria. Actual progress is monitored against these targets. Shortfalls are viewed, not as an occasion for disciplinary action, but as an opportunity for supportive diagnosis of cause and joint prescription of remedial actions.

There is, however, an increasing recognition in development circles that the targets or criteria against which performance is evaluated must be very carefully specified. If, as is too often the case, evaluations are based on the number of forms filled out, the attendance at meetings, or the adherence to standard operating procedures, then the program participants will "learn" to fill out forms, attend meetings, and follow procedures. If evaluations are based on maximizing numbers of farmers visited, then people will learn how to visit—or report visiting—many farms. These are obviously counterproductive evaluation measures. Recent experience in family planning (Korten and Korten 1977), in the delivery of integrated health packages (Pyle 1979, 1981), and in agricultural extension (Chambers 1974) has shown that much more effective learning can be achieved when evaluation targets are defined in terms of the actual results desired of the development program. Monitoring results is often more difficult than monitoring procedures, but improvements in the learning process will often justify the costs.[80]

Evaluation of program performance, as well as people performance, is necessary if an effective learning process is to be carried out. Demonstration programs, research programs, pilot programs, and the like are often put forward as means of accomplishing such evaluations. As Pyle (1979) has pointed out, however, it is important to recognize that each of these programs serves a radically different function.

Demonstration programs are designed to *convince* someone (who may be a poor farmer or a high development official) that a given specific program is both feasible and desirable. We argued in chapter 1 that social interactions are supposed to help people learn what they want; and we showed in chapter 3 that it is altogether rational for a farmer to insist on a credible demonstration of a new technology before he risks a year's crop on it. Convincing demonstration programs therefore have an essential place in the larger learning process of development. They are appropriate, however, only where someone already has an answer and is trying to teach it to someone else.

Research programs and pilot programs have a more obviously important role to play in helping people learn about development. It is crucial to emphasize, however, that formal experimental methods are useful only when con-

---

[80] We would hope, however, that the advocacy of "results-oriented" over "procedures-oriented" evaluation approaches does not become uncritically accepted dogma in development circles. A thriving literature on program evaluation in the developed countries warns that there are numerous instances in which evaluation by procedural criteria is to be preferred. Majone (1979), for example, points out how badly an insistence on evaluation by results would serve modern medical or legal practice.

fined to situations in which the classical scientific notions of "test" and "experimenter" make sense. This is certainly the case when an extension service wants to evaluate the growth potential of a new rice variety. It is likewise credible when a new oral-rehydration technique is being field "tested" for the first time. In such cases, the experiment is clearly defined, and the learning is properly acruing to the senior facilitator people who will be responsible for revising or distributing the tested innovation.

Classical "research" and "pilot" approaches are less useful—and often counterproductive—when applied to programs in which the major need is to develop a local capacity for sustained development action. In such cases, program success requires that the local people and their field-level facilitators learn how better to organize themselves to deal with a continuing problem area. All too often, this distinction is overlooked by planners or donors intent on "demonstrating," "testing," or "proving" the merits of a particular blueprint for subsequent program organization. Temporary staff and structures are brought in to assure program success and an adequate control of presumed key variables. The result is that the learning acrues to the wrong people. Once the experiment is completed, and the approach "proven," the team of imported managers, specialists, and consultants takes the lessons it has learned on to its next assignment, leaving the local groups as ignorant and inexperienced as they were to begin with. The attempted "transfer" usually fails, leaving little sustained problem-solving capacity in its wake (Lele 1975, chap. 8).

Treatment of pilot projects as "tests" of development "hypotheses" retains a flavor of what we earlier called "physics envy" when it is applied in any but the most narrowly defined development contexts. Korten (1980a, p. 493) has suggested that the concept of a "learning laboratory" is a more generally appropriate means of learning from the interactive experience of development. Using the example of the Philippine National Irrigation Administration, Korten argues that the explicit purpose of a "learning laboratory" is to provide an error-embracing environment in which the local people and facilitators are helped to evaluate their own performance and to benefit from their own experience. The role of the subject-matter specialist or development planner is transformed from one of problem-solver and evaluator to what Korten calls one of capacity builder. The goal is to facilitate a learning sequence of organizational growth.

There is a growing recognition of the need to view rural development as a continuing, dynamic learning process. PIDER, the Investment Program for Rural Development in Mexico, provides an interesting example. Since its inception in 1973, PIDER has made provision for monitoring and evaluation to draw lessons from ongoing experience and to guide the redesign of programs so as to enhance their future effectiveness. The Mexican government, in collaboration with the World Bank and the Inter American Development Bank, has acted to institutionalize applied research and evaluation by setting up CIDER, a research center for rural development. By 1978 this interdisciplinary organization had a staff of nearly fifty professionals. It is expected to devote a substantial part of its work to the analysis and evaluation of PIDER's field programs (Cernea 1979). A "midterm evaluation" carried out jointly by PIDER and CIDER (and with participation by the World Bank) concluded, for example, that an important shortcoming of the program was a lack of feasible and profitable technological "packages" adapted to Mexico's rainfed farming areas. A substantial Rainfed Agricultural Development Project is now underway in order to overcome that major deficiency.

We shall see in chapter 6 that the notion of development as a learning process is equally appropriate for redesigning national development strategies.

CHAPTER SIX

Adaptive Strategies:
A Three-pronged Approach

In the preceding chapters we have considered specific interventions for the redesign of production, consumption, and organization programs. In this concluding chapter we consider the interrelationships between those interventions and confront the problem of combining them into effective strategies for rural development.

The resource and structural-demographic constraints examined in chapter 2 make it painfully obvious that late-developing countries cannot do everything at once. "Limited resources force compromise and choice." Thus Wildavsky (1979, p. 391) emphasizes that even in affluent economies, wants and needs exceed resources and it is therefore irresponsible to pursue objectives attainable only at exorbitant political, economic, or social cost. Because opportunity cost is a ubiquitous fact of life, setting priorities is necessary for any effective development strategy. Undertaking low-priority programs, however desirable they may appear to be when considered in isolation, means a commitment of resources which will almost inevitably be at the expense of higher-priority objectives. Similarly, a short-sighted focus on relieving immediate suffering often levies excessive cost on posterity. Lele's findings in the context of East Africa are echoed throughout the developing world: "a substantial allocation of essential resources to social services frequently occurs at the cost of more immediately productive investments in rural areas, and therefore, may prove self-defeating in the long run" (1975, p. 123).

All too frequently, however, the need for priorities becomes an excuse for simplistic absolutes: "Food First," "Steel First," "First the Revolution." In the unsimple real world there exist both complementary and competitive relationships between production, consumption, and organization-oriented activities. Indeed, we argue in this chapter that preoccupation with any single program area is likely to be self-defeating.

A major concern of policy analysis, we have seen, is to adjust both ends and means, reflecting a realistic view and a continuing reassessment of prevailing constraints. Merely to lower expectations in order to achieve a balance between resources and objectives is a counsel of despair, a recipe for perpetuating poverty and its deprivations. What leads us to a concern with multiple objectives is not a penchant for grandiose plans but the nature of the problem faced by the late-developing countries: it is essential to achieve as much progress as possible in realizing the interrelated objectives of accelerating the growth of output, expanding employment opportunities, reducing severe deprivations such as malnutrition and excessive morbidity, and slowing population growth. And those objectives cannot be realized without sustained efforts to build the organizational, problem-solving capacity to implement the required production and consumption programs.

A country's development progress may be unsatisfactory because policymakers focus too narrowly on growth or because they opt for an unrealistically wide range of activities. In either case, program implementation may fail to significantly improve the well-being of the mass of the population. Later in this chapter we argue that the problem of achieving a workable consensus on which activities to undertake is bedeviled by competing claims which err in both directions—an excessively narrow view of the objective of accelerating the growth of output, and unrealistically expansive proposals to satisfy basic needs directly. This failure to reach a workable consensus on longer-term strategic objectives often results in efforts that are so sporadic that little change of any sort is actually accomplished.

We have seen that one of the basic tasks of calculation and control to be performed by organizations is the distribution of resources among competing claims. Policymakers at the national level confront especially formidable problems in striking an appropriate balance among the various components of a strategy for rural development. The choices are inevitably difficult because of the need to be concerned simultaneously with production, consumption, and organization. The mutual adjustment of ends and means therefore requires that some highly desirable ends be deferred. It also requires selecting means which economize on the scarcest resources and are effective in attaining multiple objectives.

We begin our discussion with a critical examination of the techniques available for affecting mutual adjustment of means and ends at the national level. We consider not only intellectual techniques such as planning, budgeting, and systems modeling but also interactive techniques associated with various kinds of markets. Our conclusion, echoing earlier themes from chapter 1, is that neither cogitation nor interaction alone can provide adequate guidance for the design of national development strategies. The central challenge for today's planners and policymakers is to combine the two approaches more effectively, thus better to guide and to learn from the ongoing process of development.

Our emphasis on development as a learning process notwithstanding, we recognize with Caiden and Wildavsky that "correcting mistakes and building up from limited success are slow and time-consuming" (1974, p. 310). It is therefore important to make as much use as possible of what is presently known regarding the variables, interrelationships, and constraints relevant to the design of development strategies. This requires the critical if tentative application of intellectual, analytic approaches which draw upon theoretical insights and upon evidence from past experience.

Our analyses in previous chapters focused individually on production, consumption, and organization programs. We noted in passing, however, numerous ways in which these programs affect and depend upon one another. In this chapter we summarize our analyses, focusing on the interrelationships per se. This leads us to emphasize that programs can have complementary as well as competitive impacts on each other and on the well-being of the rural poor. We sketch a three-pronged strategic perspective which assigns simultaneous and high priority to programs that promote broadly based improvements in agricultural production and rural employment; strengthen social services through an emphasis on health, nutrition, and family planning; and increase the efficacy of organizational structures and procedures. We argue that such a three-pronged approach is more likely to promote tangible and sustained benefits to the rural poor than are many of the alternative, more narrowly focused strategies now being promoted. Food-subsidy programs and relief-and-welfare approaches to foreign aid are singled out as particularly inappropriate foundations on which to base rural development policies.

As we stressed in chapter 1, the ultimate plan is to act. In the concluding section of this chapter we advance some thoughts on the directions that action might profitably take and on the role of patience and persistence in helping actions and their results contribute to an adaptive strategy of rural development.

Approaches to National Policy Design

Many techniques have been utilized to provide guidance in setting priorities and allocating scarce resources among programs. Some of these received attention in chapter 5; here our focus is on strategic policymaking at the national level. The most conspicuous policymaking techniques at the national level are various procedures for planning and budgeting. Both are examples of what we earlier called the intellectual-cogitation, or thinking-through, approach to social problem-solving. Less conspicuous but at least as important, however, are approaches to policymaking through social interaction. These include political and bargaining techniques plus market and price mechanisms, which attain special significance at the national level. As we argued in chapter 1, there is a pressing need to achieve a more effective integration of intellectual cogitation and social interaction as complementary approaches to strategic problem-solving.

Thinking-through Approaches
Planning. No one approach can be expected to provide totally satisfactory guidance to national policymakers. Nonetheless, great hopes have been placed on comprehensive economic planning as a major instrument for achiev-

ing more rational and more rapid development. Those high hopes, however, have not been fulfilled; the shortcomings of planning are now generally recognized. Some of the general reasons for these shortcomings were considered in chapter 1. A number of the specific shortcomings of development planning were examined in detail in a pioneering study by Waterston (1965). Arthur Lewis's *Development Planning* (1966) is essentially a how-to-do-it book written in response to a need: most of the developing countries have adopted the practice of preparing a Development Plan, usually at five-year intervals. In contrast to the enthusiasm for planning which prevailed in the 1960s, however, Lewis offers no more than two cheers for formal planning. He asserts that "the secret of successful planning lies more in sensible politics and good public administration" than in the techniques of planning. Furthermore, "comprehensive planning is more important to advanced economies than it is to underdeveloped economies" (Lewis 1966, Preface and p. 242).

The most devastating critique of planning is presented in Caiden and Wildavsky's *Planning and Budgeting in Poor Countries* (1974), an insightful book which gives equal attention to the budget process. Their general conclusion is that "formal planning fails . . . in virtually all poor countries most of the time" (p. 288). Comprehensive approaches to planning have remained unimplemented. They require too many data and too many skills which do not exist. The resources that would be required to fulfill the plan usually exceed the resources available. Many items included in the development plan are therefore never actually funded. In his review of Caiden and Wildavsky (1974), Mead (1977) concedes that planning has failed in the sense of "future control." He argues, however, that the process of planning can nevertheless serve a useful purpose. To be sure, systematic efforts to look forward and to assess the consistency between the availability of resources and the goals that are adopted have the potential to improve the quality of policymaking. But do the benefits exceed the costs? Caiden and Wildavsky (1974, pp. 283–89) argue persuasively that they often do not. National economic planning is nonetheless here to stay. The challenge, we believe, is to recognize the inevitable limitations of synoptic planning and to apply the scarce and expensive planning skills which are available to the analysis of those issues for which central-government decisions will make the most difference. This includes the decisions which, as we noted in chapter 3, establish the policy environment and incentives to which farmers and other producers respond. It also includes all-important "details": strengthening the organizational capacity for implementing programs and designing the sequential investments in research, in infrastructure, and in social services which provide the "public goods" so essential to the development process.

d for a more effective approach to planning is especially evident in the design and implementation of strategies for rural development. planning typically fails to take account of realities at the local level. because of their backgrounds and interests, too often are inclined to spend most of their time in the capital city, remaining ignorant of the rural sector in general and of semisubsistence farming in particular. As an extreme example, in 1972 there were seventy-four established posts for economists in Lusaka, Zambia's capital, but "not a single economist or planning specialist in the provinces" (Chambers 1974, p. 117). Planners have rarely attended seriously to allocating the scarce resource represented by the analytical skills which they possess. Too little time and effort have been devoted to adapting national targets and budget allocations in the light of the actual conditions and changes taking place at the local level. Even the techniques for tapping local knowledge and for learning from the experience of actually implementing programs are poorly developed. On those occasions when efforts have been made by central planners to request local plans, the result has been the preparation of shopping lists of projects. But planners have given little attention to devising practicable means of "handling the resulting voluminous and inconsistent lists of requests. Mounds of papers mouldering and gathering dust in the back rooms of ministries and disillusioned field staff are the two main relics of this approach" (Chambers 1974, p. 141).

It is in the area of planning for rural development that the need to recognize the limitations of synoptic planning and to devise more effective means of combining the two approaches of intellectual cogitation and social interaction is particularly important. The continuing process of formulating and adapting plans for strengthening organizational capacity and for investments in research, in agricultural extension, in infrastructure, and in social services to provide the "public goods" so essential to production and consumption programs will require increased attention to the farm-level investigations and assessment surveys that we have emphasized in chapters 3 and 5. In brief, planning activities, in individual ministries as well as in central planning agencies, can and should contribute to the learning process that is so essential for the design and redesign of feasible and effective programs for rural development.

Budgeting. The limitations of comprehensive budgeting are also severe, though they have received less attention than the failures of planning. Formal budgeting has a number of conservative biases. A country's finance ministry is bound to be sensitive to "the problem of poverty: too few resources and too many needs" (Caiden and Wildavsky 1974, p. 158). In most developing countries it also confronts a great deal of uncertainty. These conditions give rise to defensive strategies. "The task of the treasury is to have money available; if it runs out the finance ministry gets the blame. If money is left over, no one will say mismanagement has occurred" (Caiden and Wildavsky 1974, p. 69). A common response is to underestimate revenue and overestimate expenditure.

Operating departments adopt their own defensive strategies. They seek special funds under their own control or attempt to set up autonomous organizations outside the normal budgeting process. Frequently, they pad their estimates of expenditure as a hedge against expected cuts. This give-and-take bargaining between the finance ministry and the other ministries, each of which seeks to expand its share of the limited funds available, has many unfortunate consequences: "departments spend more than is needed at the end of the budget period for fear of forfeiting funds; they have difficulty pacing expenditure throughout the year; their recurrent estimates are quickly exhausted while capital funds remain unspent" (Caiden and Wildavsky 1974, p. 159). Another consequence of the conservativism of formal budgeting is the tendency for the process to become entirely routine. Bids for funds by ministries, by regions, and by local entities tend to be based on the previous year's budget. Allocations typically are slightly above those of the previous year, with little systematic evaluation of past experience (see Chambers 1974, p. 140; and Caiden and Wildavsky 1974, p. 30).

The technique of "program budgeting" has been viewed by some as a means to overcome the deficiencies of formal budgeting. Program budgeting is supposed to focus on the objectives of an organization rather than on the traditional "input" categories of personnel, maintenance, and supplies. The idea of being able to determine expenditure priorities according to a ranking of objectives is appealing to advocates of program budgeting. The data and other requirements for achieving the remarkable outcome that they claim are so great, however, that the technique is not workable in practice. Results have been dismal in both developed and developing countries (Caiden and Wildavsky 1974, pp. 159–60).

Although the condemnation of centralized efforts at program budgeting appears to be valid, there is considerable scope for devising techniques to improve programming, budgeting, and management at lower levels of administration. These possibilities relate to situations in which there is some devolution of programming and budgeting responsibilities and authority to the district, block, or other local level. Thus, the previously mentioned techniques evolved by Belshaw and Chambers deal with recurrent budgeting decisions as well as the work of field staff (Chambers 1974, pp. 41–54). The approach appears promising, but it still needs to be tried, tested, and adapted under various local conditions.

Benefit-cost analysis and project evaluation. Benefit-cost analysis, say two well-known practitioners, is "the principal analytical framework used to evaluate public expenditure decisions" (Stokey and Zeckhauser 1978, p. 134). This generalization may describe the situation in the United States. It would be disturbing if it were true of less developed countries, however, because of the limitations of benefit-cost analysis in providing guidance on many of their important problems. There is no question that benefit-cost analysis of specific, time- and space-bounded projects has an important role to play. When appropriately applied, its calculations can mitigate the risk that scarce resources will be allocated on the basis of slipshod assessments influenced by a few special interests.

In the rural development context, however, the recent tendency to impose elaborate appraisal procedures smacks of the folk science we described in chapter 1. While providing reassurance for a body of believers, this pseudosophistication places excessive demands on the limited planning and administrative capacity available, thereby causing delays and a shortage of good projects (Chambers 1977). More fundamental, relying on the resulting project-oriented evaluations without seriously considering other types of evidence inevitably leads to "suboptimization," for two important reasons. First, if individual projects are considered in isolation, interactions and complementarities are ignored; the effectiveness of a rural development strategy depends, however, on a satisfactory mix and balance among its components. Second, even for a single project, some of the benefits that should be considered are difficult or impossible to quantify. In particular, as we noted in chapter 4, the benefits resulting from social-service programs in nutrition and health are frequently impossible to quantify in any meaningful way. The resulting increases in productivity are extremely difficult to measure. Moreover, they are less significant than the contributions to individual well-being associated with improved vigor and reduced suffering and other contributions that are even more difficult to measure. As only one example, high rates of child mortality impose serious psychological costs on individual families and appear to have high social costs as a source of resistance to family planning. How can benefit-cost analysis pretend to quantify the "value" of health programs which improve child survival?

Formal benefit-cost analysis is of little value in guiding the strategic debate over, for example, the priority that should be given to nutrition, health, and family planning programs or the choice between unimodal and bimodal agricultural development. Although benefit-cost analysis is a potentially useful tool for aiding tactical choices among individual projects, it can offer little but self-delusion when it is applied to the larger problems of redesigning rural development.

"Systems" models. The principal response of economists and policy analysts to the strategic shortcomings of benefit-cost analysis has been the elaboration of a variety of macro and sector models. More generally, a tendency to attach great importance to formal models and model-building exercises has been a common characteristic of government planners and university-based development economists. The economist in charge of demographic research at ILO has argued that because of the complex interactions among variables and the importance of indirect as well as direct effects, "we need more complex analytical techniques—models which incorporate as many of the relevant relationships as possible are more likely to give useful insights and guidelines for policy than are simpler approaches" (Rodgers 1977, p. 24).

This is nonsense. Furthermore, it is so contrary to common sense that only strong vindication from practical experience would justify its propagation. But experience with large-scale, "black-box" models has been neither extensive nor encouraging. In the first place, most of the models have been flawed by technical deficiencies and questionable assumptions. Beyond that, it is doubtful whether such large-scale models can be useful even if technical deficiencies are removed. Arthur and McNicoll's (1975) and Sanderson's (1978, 1980) critical analyses of the various TEMPO models, of ILO's BACHUE model for the Philippines, and of the Adelman-Robinson model for South Korea illustrate the problems. One common difficulty is that a mantle of false complexity often cloaks simplistic structural assumptions. For example, the TEMPO model's "robust" conclusion that slower population growth translates into more rapid growth of per capita GNP is in fact nothing more than the necessary result of including a Cobb-Douglas production function in the model (Arthur and McNicoll 1975, p. 257).

In addition, both the BACHUE and the Adelman-Robinson models purport to demonstrate that slowing population growth has beneficial effects only after thirty years. Prior to that, it is alleged, "there is a slight tendency for population policies to lead to a deteriorating income distribution and increasing poverty" (Adelman et al. 1976, p. 46). But again, this "counterintuitive" result is a consequence of assumptions built into the model. In this case, the relevant assumptions ensure that a slower rate of population growth will mean a worsening of agriculture's terms of trade because of the slower growth in demand for food. And since the bulk of poverty is located in rural areas, the welfare gain of the urban poor from lower food prices is more than offset by the reduction in income for rural households. That implicit assumption of the model is in sharp contrast with the explicit view of Mellor (1976) and others that governments' concern about the possibility of a rapid rise in urban food prices has often deterred them from pursuing employment-oriented development policies. Again, either assumption may be argued, and indeed the implications of both should be explored as part of the policy debate. But modeling approaches which obscure rather than illuminate the assumptions from which their conclusions derive are likely to be counterproductive.[1] This is particularly true when, as in the BACHUE case, there are serious conceptual and technical errors (Sanderson 1978, p. 71), coupled with a disregard of elementary validation criteria.

When models are complex or badly documented or are treated as holy scripture to be interpreted only by the suitably initiated, then their inevitable technical and conceptual errors will go undetected. Moreover, they will be unusable as a guide for learning. Too often, even the model-builders have only a limited understanding of the assumptions and relationships that drive "their" models.

---

[1] Julian Simon (1976) claims that his demographic-simulation model "demonstrates" that "population growth may be good for LDCs in the long run." In fact, his conclusion derives from highly dubious assumptions built into the model. For example, he assumes that a doubling or quadrupling of infrastructure investment will double or quadruple output; and that an increase in the size of the work force will automatically induce a proportional increase in infrastructure (Sanderson 1978, pp. 98–99).

An early infatuation with big models and systems analysis has been a common phenomenon; a number of more mature fields have now outgrown it. Military planning in the 1950s, water resource planning in the 1960s, urban and environmental planning in the 1970s—each initially developed large-scale simulation approaches to cope with their complex problems. In each field, practical experience with the actual results of these initial efforts eventually forced a reassessment of the desirable and the feasible. In each field, maturity led to a remarkable convergence of opinion which recognized the strengths and limitations of model analyses and, most importantly, their limited role in the overall process of policy design, implementation, and improvement.[2]

Common lessons of this convergence are illustrated by the practical evaluations of various model-based approaches to environmental policy design recently conducted under the auspices of the International Institute for Applied Systems Analysis (IIASA) by C. S. Holling and his co-workers. The dominant and recurring finding of this work is the need for simplification at all stages of the modeling and analysis effort. Such simplifications are essential "to encapsulate understanding and help intuition play its central role in the analysis" and "to facilitate communication" (Clark, Jones, and Holling 1979, p. 22). Models or any other analytical approach hoping to assist in policy design are of little value unless they contribute to constructive interaction between policy analysts, managers, and decision-makers.

The IIASA group stresses that the problems it addressed "are comprised of an immense array of interacting variables, conflicting objectives and competing actions." Their conclusion, which applies with even greater force to the messy problems of rural development, is that "attempts to comprehensively model such complexities are futile. At best they produce models as intricate and unfathomable as the real world. More likely, they founder in a limbo of unending data requirements, impossible 'debugging' problems, and general ineffectiveness" (Clark, Jones, and Holling 1979, p. 7). In place of a spurious "comprehensiveness," they argue, "the variables selected for system description must be the minimum that will capture the system's essential qualitative behavior in time and space" (Clark, Jones, and Holling 1979, p. 7). The resulting models often are initially cast as simulations, principally to avoid the premature sacrifice of realism for mathematical tractability. But the simulations are in turn simplified through rigorous qualitative analysis, mathematical programming, and above all, graphical presentation of key assumptions and consequences. Such analytic simplifications can be technically challenging. They inevitably require that initial model formulation be sparing of extraneous detail. And they are the single factor which the IIASA group judged most re-

---

[2] See Cline (1961) and Quade (1964) for the military experience, Fiering (1976) and Ackerman et al. (1974) for water resources, Brewer (1973) and Lee (1973) for urban and regional planning, and Holcomb Research Institute (1976) and Holling (1978) for ecological and environmental applications.

sponsible for occasional practical successes in improving ongoing policy debate.

The development field does have a few examples of models which are sufficiently simple and transparent to be critically analyzed and utilized. For example, current efforts to modify the Kelley-Williamson-Cheetham model (1972) so as to achieve greater policy relevance seem promising (Kelley and Williamson 1980). The linear programming models developed by Gotsch et al. (1975) also provide good examples of the use of formal, quantitative techniques to illuminate certain specific issues of agricultural policy.

The optimization fetish is a particularly acute form of infatuation with modeling. For the ill-structured problems of rural development, however, attempts to determine the "optimal" are inane. In fact, "the first responsibility of policy design is to generate and explore a strategic range of alternative approaches to the management problem" (Clark, Jones, and Holling 1979, p. 28). Real decisions will be shaped by local constraints, by particular institutions and organizational structures and procedures, and by unique personalities.[3] Development choices are based on what is *perceived* to be technically feasible and politically implementable at the time. In a very real sense, a policy analysis therefore shapes the decision-maker's preferences by arguing what can and cannot be obtained. Of great importance are continuing heuristic modifications of an initial policy design which draw upon additional information and insights.

Professional social inquiry. Our reservations about large models and other formal analytical techniques reflect a more general problem. Social scientists and practitioners of what Lindblom and Cohen (1979) refer to as "professional social inquiry" (PSI) have a tendency to exaggerate the importance of their approach to social problem solving. It is well to keep in mind that PSI is "only one among many routes to solutions." Practitioners of PSI, however, "greatly overestimate the amount and distinctiveness of the information and analysis they offer." In fact, PSI plays only a limited role "alongside ordinary knowledge, social learning, and interactive problem solving" (Lindblom and Cohen 1979, p. 12). Moreover, there are many types of problems that PSI cannot handle. For all of these reasons, both the "conclusiveness" and the "authoritativeness" of the results of investigations and analyses by social scientists are distinctly limited. Contrary to the optimistic claims of many practitioners, investing resources in PSI is at least as likely to lead to a divergence of views as to a convergence. PSI therefore not only "fails to do as well as it might" but "often positively obstructs social problem solving" (Lindblom and Cohen 1979, p. 86). Especially pertinent to research and analysis on development issues is that "problem complexity denies the possibility of proof" (p. 81). Formal models and analyses of survey data, however rigorous the statisti-

---

[3] Allison's (1971) analysis of the Cuban missile crisis provides the classical example of this view, illustrating the shortcomings of relying exclusively on a "rational actor model."

cal methods for hypothesis testing, can at most offer useful evidence in support of an argument. An earlier essay by Helmer and Rescher (1959) emphasized this point, arguing that although formal analytical techniques have an important role to play, in their application to "inexact" fields of social science they need to be supplemented by "reasoned methods of explanation and prediction" which take account of many types of evidence. Much of that evidence is based on the practical experience gained through processes of social interaction.

Acting-out Approaches

Because of the inevitable shortcomings of comprehensive models in particular and of intellectual cogitation in general, decisions must also be shaped by techniques of social interaction. The role of political and bargaining techniques by which various interest groups make and enforce their claims was considered at some length in chapter 5. Attention was also given to exchange mechanisms as a social technique of calculation and control. It was noted, for example, that exchange within networks of patron-client relationships is often of great importance in traditional rural communities. In more developed modern economies, however, markets and prices become an increasingly important mechanism of social interaction and therefore an increasingly important complement to intellectual cogitation.

A distinctive and highly significant feature of the development process is the expansion and evolution of markets—markets for consumer goods and services, for an increasing variety of intermediate products (raw materials, steel, industrial chemicals), for labor services, for land, for capital, and for financial services. Even in centrally planned economies, the growth of markets is an essential feature of the processes of division of labor, differentiation of function, and growth of interindustry specialization. These processes of specialization and of growth of exchange and interdependence in turn are critical to the increases of productivity upon which economic progress depends.[4] Market mechanisms and market-determined prices come to play a crucial interactive role in guiding and harmonizing decisions by producers and consumers within an integrated national (and international) economy.

Nearly everyone would agree that a market system is a uniquely parsimonious means of calculation and control. The controversy is over the results thereby obtained, and their relation to the equity goal of social policy. A price system is a very efficient mechanism for generating and transmitting information to guide the decisions of individual producers and consumers. Even in developed economies, the range of information that could be handled by the alternative means of communication which are available or which could be created without excessive cost is limited (Arrow 1974, chap. 4). Moreover, decentralized decision-making by individual producers has especially signifi-

---

[4] See Johnston and Kilby (1975, chap. 2) and Kuznets (1971).

cant advantages in the agricultural sector, for reasons that we examined in chapter 3. It is also worth emphasizing that the trial-and-error "experiments" carried out by numerous individual farmers in response to price changes, technical innovations, and other changes in their environment can and should be an important part of the learning process which is such a significant feature of agricultural development. Hence, market-determined prices which reflect the scarcity value (social opportunity cost) of resources have an exceptionally significant role to play in facilitating efficient production of farm products. Efficient production is critical because the cost of inefficiency is exceedingly high in poor countries. Furthermore, efficiency is unlikely to be obtained by other means. It has no constituency and is readily (if implicitly) sacrificed by planning, budgeting, and other social techniques of calculation and control. Voting systems, as we noted earlier, are notorious for allocating "too large" a proportion of resources to current consumption.

Many developing countries are nonetheless ambivalent about the role of market mechanisms. There are numerous reasons why this is so. The tendency to equate reliance on markets with "capitalism" has been an important factor where a colonialist "capitalist system" is viewed, with some justification, as responsible for the perpetuation of poverty and underdevelopment. A second factor has been a reaction against the reduced national autonomy which results from dependence on international prices. Another, noted in chapter 3, is a political bias towards artificially low food prices because of the power and influence of urban groups. Most important, however, is the prevalent goal of seeking to accelerate industrial growth by the "industrialization-first" strategy, discussed in chapter 3. Market interventions motivated by that strategy typically have resulted in severe price distortions because of high levels of protection, overvalued exchange rates, underpricing of capital, and attempts to apply a host of direct controls on trade and investment. Because prices have not reflected the social opportunity cost of resources, they have had serious adverse effects on efficiency, on the growth of output and especially of employment, and on the distribution of income. Pursuit of such policies has created numerous groups with a vested interest in the perpetuation of industrial protection and other policies which benefit privileged enclaves at the expense of the broader public interest and, especially, the rural sector.

Wide support might be expected for moves toward price policies that would lessen the adverse effects on production incentives and on agriculture's terms of trade. Practical experience in countries such as Taiwan and South Korea confirms the theoretical expectation that relative prices which reflect social opportunity cost more accurately do in fact contribute to a more buoyant economywide expansion of output and employment. But the industrialists and workers in the "modern" sector, who benefit from the existing price distortions, are well organized and capable of exerting considerable influence on government policy. Moreover, their resistance is often reinforced by government policymakers and administrators who benefit from the system of direct controls. The rural poor and workers outside the modern sector are numerous but unorganized and lack political power. In addition, lowering wages, even if it is confined to a privileged enclave, is likely to be regarded as reactionary.

Moves toward higher interest rates also tend to be regarded as reactionary; they are to be "identified with redistribution favorable to owners of capital and to the banks, at the cost of poor debtors" (Sheahan 1980, pp. 275–76). The alleged benefits of low interest rates for small farmers receive much attention. But the great majority of small borrowers do not have access to low-interest credit from institutional sources; they must pay exorbitant interest charges to noninstitutional lenders or do without credit altogether. Hence the reality: low-interest-rate programs which are ostensibly adopted to benefit the small farmer in practice benefit the large and influential.

Steps to "get prices right" in the interest of greater efficiency may nevertheless be condemned on distributional grounds. The effective demand which interacts with supply to determine the allocation of resources and relative prices is, of course, a function of the existing income distribution. And income distribution is highly unequal in most developing countries. One consequence is that using the growth of aggregate national income as a measure of development "implies giving 10 to 20 times as much weight to a 1 percent increase in the incomes of the rich as to a 1 percent increase in those of the poor" (Chenery 1980, p. 27; Ahluwalia and Chenery 1974, pp. 39–42). Superficially, it might seem that substituting a system of government-administered prices for market-determined prices would enable a society to achieve a more equitable outcome. But the problem is not that simple. In fact, practical experience demonstrates that failing to use market-determined prices which accurately reflect the social opportunity cost of resources has very adverse effects on efficiency. And we have seen that the price distortions which are introduced typically exacerbate poverty as well.[5]

One reason why reliance on government-administered prices has had such a dismal record is that such attempts place a very heavy burden on administra-

[5] Development economists commonly advocate government interventions to influence prices, with little or no attention to the political factors which make it so likely that the result will be a distorted structure of relative prices highly adverse to the interests of the great majority of the farm population. Robert Bates, an able political scientist who has studied political intervention in African markets, argues that in order to understand the content of agricultural policies in less developed countries, it is necessary to utilize three models of government decision-making. The first "emphasizes the role of the state as an agency for fulfilling social purposes and interprets agricultural policies as choices made in efforts to secure public objectives." The second "emphasizes the role of the state in aggregating political demands and interprets agricultural policies as choices made in response to the pressures of private interests." And the third "looks at the ways in which governments attempt to use markets as instruments of political control." Even though the price distortions caused by market interventions lead to inefficiency and inequities, these "agricultural policies nonetheless generate political resources by which those in charge of these programs build loyal constituencies, create political followings, and thereby remain in power" (Bates 1980, pp. 38, 39).

tive systems handicapped by a lack of managerial talent. John Kenneth Galbraith, who can hardly be characterized as an ideologue of the price system, stresses that market mechanisms "economize on scarce and honest administrative talent," whereas reliance on prices which are administratively determined jeopardizes the prospects for rapid and efficient economic growth. He stresses the administrative problem in these terms: "The consequence—reliance on a large, centrally planned and administered public sector—is that the greatest possible claim is placed on the scarcest possible resource. That is administrative talent, with its complementary requirements in expert knowledge, experience, and discipline" (Galbraith 1979, p. 111). Thus the attempt to rely on government-administered prices has a high opportunity cost in addition to its adverse effects on the efficient allocation of scarce resources.

It is not only because administrative talent is scarce in late-developing countries that the opportunity cost of burdening the central administration with management of a system of government-administered prices is high. Our examination of production, consumption, and organization programs in the preceding chapters underscores the fundamental importance of a wide range of activities in which direct government action is indispensable because markets would perform poorly if at all.

In chapter 3 we emphasized that a unimodal pattern of agricultural development can promote widespread increases in farm productivity and income and thereby advance both output and equity objectives of development. The success of efforts to promote broadly based agricultural development depends in large measure, however, on the level and quality of support services such as agricultural research and extension and on government programs for investment in infrastructure such as irrigation and a rural road network. Our treatment of consumption-oriented activities in chapter 4 stressed the need to give a high priority to social-service programs for education and to provide broad coverage of a country's population in terms of access to health, nutrition, and family planning services. In the jargon of economics, all of those activities are "public goods": they are characterized by indivisibility, externality, and jointness in supply and utilization (Kaneda 1980, p. 27). To rely on the response of markets to private demands for such services represents a grossly inefficient, highly inequitable approach to providing those services. That is, because they have the characteristics of public goods, they will not be made available at socially optimal levels without interventions by publicly supported organizations. Moreover, as we argued in chapter 5, the performance of the "facilitator organizations" required to meet those needs will be unsatisfactory unless serious and sustained attention is given to the complex and important issues of organizational design and management. We also stressed in chapter 5 that progress in the design and management of more effective organizations and programs depends much more on learning from experience—the "acting-out" approach to social interaction—than on intellectual cogitation.

Learning Approaches

Intellectual cogitation and social interaction both have significant strengths and weaknesses.[6] In its extreme version, cogitation leads to the vision of an intellectually guided society. It is based on an optimistic view of man's intellectual capacities, reflecting unlimited confidence in his abilities to produce a comprehensive theory of social change and to guide society by "thinking through" optimal policy designs. Social interaction, on the other hand, is based on a pessimistic view of man's intellectual capacity. It therefore relies on an interactive approach to policy guidance and on a "strategic" approach to problem resolution. In deference to the limits of intellectual competence, interaction emphasizes incremental learning as a complement to inevitably incomplete analyses. Uncertainty is inevitable because of the complexity of social problems and because problems and possibilities for problem-solving interventions are changing constantly. Because they recognize the difficulty of good analysis, interactive approaches are selective, discriminating, and economical of analytical talent.

Reliance on intellectual cogitation implies an underlying harmony of interest which can be known to an elite—an elite which can therefore claim to *discover* the single "correct" solution which best provides for the needs of people. Social interaction assumes a conflict-ridden society in which a harmony of interest is not only unknown but nonexistent. Interactive processes therefore aim to clarify and to cope with conflict. Since elites cannot know what is "correct" in any absolute sense, conflict serves the useful purposes of forcing an examination of possibly mistaken policies and of emphasizing the need for institutions that hold fallible leaders accountable.

When viewed as extreme alternatives between which a choice must be made, cogitation and interaction are in effect another pair of the grand isms we discussed in chapter 5. As we have argued repeatedly, policy analysis seeks to integrate intellectual cogitation and social interaction in a way that recognizes the strengths and weaknesses of each. Mistakes or failures of policy design are inevitable. Since it is impossible to eliminate uncertainty, the realistic goal is to accommodate it more effectively. This calls for more tentative attitudes and a shift away from a focus on certainty and definitive answers towards a learning process of adaptive policy design and redesign. An essential feature of such an approach is to view the inevitable failures encountered in development programs as costly but potentially invaluable experience and the source of priceless lessons. The need is twofold, as expressed in the title of a provocative book by Donald Michael (1973), *On Learning to Plan—and Planning to Learn*. An

---

[6] This discussion draws heavily on Lindblom (1977, chaps. 19 and 23). In those chapters, Lindblom contrasts two idealized models of how a society might be organized and what he refers to as "synoptic" and "strategic" planning. We will focus here on the more general contrast between cogitation and interaction.

important aspect of learning to plan is learning to fail. Planning to learn is planning to fail in a manner such that we both survive the experience and gain as much information as possible from it.

The barriers to adopting a learning approach are tremendous—at the political, professional, and personal levels. The first step in overcoming these barriers is to admit that they are there. Wherever we look, the most obvious trappings of power and competence involve *appearing* to be in control and *appearing* to be right. However illusory these appearances may be, maintenance of the illusion is accorded very high priority by governments, institutions, and our own personal psyches. Instead of associating competence with a well-manicured record of correct decisions, we need to view it as the ability to fail creatively, and to learn from the experience.

Such prescriptions are not pipe dreams. Even at the national political level there are examples of a pragmatic, "learning by doing" approach. China's approach to rural development has often given evidence of a willingness to recognize mistakes and modify policies. A case in point is the readoption of the small production team as the principal unit of decision-making in the early 1960s after the setbacks associated with the Great Leap and the creation of the rural communes. The decision of General Chiang Kai-shek's administration in Taiwan to implement an effective land reform in the early 1950s is another interesting example. That regime had just gone through what John Brewster (1967) has aptly described as a "catastrophic learning experience" in its defeat by the Chinese Communists and expulsion from the mainland. One of the key lessons learned through that painful experience was the importance of maintaining the support of the farm population. Land reform and output-increasing measures were therefore taken seriously, and have been highly effective (see chapter 3). In the area of rural health programs, the Indian government acted promptly to commission a number of evaluation studies of its Rural Health Scheme, initiated in 1977. These studies are designed to support a continuing effort of policy redesign and managerial improvement for that complex and challenging program.

Trial-and-error learning through the various techniques of social interaction is a necessary but costly and time-consuming process. The analysis and interpretation of historical success and failure is an important aspect of interactive learning which can be exploited by late-developing countries; that is the reason for our emphasis throughout this essay on the retrospective assessment of past program performance.

Looking to the future, the challenge is to use these lessons of the past to redesign our successive trials of rural development strategy. Learning to design more productive trials for subsequent interactive evaluation requires all the limited skills and insights that cogitation can bring us. We sketch the conclusions derived from our own cogitation-plus-interaction process in the remainder of this chapter.

Strategies for Rural Development

In this section we review some of the more prominent specific strategies for rural development now being debated by development scholars, and practiced by development workers. We begin by summarizing our own analysis, which leads to our recommendation for a three-pronged strategy which simultaneously emphasizes programs for production, consumption, and organization. We describe the complementary and competitive interrelationships between these programs which make their simultaneous consideration such an important aspect of strategic design.

We then consider some alternative views which hold that multiple-objective strategies are infeasible or undesirable. We concentrate particularly on those strategies which make either growth or equity considerations the prime determinant of program structures. We argue that the growth-versus-equity dichotomy is often unnecessary: both can be achieved if development programs devote sufficient attention to the rate *and* bias of technical change.

Finally, we consider those strategies which propose relief-and-welfare approaches to rural development. We reiterate our arguments of earlier chapters that such approaches sacrifice long-term gains for short-term objectives, thus undercutting the long and arduous process of broad-based development. We note particularly the roles that foreign aid can and cannot be expected to play in such strategies.

A Three-pronged Approach: Production, Consumption, and Organization

Because of the limitations of formal evaluation procedures, judgment and intuition must play a major role in the design of rural-development strategies. But judgment and intuition are often wrong. Moreover, the problems encountered in reaching the degree of consensus required for effective action are compounded when the debate involves different judgments about benefits, costs, and feasibility.

It has been argued, for example, that priorities for health programs should be determined by criteria such as the "magnitude, severity, and social consequences of a *health* problem; feasibility, costs and effectiveness of the *health* action; and demand for care and acceptance of [health] services by the community" (WHO 1976, p. 32 [italics added]; see also Bengoa 1973). These are indeed relevant considerations. There are significant advantages, however, in considering such issues within a broader framework that directs attention to the interrelationships among the major components of a rural development strategy. Explicit and systematic consideration of those relationships improves the chances that the strategy resulting from a series of judgmental decisions will be both feasible and effective.

Our analysis of the interrelationships between the determinants of rural well-being has emphasized that there are both competitive and complementary relationships among the multiple objectives of development. This raises the prospect of redesigning the production, consumption, and organization components of a rural development strategy in a way that maximizes their capacity for mutual support while minimizing the risk that action in one program area will compromise actions in others. We propose one such design in the following pages—an adaptive, three-pronged strategy for rural development.

The first "prong" of our proposal is a broad-based, or unimodal, approach to agricultural development. Its multiple benefits derive from opportunities to simultaneously expand the growth of output and employment, both within and outside agriculture. Expansion of opportunities for productive employment, including self-employment in agriculture, must be a central objective of development. Fuller and more efficient utilization of the relatively abundant resource of human labor facilitates the expansion of output and at the same time generates the incomes that enable the poor to improve their level of consumption.

The most feasible and effective means of reducing poverty among the low-income households which are so dependent upon labor income is to ensure that opportunities for productive employment in agriculture, manufacturing, and service activities increase faster than the size of the work force seeking employment (see Binswanger and Ryan 1977). The historical experience reviewed in chapter 3 emphasized how important it is to tighten the labor supply/demand situation if increases in returns to labor and a narrowing of inequalities in income distribution are to be achieved. Later in this chapter, we stress that in order for the level of per capita income to be raised, the expansion of employment opportunities must also be associated with widespread increases in productivity.

The second prong of our development strategy involves programs to strengthen social services—education, health, nutrition, and family planning. Such programs also offer the possibility of multiple benefits. For reasons summarized in chapter 4, we believe that the potential advantages of linking health, nutrition, and family planning activities can be great enough to justify the increased difficulties of organizing a more complex program. Only carefully monitored experience can determine whether, and under what conditions, that potential can be realized. It is clear, however, that measures to ᵒve nutrition and health must be paralleled by action to promote family ᵗ. We have seen that better birth spacing and smaller families have ᶜfects on the health and well-being of mothers and children. Furᵗntinuation of rapid rates of population increase aggravates the ᵐployment opportunities fast enough to accommodate the of working age. The most obvious way in which high ᵗe distribution is through increasing the supply of labor relative to the supply of land and other factors of production, "thus restraining the growth of real wages, perhaps even reducing them" (Birdsall et al. 1979, p. 261). A disturbing feature of the decline in fertility occurring in some developing countries is that it is confined mainly to the wealthier segments of the population. Unless family planning spreads among low-income rural households, the relative surplus of unskilled labor, with its depressing effect on labor incomes, will become even more pronounced.

The third prong of our development strategy concerns organization programs designed to enhance the institutional infrastructure and managerial skills needed for rural development. It is somewhat unorthodox to single out organization programs as meriting an emphasis similar to that accorded production and consumption programs. For reasons implicit throughout this essay, and explicit in chapter 5, we believe the unorthodoxy is long overdue. Even a decade and a half ago, S. C. Hsieh and T. H. Lee could assert that "the main secret of Taiwan's development" was "her ability to meet the organizational requirements" (Hsieh and Lee 1966, pp. 103, 105). They suggested that the organizational aspect of Taiwan's development was possibly "unique" and therefore not transferable to other countries. One of us responded at that time that "the real point [is] that there are organizational requirements that must be fulfilled, institutional and other obstacles that must be overcome, not that these are capacities possessed only by the Taiwanese, the Japanese, or certain other population groups" (Johnston 1966, p. 300). Subsequent experience demonstrates, however, that organizational requirements are *not* easily fulfilled and indeed are unlikely to be satisfied unless they receive serious and persistent attention. Moreover, neglect of the organizational requirements for rural development will adversely affect implementation of the programs for agricultural development and social services which we have emphasized as the first and second "prongs" of an effective strategy for rural development.

We discussed various relationships between the production, consumption, and organization prongs of our development strategy in earlier chapters dealing with individual program areas. Those interrelationships can now be made clearer, and their central relevance to strategies of rural development more evident, by shifting our perspective and focusing on them directly. In figure 6.1 we offer—with some trepidation—one such "systems" perspective on the interrelated determinants of rural well-being.

The figure summarizes much of our preceding analysis of development programs. As we emphasized in chapter 2, however, that analysis has been far from comprehensive. In order to focus our discussion and highlight certain key points, we have intentionally omitted such important considerations as the new international economic order and energy and environmental concerns. Moreover, the important relationships between agriculture and industrial development which we did discuss in chapter 3 do not lend themselves to effective representation in the format of figure 6.1. Finally, the central role of organization—political and economic, administrative and traditional—which we described in chapter 5 is portrayed here not so much as a leading actor but rather as the stage that supports and constrains the continuing play of development. We emphasize that this is a shift in perspective, not priorities. We have aimed to present a complementary—not an alternative—view of the evidence we have been discussing throughout the essay.

Figure 6.1 directs attention to the major causal linkages and feedback effects which previous chapters have shown to be important in determining the well-being of a country's rural population. In brief, the well-being of the rural population is a function of the growth, distribution, and composition of per capita consumption of goods and services. It can be enhanced directly by effectively implemented production- and consumption-oriented activities and indirectly by the interactive effects of these activities on the rate of natural increase of the rural population, on migration flows, and on human capital formation.

The rate and pattern of rural development. The top of the diagram draws attention to the effects of production programs—implemented through appropriate organizational designs—on the rate and pattern of rural development. These in turn influence employment opportunities, the income derived from wage employment, the sale of farm products, and the income in kind represented by production for home consumption. For reasons we examined in chapter 3, a broadly based, or unimodal, pattern of development will lead to a more equal distribution of income than will a bimodal pattern. This contrast is especially striking when unimodal policies can be accompanied by a

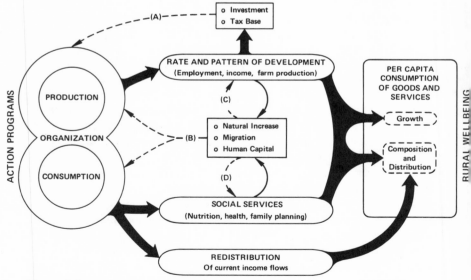

Figure 6.1. The Determinants of Rural Well-Being.

Note: Heavy solid arrows denote direct effects; light solid arrows, indirect effects; and dotted arrows, major feedbacks.

redistributive land reform program whereby marginal and landless farm households are able to augment their labor income with resource rents resulting from their ownership of land.[7] We also argued, however, that land reform is neither a necessary nor a sufficient condition for achieving the more widespread increases in productivity and income which are attainable under a unimodal pattern of agricultural development. Furthermore, as we noted in chapter 5, depending upon the institutional structures available and the distribution of power within them, land reform may not be feasible.

In chapter 4 we showed that the more equal income distribution associated with a unimodal approach will be reflected in relatively high levels of food consumption, with favorable effects on nutrition. This more rapid growth in demand for food means that the growth of agricultural output can be faster with a unimodal pattern of development. Whether that potential is realized depends on the level and orientation of investments in agricultural research, extension programs, and infrastructure and on the effectiveness of organizational programs in influencing the growth of farm productivity and output.

The monetary component of the net income flows generated by production programs will be divided mainly between consumption expenditures and investment outlays. However, farm cash income is also a major source of government tax revenues in the predominantly agrarian economies of the late-developing countries. The feedback emphasizes that the level and administrative allocation of these investment funds and tax revenues will affect future production, as well as the level of future consumption-oriented programs.

It should be noted that the causal linkages associated with the rate and pattern of development are not limited to the direct effects on the growth, distribution, and composition of per capita consumption. The indirect effects on the rate of natural increase, on rural-urban migration, and on human capital formation are also significant.

We suggested in chapter 4 that broad participation of the rural population in processes of technical and economic change creates an environment that is relatively favorable to the changes in attitudes, motivation, and behavior required for the spread of family planning and the slowing of population growth. Rural-urban migration flows will be influenced both by the rate of natural increase of the rural population and by the various factors that determine the relative attractiveness of the income-earning opportunities available in rural and urban localities. The rate of growth of the total population of working age, in combination with the rate of out-migration from agriculture, will, as we noted in chapter 2, influence both the growth rate of the rural labor force and the time required to reach the turning point when that labor force will begin to decline in absolute size.

Finally, unimodal agricultural development creates a more favorable environment for human capital formation than does bimodal development. In

[7] For an illuminating discussion of the importance of resource rents and other types of economic rents, see Reynolds (1980).

part this is a consequence of the opportunities for "learning by doing": the great majority of the farm population acquires increased familiarity with the calculation of costs and returns and with the evaluation of a flow of innovations. In addition, broad participation of the farm population in technical and economic change promotes the creation and strengthening of a variety of local organizations and "facilitator" organizations. As we emphasized in chapter 5, this can become a self-amplifying process in which such reorganization of the rural population in turn promotes even more effective and more broadly based development (feedback B in figure 6.1). We therefore believe that a unimodal approach will provide a more favorable environment than will bimodal development for the individual and organizational learning processes which are such important ingredients of development.

Broad participation of the farm population in improved income-earning opportunities and in the institutions that facilitate agricultural development can also be expected to change the rural power structure and political institutions. Those changes have significant implications with respect to the political and financial support for rural schools and thereby have additional effects on human capital formation.[8] As we will argue shortly, investments in education can be expected to contribute to the success of programs to expand agricultural production. But there are also important interactions between investments in agricultural research and returns to education. Many empirical studies in both developed and developing countries report significant positive effects of education on farm output. Some of the studies in developing countries, however, fail to show this effect. Welch (1978) reviews these studies and offers a convincing explanation. He emphasizes that education is not productive independently of other factors; instead, its value lies in enhancing the ability of farmers to learn and to make judgments about alternatives. From this perspective, it is not surprising to find that in situations where research programs are generating new production possibilities there are significant returns to education, whereas in stagnant situations where locally adapted technical innovations are not available education seems to have little effect on farm productivity. This interpretation is supported by an analysis of empirical data from a number of developing countries carried out by Lockheed, Jamison, and Lau (1980).

Social services and income redistribution. The lower portion of figure 6.1 emphasizes that the allocation of resources for consumption-oriented activities involves a trade-off between the strengthening of social services and measures to redistribute current income flows. For social services, both the

---

[8] This is just one example of the reciprocal interactions between the effects of the pattern of rural development on the distribution of political power and the influence of the power structure on the choice of development strategy. In chapters 3 and 5 we considered briefly other interactions between "political constraints" and the decision-making process that determine the pattern of development. These issues are examined in more detail in Johnston and Kilby (1975, pp. 153–73).

indirect and the longer-term feedback effects may be even more important than the direct increases in per capita "consumption" of education and health services.

We have emphasized that social services in the form of education, health, nutrition, and family planning programs represent "public goods" which have significant effects on human capital formation, the rate of natural increase, and the rate of rural-urban migration. Migration flows may also be affected by the differential availability of such services in rural and urban locations. Recall from chapter 2 that rapid growth of population and labor force means that the late-developing countries will face increasingly serious problems of either "rural overpopulation" or "hyperurbanization," depending on the rate of out-migration from the rural sector. However, a pattern of rural development which fosters a relatively decentralized pattern of industrial growth can lessen the concentration of the urban population in one or a few major cities (see Kaneda 1979).

Social services also eventually affect the rate and pattern of rural development via their impact on the rate of rural population growth and human capital formation (feedback C in figure 6.1). Their effects on future increases in per capita incomes are, of course, especially noteworthy. In turn, slower growth of the rural population has an obvious influence on future prospects for improving the coverage and quality of both social-service and income-redistribution measures. The feedback effect of human capital formation on the strengthening of social-service programs is particularly important (feedback D in figure 6.1). This is realized in part through improved availability of teachers, health professionals, auxiliaries, and village-level health workers. In addition, however, improving the quality of human resources can directly aid the beneficiaries of social-service programs. Most obvious, as noted in chapter 2, is the improved performance of school children whose physical and cognitive development is not impaired by malnutrition and excessive morbidity. Improved education and health of rural children also has a favorable impact on production in the nonfarm sectors, where a growing number of more capable children from farm households will be able to find productive employment.

Programs to strengthen and achieve broader coverage of education, health, and nutrition services have direct effects on all dimensions of rural well-being: increased availability of those services, better distribution, and a change in composition toward meeting needs that are "basic." Improving access of the rural population to health services is especially significant in reducing a very important dimension of inequality between rural and urban populations.[9] Once again, however, designing appropriate organizations to implement such broadly based health programs is both essential and difficult. The poor have

---

[9] Pyle (1981, p. 199) reports that in India some 80 percent of the physicians are located in cities, where only about 20 percent of the population resides; and an urban resident is nine times more likely to receive medical attention than a villager.

neither the political nor the economic means to shift a country's resources from urban hospitals which cure diseases to rural programs which promote health. Here as elsewhere, serious and sustained support from public and private organizations at the national and international level will be a necessary component of strategies to effect widespread improvements in rural well-being.[10]

Programs to redistribute current income flows have a narrower range of impacts. In figure 6.1 we limit the effects of redistributive measures such as food subsidies and supplementary feeding programs to direct impacts on the distribution and composition of consumption. Such measures do not have the significant effects on growth (especially growth in per capita consumption) that can be expected from education, health, and family planning activities. We conclude that when resources must be shared among them, programs which redistribute current income flows generally deserve lower priority in strategies for rural development than do programs which strengthen social services. We explore this critical trade-off in more detail later in this chapter.

Integration and organization. What is the relationship between our three-pronged strategy and the concept of "integrated rural development," which has received considerable attention in recent years? To answer this question would require an operational definition of what is meant by "integrated rural development." Unfortunately, we have been unable to discover such a definition. Generally speaking, the concept is indeed distinguished by a focus on rural rather than agricultural development, as well as an emphasis on integration. The World Bank's version emphasizes a broad range of factors influencing the well-being of a target population, defining "rural development" as a "strategy designed to improve the economic and social life of a specific group of people—the rural poor" (1975, p. 3).[11] And Kötter (1978, p. 105) states that integrated rural development "means the integration of the left out

---

[10] The decision by the government of India to initiate a Community Health Worker Program in 1977 in order to achieve broad coverage of its rural population is an especially important example of an attempt to move to a more appropriate and more equitable allocation of resources for health programs. India's five-year plan for 1978–83 states explicitly that the "Western model" of medical care and health services, based on curative rather than preventive and promotional activities, is inappropriate. Great difficulties have been encountered, however, in implementing that program and in reversing the bias against rural areas. Health manpower and expenditures concentrate in urban areas in part simply because the politically powerful are more likely to demand specialized hospital care rather than public-health clinic care. Although the poor, and especially the rural poor, are more numerous, they "do not have sufficient political influence to determine policy or implementation in favor of more appropriate and needed public health inputs" (Pyle 1981, p. 202).

[11] The concept of integrated rural development is also advocated as a means of linking economic and social development by combining programs for expanding health services and improving road networks with activities aimed directly at increasing production. Presumably, the main impetus for this type of integration is the greater ease of obtaining foreign aid for social services when they are linked with a project aimed at increasing agricultural production. An important disadvantage is that such "integrated area development projects" typically involve commitments of funds and manpower at levels too high to be replicated in national programs (Johnston 1979).

into society and the economy as a whole," thus defining integrated rural development as a desired end result. In fact, integrated rural development is a concept that can take on an infinite variety of forms depending on the scope and degree of integration involved (Das Gupta 1979). Rather than trying to describe what others mean by "integrated rural development," it will therefore be more useful to describe what place integration has in our view of rural development.

In this context, the distinctive feature of our three-pronged strategy is that it is indeed *strategic*. It emphasizes the advantages of pursuing production, consumption, and organization programs simultaneously, with explicit recognition of their interrelationships. Ours is not, however, an argument for tactical integration of all development activities. We share Hunter's view that "considerable confusion and harm" can result from attempts to integrate administratively or institutionally an arbitrarily wide range of activities (Hunter 1978a, p. 98; see also Ruttan 1975).[12] We noted in chapter 5, for example, that integrating production and social-service activities in a single organization is more than likely to be disastrous for the poor. In figure 6.1, our embedding of production and consumption programs within a single organizational framework is meant to reflect the ubiquitous linkages between the social, political, economic, and administrative channels through which all development activities must be implemented. But the figure's partial separation of that organizational framework into one component concerned largely with production-oriented programs and another component concerned largely with consumption-oriented programs emphasizes our belief that those linkages neither are nor should be completely intertwined.

Effective development is ultimately a matter of details. Strategic plans and perspectives ignore this reality at peril of irrelevance. We stressed throughout chapter 5 that the redesign of more effective development requires that certain specific programs be closely linked at certain organizational levels and other specific programs be kept organizationally separate. We emphasized that

---

[12] Hunter and his colleagues at the Overseas Development Institute have since enlarged on the problems related to the concept of integrated rural development (ODI 1979). A comprehensive review of that paper by Richter (1980) is of considerable interest. He suggests that an important contribution of experience with integrated rural development projects has been to promote greater awareness of how-to questions, which, as we argue throughout this essay, are just as important as the what-to questions. Richter argues that a major reason for implementation failures has been "quantitative as well as qualitative inadequacy of rural development personnel." His emphasis on the need for more attention to training and increasing the problem-solving capabilities of field staff is well taken. We believe, however, that inadequate performance on the part of the "facilitators" of rural development is affected even more by the questions of institutional structure and managerial procedures that we examined in chapter 5. Our main disagreement with Richter's analysis relates to his failure to distinguish between the strategic importance of the interrelationships between the components of a rural development strategy and the tactical integration of the administration of a wide range of development activities. In particular, we believe that his assertion of "the need for full coordination and collaboration between the various 'change agents' " is misleading and, if taken seriously, could have disastrous effects on efforts to design more effective organization programs (Richter 1980, pp. 311, 314).

knowledge of *which* specific programs should be linked in *which* manner at *which* organizational level must ultimately be based on detailed field-level assessments followed by a trial-and-error learning process. Nonetheless, it is important to recognize that the potential for technical complementarities among certain programs does exist, and that knowledge of this potential can form a useful foundation upon which to build assessments of specific situations.

For example, a notable virtue of the Training and Visit approach to agricultural extension, discussed in chapters 3 and 5, is that it promotes better coordination between agricultural research and extension programs: it increases the relevance of research to the needs of small farmers and at the same time ensures that extension staff have worthwhile innovations to extend. The considerable consensus that is emerging concerning the need for greater devolution of programming and financial authority is probably related to increased awareness of the need to make greater use of local knowledge and organizational capabilities and to adapt program designs to fit specific local conditions (Krishna 1978; Hunter 1978a). But decentralization can also facilitate better coordination in the planning and implementation of interrelated activities within, say, a district or the command area of an irrigation project. We have also suggested that health, nutrition, and family planning activities are so closely interrelated and potentially so reinforcing that they may constitute an instance in which a range of activities should be integrated administratively.

A related example is provided by one of the conclusions of a workshop on Meeting Basic Health Needs organized by the World Bank in October 1980. The participants in that workshop agreed that rural water-supply projects should, in general, receive priority only when there is a reasonable expectation that complementary action to improve hygiene and sanitation will ensure furtherance of health objectives, as well as save time and reduce drudgery.[13] In general, however, even the requirements for coordination should be held to the minimum necessary to ensure that "requisites" that must be satisfied simultaneously—such as the availability of high-yield, fertilizer-responsive varieties and the timely distribution of fertilizer—are in fact satisfied. Efforts to administer a range of multisectoral activities in an integrated way will almost certainly exceed the organizational capacities available.

Beyond the administrative difficulties, we believe that it is important to stress that the usual concept of integrated rural development seems incompatible with our view of rural development as a learning process. Most of the proposals for integrated rural development are based on an implicit assumption that we *know* which activities should receive priority and how they should be integrated within organizations designed to facilitate rural development. The reality, as we argued at length in chapter 5, is that this is an area where knowledge is sadly deficient. Attempts to impose a blueprint in the form of a

---

[13] A report on the workshop is available from Fredrick L. Golladay, Transportation, Water, and Telecommunications Department, the World Bank.

program of "integrated rural development" would be counterproductive and would reduce the opportunities for learning from a more adaptive approach to the problems of organizational design and management. We return to this theme in the final section of this chapter. First, however, it is necessary to consider some of the other, more narrowly focused strategies of development currently being considered. We will argue that these are less likely than our three-pronged approach to secure long-term improvements in the well-being of the rural poor.

Growth or Equity Approaches: An Unnecessary Dichotomy

Designing rural development strategies to attain multiple objectives is important but difficult. Even the first step—creating a sufficient consensus to initiate high-priority programs—is problematic. These difficulties have been compounded because the development debate has been polarized into a misleading dichotomy between "growth" and "equity." This polarization has diverted attention from the possibility of designing strategies to advance simultaneously growth and equity objectives. How can such multiple objectives be achieved? A critical requirement, in our judgment, is that program choices be made with due regard to both the rate *and* the bias of technical change.

Technical progress and increases in total factor productivity are essential to permit the rapid increases in output that are desperately needed when average incomes are extremely low and poverty is widespread. By reducing the resource requirements for producing a given level of output, technical progress opens up the possibility of reallocating resources. New goods and services can thereby be produced, and the output of the existing mix of consumption and investment goods can be expanded. Hence a rapid *rate* of technical change is much to be desired. However, if the *bias* of that technical change is in a labor-saving, capital-using direction, it will be impossible for the great majority of a country's rural population to participate in the gains in productivity and income. Inappropriately capital-intensive technologies can be criticized because they displace much more labor than do more "appropriate" technologies. Given the relative abundance of labor and scarcity of capital, they also waste capital in comparison with technologies which are economically efficient. This waste has a high social cost because it deprives the economy of possibilities that would otherwise exist for creating new jobs and achieving more rapid as well as more widespread growth. Efforts simultaneously to accelerate the growth of farm output and to expand employment opportunities require simultaneous concern for the rate and the bias of technical change. To concentrate only on the rate *or* the bias of technical change is an inefficient means of reducing poverty in low-income countries.

Growth perspectives. Some economists, however, have challenged the proposition that a development strategy should be designed with the aim of attaining multiple objectives. For example, Hopper has argued that developing countries "cannot afford the luxury of mixed goals" and hence "the production of food must be accepted as *the* priority objective." He is especially critical of "policies to discourage the development of mechanized agriculture because of its assumed impact on rural labor-force employment" (Hopper 1968, p. 105). In a more recent discussion of these issues, Hopper (1978) emphasizes particularly the irrationality and adverse effects of an outright prohibition of tractors or certain other types of equipment.[14] However, in citing Brazil as a shining example of a country "where farm-output growth has been high under essentially market conditions," Hopper ignores the fact that the adoption of inappropriately capital-intensive technologies by a subsector of large-scale farm units has been encouraged by their privileged access to credit from institutional sources (1978, p. 77). The subsidized loans provided for purchase of tractors in Brazil and many other developing countries have often represented *negative* real rates of interest and an income transfer to a relatively affluent segment of the population (Abel 1978, p. 193; Gonzalez-Vega 1976).

The "crash modernization" of large and relatively capital-intensive farm units can indeed achieve high levels of labor productivity within an enclave of "modern agriculture." But as we saw in chapter 3, such growth by-passes the great majority of farm households. In the process, it intensifies the cash-income and purchasing-power constraints which are a consequence of the structural-demographic characteristics of late-developing countries. In contrast, the progressive modernization of essentially all farm households under a well-conceived, broadly based approach can yield an efficient and equitable expansion path for the entire agricultural sector.[15] If technical innovations and gradually enlarged use of purchased inputs which complement rather than displace labor are emphasized, the resource cost of expanding agricultural output is minimized. The widespread increases in farm productivity and incomes also stimulate the expansion of output and employment by local manufacturing firms employing labor-using, capital-saving technologies.

In addition to these economic aspects, it is important to stress the social advantages of such an approach: more rapid expansion of employment opportunities promotes higher returns to labor and a narrowing of income inequality. We have also argued that broadly based agricultural development creates a more favorable environment for human capital formation, for improved nutrition, and for the spread of family planning.

Equity perspectives. Giving undue weight to equity considerations can

---

[14] Economists are understandably concerned about prohibitions that have the effect of placing an infinite price on a productive input. To our knowledge, however, the only example of such an action is the recent prohibition of combine-harvesters in India. It seems difficult to fault that decision, because combine-harvesters do not raise crop yields, whereas in India and other low-income countries they will doubtless damage the income-earning opportunities of the poorest rural households.

[15] Especially relevant are the large increases in factor productivity in Japan and Taiwan, which we discussed in chapter 3. It must be reemphasized, however, that the evidence from past experience is more persuasive for agricultural economies which rely mainly on irrigated production than for those where rainfed cultivation predominates.

also have adverse effects on development, especially when it is coupled with a narrow view of the effects of technical change. The resource-saving effects of technical change can generate new employment opportunities, together with increased output of goods and services. Because they ignore this potential, partial, static analyses are likely to condemn any technical change that eliminates income-earning opportunities of low-income households.

The issues are well illustrated by controversy concerning the choice of technology for rice milling in Indonesia. A clear and well-quantified analysis of alternative technologies by Timmer (1974) challenged recommendations for major investments in large-scale mills. Timmer demonstrated that given the relative prices of labor and capital prevailing in Indonesia, small rice hullers represented the economically efficient choice. His analysis was apparently helpful in rejecting an investment program for large bulk facilities which an international consulting firm had recommended on the basis of the modernity and technical efficiency of the capital-intensive alternative. Timmer's conclusions subsequently were criticized on equity grounds. It was argued that even the relatively labor-intensive small mills which he had shown to be economically optimal were inappropriate: they were causing a serious loss of income from hand-pounding of rice, a significant source of cash income for poor households (Collier et al. 1974). It was estimated that the small mills which were rapidly replacing hand-pounding would result in an annual loss of some 125 million woman-days of wage labor and earnings equivalent to about $50 million. In his reply, Timmer emphasizes that "banning small rice mills (thus forcing a return to hand-pounding) would be an enormously costly way of helping the displaced women. . . . We must set the $50 million loss to these women against a gain to society of more than $450 million." (1974, p. 20).

Concern with the plight of the poor often leads to condemnation of any technical change which has some adverse affect on a significant number of poor households. In this view, such changes should be tolerated only if they are coupled with mechanisms to redistribute enough of the social gain from the innovations to compensate the groups that experience a loss of income. This is in accord with the orthodox view of welfare economics, which is to argue for "the efficient choice" and then to supplement that decision with "the necessary distributional adjustment through a tax-transfer mechanism" (Musgrave 1969, p. 804). Our emphasis on the rate and bias of technical change is motivated in part by the realities which make it so unlikely that such a distributional adjustment will actually be carried out. Poverty is such a huge and pervasive problem in late-developing countries, and the lack of resources so acute, that any distributional adjustment will almost certainly be impossible to implement on a sufficient scale to be of substantial benefit to the poor. Moreover, it is usually infeasible to administer organizational schemes which would compensate a specific group for loss of income resulting from a specific innovation. In agriculture even more than in a processing industry such as rice milling, such schemes would demand extraordinary organizational support capable of identifying and assessing who is affected, in what way, and over which period by the various innovations adopted by farmers in a complex and continuing process of technical change. Such organizations do not exist and could be created—if at all—only at enormous opportunity cost for other organizational functions.

It seems likely that the consultants who recommended major investments in large-scale rice mills in Indonesia would have asserted that those modern mills represented "the efficient choice." Fortunately, Timmer's analysis demonstrated that given the price of labor relative to the price of capital, technical efficiency did not imply economic efficiency, despite the "modernity" of the large mills. On the other hand, to proscribe the spread of small-scale, economically efficient rice hullers in order to maintain the level of employment in hand-pounding of rice would also have sacrificed a long-term increase in the well-being of a substantial number of rural poor for adherence to an inappropriate ideal.

Condemnation of export crops. Another narrow, partial viewpoint which ignores the need to be concerned with both growth and equity is that of nutritionists and others concerned with the immediate welfare of the rural poor who condemn "cash crop agriculture," especially production of export crops. Their argument, in brief, is that malnutrition is aggravated because farmland is being used to produce coffee, tea, or other export crops rather than food crops. Thus the report of a WHO Expert Committee on Maternal and Child Health asserts that the commercialization of agriculture has "worsened the health situation in rural areas. Subsistence-style farming, for instance, has been largely replaced by cash crop agriculture geared to external markets rather than to the needs of the rural population. This has contributed significantly to changed nutritional habits and in many cases has severely impaired the ability of rural people to satisfy their own nutritional needs" (WHO 1976, p. 13).

There are situations in which this viewpoint has some validity. When production of export crops is concentrated on plantations or estates, the profitability of export enterprises may accentuate the other forces that lead to a bimodal agricultural structure and to a concentration of farmland in large-scale units. This intensifies the limited access to resources, which is such an important contributor to the poverty of the majority of the farm population. In Jamaica, for example, plantations producing sugar occupy a large percentage of the level, fertile land. The country's smallholders depend mainly on cultivation of the hillsides, where productivity is low as a result of soil erosion and related problems. A similar situation has existed in El Salvador. Much of the best farmland has been held by large estates producing cotton for export, and the bulk of the farm population has been obliged to eke out meager incomes cultivating small plots on steep and rocky hillsides.

In other situations, however, the blanket condemnation of export crops is out of place. In many African countries, for example, the economic innovation represented by the introduction of cocoa, coffee, cotton, and other export crops accelerated the growth of agricultural output and export earnings. Furthermore, because smallholders account for most of the export production, these innovations also lead to widespread increases in farm incomes (Anthony et al. 1979, chap. 2). A recent study in Kenya represents one of the few empirical analyses of the relationship between cash cropping and malnutrition. Data from Kenya's Integrated Rural Survey and a National Nutrition Survey provided the basis for this analysis of the relationship between cash cropping and nutritional status in essentially all of the country's smallholder farming areas. Two sugar-producing localities were the only areas where there was a correlation between cash cropping and malnutrition, and in only one of those areas was the correlation statistically significant.[16] Despite such evidence and the general presumption concerning the benefits that result from smallholder production of export crops, the condemnation of export-crop production is as common in the African as in the Latin American context. As noted in chapter 1, the debate proceeds along undeclared ideological tracks, failing to accumulate or contend with facts.

The concentration of land and other resources in large-scale farm units—a characteristic feature of bimodal patterns of agricultural development—often does accentuate the nutritional and other problems faced by the great majority of the rural population because of their limited access to productive resources. More generally, modifications of traditional patterns of subsistence production undoubtedly do increase the importance of nutrition education. But a general condemnation of export crops is based on a misleading, partial analysis of the situation. It ignores the fact that in many developing countries expanded production of such crops has made possible a very significant increase in cash and total income among small farmers, thus making an important contribution to rural well-being, as well as earning foreign exchange—one of the scarcest resources in most developing countries. Imposing restrictions on production of export crops would reduce the welfare of farm households by preventing them from using their land and other resources so as to maximize their net income.[17] The fundamental requirement is to increase productivity so as to enable farm households to expand their commercial production while simultaneously increasing their output of food for home consumption. As we emphasized in chapter 3, subsistence agriculture is inevitably condemned to a low level of productivity. Achieving the increases in farm productivity and output required to support economic and social development requires a tran-

[16] In that locality sugar cane was being grown on such a small fraction of the land of the households affected that competition for available resources of land and labor could hardly be the explanation. The plausible hypothesis is offered that the increased availability of sugar cane in the area had encouraged consumption of sugar by small children as a substitute for maize and other more nutritious food, thus giving rise to a higher incidence of protein-calorie malnutrition (Kenya 1979b, p. II.3).

[17] The same criticism applies to a recommendation by Joy and Payne that "resources should not be diverted to the production of luxury foods" (1975, p. 49).

sition from a traditional "resource-based" agriculture to a more productive "science-based" agriculture. This in turn requires a gradual expansion in the use of new, purchased inputs such as fertilizers and seed for high-yield, fertilizer-responsive varieties (Hayami and Ruttan 1971; Johnston 1978). Probably the most valid criticism of emphasis on export crops is that the priority given to crops such as coffee, cocoa, and cotton has contributed to the neglect of research on food crops (Anthony et al. 1979, chap. 8).

Some of the extreme recommendations concerning the orientation of agricultural research towards the needs of small farmers fall into the same trap of partial, tactical analysis. By and large, "zero input" technologies (that is, those involving no requirements for purchased inputs) simply will not yield the increases in farm productivity and output that are required (Oram 1978). There are some instances in which new varieties or certain other innovations can increase productivity and output with virtually no increase in purchased inputs. Perhaps the most important example is the potential for breeding high- and stable-yield varieties of cassava, building on recent work at the International Institute for Tropical Agriculture (IITA), in Nigeria, and at the Centro Internacional de Agricultura Tropical (CIAT), in Colombia. There has been such neglect of research on cassava that "the potential payoff from breeding and associated support research appears to be enormous" (Flinn 1979, p. 87). In general, however, the need is for strengthening research to generate a sequence of innovations each of which requires only a gradual increase in the use of *divisible* inputs that complement rather than displace the relatively abundant resource of farm labor. Nonspecialists commonly condemn the Green Revolution because the improved varieties of rice and wheat require more purchased inputs to realize their yield potential. This criticism, however, ignores the labor-using, capital-saving bias of fertilizer and other inputs essential to the core technology of that "revolution," which is more accurately described as a seed-fertilizer revolution.

Towards strategic integration. In contrast to narrow arguments for growth *or* equity, we have advocated throughout this essay a more strategic response to the serious problems of rural underemployment and unemployment. For example, it is likely to be both desirable and feasible for governments to undertake labor-intensive rural-works programs for the twofold purpose of providing supplementary income-earning opportunities for the most disadvantaged rural families and improving the rural infrastructure through building roads and similar activities. A major Kenyan project for building rural access roads is of interest not only because it "proved that labour-intensive construction methods are economical and technically viable" but also because it demonstrated that organizational and management techniques can be adapted to facilitate such methods (de Veen 1980, p. 1). Despite such evidence in support of the feasibility and desirability of a strategically integrated approach to rural development, a variety of contrary views persist. In one of the most sophisticated of these, Schuh (1978) argues that the choice of technologies for expanding production should not be influenced by concern with their impact on income distribution. As Castle (1978, p. 328) puts it, "Schuh's major thesis is that policies to promote the generation of additional income streams should be uncoupled from policies to redistribute income or wealth."

Schuh argues that "the relative-income problem requires a different set of policies than to deal with the output problem." In his view, the introduction of new production technologies in agriculture should be viewed solely as a means of expanding output. He rightly condemns the viewpoint of "social scientists who would throw the baby out with the bath water by abandoning technical change altogether" (Schuh 1978, p. 322). But Schuh overlooks the fact that there are different *kinds* of technical change. And in late-developing countries the kinds of change appropriate to a unimodal pattern of agricultural development are likely to receive high marks for their effects on both the rate and the bias of technological change.

Schuh would place the entire burden of alleviating poverty and unequal income distribution on policies affecting human capital formation and the performance of factor markets. His emphasis on underinvestment in schooling and in health programs for the rural population is similar to the thrust of the second "prong" of our strategy: both advocate a high priority for social-service programs related to education, health, nutrition, and family planning. However, we believe that it is a misleading oversimplification to suggest that members of the rural labor force have limited labor opportunities outside agriculture because they "do not have the human capital to obtain alternative employment" (Schuh 1978, p. 319).

The major thrust of Schuh's argument is that to try to increase employment in agriculture rather than to attack the fundamental problems causing low labor absorption in the industrial sector is to deal with symptoms rather than fundamental causes. And his general conclusion is that "policies for alleviating rural poverty must be directed to giving rural workers the skills they need for alternative employment, to promoting more efficient labor markets, and to removing the anti-employment bias of development policy by reducing the factor-price distortions in the economy at large" (Schuh 1978, pp. 321–22). Certainly the elimination of price distortions that have an antiemployment bias is important. And as structural transformation proceeds, expansion of employment opportunities in industry will have an increasingly important role to play in alleviating problems of rural poverty.

However, to ignore the possibilities for absorbing labor into productive employment in agriculture and to concentrate entirely on labor absorption in the industrial sector is a mistake. This ignores the fundamental constraint that derives from the structural-demographic characteristics of late-developing countries, where some 60 percent to 80 percent of the labor force is still dependent on agriculture. It is that constraint, in combination with the extremely low levels of per capita income, which makes it so important to give explicit attention to the *rate* and *bias* of technical change in programs designed to spur the growth of a more broadly-based *pattern* of agricultural development.

Relief-and-Welfare Approaches: Food Subsidies and Foreign Aid

We have seen that a critical issue in the continuing redesign of development strategies concerns the "appropriate" balance of resources between strengthening social services and redistributing current income flows. The issue is critical in part because redistribution schemes are usually considered in an ad hoc manner which ignores the inevitable competition for scarce resources.

In this section we consider measures for redistributing current income flows to directly and quickly increase food consumption. Quick solutions to an immediate and pressing problem such as malnutrition seem so desirable that the temptation to gloss over the question of feasibility is strong. The desirability of quick solutions encourages a related tendency to assume that expanded foreign aid will be forthcoming to offset the lack of domestic resources. If policy analysis is to contribute to the design and implementation of policies that are truly beneficial to the poor, it is essential to confront explicitly the trade-offs that are implicit in alternative strategic designs. This was the main reason for presenting our "systems view" of the interrelated determinants of rural well-being. It is also a principal reason underlying our focus on problems of rural development: it is the rural poor who are likely to suffer from an undue concentration of attention and resources on a relief-and-welfare approach. Our critique of redistributive measures in this section is not motivated by doubts about their desirability. On the contrary, we regard such measures as highly desirable in industrialized countries such as the United States and in a number of middle-income countries where financial and manpower constraints are not too binding. We do contend, however, that in late-developing countries such measures should be given a relatively low priority until even more urgent and competitive needs have been met. That contention derives support, we believe, from our analysis of the interrelationships among the determinants of rural well-being: measures such as food subsidies will not have the significant effects on development that can be expected to result from education, health, nutrition, and family planning programs which achieve broad coverage of a country's rural as well as its urban population.

The search for shortcuts. In his influential book *The Nutrition Factor*, Alan Berg cites conditions in India while arguing the case for direct action to eliminate malnutrition: "Unless a new strategy is evolved to shortcut the traditional means of providing nutrition, it will be near the turn of the century before the poorest third of India's population can afford a minimum adequate diet" (1973, p. 12). Unfortunately, as we showed in chapter 4, little progress has been made in reaching a consensus concerning the practical components of such a "new strategy." Writing in 1973, Berg was still considerably influenced by the "protein gap" view of the world food problem. Accordingly, he gave a good deal of attention to new foods such as single-cell protein and fish-protein concentrate and to fortification as means of short-cutting reliance on income growth as a means of improving diets (Berg 1973, pp. 132–42).

In recent years, with the greater recognition of the need to increase consumption of *food* to overcome energy deficits, the principal interventions advocated for increasing food intake directly have been supplementary feeding schemes and especially food price subsidies or food stamp programs. The report of a Presidential Commission on World Hunger established by President Carter in 1978 is a good example of the current emphasis on direct measures to achieve immediate results. The report recognizes the importance of attacking the causes of hunger by promoting equitable economic growth, by establishing national and international food reserves, and by reducing the rate of population growth. More or less equal attention is given, however, to "alleviating hunger under conditions of continued poverty and underdevelopment" by "treating the symptoms" The first objective considered under that rubric is "assuring that people who are poor need not be hungry as well." The text includes an endorsement of a food stamp approach, which "enables needy people to buy additional food while stimulating rather than depressing demand for local supplies." (Presidential Commission on World Hunger 1980, pp. 40–41).[18] As we will note shortly, a food-stamp plan may have the advantage of being less costly than a general food-subsidy program. Both types of programs appear to be inappropriate, however, under the conditions prevailing in late-developing countries.

The advocacy of direct measures for "treating the symptoms" of poverty is influenced by calculations that purport to demonstrate that the cost of immediate action to eliminate hunger would be relatively modest. For example, the report of the Presidential Commission on World Hunger cites an FAO projection that some 416 million people will be subject to malnutrition in 1990 and that 32 million tons of grain above and beyond the quantities required to meet commercial demand would be sufficient to cover the deficit between energy requirements and projected levels of food intake.[19] The commission report suggests that "special feeding programs or food subsidy schemes to feed these people adequately" would be quite manageable because the cost of producing

[18] The World Food Council has advocated similar programs, especially an "international food-entitlement scheme." Its proposals also gloss over the opportunity cost of such programs on the assumption that they would be financed by additional foreign-aid allocations (World Food Council 1980). It is also worth mentioning that an urban food-stamp plan is the principal intervention program recommended in the World Bank's first major publication on nutrition, *Malnutrition and Poverty*, by Reutlinger and Selowsky (1976).

[19] The report does not cite the FAO source for these projections. We pointed out in chapter 2 that large variations in the estimates that have been made of the number of persons subject to Protein-Energy Malnutrition are related to uncertainties about methodology as well as about current and future levels of food production. FAO's *The Fourth World Food Survey* presents calculations based on several approaches (1977, pp. 59–65). These estimates suggest that the 32-million-ton figure used in the report of the presidential commission is on the low side. In our judgment, however, that discrepancy is relatively unimportant as compared with the other problems discussed in the text.

the additional grain would be about $8 billion—approximately the cost of the U.S. Food Stamp Program in 1979. What the report fails to mention is that the current level of expenditure in the United States for food stamps reflects a remarkable increase in the level of social-welfare expenditures since President Johnson launched the War on Poverty in 1965. The increase in expenditures for the food stamp plan has been especially large—from $33 million in 1965 to a little over half a billion dollars in 1970, $4.4 billion in 1975, and close to $8 billion in 1979 (Presidential Commission on World Hunger 1980, p. 34; Wildavsky 1979, p. 88).

The body politic in the United States seems to have accepted the idea that "people who are poor need not be hungry as well." With a GNP of well over $2 trillion in 1979, the United States had invested only one third of 1 percent of its GNP in its food stamp program. The fiscal burden of food subsidy schemes in developing countries that have adopted such schemes is much greater. Government expenditures for food subsidies in Pakistan amounted to 1.9 percent of the GNP in the early 1970s; the central government's expenditures for education and health were only 1.3 percent of the GNP, although the figure rises to 3.1 percent of the GNP when expenditures at all levels of government are included. We noted in chapter 4 that among the low-income countries, Sri Lanka has relatively strong education and health programs. In the early 1970s government expenditures for these two social-service programs represented approximately 4.8 percent of the GNP; but government expenditures for food subsidies were nearly as large, amounting to 4.5 percent of the GNP. The extreme example is Egypt, where in 1974 food subsidies amounted to 10 percent of the GNP, one and a half times public spending on education and health (Meerman 1980, pp. 127, 149). (We return to Egypt's experience in the next section, on foreign aid and welfare measures.)

The countries that we have cited are extreme examples. Once food subsidies are introduced, however, there is a tendency for pressure groups in urban areas to push for their expansion. The heavy burden of financing such programs is likely to preclude the government's undertaking many alternative activities. The large demands on budget resources are also likely to tempt governments to set low domestic procurement prices for the locally produced foods included in the program, thereby depressing agricultural incentives and incomes (Meerman 1980, p. 149).

Another shortcoming is that food subsidy programs in late-developing countries typically fail to reach many of the poorest households which have the most serious nutritional problems. In Peru, for example, less than 15 percent of the total food subsidy is consumed by the poorest 40 percent of the population (Meerman 1980, p. 150). This is mainly because the principal beneficiaries of food subsidies are urban consumers. In the case of Bangladesh, the rationing system which distributes rice and wheat at subsidized prices reaches less than 25 percent of the country's population. Some 70 percent of the food which is distributed through the rationing system goes to urban consumers;

the 80 percent of the population in rural areas benefits very little. Even among the urban population, only a little over one fourth of the poorest and most malnourished families have access to the system (Levinson 1979, pp. 13–14).

Advocates of a food stamp program (or food entitlement scheme) emphasize that costs could be reduced substantially as compared to a general food subsidy by confining the subsidized distribution to specific target groups of low-income families. Difficult political and administrative problems arise, however, in attempting to implement such schemes. Assessing need in order to determine eligibility for participating in a food stamp program is difficult in urban areas.[20] It would be enormously more difficult for rural households that satisfy a substantial percentage of their food needs by their own subsistence production: the adequacy of home-produced supplies varies seasonally and from year to year depending on weather conditions and many other factors influencing crop production.

Despite their shortcomings, food-subsidy programs are often advocated. Thus a recent report by the International Food Policy Research Institute, Washington, D.C., states "that broad food subsidy programs are, despite the high cost, a promising means of improving the welfare of large numbers of poor people" (IFPRI 1978, p. 6). That view is reiterated by a senior IFPRI staff member, J. D. Gavan, in an *IFPRI Report* which includes an explicit recognition that the cost of food subsidy schemes exceeds the resources of low-income countries. It is therefore asserted that "foreign assistance must meet a major part of the burden" and that "funds to help maintain farm prices must be forthcoming as well" (Gavan 1979).

Foreign aid and short-term welfare measures. Most discussions of a "basic needs strategy" also emphasize an important role for foreign aid in augmenting domestic resources. Thus Streeten and Burki (1978, p. 415) state that "poor countries will not be able to satisfy basic needs on their own within a reasonable time span, without substantial assistance from outside." The assertion is often made that the availability of aid could be increased substantially if donor countries could only be assured that the aid provided would mainly benefit the poorer segments of a developing country's population.

Proposals for a "global compact" which would increase aid flows by means of a more explicit antipoverty orientation have received considerable atten-

[20] Although the problems of administering a food stamp plan, food subsidies, or other redistributive schemes are less severe in urban areas, it does not follow that they merit priority even in those areas. The enormous growth of cities which is in prospect in the developing countries, which we noted in chapter 2, means that problems of management and poverty reduction in urban areas will place heavy demands on scarce financial and manpower resources. It is therefore not surprising that an analysis of these problems by the coordinator of the World Bank's Urban Poverty Task Force, the director of its Urban Projects Department, and two of their colleagues concludes that priority should be given to production- and employment-oriented programs and to the strengthening of social services. Indeed, they assert that "there is little that can be done specifically to alleviate the problems of the [urban] poor. Well-meant but inappropriate programmes would dissipate extremely scarce resources necessary for national growth" (Beier et al. 1976, p. 398).

tion. Rich and poor countries would concert their efforts to satisfy the basic needs of low-income households in poor countries, and the "compact" would somehow spell out the changes in policies "that must be made" in both donor and recipient countries in order to achieve the objectives of a basic needs strategy.[21]

There is a good deal of self-delusion involved in these heady discussions of a "global compact" and a large expansion of foreign aid. External aid can and should supplement the financial and manpower resources available within the low-income countries to a much greater extent than at present. And there is probably some validity in the view that support for economic and technical assistance within donor countries would be increased if there were more confidence that aid was contributing to the reduction of poverty. Unfortunately, recent experience does not justify optimistic expectations. The official development assistance provided by the United States, Canada, Japan, and the European members of the Organisation for Economic Co-operation and Development (OECD) in 1977 amounted to $14.7 billion. This represented only 0.31 percent of their GNP, less than half of the 0.7 percent target endorsed by the U.N. General Assembly in 1970. Moreover, given the problems of inflation, concern with the world energy problem, and the current climate of opinion in the industrialized countries, the future prospects for the expansion of aid are not encouraging. In principle, there is a large potential for expanding the level of foreign aid if the enormous outlays for military expenditure could be reduced even moderately.[22] But the prospects for such a reduction are bleak. In the early 1970s a rapid expansion of official development assistance from the OPEC countries provided a substantial addition to the aid flows from the industrialized countries. But during 1975–77 the aid from OPEC countries leveled off at about $5.6 billion per year and, as a percentage of GNP, declined from 2.7 percent in 1975 to 2.0 percent in 1977 (World Bank 1979, p. 8).

The emphasis on a "basic human needs" approach has been especially prominent in discussions of aid in the United States. The emphasis raises some important issues because of the large though declining share of U.S. aid programs in the total flows of official development assistance to less developed countries. In 1965 U.S. foreign assistance was equivalent to about 0.5 percent of the country's GNP and represented 58 percent of the official development assistance of the OECD member countries. By 1977 U.S. foreign aid amounted to only 0.22 percent of the GNP and accounted for but 28 percent of the total aid flows from OECD countries (World Bank 1979, pp. 156–57). Moreover, Egypt and Israel have received more than 40 percent of the total foreign-assistance budget because of their special significance to U.S. foreign-policy objectives. Although there is a possibility that orienting U.S. aid programs

---

[21] For a brief discussion of the apparently insuperable difficulties that would arise in defining and reaching agreement on such a compact, see Bhagwati (1977, p. 11).

[22] As we noted in chapter 2, this was a major theme of the report of the Independent Commission on International Development Issues chaired by Willy Brandt (1980).

toward the objective of meeting basic human needs will make it easier to reverse the declining trend in U.S. assistance, there is also a danger that a narrow preoccupation with programs aimed at directly satisfying basic needs will have adverse effects on the less developed countries.

In recent years there has been a reluctance on the part of the United States to support major investments in irrigation and other rural infrastructure projects on the grounds that such activities would not directly benefit the poor. It is not surprising that some representatives of less developed countries have interpreted the recent emphasis in the United States on basic human needs as a cynical ploy to give lip service to the plight of poor families while stinting on support for costly investments in infrastructure and for long-term institution-building activities. We believe that an emphasis on short-term welfare measures will reduce the effectiveness of the foreign-aid program. And this may weaken the longer-term support for U.S. efforts to provide assistance to developing countries.

Food aid versus alternative forms of assistance. Another consideration concerns the effectiveness and opportunity cost of different forms of aid in furthering the multiple objectives of development. Just as there are trade-offs in the allocation of domestic resources, so there are inevitably trade-offs in the allocation of foreign aid. Programs to raise consumption levels directly compete with programs to strengthen a country's own capacities for increasing production and providing social services. Food aid may result in a saving in foreign exchange; but it is most commonly justified as a means of raising consumption levels. Despite fluctuations, food aid has consistently accounted for a sizable fraction of the development assistance provided by the United States.[23]

Food aid is often said to be less costly in terms of "political resources" than other forms of aid because agricultural surpluses are generated as a by-product of domestic programs for supporting farm prices. There is considerable truth in this view, especially as a short-term interpretation of U.S. congressional decision-making. It is, however, less true at the present than in the 1950s and the 1960s.[24]

There are, of course, circumstances in which food aid is an extremely valuable form of assistance. In emergency situations such as that in Cambodia in

[23] The gross cost of financing food-aid shipments typically has been equal to about one third of the total official development assistance provided by the United States. The $1.2 billion food aid in 1977 was 29 percent of the total; but in 1965 and 1975 the share of food aid reached 61 percent and 41 percent of the total, respectively (USDA 1979, table 6; World Bank 1979, p. 156).

[24] Witt (1977, p. 86) suggests that "food aid in the 1950s and 1960s could be characterized as a marriage of convenience enabling grain exporters to bypass the problems of excess production capacity and grain importers to avoid facing the problems of inadequate production capacity." In the United States, "non-recourse loans" frequently led to the accumulation of government-held stocks representing burdensome surpluses. These were transmuted into a valuable resource through the Public Law 480 Food for Peace Program. Recent years have witnessed a deemphasis of non-recourse loans. Commercial demand for agricultural exports has grown, as has interest in enlarging export earnings from farm products because of the U.S. balance-of-payments problems.

1979/80, the food crises in Bangladesh in the 1970s resulting first from civil war and then from severe flood damage, or the drought-induced food shortages in India in the mid-1960s and subsequently in the African Sahel, the need is for food that is immediately available to avert starvation and to lessen the disease problems aggravated by severe malnutrition.

In terms of promoting the longer-term objectives of development, however, there is little doubt that food aid is not as effective as many alternative forms of economic and technical assistance.[25] Even among commodity-aid programs, financing fertilizer imports will almost certainly have a considerably greater positive impact. Each dollar invested in fertilizer permits a severalfold increase in the value of food produced in the recipient country and permits increases in food consumption among both the farm and the nonfarm population.[26] Moreover, the growth in domestic-farm cash income resulting from expanded commercial sales has important multiplier effects, leading to further increases in productivity, output, and employment within and outside agriculture.

The interacting effects of foreign aid and short-run domestic political pressures are illustrated clearly by events in Egypt. By 1975 a sequence of decisions had led the Egyptian government to allocate approximately 11 percent of the country's Gross Domestic Product to food subsidy programs. This outcome was certainly not based on a judgment that such an enormous fraction of the country's resources should be invested in food subsidies. The initial cost of the program was much less. And the availability of large food-aid shipments from the United States contributed to the decision to undertake the program and lessened the fiscal burden on the Egyptian government. However, the costs of the program escalated with the sharp rise in world grain prices between 1972 and 1974. Once a government is committed to such a program, it is difficult to terminate or even to curtail it. A decision to cut back on the subsidy program was reversed in January 1977 because of strong and highly visible protests in Cairo and other major cities (L. Taylor 1977, pp. 35–36). There is little doubt that in this extreme instance the program represented an inefficient allocation of both domestic and external resources. One indication of the misallocation is the shipment of substantial quantities of cheap, subsidized bread to rural areas, where it is used as poultry feed.[27]

Superficially, it might seem that the recent focus on poverty and basic needs by aid agencies would be beneficial to the poor in less developed countries. And no doubt there is some scope for donor agencies to apply leverage that

[25] P.L. 480 and similar food-aid programs are a form of "aid-tying," in which the aid is tied to a particular set of commodities as well as to purchases in a particular country. The proposition that reducing the extent of aid-tying will increase the value of a transfer of external resources to the aid-receiver would seem to apply as much to food aid as to other forms of assistance.

[26] In a study of the impact of the seed-fertilizer revolution in Pakistan it was estimated that the grain-nutrient response ratio was ten to one on a weight basis, and two to one or three to one on a value basis (Cownie, Johnston, and Duff 1970, p. 63).

[27] Inasmuch as this bread is resold illegally at black-market prices, the practice is not well documented; but we have confidence in reports suggesting that it is a common practice.

strengthens domestic groups which emphasize, for example, increasing the incomes of small farmers rather than capital-intensive, labor-displacing investment in the large-scale subsector of agriculture.

There is serious risk, however, that on balance the new orientation of foreign assistance will have detrimental effects on the rural poor. This is in part because of the understandable but dangerous impatience for quick results that is too often a characteristic of donor agencies in the era of New Directions and Basic Human Needs. It seems all too likely that instead of strengthening a longer-term perspective and providing support for the sustained effort required to achieve development objectives, external donors will reinforce the domestic political pressures which so often given rise to an urban bias and a focus on short-term tactical solutions which compromise the prospects for attaining strategic objectives.[28]

To reiterate, we believe that the opportunity cost of emphasis on a relief-and-welfare approach is likely to be very high. Preoccupation with attempts to achieve quick results by such measures is found to divert both resources and attention away from more fundamental measures. Our emphasis on a strategic perspective and on the three-pronged strategy for rural development outlined in this chapter is intended to focus attention on the trade-offs that should be confronted in considering relief-and-welfare measures. More realistic recognition of the competitive and complementary interrelationships which we emphasized in arguing for a three-pronged approach can, we believe, contribute to a consensus on the essential elements of production, consumption, and organization programs which will be both feasible and effective in promoting development and reducing rural and urban poverty.

From Reflection towards Action

If you, our readers, have arrived at the close of this essay expecting a succinct prescription for the redesign of rural development, you will be disappointed. So will we. For we have argued repeatedly that thinking about development is only part of the process of making development happen. No analysis of the sort we have attempted here can be more than a guide, an aid, to better policy design. Without effective implementation of specific program interventions, it remains nothing more than a rhetorical self-indulgence. At this point we therefore pass our reflective exercise on to those of you who are the practitioners of development. What you do with it will determine its rele-

---

[28] The tendency for a government's priorities to be dominated by a current or recent crisis is illustrated by Timmer's (1973) analysis of rice policy in Indonesia: preoccupation with a sharp rise in food prices and with the reactions of urban consumers led to a dominant concern with price policy and relative neglect of production programs. It was suggested in chapter 3 that the short-term perspective of policymakers has been an especially serious problem in the countries of Sub-Saharan Africa. Lele (1981, pp. 552–53) argues explicitly that policies of donor agencies have often reinforced this tendency.

vance to rural well-being in the late-developing countries. We hope only that some of what we have said will help some of you better to reflect on your own past experience, and better to plan your own future actions. We emphasize the planning of actions, for make no mistake about it, if planning is to make a difference in development, the ultimate plan must be to act.

The plan is to act and, as we have argued throughout our essay, to act *strategically*: to act in recognition of the interconnected determinants of rural well-being and the consequent need for better program integration; to act in recognition of the long time scales required for fundamental change and the consequent need for more patience and persistence; to act in recognition of the limited scope of theory and analysis and the consequent need for improved trial-and-error learning. Let us conclude by briefly recapitulating our arguments concerning these interrelated components of our strategic perspective on rural development.

The goal of development programs is to improve the well-being of people. Neither ideological nor technical disagreements over how best to go about this task should obscure the overriding need to get on with the job as quickly, effectively, and efficiently as possible. The determinants of well-being, however, are interconnected in ways that can make piecemeal interventions an inefficient and often counterproductive approach to overall policy design. Throughout the history of development, individual program actions have exhibited both complementary and competitive effects on one another. This suggests the desirability of a strategic perspective from which *packages* of programs mutually adjusted to one another's requirements, strengths, and weaknesses can be more readily perceived and designed.

We have described one such strategic perspective. Our three-pronged approach to rural development emphasizes concurrent, mutually supportive programs relating to production, consumption, and organization. In particular, we stress the desirability and feasibility of actions to achieve broadly based advances in rural employment opportunities and agricultural development; to promote widespread rural coverage of services relating to health, nutrition, and family planning; and to improve the institutional structures and managerial procedures through which rural people resolve local problems and are linked into the broader social system.

Few, we suspect, will question the desirability of these activities; many, however, will doubt their feasibility. Such doubts are not unfounded: given the myriad obstacles to improving rural well-being, the odds are steep against *any* approach, ours included. We argue only that a three-pronged strategic perspective of the sort we have described is more likely than its alternatives to promote the broad-based changes which are so desperately needed.

The greatest danger of this three-pronged perspective is that its synoptic scope will be taken for a recommendation to adopt any and all programs that may be advocated in the production, consumption, or organization areas. No interpretation could be further from our actual intent. On the contrary, widespread and sustained progress towards improving rural well-being requires that only a very few of the highest priority, most mutually reinforcing programs should be undertaken at all. Strategic choice means choosing *not* to do a vast number of tactically attractive things. Our emphasis on the necessity of an appropriate balance between production- and consumption-oriented activities highlights this key requirement of strategic design.

An emphasis on schemes such as supplementary feeding or food stamp programs is likely to be reinforced by a desire on the part of donor agencies and foreign advisors "to get on with it" and "to do what can be done." Those are commendable attitudes, especially in an environment in which resource constraints are not too severe. However, late-developing countries face severe resource constraints. Political pressures all too often encourage an "urban bias" and a preoccupation with immediate concerns. Considering the staggering problems faced by poor countries, the opportunity cost of concentrating attention and resources on short-term welfare measures is enormous. To be sure, some immediate deprivations of certain target groups can be alleviated. However, the pervasive problems of poverty—especially among the hard-to-reach rural population—are likely to be accentuated because the commitment of resources to redistributive measures is almost certain to be at the expense of even more important programs. The problems of rural poverty will surely become more widespread and more intractable unless actions are relentlessly focused on programs that strengthen indigenous capacities to accelerate the growth of output, expand employment opportunities, improve health and nutrition, and slow population growth—to repeat our fourfold litany one last time.

The need to conserve scarce resources, to undertake only those tasks most central to the improvement of rural well-being, is equally acute when we consider the organizational components of a development strategy. A strategic perspective does not mean an ever-growing staff of master planners sequestered in national capitals. Nor does it imply tactical integration of all development activities. On the contrary, our three-pronged approach advocates explicit separation of some activities and suggests a need for closely coordinated administration of others.

A strategic perspective does mean using all available forms of social organization—including political, market, and traditional structures—for the tasks which they can be made to perform reasonably well, while preserving scarce administrative talent for focused intervention when and where it can do the most good. Above all, our strategic perspective emphasizes that effective production and consumption programs can be expanded only with the growth of organizational capacity for their effective implementation. This focus on the importance of time and timing brings us to the second major theme of our strategic perspective.

Improving rural well-being is an inherently time-consuming process. Historical experience teaches that at best, broadly based and sustainable progress will be measured in decades, not years. In part, the pace of development is limited by fundamental structural-demographic constraints: we showed that even under the most optimistic of assumptions, today's late-developing countries will remain predominantly rural societies into the twenty-first century. Perhaps even more significant for policy design, however, is that development is essentially a learning process: the growth of organizational competence and personal knowledge are as fundamental a requirement as the growth of capital in the conventional sense. Because most of the "answers" to development questions aren't known by anyone, because even those answers which are known by some must be laboriously passed on to others, because all answers must be adapted to specific places and times, the learning process of development necessarily entails a great deal of trial and error. Extraordinary patience and persistence are required to mold this trial-and-error process into a continually improving sequence of program designs.

This much needed persistence has too often been lacking in rural development strategies. The desire to by-pass the errors, to teach answers instead of facilitating learning, is as strong—and as disastrous a long-term strategy—in rural development as in child rearing. In particular, an impatience for immediate results has often encouraged a relief-and-welfare approach to improving rural well-being. Such short-term activities, however, almost invariably lead to the neglect of more fundamental long-term tasks: building organizational and technical capabilities and strengthening the capacities of local people to meet their own needs.

Our emphasis on the time-consuming realities of development should not be interpreted as a lack of awareness or concern with the deprivations of widespread poverty in late-developing countries. Rather, it reflects our conviction that short-term, tactical solutions emphasizing a relief-and-welfare approach are simply not equal to the task of eliminating poverty in low-income developing countries. Moreover, we believe that failure to pursue rural development strategies which are directed at correcting the root causes of poverty will mean that the number of people in these countries suffering from malnutrition and related deprivations will continue to increase.

Relief-and-welfare approaches are at least grounded in a concern to relieve immediate suffering. Less defensible and equally destructive are the frequent fads of the year which continue to plague rural development. Most new directions have involved cutting off or drastically curtailing existing programs after only a few years of trial—far too short a period for any but the most superficial organizational development and personal learning to have occurred. Of course some programs should be terminated—indeed they must be if resources are to be available for supporting the few ventures which turn out to really make a difference. Nonetheless, a great deal of premature termination and meaningless "testing" stem from development workers' infatuation with inappropriate experimental methods drawn from the natural sciences. We have argued, however, that there is little to be learned from short-term attempts to "prove" or "demonstrate" the virtues of rigidly controlled development-program designs. Much more effective is sustained, long-term support for organizational structures and managerial procedures which facilitate adaptive learning and continuing program redesign.

Who is to provide the persistent support of long-term strategy which is so necessary for sustained, broad-based progress in rural development? One commonplace has it that since politicians and their appointees are always preoccupied with staying in office, only donor agencies and independent scholars can afford the luxury of long perspectives. But such a view, however common, is wrong.

A sizable proportion of the success stories reviewed in this essay were intimately bound to politicians (and political organizations) in the developing nations who *did* persist in their chosen strategies through ten or even twenty years of slow and painful learning. And a sizable proportion of the terminal failures reviewed in this essay were intimately bound to exotic projects which came and went with the effervescent fads and internecine strife of the professional development community. And between these blatantly caricatured extremes are to be found all manner of intermediate cases—some, to be sure, inhabited by short-sighted politicians and others by long-visioned scholars. Our aim is not to cast any group as angels or demons but rather to stress that assigning the blame for past failures to stereotypes does nothing but poison the debate.

The short-sighted politicians who undoubtedly exist in worlds both developing and developed can be reasoned with, cajoled, and induced by offers of conditional aid. Historical experience warns us neither to expect too much from such efforts nor to scorn them entirely. But the professional development community should not exert too much energy berating the politicians before it sets its own house in order.

The development "failures" just described are failures about which something can be done. One important source of failure which needs attention is the existing structure of incentives and policies in a number of aid agencies as well as in academic circles. These incentives and policies continue to encourage elaborate but immature model-building exercises, costly but often meaningless field experiments, and short but expensive appraisal visits which are uninformative because they focus on isolated projects independent of their strategic context.

Of course, there are important exceptions. The World Bank's African Rural Development Study, carried out by Uma Lele and a team of research workers, was a novel and serious attempt to learn from past experience and to consider questions of both *what* programs to adopt and *how* to implement them effectively. But that study was completed in 1975, and few if any similar comparative retrospectives focused on other regions or problem areas have yet been initiated.

Surely it is high time for the development community—scholars, practitioners, and politicians—to appreciate more fully and to support more persistently a strategic perspective on rural development which recognizes the inevitable limitations of knowledge and understanding. Surely it is time for a perspective that emphasizes the consequent need for an adaptive, sequential learning process of policy redesign. Surely it is time for a perspective that stresses the necessity of building cumulative development capabilities from a combination of trial-and-error experience, novel ideas, increased organizational capacity, and enhanced individual talents. We are under no illusion that the reorientation of scholarship, analysis, and policymaking which such a perspective implies will be easy or quick to come. We do believe that until such a reorientation occurs, many short-term development "solutions" will continue to contribute to the long-term problems of development.

Many have argued that *no* long-term solutions are possible—that the factors militating against real progress in the late-developing countries are simply overwhelming. Some have invoked numbers and logic to prove that the present situation is hopeless. Such conclusions may indeed be justified, even if their claims and ultimate authoritativeness are not.

Our perspective, however, is more ambivalent. Yes, the numbers and needs are appalling. No, there are no simple and instant solutions—neither the dreams of revolutionaries nor the fantasies of technological fixers are going to whisk away the myriad obstacles to rural development. Perhaps, however, there still remains between these stark perceptions of reality some room for what A. O. Hirschman has characterized as a "bias for hope."

Ultimately, development is about neither numbers nor solutions; rather, it is about people. Our bias for hope derives from our inclination to see people not only as the ends of development programs but also as the means for those programs' effective implementation. And as Mosher has pointed out, people, viewed as problem-solving agents capable of acquiring increased competence and confidence, constitute a uniquely abundant and self-renewing resource. The very real prospect of exploiting this unique resource more broadly and effectively is among the most cogent and underrated justifications for hope available to contemporary development workers. Why? Because what individual people choose to do about development does make a difference.

That people *can* make a difference has been a recurrent theme of our three-pronged strategy for rural development. We have shown that such a perspective suggests sequences of feasible, incremental steps through which production, consumption, and organization programs can be pursued, and by which their complementary effects on rural well-being can be realized.

That people *have* made a difference is a central fact of development's history. It must not be forgotten that only a decade or two ago many of today's middle-income countries faced constraints and conditions comparable to those of today's low-income countries. Much of these countries' growth, much of the improved well-being of their people, is because their people *did* pursue strategies for rural development emphasizing vigorous and sustained production, consumption, and organization programs similar to the three "prongs" of the strategy that we have advocated. China and Taiwan are only two of the specific examples we have discussed in which these critical choices played a pivotal role.

We believe that the efforts of today's low-income countries to emulate such successes will be facilitated to the extent that the development debate within these countries and the international development community can be focused constructively on fundamental constraints and opportunities, on the longer-term implications of strategic policy decisions, and on systematic efforts to learn from both successes and failures. In that way, the actions and under-standing of the people who make development happen can become increasing-ly efficacious in their contributions to the continuing process of policy redesign.

References

Abel, M. E. "Hard Policy Choices in Improving Incentives for Farmers." In *Distortions of Agricultural Incentives*, edited by T. W. Schultz. Bloomington and London: Indiana University Press, 1978.

Acharya, S. N. "Perspectives and Problems of Development in Low Income, Sub-Saharan Africa." In *Two Studies of Development in Sub-Saharan Africa*. World Bank Staff Working Paper no. 300. Washington, D.C.: World Bank, 1978.

Ackerman, B. A.; Ackerman, S. R.; Sawyer, J. W., Jr.; and Henderson, D. W. *The Uncertain Search for Environmental Quality*. New York: Free Press, 1974.

Ackoff, R. L. *Redesigning the Future: A Systems Approach to Societal Problems*. New York: Wiley-Interscience, 1974.

Adelman, Irma. "Development Economics—A Reassessment of Goals." *American Economic Review* 65, no. 2 (1975), pp. 302–9.

———, et al. *The Political Economy of Egalitarian Growth*. Geneva: International Labour Office, 1976.

Ahluwalia, M. S., and Chenery, H. "The Economic Framework." In *Redistribution with Growth*, by H. Chenery et al. London: Oxford University Press, 1974.

Alchian, A. A. "Uncertainty, Evolution, and Economic Theory." *Journal of Political Economy* 57, no. 3 (1950), pp. 211–21.

Alfonso, F. B. "Assisting Farmer Controlled Development of Communal Irrigation Systems." In *Bureaucracy and the Poor: Closing the Gap*, edited by D. C. Korten and F. B. Alfonso. Singapore: McGraw-Hill, 1981.

Allison, G. T. *Essence of Decision: Explaining the Cuban Missile Crisis*. Boston: Little, Brown & Co., 1971.

Almond, G. A., and Verba, S. *The Civic Culture*. Boston: Little, Brown & Co., 1965.

Anden-Lacsina, Teresa, and Barker, R. "The Adoption of Modern Varieties." In *Changes in Rice Farming in Selected Areas of Asia*, by International Rice Research Institute. Los Baños, Philippines: International Rice Research Institute, 1978.

Anthony, K.R.M.; Johnston, B. F., Jones, W. O.; Uchendu, V. C. *Agricultural Change in Tropical Africa*. Ithaca: Cornell University Press, 1979.

Anthony, K.R.M., and Uchendu, V. C. "Agricultural Change in Mazabuka District, Zambia." *Food Research Institute Studies* 9, no. 3 (1970), pp. 215–67.

Arrow, K. J. *The Limits of Organization*. New York: Norton, 1974.

Arthur, W. B., and McNicoll, G. "Large-Scale Simulation Models in Population and

273

Development: What Use to Planners?" *Population and Development Review* 1, no. 2 (1975), pp. 251–65.

Asian Development Bank. *Rural Asia: Challenge and Opportunity.* New York: Praeger, 1978.

―――. *Sector Paper on Agriculture and Rural Development.* Manila: Asian Development Bank, 1979.

Ayer, H. W., and Schuh, G. E. "Social Rates of Return and Other Aspects of Agricultural Research: The Case of Cotton Research in São Paulo, Brazil." *American Journal of Agricultural Economics* 54, no. 4, pt. 1 (1972), pp. 56–67.

Bagadion, B. U., and Korten, F. F. "Developing Viable Irrigators' Associations: Lessons from Small Scale Irrigation Development in the Philippines." *Agricultural Administration* 7, no. 4 (1980), pp. 273–87.

Bardach, E. *The Implementation Game.* Cambridge, Mass.: MIT Press, 1977.

Bardhan, P. K. "Size, Productivity, and Returns to Scale: An Analysis of Farm-Level Data in Indian Agriculture." *Journal of Political Economy* 81, no. 6 (1973), pp. 1370–86.

―――. "Wages and Unemployment in a Poor Agrarian Economy: A Theoretical and Empirical Analysis." Mimeographed. Berkeley: University of California, Department of Economics, 1977.

―――, and Rudra, A. "Terms and Conditions of Sharecropping Contracts: An Analysis of Village Survey Data in India." *Journal of Development Studies* 16, no. 3 (1980), pp. 287–302.

Barnum, H.; Barlow, R.; Fajardo, L.; and Pradilla, A. *A Resource Allocation Model for Child Survival.* Cambridge, Mass.: Oelgeschlager, Gunn & Hain, Publishers, 1980.

Bates, R. H. "States and Political Intervention in Markets: A Case Study from Africa." Social Science Working Paper 345. Pasadena: California Institute of Technology, Division of the Humanities and Social Sciences, 1980.

Becker, G. S. "A Theory of the Allocation of Time." *Economic Journal* 75 (September 1965): 493–517.

Beier, G.; Churchill, A.; Cohen, M.; and Renaud, B. "The Task Ahead for the Cities of the Developing Countries." *World Development* 4, no. 5 (1976), pp. 363–409.

Bell, C.L.G., and Duloy, J. H. "Rural Target Groups." In *Redistribution with Growth*, by H. Chenery et al. London: Oxford University Press, 1974.

Bengoa, J. M. "Significance of Malnutrition and Priorities for Its Prevention." In *Nutrition, National Development, and Planning*, edited by A. Berg, N. S. Scrimshaw, and D. Call. Cambridge, Mass.: MIT Press, 1973.

Benor, D., and Harrison, J. Q. *Agricultural Extension: The Training and Visit System.* Washington, D.C.: World Bank, 1977.

Berg, A. *The Nutrition Factor.* Washington, D.C.: Brookings Institution, 1973.

Berry, R. A., and Cline, W. R. *Agrarian Structure and Productivity in Developing Countries.* Baltimore: Johns Hopkins University Press, 1979.

Bhagwati, J. N. "Introduction." In *The New International Economic Order: The North-South Debate*, edited by J. N. Bhagwati. Cambridge, Mass., and London: MIT Press, 1977.

―――, and Desai, P. *India: Planning for Industrialization.* London: Oxford University Press, 1970.

Bhattacharyya, A. K. "Income Inequality and Fertility: A Comparative View." *Population Studies* 29, no. 1 (1975), pp. 5–19.

Binswanger, H. P. *The Economics of Tractors in South Asia: An Analytical Review.* New York: Agricultural Development Council; Hyderabad, India: International Crops Research Institute for the Semi-Arid Tropics, 1978.

————, and Ryan, J. G. "Efficiency and Equity Issues in *Ex Ante* Allocation of Research Resources." *Indian Journal of Agricultural Economics* 32, no. 3 (1977), pp. 217–31.

————. *Village Level Studies as a Focus for Research and Technology Adaptation.* Hyderabad, India: International Crops Research Institute for the Semi-Arid Tropics, 1979.

Binswanger, H. P.; Ghodake, R. D.; and Thierstein, G. E. "Observations on the Economics of Tractors, Bullocks, and Wheeled Tool Carriers in the Semi-Arid Tropics of India." In *Proceedings of the International Workshop on Socioeconomic Constraints to Development of Semi-Arid Tropical Agriculture, 19–23 February 1979, Hyderabad, India.* Patancheru, A.P., India: International Crops Research Institute for the Semi-Arid Tropics, 1980.

Binswanger, H. P.; Jodha, N. S.; and Barah, B. C. "The Nature and Significance of Risk in the Semi-Arid Tropics." In *Proceedings of the International Workshop on Socioeconomic Constraints to Development of Semi-Arid Tropical Agriculture, 19–23 February 1979, Hyderabad, India.* Patancheru, A.P., India: International Crops Research Institute for the Semi-Arid Tropics, 1980.

Binswanger, H. P.; Virmani, S. M.; and Kampen, J. *Farming Systems Components for Selected Areas in India: Evidence from ICRISAT.* ICRISAT Research Bulletin no. 2. Andhra Pradesh, India: International Crops Research Institute for the Semi-Arid Tropics, July 1980.

Birdsall, Nancy; Fei, J.; Kuznets, S.; Ranis, G.; and Schultz, T. P. "Demography and Development in the 1980s." In *World Population and Development: Challenges and Prospects*, edited by P. M. Hauser. New York: Syracuse University Press, 1979.

Blau, P. M. *Exchange and Power in Social Life.* New York: John Wiley, 1964.

Blaug, M. "The Quality of Population in Developing Countries, with Particular Reference to Education and Training." In *World Population and Development: Challenges and Prospects*, edited by P. M. Hauser. New York: Syracuse University Press, 1979.

Bogue, D. J., and Tsui, A. O. "Zero World Population Growth?" *The Public Interest*, no. 55 (Spring 1979), pp. 99–113.

Boothroyd, H. *Articulate Intervention.* London: Taylor and Francis, 1978.

Bose, A., et al. *An Assessment of the New Rural Health Scheme and Suggestions for Improvement.* Delhi: Demographic Research Centre, Institute of Economic Growth, University of Delhi, 1978.

Bower, J. L. *Managing the Resource Allocation Process: A Study of Corporate Planning and Investment.* Boston: Harvard University Graduate School of Business Administration, 1970.

Boyce, J. K.; and Evenson, R. E. *National and International Agricultural Research and Extension Programs.* New York: Agricultural Development Council, 1975.

Brewer, G. *The Politician, the Bureaucrat, and the Consultant.* New York: Basic Books, 1973.

Brewster, J. M. "The Machine Process in Agriculture and Industry," *Journal of Farm Economics* 32, no. 1 (1950), pp. 69–81.

———. "Traditional Social Structures as Barriers to Change." In *Agricultural Development and Economic Growth*, edited by H. M. Southworth and B. F. Johnston. Ithaca: Cornell University Press, 1967.

Brooks, H. "Expertise and Politics: Problems and Tensions." *Proceedings of the American Philosophical Society* 119 (1975): 257–61.

Brown, H. *The Human Future Revisited: The World Predicament and Possible Solutions*. New York: W. W. Norton & Company, 1978.

Bustillo, J. "Discussion of Korten." In *Population and Social Development Management: A Challenge for Management Schools*, edited by D. C. Korten. Caracas: Instituto de Estudios Superiores de Administración-IESA, 1979.

Caiden, Naomi, and Wildavsky, A. *Planning and Budgeting in Poor Countries*. New York: John Wiley & Sons, 1974.

Calloway, Doris H. "Working Paper: Proposal for Research." *PAG Bulletin* 7, nos. 3–4 (1977), pp. 53–58.

Carr, Marilyn. "Technology and Rural Women in Africa." Draft paper prepared for the International Labour Office Technology and Employment Programme, Geneva, January 1979. Mimeographed.

Carter, L. J. "Global 2000 Report: Vision of a Gloomy World." *Science*, August 1, 1980, pp. 575–76.

Cassen, R. H. "Current Trends in Population Change and Their Causes." *Population and Development Review* 4, no. 2 (1978), pp. 331–53.

Castle, E. N. "Comment" on "Approaches to 'Basic Needs' and to 'Equity' that Distort Incentives in Agriculture," by G. E. Schuh. In *Distortions of Agricultural Incentives*, edited by T. W. Schultz. Bloomington and London: Indiana University Press, 1978.

Cernea, M. M. *Measuring Project Impact: Monitoring and Evaluation in the PIDER Rural Development Project—Mexico*. World Bank Staff Working Paper no. 332. Washington, D.C.: World Bank, 1979.

Chafkin, S. "Nutrition Policies, Programs, and Politics." *American Journal of Agricultural Economics* 60, no. 5 (1978), pp. 806–9.

Chambers, R. *Managing Rural Development: Ideas and Experience from East Africa*. Uppsala: Scandinavian Institute of African Studies, 1974.

———. "Simple is Practical: Approaches and Realities for Project Selection for Poverty-Focused Rural Development." Paper presented at a seminar on the Implications of the Employment and Income Distributions Objectives for Project Appraisal and Identification, Kuwait, April 5–6, 1977.

———. *Rural Poverty Unperceived: Problems and Remedies*. World Bank Staff Working Paper no. 400. Washington, D.C.: World Bank, 1980.

———; Longhurst, R.; Bradley, D.; and Feachem, R. "Seasonal Dimensions to Rural Poverty: Analysis and Practical Implications." Institute of Development Studies Paper no. 142. Brighton, England: University of Sussex, 1979.

Chandler, A. D., Jr. *Strategy and Structure: Chapters in the History of the American Industrial Enterprise*. Cambridge, Mass.: MIT Press, 1962.

Chandra, R. K. "Malnutrition and Infection." Paper presented at the MIT International Nutritional Program Conference on Interface Problems between Nutrition Policy and Its Implementation, Cambridge, Mass., November 5–8, 1979.

Chávez, A., and Martínez, Celia. "Behavioral Effects of Undernutrition and Food Supplementation." In *Behavioral Effects of Energy and Protein Deficits*, edited by J. Brožek. NIH publication no. 79-1906. Washington, D.C.: U.S. Government Printing Office, 1979.

Chayanov, A. V. *The Theory of Peasant Economy*. Homewood, Ill.: R. D. Irwin, 1966.

Chen, Pi-chao. "Translator's Introduction" to "Birth Planning in China," by Chen Muhua. *Family Planning Perspectives* 11, no. 6 (1979), pp. 348–49.

Chenery, H. B. "Poverty and Progress: Choices for the Developing World." In *Poverty and Basic Needs*, by World Bank. Washington, D.C.: World Bank, 1980.

———, ed. *Studies in Development Planning*. Cambridge, Mass.: Harvard University Press, 1971.

Chenery, H., Ahluwalia, M. S.; Bell, C.L.G.; Duloy, J. H.; and Jolly, R. *Redistribution with Growth*. London: Oxford University Press, 1974.

Cheung, S.N.S. *The Theory of Share Tenancy*. Chicago: University of Chicago Press, 1969.

Chinn, D. L. "Income Distribution in a Chinese Commune." *Journal of Comparative Economics* 2, no. 246 (1978), pp. 246–69.

Chiu, C. H. "Food Supply and Nutrition Requirements in Taiwan." Mimeographed. Taipei: Joint Commission on Rural Reconstruction, Rural Health Division, August 20, 1976.

Clark, W. C.; Jones, D. D.; and Holling, C. S. "Lessons for Ecological Policy Design: A Case Study of Ecosystem Management." *Ecological Modeling* 7 (1979): 1–53.

Cleave, J. H. *African Farmers: Labor Use in the Development of Smallholder Agriculture*. New York: Praeger Publishers, 1974.

Cline, R. "A Survey and Summary of the Mathematical and Simulation Models as Applied to Weapons System Evaluation." Aeronautical Systems Division Technical Report 61–376. Wright Patterson Air Force Base, Ohio: Air Force System Command, 1961.

Clinton, J. J., and Baker, Jean, eds. *East Asia Review 1978–79*. Studies in Family Planning 11, no. 11 (1980), pp. 311–50.

Cohen, J. E. "Mathematics as Metaphor." *Science*, May 14, 1971, pp. 674–75.

Cohen, J. M., and Uphoff, N. T. *Rural Development Participation: Concepts and Measures for Project Design, Implementation and Evaluation*. Rural Development Committee Monograph Series no. 2. Ithaca: Cornell University Center for International Studies, 1977.

Collier, W. L.; Colter, J.; Sinarhadi; and Shaw, R. d'A. Comment on *Choice of Technique in Rice Milling in Java*, by C. P. Timmer. New York: Agricultural Development Council Research and Training Network Reprint, 1974.

Cownie, J.; Johnston, B. F.; and Duff, B. "The Quantitative Impact of the Seed-Fertilizer Revolution in West Pakistan: An Exploratory Study." *Food Research Institute Studies* 9, no. 1 (1970), pp. 57–95.

Crocombe, R. G. "Social Aspects of Cooperative and Other Corporate Land-Holding in the Pacific Islands." In *Two Blades of Grass: Rural Cooperatives in Agricultural Modernisation*, edited by P. Worsley. Manchester: Manchester University Press, 1971.

Dahl, R. A., and Lindblom, C. E. *Politics, Economics, and Welfare*. New York: Harper & Brothers, 1953.

Darrow, K., and Pam, R. *Appropriate Technology Sourcebook*. Vol. 1. Stanford: Volunteers in Asia, Stanford University, 1978.

Das Gupta, J. "Rural Development, Policy Design, and Policies in Action." Pt. 2 of "Rural Development, Strategies: A Survey of Policy Options and the Concepts of Integration and Basic Needs." Report submitted to the U.S. Agency for International Development Office of Rural and Administrative Development, Contract no. DSAN C-0016. Washington, D.C., 1979.

DaSilva, E. J. "Biogas Generation: Developments, Problems, and Tasks: An Overview." In *Bioconversion of Organic Residues for Rural Communities. Food and Nutrition Bulletin*, supp. 2. Tokyo: United Nations University, 1979.

Dasmann, R. F.; Milton, J. P.; and Freeman, P. H. *Ecological Principles for Economic Development*. London: John Wiley & Sons, 1973.

David, M.; Oyugi, W.; and Wallis, M. "SRDP as an Experiment in Development Administration." In *Second Overall Evaluation of the Special Rural Development Programme*. Institute of Development Studies Occasional Paper no. 12. Nairobi: University of Nairobi, 1975.

Davis, L. E., and North, D. C. *Institutional Change and American Economic Growth*. Cambridge: Cambridge University Press, 1971.

de Jesus, E. "Local Linkage Building in a Small Farmer Development Program." In *Bureaucracy and the Poor: Closing the Gap*, edited by D. C. Korten and F. B. Alfonso. Singapore: McGraw-Hill, 1981.

de los Reyes, R., et al. *Management of Communal Gravity Irrigation Systems*. Quezon City: Institute of Philippine Culture, 1979.

Demeny, P. "On the End of the Population Explosion." Center for Policy Studies Working Paper no. 39. New York: Population Council, 1979.

Dernberger, R. F. "Micro-Economic Analysis of the Farm in the P.R.C." Paper presented at the Conference on Agricultural Development in China, Japan, and Korea, Taipei, Taiwan, December 17–20, 1980.

de Veen, J. J. *The Rural Access Roads Programme: Appropriate Technology in Kenya*. Geneva: International Labour Office, 1980.

Dixon, Ruth B. "On Drawing Policy Conclusions from Multiple Regressions: Some Queries and Dilemmas." *Studies in Family Planning* 9, nos. 10–11 (1978), pp. 286–87.

Dore, R. F. "Modern Cooperatives in Traditional Communities." In *Two Blades of Grass: Rural Cooperatives in Agricultural Modernisation*, edited by P. Worsley. Manchester: Manchester University Press, 1971.

Dosik, R. S., and Falcon, W. P. "Energy and Agriculture in Developing Countries." Draft manuscript. Stanford: Food Research Institute, Stanford University, 1978.

Drucker, P. F. *Management: Tasks, Responsibilities, Practices*. New York: Harper & Row, 1974.

Duff, B. "Providing Assistance in the Mechanization of Small Farms." Paper presented at the Seminar on Mechanization of Small-Scale Peasant Farming, Sapporo, Japan, July 7–12, 1980.

Easterlin, R. A. "Relative Economic Status and the American Fertility Swing." In *Family Economic Behavior: Problems and Prospects*, edited by Eleanor Bernert. Philadelphia: J. B. Lippincott, 1973.

_____. "An Economic Framework for Fertility Analysis." *Studies in Family Planning* 6, no. 3 (1975), pp. 54–63.

————. "The Economics and Sociology of Fertility: A Synthesis." In *Early Industrialization, Shifts in Fertility and Changes in Family Structure*, edited by C. Tilly. Princeton: Princeton University Press, 1977.

Eckstein, S.; Donald, G.; Horton, D.; and Carroll, T. *Land Reform in Latin America: Bolivia, Chile, Mexico, Peru, and Venezuela*. World Bank Staff Working Paper no. 275. Washington, D.C.: World Bank, 1978.

Epstein, T. Scarlett. *South India: Yesterday, Today and Tomorrow*. New York: Holmes and Meier, 1973.

Esman, M. J., and Montgomery, J. D. "The Administration of Human Development." Pt. 3 of *Implementing Programs of Human Development: A Background Paper for World Development Report, 1980*, edited by P. T. Knight. World Bank Staff Working Paper no. 403. Washington, D.C.: World Bank, 1980.

Etzioni, A. "Beyond Integration, Toward Guidability." In *World Population and Development: Challenges and Prospects*, edited by P. M. Hauser. New York: Syracuse University Press, 1979.

Evenson, R. E. "The Organization of Research to Improve Crops and Animals in Low Income Countries." In *Distortions of Agricultural Incentives*, edited by T. W. Schultz. Bloomington and London: Indiana University Press, 1978.

————; Waggoner, P. E.; and Ruttan, V. W. "Economic Benefits from Research: An Example from Agriculture." *Science*, September 14, 1979, pp. 1101–7.

Feyerabend, P. *Science in a Free Society*. London: New Left Books, 1978.

Field, J. O. "The Soft Underbelly of Applied Knowledge: Conceptual and Operational Problems in Nutrition Planning." *Food Policy* 2, no. 3 (1977), pp. 228–39.

Fiering, M. B. "The Role of Systems Analysis in Water Program Development." *Natural Resources Journal* 16 (1976): 759–71.

Finkle, J. L., and Crane, Barbara B. "The World Health Organization and the Population Issue: Organizational Values in the U.N." *Population and Development Review* 2, nos. 3–4 (1976), pp. 367–93.

Flinn, J. C. "Agroeconomic Considerations in Cassava Intercropping Research." In *Intercropping with Cassava: Proceedings of an International Workshop held at Trivandrum, India, 27 November–1 December 1978*, edited by E. Weber, B. Nestel, and Marilyn Campbell. Ottawa: International Development Research Centre 1979.

Food and Agriculture Organization of the United Nations (FAO). *The Fourth World Food Survey*. Rome: FAO, 1977.

————. "Special Feature: FAO Indices of Food and Agricultural Production." *FAO Monthly Bulletin of Statistics* 2 (1979a): 10–48.

————. *Nutrition in Agriculture*. Fifth Session of the FAO Committee on Agriculture, April 18–27, 1979. Rome: FAO, 1979b.

————. *Agriculture toward 2000*. Rome: FAO, 1979c.

FAO/WFC/ECA Inter Agency Working Group. "Proposals for a Programme of Action for the Developmenet of Food and Agriculture in Africa 1980–85." Prepared for consideration by the OAU Extraordinary Economic Summit. Rome: FAO, February 1980.

FAO/WHO. *Energy and Protein Requirements*. Report of a Joint FAO/WHO Ad Hoc Expert Committee, March 22–April 2, 1971. FAO Nutrition Meetings Report Series no. 52; WHO Technical Report Series no. 522. Rome: FAO; Geneva: WHO, 1973.

_____. *Food and Nutrition Strategies in National Development*. Report of the 9th Session Joint FAO/WHO Expert Committee on Nutrition. FAO Nutrition Meetings Report Series no. 56; WHO Technical Report Series no. 584. Rome: FAO; Geneva: WHO, 1976.

Franda, M. *Small is Politics: Organizational Alternatives in India's Rural Development*. New Delhi: Wiley Eastern, 1979.

Franklin, J. C.; Schiele, B. C.; Brožek, J.; and Keys, A. "Observations on Human Behavior in Experimental Semistarvation and Rehabilitation." *Journal of Clinical Psychology* 4 (1948): 28–45.

Freedman, R. "Theories of Fertility Decline: A Reappraisal." In *World Population and Development: Challenges and Prospects*, edited by P. M. Hauser. New York: Syracuse University Press, 1979.

Friedland, W. H. "A Sociological Approach to Modernization." In *Modernization by Design*, edited by C. Morse et al. Ithaca: Cornell University Press, 1969.

Galbraith, J. K. *The Nature of Mass Poverty*. Cambridge, Mass.: Harvard University Press, 1979.

Galenson, W. "The Labor Force, Wages, and Living Standards." In *Economic Growth and Structural Change in Taiwan: The Postwar Experience of the Republic of China*, edited by W. Galenson. Ithaca and London: Cornell University Press, 1979.

Gavan, J. D. "Commentary: Food Subsidies—Imperfect but Expedient." *IFPRI Report* 1, no. 2 (1979).

Gerhardt, J. *The Diffusion of Hybrid Maize in Western Kenya: Abridged by CIMMYT*. Mexico City: Centro Internacional de Majoramiento de Mais y Trigo, 1975.

Ghodake, R. D.; Ryan, J. G.; and Sarin, R. *Human Labor Use in Existing and Prospective Technologies of the Semi-Arid Tropics of Peninsular India*. Progress Report, Economics Program 1, Village Level Studies Series 1.3. Hyderabad, India: International Crops Research Institute for the Semi-Arid Tropics, 1978.

Gladwin, Christina H. "A View of Plan Puebla: An Application of Hierarchical Decision Models." *American Journal of Agricultural Economics* 58, no. 5 (1976), pp. 881–87.

Gonzalez-Vega, C. "On the Iron Law of Interest Rate Restrictions: Agricultural Credit Policies in Costa Rica and Other Less Developed Countries." Ph.D. diss., Stanford University, 1976.

Gopalan, C. "Adaptation to Low Calorie and Low Protein Intake: Does it Exist?" In *Progress in Human Nutrition*, edited by S. Margen and R. A. Ogar, vol. 2. Westport, Conn.: AVI Publishing Company, 1978.

_____. *The Child in India*. Thirteenth Jawaharlal Nehru Memorial Lecture. New Delhi, 1979.

Gotsch, C. H. "Economics, Institutions and Employment Generation in Rural Areas." In *Employment in Developing Nations*, edited by E. O. Edwards. New York: Columbia University Press, 1974.

_____. Book Review of *Rural Asia: Challenge and Opportunity*, by Asian Development Bank. In *Nutrition Planning* 2, no. 1 (1979), pp. 5–9.

_____ et al. "Linear Programming and Agricultural Policy: Micro Studies in the Pakistan Punjab." *Food Research Institute Studies* 14, no. 1 (1975), pp. 3–105.

Griffin, K. *International Inequality and National Poverty*. London: Macmillan Press, 1978.

————. *The Political Economy of Agrarian Reform*. 2nd ed. London: Macmillan Press, 1979.

Gupta, R. "The Poorest of the Poor: Lessons from Dharampur." In *Bureaucracy and the Poor: Closing the Gap*, edited by D. C. Korten and F. B. Alfonso. Singapore: McGraw-Hill, 1981.

Gwatkin, D. R.; Wilcox, Janet R.; and Wray, J. D. "Can Interventions Make a Difference? The Policy Implications of Field Experiment Experience." Report to the World Bank. Washington, D.C.: Overseas Development Council, 1979.

Halse, M. "Increasing the Incomes of Landless Labourers and Small-Holders—Part 1." *Agricultural Administration* 7, no. 4 (1980), pp. 259–72.

Hansen, R. D. *The Politics of Mexican Development*. Baltimore: Johns Hopkins University Press, 1971.

Haq, Mahbub ul. *The Poverty Curtain: Choices for the Third World*. New York: Columbia University Press, 1976.

Harrari, Denyse. "Employment Problems." In *Planning for Growing Populations*, edited by R. Cassen and M. Wolfson. Paris: Organisation for Economic Co-operation and Development, Development Centre, 1978.

Harrison, R. K. "Work and Motivation: A Study of Village-Level Agricultural Extension Workers in the Western State of Nigeria." Mimeographed. Ibadan: Nigerian Institute of Social and Economic Research, 1969.

Hayami, Y. *Anatomy of a Peasant Economy*. Los Baños, Philippines: International Rice Research Institute, 1978.

————, and Ruttan, V. W. *Agricultural Development: An International Perspective*. Baltimore: Johns Hopkins Press, 1971.

Healey, D. T. "Development Policy: New Thinking About an Interpretation." *Journal of Economic Literature* 10, no. 3 (1972), pp. 757–97.

Heginbotham, S. J. *Cultures in Conflict: The Four Faces of Indian Bureaucracy*. New York: Columbia University Press, 1975.

Helmer, O., and Rescher, N. "On the Epistemology of the Inexact Sciences." *Management Science* 6, no. 1 (1959), pp. 25–52.

Henderson, R. H., and Keja, J. "Selective Health Care for Developing Countries." *New England Journal of Medicine*, March 27, 1980, p. 758.

Herdt, R. W.; Te, Amanda; and Barker, R. "The Prospects for Asian Rice Production." *Food Research Institute Studies* 16, no. 3 (1977), pp. 183–203.

Herdt, R. W., and Wickham, T. H. "Exploring the Gap between Potential and Actual Rice Yield in the Philippines." *Food Research Institute Studies* 14, no. 2 (1975), pp. 163–81.

Hertford, R., and Schmitz, A. "Measuring Economic Returns to Agricultural Research." In *Resource Allocation and Productivity in National and International Agricultural Research*, edited by T. M. Arndt, D. G. Dalrymple, and V. W. Ruttan. Minneapolis: University of Minnesota Press, 1977.

Heyer, Judith. "Rural Development Programmes and Impoverishment: Some Experiences in Tropical Africa." Paper presented at the International Conference of Agricultural Economists, Banff, Canada, September 1979.

————; Maitha, J. K.; and Senga, W. M., eds. *Agricultural Development in Kenya: An Economic Assessment*. Nairobi: Oxford University Press, 1976.

Hildebrand, P. E. *Generando tecnología para agricultores tradicionales: Una metodología multidisciplinaria [Generating Technology for Traditional Farmers: A Multi-*

Disciplinary Methodology]. Guatemala City: Socioeconomía Rural, Instituto de Ciencia y Tecnología Agricolas, Sector Público Agrícola, 1976. This publication is in both English and Spanish.

Hindmarsh, P. S.; Tyler, P. S.; and Webley, D. J. "Conserving Grain on the Small Farm in the Tropics." *Tropical Science* 20, no. 2 (1978), pp. 117–28.

Hirschhorn, N. "The Treatment of Acute Diarrhea in Children: An Historical and Physiological Perspective." *American Journal of Clinical Nutrition* 33, no. 3 (1980), pp. 637–63.

Hirschman, A. O. *A Bias for Hope.* New Haven: Yale University Press, 1971.

———, and Lindblom, C. E. "Economic Development, Research and Development, Policy Making: Some Converging Views." *Behavioral Science* 7 (1962): 211–22.

Ho, S.P.S. "Decentralized Industrialization and Rural Development: Evidence from Taiwan." *Economic Development and Cultural Change* 28, no. 1 (1979), pp. 77–96.

Ho, Teresa J. "Labor Market for Married Women in Rural Philippines." Ph.D. diss., Stanford University, 1980.

Holcomb Research Institute. *Environmental Modeling and Decision Making.* New York: Praeger, 1976.

Holdcroft, L. C. "The Rise and Fall of Community Development in Developing Countries, 1950–65: A Critical Analysis and an Annotated Bibliography." Rural Development Paper no. 2. East Lansing: Michigan State University, Department of Agricultural Economics, 1978.

Holling, C. S., ed. *Adaptive Environmental Assessment and Management.* Chichester, England: Wiley-Interscience, 1978.

Hopper, W. D. "Investment in Agriculture: The Essentials for Payoff." In *Strategy for the Conquest of Hunger: Proceedings of a Symposium Convened by the Rockefeller Foundation.* New York: Rockefeller Foundation, 1968.

———. "Distortions of Agricultural Development Resulting from Government Prohibitions." In *Distortions of Agricultural Incentives*, edited by T. W. Schultz. Bloomington and London: Indiana University Press, 1978.

Hsieh, S. C., and Lee, T. H. *Agricultural Development and Its Contributions to Economic Growth in Taiwan.* Economic Digest Series no. 17. Taipei: Joint Commission on Rural Reconstruction, 1966.

Hull, T. H.; Hull, V. J.; and Singarimbun, M. "Indonesia's Family Planning Story: Success and Challenge." *Population Bulletin* 32, no. 6 (1977), pp. 3–52.

Hull, Valerie J. "Women, Doctors, and Family Health Care: Some Lessons from Rural Java." *Studies in Family Planning* 10, nos. 11–12 (1979), pp. 315–25.

Hunter, G. *Modernizing Peasant Societies: A Comparative Study in Asia and Africa.* London and New York: Oxford University Press, 1969.

———. *The Administration of Agricultural Development: Lessons from India.* London: Oxford University Press, 1970.

———. "Research on Cooperatives in East Africa: Review/Note." Mimeographed. Overseas Development Institute, London: 1971.

———. Review of *Two Blades of Grass: Rural Co-operatives in Agricultural Modernisation*, edited by P. Worsley. *Journal of Administration Overseas* 11, no. 3 (1972), pp. 192–97.

———. "Report on a Visit to India—February 1976: Programmes for Small and Marginal Farmers." Mimeographed. London. Overseas Development Institute, 1976.

———. "Report on Administration and Institutions." In *Rural Asia: Challenge and*

Opportunity. Supp. papers, vol. 4, *Administration and Institutions in Agricultural and Rural Development.* Manila: Asian Development Bank, 1978a.

————, ed. *Agricultural Development and the Rural Poor: Guidelines for Action.* London: Overseas Development Institute, 1978b.

Huntington, S. P., and Nelson, J. M. *No Easy Choice: Political Participation in Developing Countries.* Cambridge, Mass.: Harvard University Press, 1976.

Hyden, G. "Cooperatives and Their Socio-Political Environment." In *Cooperatives and Rural Development in East Africa,* edited by C. G. Widstrand. New York: Africana Publishing Corp., 1970.

Ickis, J. C. "Structural Responses to New Development Strategies." In *Bureaucracy and the Poor: Closing the Gap,* edited by D. C. Korten and F. B. Alfonso. Singapore: McGraw-Hill, 1981.

Inayatullah. *Cooperatives and Development in Asia: A Study of Cooperatives in Fourteen Rural Communities of Iran, Pakistan, and Ceylon.* Geneva: U.N. Research Institute for Social Development, 1972.

Independent Commission. *North-South: A Program for Survival.* Report of the Independent Commission on International Development Issues under the Chairmanship of Willy Brandt. Cambridge, Mass.: MIT Press, 1980.

India, Government of. *Draft Five Year Plan 1978–83.* New Delhi: Planning Commission, 1978.

International Food Policy Research Institute (IFPRI). *Recent and Prospective Developments in Food Consumption: Some Policy Issues.* IFPRI Research Report no. 2. Rev. ed. Washington, D.C.: IFPRI, 1977a.

————. *Food Needs of Developing Countries: Projections of Production and Consumption to 1990.* IFPRI Research Report no. 3. Washington, D.C.: IFPRI, 1977b.

————. *IFPRI Research Highlights 1978.* Washington, D.C.: IFPRI, 1978.

International Institute for Applied Systems Analysis (IIASA). "Health Delivery Systems in Developing Countries." Committee report to IIASA by the participants in an informal meeting (CP-79-10). Laxenburg, Austria: IIASA, 1979.

International Labour Office (ILO). *Employment, Growth and Basic Needs: A One-World Problem.* Report of Director-General of the International Labour Office to the Tripartite World Conference on Employment, Income Distribution and Social Progress and the International Division of Labour. Geneva: ILO, 1976.

————. *Towards Self-Reliance: Development, Employment and Equity Issues in Tanzania.* Addis Ababa: Jobs and Skills Programme for Africa, 1978.

International Maize and Wheat Improvement Center (CIMMYT). *CIMMYT Review 1978.* Mexico City: CIMMYT, 1978.

————. *Planning Technologies Appropriate to Farmers: Concepts and Procedures.* Mexico City: CIMMYT Economics Program, 1980.

International Rice Research Institute (IRRI). *Changes in Rice Farming in Selected Areas of Asia.* Los Baños, Philippines: IRRI, 1978.

————. *Farm-Level Constraints to High Rice Yields in Asia: 1974–77.* Los Baños, Philippines: IRRI, 1979.

International Union for Conservation of Nature and Natural Resources (IUCN). *World Conservation Strategy.* Gland, Switzerland: IUCN, 1980.

Jodha, N. S. "Effectiveness of Farmers' Adjustments to Risk." *Economic and Political Weekly,* June 24, 1978, pp. A38–A48.

Johnson, D. G. "Resource Allocation Under Share Contracts." *Journal of Political Economy* 58, no. 2 (1950), pp. 111–23.

Johnston, B. F. "Agricultural Productivity and Economic Development in Japan." *Journal of Political Economy* 59, no. 6 (1951), pp. 498–513.

———. *The Staple Food Economies of Western Tropical Africa*. Food Research Institute Studies in Tropical Development. Stanford: Stanford University Press, 1958.

———. "Agriculture and Economic Development: The Relevance of the Japanese Experience." *Food Research Institute Studies* 6, no. 3 (1966), pp. 251–312.

———. "The Japanese 'Model' of Agricultural Development: Its Relevance to Developing Nations." In *Agriculture and Economic Growth: Japan's Experience*, edited by K. Ohkawa et al. Tokyo: University of Tokyo Press, 1969.

———. "Food, Health, and Population in Development." *Journal of Economic Literature* 15, no. 3 (1977), pp. 879–907.

———. "Agricultural Production Potentials and Small Farmer Strategies in Sub-Saharan Africa." In *Two Studies of Development in Sub-Saharan Africa*. World Bank Staff Working Paper no. 300. Washington, D.C.: World Bank, 1978.

———. " 'Integration' and 'Basic Needs' in Strategies for Rural Development." Pt. 1 of "Rural Development, Strategies: A Survey of Policy Options and the Concepts of Integration and Basic Needs." Report submitted to the U.S. Agency for International Development Office of Rural and Administrative Development, Contract no. DSAN C-0016. Washington, D.C., 1979.

———. "Socioeconomic Aspects of Improved Animal-Drawn Implements and Mechanization in Semi-Arid East Africa." In *Proceedings of the International Workshop on Socioeconomic Constraints to Development of Semi-Arid Tropical Agriculture, 19–23 February 1979, Hyderabad, India*. Patancheru, A.P., India: International Crops Research Institute for the Semi-Arid Tropics, 1980.

———, and Cownie, J. "The Seed-Fertilizer Revolution and Labor Force Absorption." *American Economic Review* 59, no. 4 (1969), pp. 569–82.

———, and Kilby, P. *Agriculture and Structural Transformation: Economic Strategies in Late-Developing Countries*. New York: Oxford University Press, 1975.

———, and Meyer, A. J. "Nutrition, Health, and Population in Strategies for Rural Development." *Economic Development and Cultural Change* 26, no. 1 (1977), pp. 1–23.

Joy, L., and Payne, P. *Food and Nutrition Planning*. FAO Nutrition Consultants Reports Series no. 35. Rome: FAO, 1975.

Kaneda, H. "Issues in Policy Analysis of Agricultural Development and Internal Migration." IIASA Working Paper no. 79-109. Laxenburg, Austria: IIASA, 1979.

———. *Growth and Equity in India's Agriculture in Recent Years*. Working Paper Series no. 155. Davis: University of California, Department of Economics, 1980.

Karanjia, R. K. *The Mind of Mr. Nehru*. London: George Allen and Unwin, 1960.

Keeley, M. C. "A Comment on 'An Interpretation of the Economic Theory of Fertility.' " *Journal of Economic Literature* 13, no. 2 (1975), pp. 461–68.

Kelley, A. C., and Williamson, J. G. "Modeling Urbanization and Economic Growth." IIASA Research Report no. 80-22. Laxenburg, Austria: IIASA, 1980.

Kelley, A. C.; Williamson, J. G.; and Cheetham, R. J. *Dualistic Economic Development: Theory and History*. Chicago: University of Chicago Press, 1972.

Kenya, Republic of. *Development Plan: For the Period 1979 to 1983*. Pt. 1. Nairobi: Government Printer, 1979a.

———. *Child Nutrition in Rural Kenya*. Nairobi: Central Bureau of Statistics, Ministry of Economic Planning and Community Affairs, 1979*b*.

———. *Kenya Fertility Survey 1977–1978. First Report*. Vol. I. Nairobi: Central Bureau of Statistics, 1980.

Keyfitz, N. "Do Cities Grow by Natural Increase or by Migration?" IIASA Research Report no. 80-24. Laxenburg, Austria: IIASA, 1980. Reprinted from *Geographical Analysis* 12, no. 2 (1980), pp. 142–56.

Keys, A. B., et al. *The Biology of Human Starvation*. 2 vols. Minneapolis: University of Minnesota Press, 1950.

Kikuchi, M., and Hayami, Y. "Inducements to Institutional Innovations in an Agrarian Community." *Economic Development and Cultural Change* 29, no. 1 (1980), pp. 21–36.

King, M., ed. *Medical Care in Developing Countries: A Symposium from Makerere*. Nairobi: Oxford University Press, 1966.

Kingshotte, A. "The Organisation and Management of Agricultural Extension and Farmer-Assistance—A Note on Developments in Botswana." Pt. 1. *Agricultural Administration* 7, no. 3 (1980*a*), pp. 191–209.

———. "The Organisation and Management of Agricultural Extension and Farmer-Assistance—A Note on Development in Botswana." Pt. 2. *Agricultural Administration* 7, no. 4 (1980*b*), pp. 297–322.

Kirk, D. "A New Demographic Transition?" In *Rapid Population Growth: Consequences and Policy Implications*, by National Academy of Sciences. Baltimore and London: Johns Hopkins Press, 1971.

———. "World Population and Birth Rates: Agreements and Disagreements." *Population and Development Review* 5, no. 3 (1979), pp. 387–403.

Kocher, J. E. *Rural Development, Income Distribution, and Fertility Decline*. New York: Population Council, 1973.

———. "Socioeconomic Development and Fertility Change in Rural Africa." *Food Research Institute Studies* 16, no. 2 (1977), pp. 63–75.

———. *Rural Development and Fertility Change in Tropical Africa: Evidence from Tanzania*. African Rural Economy Paper no. 19. East Lansing: Michigan State University, Department of Agricultural Economics, 1979.

Korten, D. C. *Integrated Approaches to Family Planning Services Delivery*. Development Discussion Paper no. 10. Cambridge, Mass.: Harvard Institute for International Development, 1975.

———. "Toward a Technology for Managing Social Development." In *Population and Social Development Management: A Challenge for Management Schools*, edited by D. C. Korten. Caracas: Instituto de Estudios Superiores de Administración-IESA, 1979*a*.

———, ed. *Population and Social Development Management: A Challenge for Management Schools*. Caracas: Instituto de Estudios Superiores de Administración-IESA, 1979*b*.

Korten, D. C. "The Pilot Project: Formal Experiment or Learning Laboratory?" Manila: Ford Foundation, 1979*c*.

———. "New Issues, New Options: A Management Perspective on Population and Family Planning." *Studies in Family Planning* 10, no. 1 (1979*d*), pp. 3–14.

———. "Community Organization and Rural Development: A Learning Process Approach." *Public Administration Review* 40, no. 5 (1980*a*), pp. 480–511.

_____. "Agricultural Planning and Management for Rural Development: A View from the Field of Management." Paper presented at the Instituto Interamericano de Ciencias Agricolas, Mexico City, September 1980*b*.

_____. "Social Development: Putting People First." In *Bureaucracy and the Poor: Closing the Gap*, edited by D. C. Korten and F. B. Alfonso. Singapore: McGraw-Hill, 1981.

_____, and Alfonso, F. B., eds. *Bureaucracy and the Poor: Closing the Gap*. Singapore: McGraw-Hill, 1981.

Korten, F. F., and Korten, D. C. *Casebook for Family Planning Management: Motivating Effective Clinic Performance*. Chestnut Hill, Mass.: The Pathfinder Fund, 1977.

Kötter, H. R. "Involvement of the Rural Poor—A Key Factor in Development: The Present and Future Role of Institutions and Organizations." In *Rural Asia: Challenge and Opportunity*. Supp. papers, vol. 4, *Administration and Institutions in Agricultural and Rural Development*. Manila: Asian Development Bank, 1978.

Krishna, R. "The Next Phase in Rural Development." Address to the National Seminar on Rural Development, New Delhi, April 28, 1978.

Kuznets, S. *Economic Growth of Nations: Total Output and Production Structure*. Cambridge, Mass.: Harvard University Press, 1971.

Lakatos, I. "Falsification and the Methodology of Scientific Research Programs." In *Criticism and the Growth of Knowledge*, by I. Lakatos and A. Musgrave. Cambridge, Mass.: Cambridge University Press, 1970.

_____. "History of Science and Its Rational Reconstruction." In *Boston Studies in the Philosophy of Science*, vol. 8, edited by R. Buck and R. Cohen. Dordrecht, Holland: D. Reidel Publishing Company, 1971.

Lall, S., and Streeten, P. *Foreign Investment, Transnationals, and Developing Countries*. Boulder: Westview Press, 1977.

Landau, M. "Redundancy, Rationality, and the Problem of Duplication and Overlap." *Public Administration Review* 29 (July–August 1969): 346–58.

Lapham, R. J., and Mauldin, W. P. "National Family Planning Programs: Review and Evaluation." *Studies in Family Planning* 3, no. 3 (1972), pp. 29–52.

Latham, M. C. "Nutrition and Infection in National Development." In *Food: Politics, Economics, Nutrition, and Research*, edited by P. H. Abelson. Washington, D.C.: American Association for the Advancement of Science, 1975.

Lau, L. J., and Yotopoulos, P. A. "A Test for Relative Efficiency and Application to Indian Agriculture." *American Economic Review* 61, no. 1 (1971), pp. 94–109.

Lee, D. B., Jr. "Requiem for Large-Scale Models." *AIP Journal*, 1973, pp. 163–78.

Lee, T. H. *Intersectoral Capital Flows in the Economic Development of Taiwan, 1895–1960*. Ithaca: Cornell University Press, 1971*a*.

_____. "Strategies for Transferring Agricultural Surplus Under Different Agricultural Situations in Taiwan." Paper presented at the Japan Economic Research Center Conference on Agriculture and Economic Development, Tokyo and Hakone, September 1971*b*.

Leibenstein, H. "An Interpretation of the Economic Theory of Fertility." *Journal of Economic Literature* 12, no. 2 (1974), pp. 457–79.

Lele, Uma J. "The Role of Credit and Marketing in Agricultural Development." In *Agricultural Policy in Developing Countries*, edited by N. Islam. London: Macmillan, 1974.

————. *The Design of Rural Development: Lessons from Africa.* Baltimore and London: Johns Hopkins University Press, 1975.

————. "Rural Africa: Modernization, Equity, and Long-Term Development." *Science*, February 6, 1981, pp. 547–53.

Leonard, D. K. *Reaching the Peasant Farmer: Organization Theory and Practice in Kenya.* Chicago and London: University of Chicago Press, 1977.

Levine, M. M., et al. "Variability of Sodium and Sucrose Levels of Simple Sugar/Salt Oral Rehydration Solutions Prepared under Optimal and Field Conditions." *Journal of Pediatrics*, in press.

Levinson, F. J. "Incorporating Nutrition in Agricultural, Food and Health Policies and Programs in South Asia." Paper presented at the U.N. Economic and Social Commission for Asia and the Pacific Regional Seminar on an Integrated Approach to Population, Food and Nutrition Policies and Programs for National Development, Bangkok, July 24–31, 1979.

Levitsky, D. A. "Ill-Nourished Brains." *Natural History* 85 (1976): pp. 6–11.

Lewis, J. P. Organisation for Economic Co-operation and Development (OECD). *Development Co-operation: Efforts and Policies of the Members of the Development Assistance Committee.* Paris: OECD, 1980.

Lewis, S. R., Jr. "Agricultural Taxation and Intersectoral Resource Transfers." *Food Research Institute Studies* 12, no. 2 (1973), pp. 93–114.

Lewis, W. A. *Development Planning: The Essentials of Economic Policy.* New York: Harper & Row, Publishers, 1966.

————. *The Evolution of the International Economic Order.* Princeton: Princeton University Press, 1978.

Leys, C. "Political Perspectives." In *Development in a Divided World*, edited by D. Seers and L. Joy. Middlesex: Penguin Books, 1971.

Lindblom, C. E. *Politics and Markets.* New York: Basic Books, 1977.

————. *The Policy Making Process.* 2d ed. New York: Prentice Hall, 1979.

————, and Cohen, D. K. *Usable Knowledge: Social Science and Social Problem Solving.* New Haven: Yale University Press, 1979.

Lipton, M. *Why Poor People Stay Poor: A Study of Urban Bias in World Development.* London: Temple Smith, 1977.

————. "Inter-Farm, Inter-Regional and Farm-Non-Farm Income Distribution: The Impact of the New Cereal Varieties." *World Development* 6, no. 3 (1978), pp. 319–37.

Little, I.M.D. "An Economic Reconnaissance." In *Economic Growth and Structural Change in Taiwan: The Postwar Experience of the Republic of China*, edited by W. Galenson. Ithaca and London: Cornell University Press, 1979.

Little, I.; Scitovsky, T.; and M. Scott. *Industry and Trade in Some Developing Countries.* London: Oxford University Press, 1970.

Livingstone, I., and Pala, A. "The Family Planning Programme in Vihiga/Hamisi, Kakamega District." In *Second Overall Evaluation of the Special Rural Development Programme.* Institute for Development Studies Occasional Paper no. 12. Nairobi: University of Nairobi, 1975.

Lockheed, M. E.; Jamison, D. T.; and Lau, L. J. "Farmer Education and Farm Efficiency: A Survey." *Economic Development and Cultural Change* 29, no. 1 (1980), pp. 37–76.

Lodge, G. C. *Engines of Change: United States Interests and Revolution in Latin America*. New York: Alfred A. Knopf, 1970.

Lofchie, M. F. "Agrarian Crisis and Economic Liberalisation in Tanzania." *Journal of Modern African Studies* 16, no. 3 (1978), pp. 451–75.

Lynam, J. K. "An Analysis of Population Growth, Technical Change, and Risk in Peasant, Semi-Arid Farming Systems: A Case Study of Machakos District, Kenya." Ph.D. diss., Stanford University, 1978.

McDowell, J. "Appropriate Technologies for Tackling Malnourishment." In *Community Action-Family Nutrition Programmes*, edited by D. B. Jelliffe and E. F. Patrice Jelliffe. New Delhi: UNICEF, 1978.

McKay, H., et al. "Improving Cognitive Ability in Chronically Deprived Children." *Science*, April 21, 1978, pp. 270–78.

McQueen, A. J. "Urban Youth on the Margins of Nigerian Society: Research and Theoretical Perspectives on School-Leavers." In *Education and Politics in Tropical Africa*, edited by V. C. Uchendu. New York: Conch Magazine, 1979.

Madigan, F. C. "Final Report (Summary of Discussions)." In *Seminar on Infant Mortality in Relation to the Level of Fertility*. Paris: Committee for International Coordination of National Research in Demography, 1975.

Majone, G. "The Feasibility of Social Policies." *Policy Sciences* 6 (1975): 49–69.

_____. "The Uses of Policy Analysis." In *Russell Sage Foundation: The Future and the Past: Essays on Programs*. New York: Russell Sage Foundation, 1977.

_____. "Process and Outcome in Regulatory Decision-Making." *American Behavioral Scientists* 22, no. 5 (1979), pp. 561–83.

March, J. G., and Olsen, J. P. *Ambiguity and Choice in Organizations*. Bergen: Universitetsforlaget, 1976.

Margen, S. "Comment" on "The Nature of the Nutrition Problem," by Leonardo Mata. In *Nutrition Planning: The State of the Art*, edited by L. Joy. London: IPC Science and Technology Press, 1978.

Martorell, R. "Nutrition-Infection Interactions and Human Growth." Paper presented at the Annual Meeting of the Human Biology Council, San Francisco, April 4, 1979a.

_____. "Responses to Chronic Protein-Energy Malnutrition: Adaptation or Malady?" Paper presented at the 48th Annual Meeting of the American Association of Physical Anthropologists, San Francisco, April 4–7, 1979b.

_____; Yarbrough, C.; Klein, R. E.; and Lechtig, A. "Malnutrition, Body Size, and Skeletal Maturation: Interrelationships and Implications for Catch-Up Growth." *Human Biology* 51, no. 3 (1979), pp. 371–89.

Martorell, R., et al. "Protein-Energy Intakes in a Malnourished Population after Increasing the Supply of the Dietary Staples." *Ecology of Food and Nutrition* 8, no. 3 (1979), pp. 163–68.

Maru, R. M. "Health Manpower Strategies for Rural Health Services in India and China: 1949–1975." *Social Science and Medicine* 11 (1977): 535–47.

_____. "Organizing for Rural Health." In *Bureaucracy and the Poor: Closing the Gap*, edited by D. C. Korten and F. B. Alfonso. Singapore: McGraw-Hill, 1981.

Mata, L. J. *The Children of Santa Maria Cauque: A Prospective Field Study of Health and Growth*. Cambridge, Mass.: MIT Press, 1978.

_____, and Mohs, E. "As Seen from National Levels: Developing World." In *Progress in Human Nutrition*, edited by S. Margen and R. A. Ogar, vol. 2. Westport, Conn.: AVI Publishing Company, 1978.

Mauldin, W. P. "Population Trends and Prospects." *Science*, July 4, 1980, pp. 148–57.

————, and Berelson, B. "Conditions of Fertility Decline in Developing Countries, 1965–1975." *Studies in Family Planning* 9, no. 5 (1978*a*), pp. 90–147.

————. "Reply" to R. B. Dixon. *Studies in Family Planning* 9, nos. 10–11 (1978*b*), p. 288.

Mead, D. C. "Review" of *Planning and Budgeting in Poor Countries*, by N. Caiden and A. Wildavsky, and *Planning for Development in Sub-Saharan Africa*, by A. Seidman. In *Economic Development and Cultural Change* 25, no. 2 (1977), pp. 376–82.

Meerman, J. "Paying for Human Development." In *Implementing Programs of Human Development: A Background Paper for World Development Report, 1980*, edited by P. T. Knight. World Bank Staff Working Paper no. 403. Washington, D.C.: World Bank, 1980.

Mellor, J. W. *The New Economics of Growth: A Strategy for India and the Developing World*. Ithaca: Cornell University Press, 1976.

————. "Food Price Policy and Income Distribution in Low-Income Countries." *Economic Development and Cultural Change* 27, no. 1 (1978), pp. 1–26.

————. *World Food Strategy for the 1980s: Context, Objectives, and Approach*. Washington, D.C.: International Food Policy Research Institute, 1979.

Michael, D. N. *On Learning to Plan—and Planning to Learn*. San Francisco: Jossey-Bass Publishers, 1973.

Migdal, J. S. *Peasants, Politics, and Revolution: Pressures toward Political and Social Change in the Third World*. Princeton: Princeton University Press, 1974.

Miró, Carmen. "Two and a Half Years after Bucharest: Searching for Means and Ways to Implement the World Population Plan of Action (WPPA)." In *Bellagio IV Population Conference*. New York: Rockefeller Foundation, 1977.

Mora, J. O.; Clement, J.; Christiansen, N.; Ortiz, N.; Vuori, L.; and Wagner, M. "Nutritional Supplementation, Early Stimulation, and Child Development." In *Behavioral Effects of Energy and Protein Deficits*, edited by J. Brožek. NIH Publication no. 79-1906. Washington, D.C.: U.S. Government Printing Office, 1979.

Morawetz, D. "Employment Implications of Industrialisation in Developing Countries: A Survey." *Economic Journal* 335, no. 84 (1974), pp. 491–542.

Morgan, M. G. "Bad Science and Good Policy Analysis," *Science*, September 15, 1978, p. 971.

Morley, D. "The Under-Fives Clinic." In *Medical Care in Developing Countries: A Symposium from Makerere*, edited by M. King. Nairobi: Oxford University Press, 1966.

Mosher, A. *Technical Cooperation in Latin-American Agriculture*. Chicago: University of Chicago Press, 1957.

Mott, F. L., and Mott, S. H. "Kenya's Record Population Growth: A Dilemma of Development." *Population Bulletin* 35, no. 3 (1980), pp. 3–43.

Mueller, Eva. "Agricultural Change and Fertility Change: The Case of Taiwan." Mimeographed. Ann Arbor: University of Michigan, 1971.

Muhua, Chen. "Birth Planning in China." *Family Planning Perspectives* 11, no. 6 (1979), pp. 348–54.

Murdoch, W. W. *The Poverty of Nations: The Political Economy of Hunger and Population*. Baltimore and London: Johns Hopkins University Press, 1980.

Musgrave, R. A. "Cost-Benefit Analysis and the Theory of Public Finance." *Journal of Economic Literature* 7, no. 3 (1969), pp. 797–806.

Myrdal, G. *Asian Drama: An Inquiry into the Poverty of Nations.* Vol. 3. New York: Pantheon, 1968.

Myren, D. T. "Integrating the Rural Market into the National Economy of Mexico." Land Tenure Center no. 46. Mimeographed. Madison: University of Wisconsin, 1968.

National Academy of Sciences (NAS). "Report of Study Team 4: Resources for Agriculture." In *Supporting Papers: World Food and Nutrition Study,* vol. 2. Washington, D.C.: Commission on International Relations, National Research Council, 1977.

Ness, G. D. "Organizational Issues in International Population Assistance." In *World Population and Development: Challenges and Prospects,* edited by P. M. Hauser. New York: Syracuse University Press, 1979.

Newbery, D. "The Choice of Rental Contract in Peasant Agriculture." In *Agriculture in Development Theory,* edited by L. G. Reynolds. New Haven: Yale University Press, 1975.

Norman, D. W. *Inter-Disciplinary Research on Rural Development: The Experience of the Rural Economy Research Unit in Northern Nigeria.* American Council on Education Overseas Liaison Committee Paper no. 6. Washington, D.C.: American Council on Education, 1974.

Nortman, Dorothy L., and Hofstatter, Ellen. *Population and Family Planning Programs: A Compendium of Data through 1978.* 10th ed. New York: Population Council, 1980.

Oechsli, F. W., and Kirk, D. "Modernization and the Demographic Transition." *Economic Development and Cultural Change* 23, no. 3 (1975), pp. 391–419.

Ojala, E. M. "The Programming of Agricultural Development." In *Agricultural Development and Economic Growth,* edited by H. M. Southworth and B. F. Johnston. Ithaca: Cornell University Press, 1967.

Olson, Mancur, Jr. *Logic of Collective Action: Public Goods and the Theory of Groups.* Rev. ed. Cambridge, Mass.: Harvard University Press, 1971.

O'Mara, G. T. "A Decision-Theoretic View of the Microeconomics of Technique Diffusion." Ph.D. diss., Stanford University, 1971.

Oram, P. A. "Comment" on "The Changing Patterns of Constraints on Food Production in the Third World," by Sir Charles Pereira. In *Distortions of Agricultural Incentives,* edited by T. W. Schultz. Bloomington and London: Indiana University Press, 1978.

Oram, P.; Zapata, J.; Alibaruho, G.; and Roy, S. *Investment and Input Requirements for Accelerating Food Production in Low-Income Countries by 1990.* IFPRI Research Report no. 10. Washington, D.C.: International Food Policy Research Institute, 1979.

Overseas Development Council (ODC). *The United States and World Development: Agenda 1977.* New York: Praeger Publishers, 1977.

Overseas Development Institute (ODI). "Integrated Rural Development Briefing Paper." No. 4. London: ODI, 1979.

Oyugi, W. O. "Participation in Development Planning at the Local Level." In *Rural Administration in Kenya: A Critical Appraisal,* edited by D. K. Leonard. Nairobi: East African Literature Bureau, 1973.

Parikh, J. K., and Parikh, K. S. "Mobilization and Impacts of Bio-Gas Technologies." IIASA Research Memorandum 77-26. Laxenburg, Austria: IIASA, 1977. Reprinted from *Energy*, vol. 2. Pergamon Press, 1977.

Pearson, S. R.; Stryker, J. K.; Humphreys, C. P., et al. *Rice in West Africa: Policy and Economics*. Stanford: Stanford University Press, 1981.

Perkins, D., et al. *Rural Small-Scale Industry in the People's Republic of China*. Berkeley: University of California Press, 1977.

Peterson, W. L. "International Farm Prices and the Social Cost of Cheap Food Policies." *American Journal of Agricultural Economics* 61, no. 1 (1979), pp. 12–21.

Polyani, M. "Manageability of Social Tasks." In *The Logic of Liberty*. London: Routledge & Kegan Paul, 1951.

Potter, J. E.; Myríãm, Ordóñez G.; and Measham, A. R. "The Rapid Decline in Colombian Fertility." *Population and Development Review* 2, nos. 3–4 (1976), pp. 509–28.

Powelson, J. P. *Institutions of Economic Growth: A Theory of Conflict Management in Developing Countries*. Princeton: Princeton University Press, 1972.

Presidential Commission on World Hunger. *Overcoming World Hunger: The Challenge Ahead*. Washington, D.C.: U.S. Government Printing Office, 1980.

Pressman, J. L., and Wildavsky, A. *Implementation: How Great Expectations in Washington are Dashed in Oakland*. Berkeley: University of California Press, 1973.

Preston, S. H. "Health Programs and Population Growth." *Population and Development Review* 1, no. 2 (1975), pp. 189–99.

————. "Mortality, Morbidity, and Development." Paper prepared for the Seminar on Population and Development in the ECWA Region, Population Division of the United Nations, September 1978.

Puffer, R., and Serano, C. *Patterns of Mortality in Childhood*. Pan American Health Organization Scientific Publications no. 262. Washington, D.C.: Pan American Health Organization, 1973.

Pyatt, G., and Thorbecke, E. *Planning Techniques for a Better Future*. Geneva: International Labour Office, 1976.

Pyle, D. F. *Voluntary Agency-Managed Projects Delivering an Integrated Package of Health, Nutrition, and Population Services: The Maharashtra Experience*. New Delhi: Prepared for the Ford Foundation, 1979.

————. "From Pilot Project to Operational Program: The Problems of Transition as Experienced in Project Poshak." In *Politics and Policy Implementations in the Third World*, edited by M. Grindle. Princeton: Princeton University Press, 1980.

————. "From Project to Program: The Study of the Scaling-Up/Implementation Process of a Community-Level, Integrated Health, Nutrition, Population Intervention in Maharashtra (India)." Ph.D. diss., Massachusetts Institute of Technology, 1981.

Quade, E. S. *Analysis for Military Decisions*. Chicago: Rand McNally & Co., 1964.

————. "Introduction." In *Systems Analysis and Public Policy*, edited by E. S. Quade and W. I. Bouchet. New York: American Elsevier Publishing Co., 1968.

————. *Analysis for Public Decisions*. New York: Elsevier, 1975.

Ranis, G. "Industrial Development." In *Economic Growth and Structural Change in Taiwan: The Postwar Experience of the Republic of China*, edited by W. Galenson. Ithaca and London: Cornell University Press, 1979.

Raup, P. M. "Land Reform and Agricultural Development." In *Agricultural Devel-*

opment and Economic Growth, edited by H. M. Southworth and B. F. Johnston. Ithaca: Cornell University Press, 1967.

Ravetz, J. R. *Scientific Knowledge and Its Social Problems*. Oxford: Clarendon Press, 1971.

Rawski, T. G. *Economic Growth and Employment in China*. New York: Oxford University Press, 1979.

Ray, A. J.; Atteri, B. R.; Sen, A. C.; and Mathur, P. N. "Quantitative and Qualitative Impact of Training and Visit System on Different Groups of Farmers—A Case Study of Hooghly District, West Bengal." *Indian Journal of Agricultural Economics* 34, no. 4 (1979), pp. 11–20.

Redclift, M. "Production Programs for Small Farmers: Plan Puebla as Myth and Reality." Mimeographed. Mexico City: Ford Foundation, 1980.

Reddy, V., and Srikantia, S. G. "Interaction of Nutrition and the Immune Response." *Indian Journal of Medical Research*, supp. to vol. 68 (1978), pp. 48–57.

Reutlinger, S., and Selowsky, M. *Malnutrition and Poverty: Magnitude and Policy Options*. Baltimore: Johns Hopkins University Press, 1976.

Revelle, R. "Energy Dilemmas in Asia: The Needs for Research and Development." *Science*, July 4, 1980, pp. 164–74.

Reynolds, C. W. "The New Terms of Trade Problem: Economic Rents in International Exchange." Mimeographed. Stanford: Food Research Institute, Stanford University, 1980.

Ricciuti, H. N. "Malnutrition and Cognitive Development: Research Issues and Priorities." In *Behavioral Effects of Energy and Protein Deficits*, edited by J. Brožek. NIH publication no. 79-1906. Washington, D.C.: U.S. Government Printing Office, 1979.

Richter, L. E. "Integrated Rural Development—A False Turning?" *Quarterly Journal of International Agriculture* 19, no. 3 (1980), pp. 304–16.

Ridker, R. G., ed. *Population and Development: The Search for Selective Interventions*. Baltimore: Johns Hopkins University Press, 1976.

Rodgers, G. B. *Demography and Distribution*. Population and Employment Working Paper no. 49. Geneva: International Labour Office, 1977.

Rogers, A. R. "Migration, Urbanization, Resources & Development." In *Alternatives for Growth: The Engineering and Economics of Natural Resources Development*, edited by H. J. McMains and L. Wilcox. Cambridge, Mass.: Ballinger, 1978.

Rogers, E. M. *Communication Strategies for Family Planning*. New York: Free Press, 1973.

Roumasset, J. A. "Risk and Uncertainty in Agricultural Development." CIMMYT Seminar Report on ADC Conference on Risk and Uncertainty, Mexico City, 1977.

Ruttan, V. W. "Integrated Rural Development Programs: A Skeptical Perspective." *International Development Review* 17, no. 4 (1975), pp. 9–16.

————. "Induced Innovation and the Green Revolution." In *Induced Innovation: Technology, Institutions and Development*, edited by H. P. Binswanger and V. W. Ruttan. Baltimore: Johns Hopkins University Press, 1978.

Ryan, J. G., and Binswanger, H. P. *Socioeconomic Constraints in the Semi-Arid Tropics and ICRISAT's Approach*. Hyderabad, India: International Crops Research Institute for the Semi-Arid Tropics, 1979.

Ryan, J. G.; Sarin, R.; and Pereira, M. "Assessment of Prospective Soil-, Water-, and Crop-Management Technologies for the Semi-Arid Tropics of Peninsular India." In

Proceedings of the International Workshop on Socioeconomic Constraints to Development of Semi-Arid Tropical Agriculture, 19–23 February 1979, Hyderabad, India. Patancheru, A.P., India: International Crops Research Institute for the Semi-Arid Tropics, 1980.

Sanderson, W. C. "On Two Schools of the Economics of Fertility." *Population and Development Review* 2, nos. 3–4 (1976), pp. 469–78.

————. *Economic-Demographic Simulation Models: A Review of Their Usefulness for Policy Analysis.* Department of Economics Memorandum no. 218. Stanford: Stanford University, 1978; also available as FAO Technical Paper 4, ES:DP/INT/73/P02, Rome, 1978.

————. *Economic-Demographic Simulation Models: A Review of Their Usefulness for Policy Analysis.* IIASA Research Memorandum 80-14. Laxenburg, Austria: IIASA, 1980.

Schönherr, S., and Mbugua, E. S. "New Extension Methods to Speed Up Diffusion of Agricultural Innovations." Institute for Development Studies Discussion Paper no. 200. Nairobi: University of Nairobi, 1974.

Schran, P. "Agriculture in the Four Modernizations." Paper presented at the Conference on Agricultural Development in China, Japan and Korea, Taipei, Taiwan, December 17–20, 1980.

Schuh, G. E. "Approaches to 'Basic Needs' and to 'Equity' that Distort Incentives in Agriculture." In *Distortions of Agricultural Incentives,* edited by T. W. Schultz. Bloomington and London: Indiana University Press, 1978.

Schultz, T. P. "An Economic Perspective on Population Growth." In *Rapid Population Growth: Consequences and Policy Implications,* by National Academy of Sciences. Baltimore and London: Johns Hopkins Press, 1971.

————. "Determinants of Fertility: A Micro-Economic Model of Choice." In *Economic Factors in Population Growth: Proceedings of a Conference Held by the International Economic Association at Valescure, France,* edited by A. J. Coale. New York: Wiley, 1976.

Schultz, T. W. *Transforming Traditional Agriculture.* New Haven and London: Yale University Press, 1964.

————. "Investment in Population Quality Throughout Low Income Countries." Human Capital Paper no. 79:1. Chicago: University of Chicago, Department of Economics, 1979.

————. "Nobel Lecture: The Economics of Being Poor." *Journal of Political Economy* 88, no. 4 (1980), pp. 639–51.

Schurmann, F. *Ideology and Organization in Communist China.* 2d ed. Berkeley and Los Angeles: University of California Press, 1968.

Scott, J. C. *The Moral Economy of the Peasant: Rebellion and Subsistence in Southeast Asia.* New Haven and London: Yale University Press, 1976.

Shah, M. M., and Willekens, F. *Rural Urban Population Projections for Kenya and Implications for Development.* Laxenburg, Austria: IIASA, 1978.

Sheahan, J. "Market-Oriented Economic Policies and Political Repression in Latin America." *Economic Development and Cultural Change* 28, no. 2 (1980), pp. 267–91.

Simon, H. A. "Designing Organizations for an Information-Rich World." In *Computers, Communications, and the Public Interest,* edited by M. Greenberger. Baltimore: Johns Hopkins Press, 1971.

_____. *Models of Discovery and Other Topics in the Methods of Science*. Dordrecht, Holland: D. Reidel Publishing Company, 1977.

Simon, J. L. "Population Growth May Be Good for LDCs in the Long Run: A Richer Simulation Model." *Economic Development and Cultural Change* 24, no. 2 (1976), pp. 309–37.

Stokey, Edith, and Zeckhauser, R. *A Primer for Policy Analysis*. New York: W. W. Norton & Company, 1978.

Streeten, P., and Burki, S. J. "Basic Needs: Some Issues." *World Development* 6, no. 3 (1978), pp. 411–21.

Sukhatme, P. V. *Nutrition and Poverty*. Ninth Lal Bahadur Shastri Memorial Lecture. New Delhi: Indian Agricultural Research Institute, 1977.

Surjaningrat, S.; Pardoko, R. H.; Sumbung, P. P.; and Soedarmadi, M. "Indonesia." In *East Asia Review 1978–79*, edited by J. J. Clinton and Jean Baker. *Studies in Family Planning* 11, no. 11 (1980), pp. 320–24.

Sussman, G. "The Pilot Project and the Design of Implementing Strategies: Community Development in India." In *Politics and Policy Implementations in the Third World*, edited by M. S. Grindle. Princeton: Princeton University Press, 1980.

Tanco, A. R., Jr. "Mobilizing National Commitment to a Multi-Agency Program: Four Critical Skills Required of Development Managers." In *Bureaucracy and the Poor: Closing the Gap*, edited by D. C. Korten and F. B. Alfonso. Singapore: McGraw-Hill, 1981.

Tang, A. M. "Food and Agriculture in China: Trends and Projections, 1952–77 and 2000." In *Food Production in the People's Republic of China*, by A. M. Tang and B. Stone. IFPRI Research Report 15. Washington, D.C.: International Food Policy Research Institute, 1980.

Tanzania, Government of. *Second Five Year Plan, July 1969–June 1974, Vol. 1: General Analysis*. Dar es Salaam: Government Printers Office, 1969.

Taylor, C. E. "Nutrition and Population in Health Sector Planning." *Food Research Institute Studies* 16, no. 2 (1977), pp. 77–90.

_____; Singh, R. D. et al. *The Narangwal Population Study: Integrated Health and Family Planning Services*. Narangwal, Punjab: Rural Health Research Center, 1975.

Taylor, L. "Research Directions in Income Distribution, Nutrition, and the Economics of Food." *Food Research Institute Studies* 16, no. 2 (1977), pp. 29–45.

Teller, C., et al. "Population and Nutrition: Implications of Sociodemographic Trends and Differentials for Food and Nutrition Policy in Central America and Panama." *Ecology of Food and Nutrition* 8, no. 2 (1979), pp. 95–109.

Tendler, Judith. *New Directions: Rural Roads*. U.S.A.I.D. Program Evaluation Discussion Paper no. 2. Washington, D.C.: U.S. Agency for International Development, 1979*a*.

_____. *Rural Electrification: Linkages and Justifications*. U.S.A.I.D. Program Evaluation Discussion Paper no. 3. Washington, D.C.: U.S. Agency for International Development, 1979*b*.

Thorbecke, E. "Agricultural Development." In *Economic Growth and Structural Change in Taiwan: The Postwar Experience of the Republic of China*, edited by W. Galenson. Ithaca and London: Cornell University Press, 1979.

Timmer, C. P. "Objectives and Constraints in the Formation of Indonesian Rice Policy: A Proto-Type Essay." Food Research Institute Rice Project Working Paper no. 2, Stanford, September 1973.

295   References

————. *Choice of Technique in Rice Milling in Java*. New York: Agricultural Development Council Research and Training Network Reprint, 1974. Pp. 1–10, 18–20.

————. "Food Policy in China." *Food Research Institute Studies* 15, no. 1 (1976), pp. 53–69.

————. "Food Prices as a Nutrition Policy Instrument." Paper presented at the MIT International Nutrition Program Conference on Interface Problems between Nutrition Policy and Its Implementation, Cambridge, Mass., November 5–8, 1979.

————, and Mullen, K. T. "Corn: Food and Fuel?" *New York Times*, December 31, 1980.

Tinbergen, J. *Economic Policy: Principles and Design*. Amsterdam: North-Holland Publishing Company, 1956.

————. *The Design of Development*. Baltimore: Johns Hopkins Press, 1958.

————. *Development Planning*. New York and Toronto: McGraw-Hill Book Company, 1967.

Tsui, Amy O., and Bogue, D. J. "Declining World Fertility: Trends, Causes, Implications." *Population Bulletin* 33, no. 4 (1978), pp. 3–55.

United Nations. *Report of the World Food Conference, Rome, 15–16 November, 1974*. New York: United Nations, 1975.

————. *Global Review of Human Settlements: A Support Paper for Habitat*. Vol. 2. Oxford: Pergamon Press, 1976.

————. *Levels of Trends of Fertility throughout the World, 1950–70*. U.N. Population Studies no. 59. New York: United Nations, 1977.

United Nations Children's Fund (UNICEF), Economic and Social Council. *Women, Children and Development: Report of the Executive Director*. Report to the UNICEF Executive Board, E/ICEF/L.1409, May 5, 1980.

United Nations Population Division. *Patterns of Urban and Rural Population Growth*. New York: United Nations, 1980.

United Nations Research Institute for Social Development (UNRISD). *Rural Cooperatives as Agents of Change: A Research Report and a Debate*. Geneva: UNRISD, 1975.

U.S. Department of Agriculture (USDA), Office of the Secretary. *Food for Peace: 1978 Annual Report on Public Law 480*. Washington, D.C.: USDA, 1979.

Uphoff, N. T., and Esman, M. J. *Local Organization for Rural Development: Analysis of Asian Experience*. Special Series on Rural Local Government no. 19. Ithaca: Rural Development Committee, Center for International Studies, Cornell University, 1974.

Uphoff, N. T.; Cohen, J. M.; and Goldsmith, A. A. "Feasibility and Application of Rural Development Participation: A State-of-the-Art Paper." Rural Development Committee Monograph Series no. 3. Ithaca: Cornell University, 1979.

Valdés, A. "The Transition to Socialism: Observations on the Chilean Agrarian Reform." In *Employment in Developing Nations*, edited by E. O. Edwards. New York: Columbia University Press, 1974.

Vallin, J. "World Trends in Infant Mortality Since 1950." *World Health Statistics Report* 29, no. 11 (1976), pp. 646–74.

Valverde, V.; Arroyave, G.; Guzmán, M.; and Flores, Marina. "Overview of Nutritional Status in the Western Hemisphere: Central America and Panama." Paper presented at the Western Hemisphere Nutrition Congress VI, Los Angeles, California, August 10–14, 1980.

Verba, S., and Nie, N. H. *Participation in America*. New York: Harper and Row, Publishers, 1972.

Vernon, R. *Storm over the Multinationals: The Real Issues*. Cambridge, Mass.: Harvard University Press, 1977.

Vyas, V. S. "Some Aspects of Structural Change in Indian Agriculture." *Indian Journal of Agricultural Economics* 34, no. 1 (1979), pp. 1–18.

Walker, T. S. "Decision Making by Farmers and by the National Agricultural Research Program on the Adoption and Development of Maize Varieties in El Salvador." Ph.D. diss., Stanford University, 1980.

Walsh, J. A., and Warren, K. S. "Selected Primary Health Care: An Interim Strategy for Disease Control in Developing Countries." *New England Journal of Medicine*, November 1, 1979, pp. 967–74.

————. "Reply" to "Selective Health Care for Developing Countries." *New England Journal of Medicine*, March 27, 1980, p. 759.

Waterston, A. *Development Planning: Lessons of Experience*. Baltimore: Johns Hopkins Press, 1965.

Watson, W.; Rosenfield, A.; Viravaidya, M.; and Chanawongse, K. "Health, Population, and Nutrition: Interrelations, Problems, and Possible Solutions." In *World Population and Development: Challenges and Prospects*, edited by P. M. Hauser. New York: Syracuse University Press, 1979.

Weick, K. E. *The Social Psychology of Organizing*. Reading: Addison-Wesley, 1969.

Welch, F. "The Role of Investments in Human Capital in Agriculture." In *Distortions of Agricultural Incentives*, edited by T. W. Schultz. Bloomington and London: Indiana University Press, 1978.

Widstrand, C. G., ed. *Co-operatives and Rural Development in East Africa*. New York: Africana Publishing Corp., 1970.

Wildavsky, A. "Discussion" of "Recent Developments: Poverty-Focused Planning," by P. Bardhan. In *Nutrition Planning: The State of the Art*, edited by L. Joy. London: IPC Science and Technology Press, 1978.

————. *Speaking Truth to Power: The Art and Craft of Policy Analysis*. Boston and Toronto: Little, Brown and Company, 1979.

Witt, L. "Food Aid, Commercial Exports, and the Balance of Payments." In *Food Policy*, edited by P. G. Brown and H. Shue. New York: Free Press, 1977.

Wittfogel, K. A. "Communist and Non-Communist Agrarian Systems, with Special Reference to the U.S.S.R. and Communist China: A Comparative Approach." In *Agrarian Policies and Problems in Communist and Non-Communist Countries*, edited by W.A.D. Jackson. Seattle and London: University of Washington Press, 1971.

World Bank. *The Assault on World Poverty: Problems of Rural Development, Education and Health*. Baltimore and London: Johns Hopkins University Press, 1975.

————. *World Tables 1976*. Baltimore and London: Johns Hopkins University Press, 1976.

————. *World Development Report 1978*. Washington, D.C.: World Bank, 1978.

————. *World Development Report 1979*. Washington, D.C.: World Bank, 1979.

————. *World Development Report, 1980*. New York: Oxford University Press, 1980*a*.

————. *Health: Sector Policy Paper*. 2d ed. Washington, D.C.: World Bank, 1980*b*.

————. *Water Supply and Waste Disposal: Poverty and Basic Needs Series September 1980*. Washington, D.C.: World Bank, 1980*c*.

World Fertility Survey. *The Kenya Fertility Survey, 1978: A Summary of Findings.* Voorburg, Netherlands: International Statistical Institute, [1979?].

World Food Council. "Toward the Eradication of Hunger: Food-Subsidy and Direct-Distribution Programmes." Report by the Executive Director, WFC/1980/ 3. Rome, February 25, 1980.

World Health Organization (WHO). *New Trends and Approaches in the Delivery of Maternal and Child Care in Health Services.* Sixth Report of the WHO Expert Committee on Maternal and Child Health, Technical Report Series no. 600. Geneva: WHO, 1976.

————. *Primary Health Care: Report of the International Conference on Primary Health Care, Alma-Ata, USSR, 6–12 September 1978.* Geneva: WHO/UNICEF, 1978.

Wortman, S., and Cummings, R. W., Jr. *To Feed This World: The Challenge and the Strategy.* Baltimore and London: Johns Hopkins University Press, 1978.

Yamada, S., and Ruttan, V. W. "International Comparisons of Productivity in Agriculture." In *New Developments in Productivity Measurement and Analysis*, edited by J. W. Kendrick and Beatrice N. Vaccara. Chicago: University of Chicago Press, 1980.

Yotopoulos, P. A. "The Population Problem and the Development Solution." *Food Research Institute Studies* 16, no. 1 (1977), pp. 1–131.

Indexes

Name Index

Welch, F., 246
Wickham, T. H., 99
Widstrand, C. G., 166
Wilcox, Janet R., 128, 129, 130, 134
Wildavsky, A., 11, 14, 162, 201, 202, 219, 221, 225, 226, 228, 229, 230, 260
Willekens, F., 111
Williamson, J. G., 234
Witt, L., 263

Wittfogel, K. A., 74
Wortman, S., 81
Wray, J. D., 128, 129, 130, 134

Yamada, S., 85
Yotopoulos, P. A., 82, 147

Zeckhauser, R., 11, 31, 230

Subject Index

Acting out, 5, 25, 150; approach, 7, 140, 150, 235, 238
Administrative capability, 28
Africa, 10, 45, 50, 55, 57, 59, 63, 71, 72, 81, 93, 100, 102, 104, 105, 110, 183, 215, 254; East, 10, 56, 99, 156, 166, 178, 196, 197, 217, 225; Sub-Saharan, 39, 76, 91, 93, 94, 106, 118; tropical, 46, 49, 59, 93, 103, 106, 110; West, 94, 96, 102
African Rural Development Study, 30
African Sahel, 264
Agency for International Development (AID), 56, 121
Agricultural and industrial development, 78
Agricultural cooperatives, 159
Agricultural development: labor-using, capital-saving, 75; marketing of products, 102; in mixed economies, 6, 70, 75; pattern of, 6, 64; priority given to, 76
Agricultural extension activities, 91, 208, 211, 218, 222, 229, 238
Agricultural incentives, 260
Agricultural infrastructure, 109
Agricultural labor force, 39
Agricultural prices, 63
Agricultural research, 6, 92, 105; expenditures for, 93; returns to, 92; support for, 105; underinvestment in, 92
Agricultural strategy, 68; and agricultural research programs, 115; bimodal, 6, 70, 71, 73, 74, 75, 79, 81, 84, 85, 114, 123, 146, 195, 198, 231, 244, 245, 246, 254, 255; choice of, 6, 70; design of, 39; unimodal, 6, 70, 71, 72, 74, 75, 76, 78, 79, 80, 81, 82, 84, 86, 88, 106, 113, 114, 115, 122, 123, 148, 195, 197, 231, 238, 244, 245, 246, 257
Agricultural surplus, 65, 263
Agriculture: government support for, 73; large-scale, 74; rate and bias of technical change in, 74; research in, 85, 238, 245, 256; resource-based, 256; science-based, 256
Agriculture-industry interactions, 76, 243

Agroclimatic environments, 93
Agrotechnical conditions, 100
Aid, opportunity cost of, 263
Animal draft power, 66, 78; land and water management utilization of, 96
Animal-powered equipment, 95, 96
Anthropometric measurements, 50
Antinatalist policy, 119
Asia, 45, 50, 55, 59, 63, 66, 71, 74, 76, 88, 91, 92, 93, 94, 99, 100, 107, 110, 178, 182, 185, 205, 215; East, 56; Middle-South, 56; South, 56, 91, 99, 107, 108; Southeast, 56, 91, 102, 107, 108; Southwest, 56
Asian Agricultural Survey, Second, 30, 65, 91
Asian Development Bank, 30, 65, 75, 91

BACHUE Model, 232
Bangladesh, 25, 37, 45, 48, 57, 58, 59, 91, 95, 127, 131, 260, 264
Bangladesh Rural Advancement Committee, 178, 194, 219, 220
Barefoot doctor program, 129, 132, 140
Bargaining arrangements, 25. See also Organization
Basic needs approach, 6, 21, 60, 116, 174, 250, 262, 263
Benefit-cost analysis, 23, 230, 231. See also Cost-benefit analysis
Benin, 38
Bihar, 88
Bimodal. See Agricultural strategy, bimodal
Bio-gas plants, generators for, 104
Biological factors, 56
Birth control, 220. See also Contraception methods
Birth rate, 43, 59, 145; crude, 49, 55, 56, 57, 58, 139, 144, 145, 146
Birth spacing. See Children, spacing of
Birth weight, 52; low, 52
Botswana, 218
Bottle feeding, and malnutrition, 125

THE JOHNS HOPKINS UNIVERSITY PRESS

Redesigning Rural Development

This book was composed in Times Roman text and News Gothic
display type by Oberlin Printing Company, from a design by Lisa S.
Mirski. It was printed on S.D. Warren's 50–lb. Sebago Cream paper and
bound in Holliston Roxite A by the Maple Press Company.